The Defeat of the Zeppelin

The Defeat of the Zeppelins
Zeppelin Raids and Anti-airship Operations 1916 -18

Mick Powis

Pen & Sword
AVIATION

First published in Great Britain in 2018 by
Pen & Sword Aviation
An imprint of
Pen & Sword Books Ltd
Yorkshire – Philadelphia

Copyright © Mick Powis 2018

ISBN 978 1 52670 249 4

Printed and bound in England by TJ International Ltd, Padstow, Cornwall.

Pen & Sword Books Limited incorporates the imprints of Atlas, Archaeology, Aviation,
Discovery, Family History, Fiction, History, Maritime, Military, Military Classics,
Politics, Select, Transport, True Crime, Air World, Frontline Publishing, Leo Cooper,
Remember When, Seaforth Publishing, The Praetorian Press, Wharncliffe Local
History, Wharncliffe Transport, Wharncliffe True Crime and White Owl.

For a complete list of Pen & Sword titles please contact

PEN & SWORD BOOKS LIMITED
47 Church Street, Barnsley, South Yorkshire, S70 2AS, England
E-mail: enquiries@pen-and-sword.co.uk
Website: www.pen-and-sword.co.uk

Or
PEN AND SWORD BOOKS
1950 Lawrence Rd, Havertown, PA 19083, USA
E-mail: Uspen-and-sword@casematepublishers.com
Website: www.penandswordbooks.com

Contents

A List of Maps

To my Nan who, when I was a little boy, told me half-remembered stories about that frightening night when she visited her Aunt Rose, and made me determined to find out more.

A Note on time

One of the problems with a book of this sort is that it relies on documents and official records from different sources, mainly British and German. This can lead to confusion about time. The British used GMT and, from 1916, British Summer Time (BST). The Germans used Central European Time and also, from 1916, daylight saving time (one hour ahead). It starts to get complicated because the British and Germans started and finished BST/daylight saving time on different dates. These are the dates:

British:

21 May 1916 to 1 October 1916

8 April 1917 to 17 September 1917

24 March 1918 to 30 September 1918

German:

30 April 1916 to 1 October 1916

16 April 1917 to 17 October 1917

15 April 1918 to 16 September 1918

This means that for most of the year German time is one hour ahead of British time, but for short periods they can be the same or two hours different. To simplify matters, I use British time throughout the book, GMT and British Summer Time on the relevant British dates. I also use a 24 hour clock system, and change quoted times to this.

Introduction

On a cold and wet Sunday on 31 January 2016, a number of commemorations took place in small towns all over the country. From Sandwell to Scunthorpe, local historians, politicians and some descendants of the victims mixed with interested onlookers to remember the centenary of the most destructive Zeppelin raid of the First World War.

On 31 January 1916, nine Zeppelin airships of the *Reichskreigsmarine*, the Imperial German Navy, set out from their bases on the north-west coast of Germany to bomb the English Midlands; though they didn't hit it, Liverpool was their primary target. In all, seventy people were killed in the bombing and about 113 were injured. I have to admit a personal interest. My grandmother was in the market town of Wednesbury, in what is now the West Midlands, that night, waiting for a tram. For the rest of her life, she remembered sheltering in a shop doorway, with two babies, covered in dust and broken glass. She was one of the lucky ones.

Two Zeppelins bombed the Black Country between Wolverhampton and Walsall: Zeppelin *L.21*, between 8.00 pm and 8.30 pm, and *L.19* at about midnight. They killed thirty-five people in Tipton, Bradley, Wednesbury and Walsall.

Three Zeppelins bombed Burton-on-Trent: probably *L.15* at about 8.30 pm, *L.20* at about 8.45 pm and *L.19* at about 9.30 pm. Fifteen people were killed.

One Zeppelin, *L.20*, bombed Loughborough, killing ten people at about 8.15 pm; it then went to Ilkeston, where another two men died at about 8.30 pm.

Zeppelin *L.13* bombed the Stoke-on-Trent area then went to the Scunthorpe area, killing three people at about 11.00 pm.

Finally, Zeppelin *L.14* bombed Derby at about midnight, killing five people.

Throughout the centenary of the Great War there have been similar ceremonies: the first in England took place in Great Yarmouth, where two people were killed by a Zeppelin on 19 January 1915, and they will go on until 13 April 2018 when we reach the centenary of the last seven people killed by a Zeppelin in Wigan. The capital cities of London and Edinburgh have their own memorials to Zeppelin victims. Great Yarmouth also commemorates an 'end' date, 5/6 August 1918, when Egbert Cadbury, of the famous chocolate family, took off from Yarmouth to shoot down the last Zeppelin to raid England.

Zeppelin raids were not confined to Britain. People were killed by them in Antwerp, Bucharest, Liege, Naples, Paris and Thessalonica, along with dozens of other places as far apart as the Balkans, the Baltic and Russia.

The Zeppelin raids led to considerable political pressure for an adequate blackout and air-raid precautions, and widespread anti-German atrocity propaganda. Several coroners' juries rendered verdicts of 'murder' by the German Kaiser and Crown Prince. The Zeppelin raids had a massive effect on morale in Britain and caused severe disruption to war production. The Government knew something had to be done to defeat the Zeppelins.

In the end, the fear, anger, economic and political pressure generated by the raids led to the development of a successful air-raid defence policy. I have covered in detail the events of the frosty foggy night of 31 January 1916 in my book *Zeppelins over the Midlands* (Pen and Sword, 2016), and in less detail what happened to the Zeppelins and their crews after this. In this book, I simply want to analyze what happened next, and put the defeat of the Zeppelins in a wider context.

While this book is a continuation of *Zeppelins over the Midlands*, it can be read as a stand-alone work, though I skip over some general information covered in detail in the first book. In both works I try to bring together two lines of research: the military and the civilian. It is perhaps surprising that far more is known about the military aspects of the raid than what happened to civilians on the ground.

Much of this information is taken from secret documents produced by GHQ (Home Forces). From various sources, interrogation of captured Zeppelin crews, spotters on the ground and police reports, they piece together the route of the airships and the destination of their bombs. These GHQ documents really give you a feel for the times; written by military men, they are wholly balanced. Describing some Zeppelin commanders as brave and skilled, others as overly cautious, they give the unvarnished facts, and a professional analysis. Each copy was a secret document, designed for a small group of senior officers; each had to be signed for. It is fascinating to read them alongside the national and local press. The concept that 'truth is the first casualty of war' certainly applies to the public, but not to those in command.

Though the newspapers at the time were subject to strict censorship and not able to give any details which could help the Germans, such as the names of the victims or the towns where raids had taken place, they do give a wonderful feel for the times, and when read with GHQ reports usually enable us to fairly accurately understand what happened. As a footnote to history, it is interesting to note that when I consulted some coroners' reports in Walsall and Wolverhampton, I found telegrams from the Under Secretary at the Home Office to the coroners. They explained that the raid could be reported provided no names, addresses or locations were indicated.

In general, local newspapers are far more accurate and useful than the national press. Most tend to report coroners' inquests almost verbatim, just leaving out places and names of victims and witnesses. The national press, and local papers reporting on other areas than their own, are unreliable, shamelessly copying other newspaper reports, leading to confusion and often inaccuracy. Reading a lot of newspapers from the time certainly disabused me of the idea that there was a golden age of fair and accurate reporting: bias and sensationalism are not new. It is interesting to note the official government position on newspaper reporting of the Zeppelin raids:

> It is undesirable that too much space should be given to describing Zeppelin raids. The actual military damage that has been done is slight, but at the same time so long as the Germans think that the raids have great effect they will be continued, and long descriptions tend to produce an impression both in England and Germany that they are of greater importance than they are in reality.

We can probably take comfort, a century later, knowing that 'spin' is not a new phenomenon, and our politicians are no more unscrupulous than their forbears.

One of the pleasures of writing this book has been that, since 2014, there has been a massive increase in First World War historical research. Many local newspapers and websites have had features about the centenary of events in their area. The Zeppelin raids, hardly discussed for 100 years, have been the subject of numerous articles and local history websites. The BBC has been very good at this, whilst regional TV stations have produced many programmes. Many websites have archive voice recordings of witnesses, some recorded up to 50 years ago. I particularly like a BBC picture from Burton-on-Trent with a modern colour picture of a street of terraced houses. In the middle of the row is a 100-year-old black and white picture of one of the houses very badly damaged by a Zeppelin, the size of the old picture adjusted so it fits exactly into place with the modern picture (see BBC

Midlands website: 109 Shobnall Street, Burton-on-Trent). The effect is so good it seems churlish to point out an error. The modern picture shows the front of the houses, the old picture the back. We can tell this by an outhouse in the backyard, standing there 'as strong as a brick outhouse' (as the more refined of us say).

In this book I give a chronological list of all Zeppelin raids on Britain, and the response to them of the Royal Flying Corps and Royal Naval Air Service. I also cover in less detail other airship operations in other theatres of war. I put all these together in chronological order, as all attacks were by the German military and part of a reasonably consistent war plan, and Zeppelins were able to move quickly from front to front according to military priority. Bombing raids on Britain are well documented; attacks in France and Belgium less so. The Eastern Front section is more complex, and even less well documented. Zeppelins took part not only in operations against Russia, but on other fronts in the Balkans and the Mediterranean, over Macedonia, Serbia, Rumania, Greece and even Africa.

Map 1: German airship bases in the West.

Chapter One

Weapons of Darkness

The Zeppelin, perhaps more than any other weapon of the Great War, symbolizes both German scientific ingenuity and brutality. At the beginning of the war, Germany was the only country that possessed a fleet of rigid airships, though their usefulness as weapons of war was in 1914 much exaggerated. The Zeppelin Company had a public relations statement which was used many times before the war by Count Zeppelin and the manager of the business, Dr Hugo Eckener, that by 1910 it ran the world's first successful airline and had an excellent safety record. The Zeppelin Company had built a number of reliable airships and set up the Zeppelin Foundation for the Promotion of Aerial Navigation and the world's first commercial airline, The German Airship Transportation Company (or Deutsche Luftschiffahrts AG, known by its German initials as DELAG). The machines built for DELAG were largely successful. Four ships - the *Schwaben*, *Viktoria Luise*, *Hansa* and *Sachsen* - had been used, and by 31 July 1914, 10,197 passengers had been carried on 1,588 voyages covering some 107,231 miles. What the firm didn't say was that most of its flights were short pleasure flights, in good weather, where well-heeled customers were wined and dined with caviar and champagne, enjoying the smooth flight of the Zeppelin and the delight of the views in the slow and low airship flight. Though it occasionally advertised city-to-city flights, the airships were too dependent on the weather to run a scheduled service: the choice of city was often dependent on the wind direction, and the service could not operate at all during the winter.

The popularity of the Zeppelin as a measure of German engineering and invention inevitably led to the development of a military role for the airship. Before the outbreak of war, Army and Navy crews were trained on the airships by DELAG. At the outbreak of war, the DELAG airships were requisitioned by the military and other airships ordered. We have a description of how the civilian ship *Sachsen* was militarized. The passenger area was stripped out and replaced by a gangway with bomb racks and a bomb release station. A good quality radio and wireless room was installed, machine guns were fitted in all the gondolas and a gun position fitted in the tail to protect from attacks from above.

The 'M' Type Zeppelin

The first Zeppelins designed and built in numbers for military service were the 'M' series. Twelve were produced: six for the Army and six for the Navy. They were large airships, 518ft long with a diameter of 48ft. They had three Maybach C-X 210-horsepower (hp) engines. In good conditions they had a top speed of about 50mph and a ceiling of about 5,000ft. With a gas capacity of about 800,000 cubic feet (ft³) of hydrogen, they could carry a potential payload of about 20,000lb. They usually had a crew of sixteen and could carry about 1,100lb of bombs. They were not comfortable to fly as they had open gondolas. It is said the reason for this was that Count Zeppelin said the Zeppelin pilots liked to feel the wind in their faces. While this may have been true over Lake Constance in July, it was certainly not the case over the North Sea in February. In comparison to the civilian airships, they were slightly bigger, had better propellers and could operate at a slightly higher altitude, but in essence they were not much different. If the civilian machines did not have the capacity to run a scheduled inter-city service, the 'M' series did not have the capacity to operate in the much more hostile environment of the battlefield.

Though the 'M' series were used in the opening months of the war, and were the first Zeppelins to bomb England, their most useful function was allowing Zeppelin commanders and crews to gain experience. Of the twelve built for the Army and Navy, four were destroyed by accident or due to the weather, six were shot down by anti-aircraft fire and two destroyed by bombing. (One of these, *LZ.37*, was the first to be bought down by an aeroplane, by Lieutenant Werneford.) Many of the airships brought down by anti-aircraft fire were hit by rifle fire; the rifle bullets would not immediately bring the Zeppelin down, but the loss of gas through holes in the gas cells would force it down. To some extent this was caused by the inexperienced commanders deliberately flying too low, but in many cases the airship could not reach a safe height, which was a particular problem in winter when ice or snow would weigh the Zeppelin down. It became apparent during 1915 that airships needed to be able to operate at higher altitudes, which led to the design and production of the 'P' and 'Q' series, the Zeppelins that went on to cause the most casualties in bombing raids.

In 1909, a rival company to Zeppelin was formed, Schutte-Lanz of Mannheim. It had the support of the German War Ministry to encourage technical competition with the Zeppelin Company. In many ways the Schutte-Lanz airships were more advanced than the Zeppelins. They were bigger, the hulls were more streamlined, they had four engines and enclosed gondolas. The most significant difference was the material used for the framework. Zeppelins had aluminium and later duralumin; Schutte-Lanz had laminated plywood, and while this was seen as an advantage by the manager of the company, Dr Johann Schutte, who argued plywood frameworks were both lighter and stronger, this view was not shared by many in the military, in particular the Navy. Wooden frameworks were affected by the weather, as moisture could alter the weight and tensile strength. For this reason, while many of the advanced features of the Schutte-Lanz designs were incorporated into later Zeppelins, there were few Schutte-Lanz ships produced.

The Zeppelin Company was given the right to use aspects of design subject to patents by the Schutte-Lanz Airship Company, and built two 'O' type and one 'N' type Zeppelins, which were three-engined transitional designs much better than the 'M' series and were relatively successful. The 'N' type works no. *LZ.26* was commissioned by the Army as *Z.XII* and commanded by Ernst Lehmann, and had a career on different fronts. It survived active service and was later used as an experimental ship, testing Siemens glider bombs. The Navy commissioned its 'O' type ship as *L.9*, the Army as *LZ.39*. Both would make a number of attacks on England, and *LZ.39* would also serve in Russia.

The 'P' and 'Q' Type Zeppelin

Early in 1915, the Zeppelin Company started mass-producing 'P' type airships, using many of the design features introduced by the 'N' and 'O' type ships. By January 1916, the Zeppelin Company had produced thirty-four of its 'P' and 'Q' type airships, with nineteen for the Army and fifteen for the Navy. By the standards of the time, these were very effective bombing machines. The 'P' type was the smaller model, developed early in 1915. Twenty two were produced, with works nos from *LZ.38* to *LZ.63*.

It is worth at this stage explaining the contradictory and confusing system of numbering Zeppelins. As every Zeppelin was built it was given a works number, in strict chronological order. They all started with 'LZ', for *Luftschiffbau Zeppelin*. These went from *LZ.1*, produced in 1901, to *LZ.114*, built in 1920. (For airships built after this, the system changes, but that is another story.) Civilian airships usually had a name: for example, *LZ.17* was *Sachsen*. Navy airships were given a service number when they were commissioned; all Navy Zeppelins were 'L' for *Luftschiffe*. For example, *LZ.45* was *L.13* and *LZ.72* was *L.31*. The Army was less consistent. When an airship was commissioned it was given a service number. Up to 1914, this was 'Z' - presumably for Zeppelin - with a Roman number. For example, *LZ.25* was *Z.IX* and *LZ.26* was *Z.XII*. In 1915, the system changed and Army airships were numbered with 'LZ'. At first, the works number and the service numbers were the same, for example *LZ.37* had the same works and service numbers. For some reason, this was changed later in 1915, with '30' added to the service number, so *LZ.42* (works no.) became *LZ.72* (service no.). For Schutte-Lanz airships, the system was simpler. The works number was 'SL', for obvious reasons, and went from *SL.1* in 1911 to *SL.24* in 1918. Navy ships had the same service number as the works number, so *SL.9* was its works and service number. The Army did the same, but used Roman numerals for the service number. So we have *SL.11* (works no.) being *SL.XI* (service no.). Despite this, the first airship shot down over England, on 2 September 1916, is almost always referred to as *SL.11*, while the Navy Zeppelin shot down on 2 October 1916 is usually known by its service number *L.31*.

The first 'P' type Zeppelin was built in March and April 1915, at Friedrichshafen, and went into Army service as *LZ.38* in April that year. It was 536ft long, with a diameter of 61ft. The hull contained sixteen gas cells with a total capacity of 1,126,400ft³ of hydrogen. It had four Maybach C-X 22.6-litre six-cylinder engines of 210hp. It had a top speed of about 55mph, could reach an altitude of about 11,000ft and carry about 4,000lb of bombs. It was formidable weapon at the time; though slower than most aircraft, it could climb faster and fly higher. *LZ.38* would have a short but eventful service life; under the command of Hauptman Erich Linnarz, it would be the first Zeppelin to bomb London on 31 May 1915. It would be destroyed in its shed at Brussels-Evere on 7 June 1915 by a British bombing raid.

The Zeppelin Works built twenty-two 'P' type airships, with twelve for the Army and ten for the Navy, the last one constructed in January 1916. The next type, the 'Q' class Zeppelin, was very similar. The only difference was that the hull was longer at 585ft, which enabled them to have eighteen gas cells with a total capacity of 1,264,100ft³ of hydrogen. This allowed them to carry a heavier bomb load and operate at a higher altitude of 12,000ft. The Zeppelin Company originally built twelve 'Q' type airships, the Navy receiving five and the Army seven. In mid-1916, the Army had five of its 'P' type ships taken out of service to be lengthened by 49ft at Dresden and have two extra gas cells added, essentially turning them into 'Q' types. They were *LZ.86*, *LZ.87*, *LZ.88*, *LZ.90* and *LZ.93*.

The Zeppelins were huge, even in relation to present day aircraft. A 'Q' type, at 585ft, was as long as two football pitches. A useful modern comparison is the Goodyear Blimp, used for advertising and television work at sporting events, which is just over 100ft long. *L.21* was five times this size. Zeppelins are still the largest combat aircraft ever to have flown. A 'Q' Zeppelin would weigh about 53,000lb empty. However, the 1,264,100ft³ of lighter-than-air hydrogen would provide useful lift, of some 39,000lb more than this, lifting the ship, crew, fuel, oil, ballast (used to control height) and war load of about two tons of bombs.

Flying these huge lighter-than-air machines has been likened to an art rather than a science. They were strongly affected by weather conditions; the temperature changed the lift generated by the hydrogen gas cells. Lift was greater in cold weather. The height achieved by the Zeppelin was controlled by a combination of static lift, dropping ballast to balance the weight of the airship against the lift of the hydrogen gas, and dynamic lift generated by the forward speed of the airship. While Zeppelins were slower than opposing fighter aircraft, their most important defensive quality was their ability to climb much faster than the aircraft opposing them in 1915 and 1916.

Probably the best way to understand how a Zeppelin flies is to recognize that technically it doesn't fly, it floats in the air. The gas bags are filled with hydrogen, making it lighter than air; it will float upwards until it reaches a point of neutral buoyancy. To rise up, the Zeppelin commander increases buoyancy, lightening the ship by dropping ballast. To go down, he makes the ship heavy by releasing hydrogen. In practice, a Zeppelin flight was a constant balancing act between height and weight. Before take-off, the commander would calculate the weight of the ship and its movable cargo, fuel, ballast and bombs, and the lift expected to be generated by the hydrogen it carried. Crew were issued with a printed book of ballast sheets, to make this calculation before any flight. Problems occurred when the ship was subject to an unexpected weight change, such as ice or snow on the hull, or when the ship lost lift due to a hydrogen leak. A Zeppelin generally got lighter as a mission went on, as fuel was used and bombs were dropped. The ship also lost hydrogen, as the gas cells expanded as the ship flew higher and the air pressure went down. Each gas cell had an automatic pressure valve to cope with this.

A Zeppelin commander would trim his ship to fly at neutral buoyancy at its cruising height, in the case of 'P' and 'Q' class ships about 9,000ft. Minor changes in height would be made using the elevator. The controls at the tail of a Zeppelin were very similar to those of an aeroplane. The ship

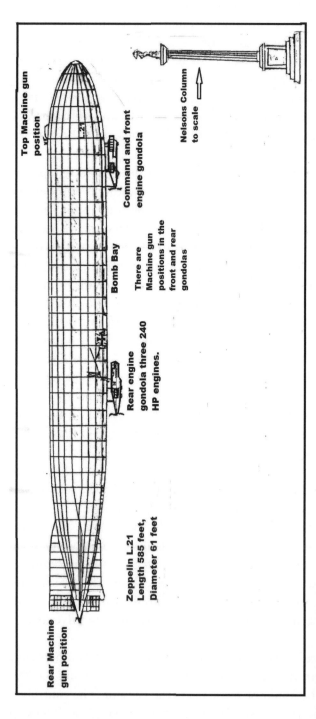

Top Machine gun position

Command and front engine gondola

Nelsons Column to scale

Bomb Bay

There are Machine gun positions in the front and rear gondolas

Rear engine gondola three 240 HP engines.

Zeppelin L.21 Length 585 feet, Diameter 61 feet

Rear Machine gun position

Map/Diagram 2: Zeppelin *L.21*

Zeppelin L.21 was a typical 'Q' class airship. 585 feet long, she carried about two tons of bombs. She had a top speed of about 60 mph, and operated a height of about 10,000 feet. She had four Maybach HSLu 240hp 19 litre six-cylinder engines, and had enough fuel for 25 to 30 hours in the air. She flew on 17 operational scouting flights and 13 raids on Britain. L.21 was built at Lowenthal in late 1915; she first flew on 10 January 1916. She was taken over by Kapitänleutnant der Reserve Max Dietrich on the 19 January 1916. He raided the English Midlands on 31 January/1 February 1916, killing 35 people. He raided York on 2/3 May 1916, killing 9 people. On 24 June 1916 a new commander took over: Hauptmann August Stelling. He flew on a number of raids but we have no record of any casualties. He was replaced by Oberleutnant zur See Kurt Frankenburg on 15 August 1916. On the 2/3 September 1916 he bombed Dodshill, killing one woman. On the 25/26 September 1916 he bombed the Bolton area, killing 13 people. His last raid was on 27/28 November 1916 and he was shot down near Lowestoft by Flight Sub-Lieutenant Edward Pulling; the crew of 17 were all killed.

Her service life of just over ten months was probably above average for a mid-war Zeppelin, as were the casualties she caused: at least 58 people killed.

had two rudders on its vertical fins, which controlled direction, and two elevators on its horizontal fins, which controlled height, or more technically the position of the nose. If the elevators were moved up, the nose rose and the ship climbed; if the elevators were moved down, the ship dived. Just like any other aircraft, a Zeppelin can use its engine power to help it climb, trading speed for height. In an emergency, like a fighter attack, a Zeppelin could climb very fast. The ship would drop ballast and put the nose up on full power. In 1916, it could out-climb any fighter.

The structure of all Zeppelins was a streamlined rigid frame made of lightweight latticed duralumin girders, with steel wire bracing. The ship was kept aloft by hydrogen-filled gas cells: huge gasbags made from cotton lined with gold beaters' skins to make them airtight. Gold beaters' skins were thin membranes from the intestines of cattle. For each gas cell, skins from some 50,000 cattle would be needed; as a result, gas cells were very expensive items, in 1916 each one costing about £2,000. A 'Q' type Zeppelin had eighteen gas cells, each containing about 70,000ft^3 of hydrogen. They were held in the frame of the Zeppelin by wire and cord netting. It is important to note that a Zeppelin was not a single bag of gas like a blimp. It had a rigid frame like an aeroplane, and the crew could move inside the envelope, climbing on ladders to machine-gun positions on top of the airship. At the bottom of the hull was a keel, which contained walkways and was where the control and engine gondoliers were attached. To some extent, a ship could be maintained and repaired in flight, and the crew had a sail-maker to repair the envelope or gas cells, and mechanics to repair the engines.

The rigid frame of the Zeppelin was covered with lightweight linen fabric, sewn and doped on the frame. The example of fabric I have seen in Nordholz Museum is natural linen, an off-white colour printed with tiny blue dots or lines, to give a light blue or grey camouflage effect. Later in the war, the undersides of Zeppelins were painted black, but this was not the case in 1915 and 1916. The airship covered in this material was therefore a very pale blue colour. This indicated why almost all eyewitnesses described them as being silver or grey in colour: seen in the reflected light of street lamps or fire from the ground, the Zeppelin would seem to be a silver grey colour. Other Zeppelins were covered in unprinted fabric, and would be a cream or very light brown colour.

Attached to the hull of the Zeppelin were a command and front engine gondola, and toward the rear, about 200ft away, was the rear engine gondola. The front gondola was the officers' station where the commander and executive officer stood. The gondola was enclosed, giving some protection from the elements, although as it was unheated it was bitterly cold. The front and sides had triplex glass or celluloid windows, which gave a very good view forward and downwards. The commander stood near the front with his map table, and had an electric telegraph to order changes in engine speed to the mechanics in the engine gondolas. He had a number of speaking tubes to communicate with the crew in different parts of the ship. Behind the commander stood the rudder man, operating a wheel to control direction and having a compass to work to. Next to him stood the elevator man with a wheel operating the elevators; he had a number of instruments to measure the height, rate of climb and inclination of the ship (whether the nose was level or pointing up or down). Zeppelins were so large and slow that they were not piloted, in the way that modern aircraft are, by one person. The commander gave orders for crewmen who turned large wheels to operate the rudders and elevators, as they would in ships, the officers and steering crew working in the enclosed front gondola of the ship. They communicated with the crew operating the engines, dropping ballast or manning the machine guns by the speaking tubes or electric telegraph.

The second in command, the executive or watch officer, operated the bomb sight and actually dropped the bombs. He used a sight manufactured by Carl Zeiss of Jena. Mounted by the front windows, it was a costly and complex instrument. It was calibrated for different weights of bomb, and could also be used to measure the drift or speed of the Zeppelin across the ground. There was a panel of electrical switches to operate the bomb release mechanism. The Carl Zeiss sight allowed very accurate bombing; the bomb aimer could hit almost anything when he could see the target, particularly when the Zeppelin was hovering. The operative words are 'see the target', as in cloud or misty conditions the Zeppelin was blind, which is why we get examples of very accurate bombing, with two bombs dropped within yards of each other, but often on the wrong city.

Behind the command section was the radio room, used by the wireless operator and generally the executive officer. It was well insulated, to keep it quiet, and hence was warm, making it the best place to work on the ship. Zeppelins were fitted with powerful Telefunken radio sets able to receive and transmit signals by Morse code. They had long trailing wire radio aerials that could be wound in and out during a flight. It was normal practice to take it in if there was any danger of lightning. The radio room had a specialist wireless operator, though the executive officer often worked there, coding and decoding messages. The radio also had another function, establishing the ship's position for navigation. The German Army and Navy had a number of direction-finding stations, most at the Zeppelin bases, but some further south at Borkum Island and Bruges to improve accuracy. To establish position, the radio operator would send a signal to these stations - each airship had its own code - and they would then measure the strength and direction of the signal, and by comparing results from the different stations by a process of triangulation, could estimate and send back their position to the Zeppelin. There were some problems with this. If the Zeppelin crew heard the position, so did the British, who had radio stations on the East Coast directly linked by telephone cable to the Admiralty in London. The second more serious problem was that the radio positioning system was of limited accuracy, and tended to lead to overconfidence about navigation among Zeppelin crews. At a range of 200-300 miles, radio location was a crude measure as it could be as much as 50 miles out.

It has to be recognized that radio, like so much else in Zeppelin technology, was in its infancy and many factors, such as the effect of atmospheric conditions on the apparent direction of radio signals, were unknown. The fact that the British could read their signals was soon understood, and by the middle of 1916 radio discipline had improved. Commanders remained dependant on the radio positioning system for navigation until the end of the war. The single most important factor in the defeat of the Zeppelins was that the British (and to a lesser extent the French) could pick up radio signals from the Zeppelins and use them to locate them, transmitting their approximate positions to the interceptors. By 1918, the Germans were developing a radio positioning system in which the Zeppelin was silent, but by then the Zeppelin was largely finished as a viable weapon, so it had only limited use.

Behind the command gondola of a 'P' or 'Q' type Zeppelin was the front engine gondola, which contained one engine, and the rear gondola, which had three engines. Each engine was controlled by a mechanic, who received his orders to set the throttle position by an electric telegraph, operated by the commander. The front gondola engine and gearbox directly drove a propeller. The three engines in the rear gondola were one behind the other, the rear engine and gearbox directly driving a propeller. The other two drove a propeller on the port or starboard side of the hull. The propellers were mounted on outriggers, a tubular structure on each side of the ship. Though these structures looked flimsy, they were practical and strong. They added drag and were less efficient than direct drive, but had the crucial advantage of allowing the propellers to reverse direction to help with low-speed manoeuvring. Each engine had its own mechanic, able to maintain and often repair them in flight. The engine gondolas had one big advantage for the mechanics – they were usually warm, though a flight next to a very noisy engine, being subject to exhaust and petrol fumes, often left mechanics deaf or with headaches for days after a flight.

The early 'P' type ships were fitted with the Maybach C-X six-cylinder 22.6-litre side valve 210hp engines. The C-X was a heavy engine with a poor power weight ratio and high fuel consumption. This limited the range or bomb load of the ships it was fitted in, but had one big advantage: it was well tested and reliable. As part of the programme to improve the performance of the Zeppelin fleet, the Maybach Company, a subsidiary of the Zeppelin Company at Friedrichshafen, developed a new engine, the HSLu, a more powerful, high compression 19-litre overhead valve six-cylinder 240hp engine. It was lighter, had a much better power-to-weight ratio and better fuel consumption. There was, however, a problem, as in early 1916 the engine was rushed from the design stage to production and installation in 'P' and 'Q' class Zeppelins without a proper testing programme. This was disastrous; everything that could go wrong with an engine did go wrong. They overheated, seized up and burned out bearings, and it was unusual for a Zeppelin to return from a mission without at least one engine out of order. On the 31 January 1916 raid, engine trouble was the main cause of the loss of Zeppelin *L.19*, and, to a greater or lesser extent, the cause of many of the problems the later model Zeppelins faced. The problems were eventually sorted, and the HSLu became the principal Zeppelin engine, with 490 being produced.

The fuel, ballast and bombs of the Zeppelin were attached to the keel, between the gondolas near the centre of gravity, so when these were used the ship remained in balance. Petrol was kept in aluminium tanks distributed along the keel; in an emergency these tanks could be jettisoned, if no other ballast was available, the tanks just dropping through the covering to the ground. Most ballast was water carried in rubberized cloth sacks attached to the keel; the water was released by the elevator man in the control gondola, pulling toggles to do so. As an example, we know that when Zeppelin *L.21* set out from Nordholz on 31 January 1916 to bomb the Midlands, it was carrying 17,720lb of ballast. This can be compared with the 4,910lb of bombs it carried.

A 'Q' class Zeppelin carried about 2 tons of bombs in a bay with an opening bomb door. Reports from the ground often talk about seeing a light inside the airship, which was probably seen through the open bomb door. The bombs hung from the keel in racks and were dropped by an electrical release mechanism, controlled by the bomb aimer in the front gondola.

The bomb release mechanism was the only thing in the Zeppelin that was directly controlled by the operator. If the release mechanism went wrong, they could be released manually by crew members stationed in the bomb bay. Bombs had to be armed after the Zeppelin took off; this was done by the bomb bay crew just after the ship left the German coast and passed over the North Sea

There were two types of bomb carried by the Zeppelin – high explosive (HE) and incendiary. HE bombs were pear-shaped, made from thick steel plate and were often called Carbonit, after the manufacturer. They had a round stabilizing fin at the tail. The bombs came in standard sizes: 10kg (22lb) 50kg (110lb) 100kg (220lb) and 300kg (660lb). They were reliable, almost always exploding if they fell on hard ground. The explosion would throw a cone of shrapnel from the steel casing dozens of yards. Most injuries were caused by the flying shrapnel, or debris thrown by the explosion. Incendiary bombs were very different: weighing only about 25lb, they were not explosive, but were in effect huge firelighters. In the centre was a tube of Thermite, which was wrapped with a coil of rope covered in tar. When the bomb ignited, the Thermite would burn with a very hot flame, which would ignite the tar and rope, which would burn for several minutes, setting fire to any building it was lodged in. Though there are a few reports of houses burning down after being hit by an incendiary bomb, it was very rare. There are more reports of people picking up burning incendiary bombs on shovels and taking them outside or covering them with earth. Most deaths and serious injuries were caused by HE bombs, either directly, by shrapnel wounds or by being hit by or buried by falling masonry. The idea of using HE and incendiary bombs together was that the HE bombs would open up buildings by blowing down walls or blowing off roof tiles, allowing the incendiary bombs to fall into them and set alight things like roof timbers.

Most Zeppelins also carried a searchlight, which could be used for finding targets or locations, but were mainly used for communication in Morse code with other airships, ships and ground stations as a safer alternative to wireless.

The other weapons the Zeppelin carried were machine guns. Most Navy airships carried six or seven 7.92mm Maxim guns. There was a gun on each side in both the front and rear gondolas. They fired through large windows, very like the waist gun positions in US B-17 bombers in the Second World War. Right at the back of the ship, behind the rudders and elevators in the cruciform tail, sat the lookout and rear gunner, who had a very cold and lonely job, communicating with the command gondola some 400ft in front of him. He had the only clear view behind the airship, so had an important role when fighters were about. The coldest position on a Zeppelin was the upper gun platform, right on top of the hull above the control gondola. This was a flat platform with two or three machine-gun positions, protected from the elements only by a canvas windbreak. They had speaking tubes and electric telegraphs to communicate with the commander. In many layers of clothes to cope with the cold, just getting to the gun position was difficult enough as they had to climb about 100ft up a ladder in an access shaft of canvas-covered duralumin rings.

'P' and 'Q' type Zeppelins had crews of up to twenty. The commander, men operating the steering controls, the radio operators and some machine-gunners worked in the control gondola. Other men were stationed in the vast envelope of the ship. There were usually two officers and two or three warrant officers in a crew, the other ranks tending to be non-commissioned officers. The officers and warrant officers remained on duty for the entire mission; the other ranks were divided into watches. Men tended to man the machine guns when off duty, which was probably a colder and more arduous task then being on watch.

Whatever they did, the crew worked in bitterly cold conditions. They wore fur-lined clothing, and fur-lined rubber or straw boots to avoid causing sparks or damaging the fragile aluminium frame of the Zeppelin. A number of photographs show officers wearing fur-lined leather flying suits. The crews had few creature comforts. A few hammocks were hung from girders in the hull, above the keel. The crews were usually well fed, much better than the blockaded civilian population. Sandwiches, sausages and chocolate were popular. Tea and coffee was available from thermos flasks, as no heating of food was possible, for obvious reasons. Ships sometimes had cans of self-heating stew or soup. A special ballast bag supplied drinking water, and brandy was usually available, though this was at the commander's discretion, and some took pride in running a 'dry' ship. Last but not least, there was a head or toilet near the back of the ship. It was quite difficult to get to for crew at the front of the ship, in bulky flying kit; it was augmented by relief tubes in most crew positions.

There are reports from the interrogation of crews who survived after being shot down – all Navy men. The intelligence reports give a lot of personal details, and are noticeably free of the 'wicked baby-killing Hun' view put over in the popular press. The crews generally come over as highly skilled and intelligent men, many former merchant seamen, going to airships as naval reservists. They tended to be mature: the crew of Zeppelin

L.15 captured in April 1916 ranged in age between 23 and 40. The commander, Kapitänleutnant Breihaupt, was 33. The average age was about 30. Much the same applied to the crew of *L.33*, shot down in September 1916. Their ages ranged between 23 and 43, and the commander, Kapitänleutnant Alois Bocker, was 37. The biographies in the reports are fascinating. While the officers were very correct, saying very little, afraid to pass on military information, many crew members were very chatty. They were proud of their skills and passed on a lot of useful information, gained by oblique conversations about seemingly non-military matters.

The Zeppelin bases were as much monuments to German scientific ingenuity as the airships themselves. The Zeppelins were kept in huge sheds, each about an eighth of a mile long. Some sheds were capable of taking two Zeppelins moored side by side. So well-built were the sheds that some are still standing today. Each Zeppelin and ground crew had a specific home shed. Many of the Army bases were in Belgium, though some were based on different parts of the Eastern Front. There were also bases in Bulgaria and Hungary. Most of the German naval Zeppelin bases were on the windswept north-west coast of Germany, though some were on the Baltic coast. There were several bases used for bombing raids: Ahlhorn near Breman; Hage near Emden, a few miles from the Dutch border; Nordholz near Cuxhaven, for most of the war the headquarters of the Airship Service; Seddin, near Danzig; Tondern in Schleswig-Holstein, near the Danish border; and Whittmund, near Wilhelmshaven.

As well as the sheds, the bigger bases also contained large gas works, using the Messerschmitt process to produce hydrogen gas by passing steam over hot iron. Each base was easily identifiable from the air. As well as having three or four huge airship hangers, they had prominent gasholders, identical in appearance to civilian gasometers. These were used to store the hydrogen used to 'top up' the Zeppelins after their missions. The gas production plant at Nordholz was capable of producing 1.5 million cubic feet of hydrogen per day. Later in the war, the bases were to become as vulnerable as the flying airships, subject to raids by carrier-borne British aeroplanes, but in early 1916 they provided a safe haven for the Zeppelins and their crews.

To service three or four Zeppelins, each base required a large ground crew of about 500 men. Though the ships required a lot of repair and maintenance, it was during take-off and landing that the large ground crew was vital. The Zeppelins could not manoeuvre on the ground like modern aircraft. Especially in windy weather, very large numbers of men were required to take each airship out of its shed and return it after its mission. For take-off, specially trained crews of 300 to 400 men would walk the airship out of its hangar, pulling it along by ropes attached to its keel. For landing, the Zeppelin would hover over the field and drop landing ropes to the ground crew, who would haul it down and walk it into its shed, using the keel ropes to pull it.

Life in a Zeppelin base must have been strange. Nordholz was a huge shore base run in accord with strict naval tradition. It was busy: the ground crew of some 800 men had plenty to do maintaining the ships. But they lived in clean dry barracks, eating far better than the civilian population. Flight crews had a gilded existence. Popular heroes, many had the Iron Cross, and food was plentiful. Officers in particular lived a very privileged existence. Some lived off the base with their families. There was an active social life around the officers' mess or casino. Men dressed for dinner and drank good wine. There was of course a price: about half the Zeppelin commanders and crews would die in action, most shot down in flames.

All Zeppelin raids on Britain took place at night, almost always when there was little moonlight. In general, Army airships would attack by flying over the Belgian coast and cross the English Channel to raid the South-East. The Navy generally attacked from further north, crossing the North Sea from the Frisian coast of Germany and flying across East Anglia or the North-East.

A typical Navy raid took twenty to twenty-four hours: about seven to eight hours crossing the North Sea, an average of about eight hours over Britain, and another seven or eight hours to get back over the North Sea. The raids were timed so the airships would cross the coast in darkness, and leave before dawn. This was not difficult in January, with the long nights, so ships took off about noon GMT. It was more difficult in the summer months, when Zeppelins took off later in the afternoon and were vulnerable crossing the coast and on the way back in the early morning dawn light.

From mid-1915, British Naval Intelligence would know at about noon there was to be a Zeppelin attack by monitoring coded wireless transmissions, which could give clues where the attack would take place. By using a system of triangulation of the direction of radio signals, they would have some idea where the airships would cross the coast. The police across the country were told an air-raid was possible. However, no public air-raid warnings were given, until the position of the airships was known. Observers on the ground, usually soldiers awaiting deployment to France, would report on the time they saw an airship, its approximate height and direction, and would telephone this information to regional command centres. For much of 1915, this was a chaotic process. There was no effective tracking system because of poor communication between the War Office and the Admiralty. After the great raid of 31 January 1916, the system was much improved and tracked an airship as it crossed the country.

The 'P' and 'Q' type Zeppelins were very effective weapons. By my calculations, of the 557 people killed in Zeppelin raids over Britain, 372 were at the hands of 'P' or 'Q' types, 139 in 1915 and 233 in 1916. The main problem when they were designed was a failure to predict the danger of aeroplane attacks. This is well illustrated in an interview Heinrich Mathy gave to the *New York Times* German correspondent in October 1915. Asked whether he had ever been attacked by an English aeroplane, Mathy said he hadn't:

> He had never been bothered by them, it took some time for an aeroplane to reach the height of a Zeppelin, 'and by then we are gone'. He said over England the crew manned the machine guns and watched for them. Personally he was not much afraid of them, and thought if they attacked he could make it interesting and take care of them.

We know of course how wrong he was, but it seems that at the time he was honestly reflecting what he thought. He was quite willing to say how much he feared anti-aircraft fire. Yet it seems crews in the airship service genuinely thought that aeroplanes were not a major threat; Zeppelins could out-climb them and if necessary fight them off.

In 1915, the searchlight and anti-aircraft gun combination was what worried the Zeppelin commanders. In reality, it was probably more important psychologically than physically. The combination of searchlights and gun fire was very frightening, and there are many incidents where commanders would turn back to escape. Mathy talked of 'searchlights like tentacles seeking to drag the Zeppelin to destruction' and the red flashes of the guns and the ominous crack of shrapnel shell, louder than the engine of the airship.

In practice, anti-aircraft artillery wasn't as dangerous as it seemed to be. There are a number of examples of Zeppelins being hit by shells and getting home, or at least landing safely. Mathy, in his 'lucky ship' *L.13*, was hit by a 6-pdr shell in September 1915 which damaged a number of gas cells, but he was able to limp home. In 1916, Joachim Breithaupt in *L.15* and Alois Bocker in *L.33* were hit by shells which damaged gas cells and forced the Zeppelins down, but most of the crews survived and were captured alive. What happened in these cases is that the shell went right through the

Zeppelin without hitting anything solid enough to make it explode. It damaged the ship, causing a loss of gas, but did not cause a fire. If the crew were unlucky and the shell hit something heavy like an engine, it would explode and the resulting hydrogen fire would leave very little behind.

The 'R' Type Zeppelin

With the seeming success of the 'P' type Zeppelin in 1915, both the German Army and Navy were enthusiastic about the introduction of a more modern and efficient airship. This was the 'R' type, called by the British the 'Super' Zeppelin, though the Germans never used this description. The new design was bigger and better, a six-engine machine that could fly further and faster, with an increased bomb load. There was opposition by the Navy to some of the design features, as the new ships would be too big for some of their existing sheds, but the High Command decided to go ahead with the ships, and alter the sheds rather than build smaller Navy airships. Though based on the 'P' type, the 'R' type was longer at 649ft and had a more streamlined hull with a diameter of 78ft. With a gas capacity of 1,949,600ft³ of hydrogen in nineteen gas cells, the 'R' type was faster at 62 mph, had better endurance and could carry almost five tons of bombs.

In general, the construction was similar to the 'P' type, the duralumin framework having a similar spacing, though the hull was more streamlined. Unlike the 'P' and 'Q' type, which had a constant diameter along most of their length, with just the bow and stern streamlined, the diameter of the 'R' type changed from bow to stern. This made construction more difficult but was better aerodynamically. The most obvious difference was the new ships had six engines. They were Maybach HSLu, high compression 19-litre overhead valve six-cylinder 240hp engines. The front engine was mounted behind the control gondola. There were three engines in the rear gondola, one driving a propeller directly, the other two driving propellers on the side brackets, which though they added drag were still seen as the best way to provide the crew with the essential ability to reverse the direction of two propellers for manoeuvring during take-off and landing. They were also useful when hovering during bomb aiming. The additional two engines were in small streamlined gondolas in the middle of the hull. The new ships had a much increased lifting capacity, and not only could they carry more bombs but more fuel and ballast, giving them the ability to fly longer missions.

The main fault of the new type was that it followed the same design philosophy as its predecessors. It could fly near the limits of anti-aircraft guns at a height that made accurate bombing possible. Aeroplanes were not seen as a major problem. The 'R' ships were very well armed, and could carry up to ten machine guns: four in the front and rear gondolas, three on top of the hull and one in the tail, like the 'P' type. It could also carry one in each of the middle gondolas, though it is doubtful if any were carried there in practice.

Seventeen 'R' type ships were made from May 1916, with fifteen for the Navy and two for the Army. *LZ.62*, commissioned as *L.30* by the Navy, first flew on 28 May 1916. Much of the commissioning and development work was done by the young but very experienced Kapitänleutnant Horst von Buttlar. When the airship was finally handed over to the Navy, Buttlar took the elderly Count Ferdinand von Zeppelin as a passenger from Friedrichshafen to Nordholz. On the way they flew over the village of Zepelin in Mecklenburg, West Pomerania, where the Zeppelin family had originated from, though he had never set foot there.

Looking at the production statistics for the 'R' type, we can see the Navy remained enthusiastic about the airship as a weapon, while the Army was increasingly dubious. There are good reasons for this in both services. The airship was (in modern parlance) a multi-use combat aircraft. The Army had used them for battlefield reconnaissance, tactical bombing and strategic bombing. They found out in 1914 they were too vulnerable for daylight reconnaissance, then 1915 and the Verdun campaign showed they were too vulnerable to ground fire for tactical bombing, which only left strategic bombing. The loss of *LZ.85* over Salonika in May 1916 and *LZ.81* over Bucharest on 27 September 1916, both to anti-aircraft fire, and the shooting down of *SL.XI (SL.11)* over London on 2 September 1916 by an aeroplane, just confirmed the position, and by June 1917 the German Army had stopped using airships. The two 'R' type machines, *LZ.113* and *LZ.120*, were transferred to the Navy: the others were scrapped.

The Navy saw things very differently. While the Zeppelin is best known as a bombing aircraft, its main naval function was aerial reconnaissance. The reason the German Navy was so enthusiastic about the Zeppelin is that it was highly efficient when used as the eyes of the fleet. Ernst Lehmann, in his semi-autobiographical work *The Zeppelins*, describes a mundane but vital task Zeppelins were involved in: mine clearance. A significant part of the British blockade was the laying of minefields. This was done at night or in stormy or foggy weather. In clear weather, a Zeppelin could locate a minefield much more quickly than a surface ship. They could destroy a single mine with machine-gun fire, or drop buoys to mark a minefield for minesweeping flotillas. They were even able to put down on the sea to pick up an officer from a minesweeper to help him get a complete idea of the extent of a large minefield, and then return him to his ship. For most of the war, the co-operation between airships and surface ships remained valuable, and though Britain's use of seaplanes and aircraft carriers would threaten the Zeppelin, they still had a useful role.

The 'height climbers'

However, Zeppelins will be remembered as the first terror bombers, and its more normal and useful military role as a naval observation aircraft remains a footnote to history. By the end of 1916, it was evident to everyone in the Naval Airship Service that aeroplanes were the real danger and that Zeppelins could not fight them off. The only answers were speed or height. Speed was briefly considered when it was suggested that two more engines could be added to 'R' type ships. This was soon disregarded, as the increase in weight would only produce a slight increase in speed with a reduction in ceiling, so the overall effect would be negative. There was no way the Zeppelin could fly faster than enemy fighters.

Height was very different. The Naval Airship Service's Leader of Airships, Fregattenkapitan Peter Strasser, strongly argued that 'high altitude was the best defence against aeroplanes'. Zeppelins were already operating near the maximum ceiling of enemy fighters, and if they could operate at an altitude of about 20,000ft they would be invulnerable to aeroplane attack. A conference took place at the German Admiralty early in 1917, when it was agreed that future Zeppelins would be built able to operate at altitudes above about 20,000ft. The main way this would be done was by a stringent policy of weight reduction. The airships resulting from this were know in Britain, for obvious reasons, as the 'height climbers', and for some time were able to roam over England free from aeroplane attack, though other problems created by operating at high altitude certainly diminished their usefulness as weapons.

There was not a specific type of high altitude Zeppelin. The first were four 'R' types coming in to service, *L.35* to *L.39*, which were modified before commissioning. The main modification was the removal of one engine from the rear gondola, a reduction in fuel capacity and the elimination of half of the bomb release mechanisms. This did not mean a reduction in the bomb load, just that the Zeppelin would carry fewer but bigger bombs. The modification of the 'R' types led to a reduction in weight of 4,000-5,000lb, with no reduction in the war load. In trials, all could reach an altitude of 16,000–17,000ft. As more Zeppelins came along the production line, other modifications were made: there was a new smaller and more streamlined rear gondola with two engines driving one propeller, which allowed the drag-producing side propeller framework to be removed. Reversing gears were fitted to engines in the middle gondolas, for low-speed manoeuvring. Later models were given different type designations, as 'S', 'T', 'U' and 'V' type machines. They remained the same size, with a gas capacity of about two million cubic feet of hydrogen. The later models had lighter and weaker duralumin frames, thinner gas cells and five rather than six HsLu engines. The later airships were more fragile and more difficult to fly, but each modification to 'add lightness' increased the useful lift and operational ceiling on bombing missions.

The height climbers were a failure, though they could operate during most of 1917 at a height unreachable by British fighters. The other problems created by operating at 20,000ft remained unsolved. The most important was altitude sickness, the symptoms of which are generally described as breathlessness, dizziness and headaches. Most debilitating is a feeling of weakness: any physical task seems to take enormous effort, leaving the individual breathless and lethargic. Crews were provided with oxygen bottles which they could suck from, but there were problems in that the oxygen was often contaminated, with oil giving it a vile taste, and the crewmen were left with symptoms similar to a hangover after a mission. There was also an attitude that taking oxygen was a sign of weakness, and crewmen put off using it until the symptoms were very bad. Later in the war, bottles of liquid air were provided, which seemed to work well, giving the individual a feeling of strength and well-being.

Altitude sickness was never completely cured on the height climbers, and the lack of oxygen combined with cold led to crewmen often incapable of performing any normal duty. It is almost as if Peter Strasser, the Leader of Airships, thought courage and determination would allow his crew to operate at high altitude without proper equipment, but Zeppelin crews were human and subject to the same laws of physiology as anyone else. Lack of oxygen and cold led to an inability by crewmen to maintain the airship in flight, which led to mechanical failure and destroyed more airships than British fighters. However, even if knowledge of aviation medicine had advanced and crews had been fitted with well-designed oxygen masks and heated clothing, there were other important failures. Zeppelins could only accurately bomb targets they could see. On most raids in 1917 and 1918, the Zeppelins were well above the clouds and couldn't navigate let alone bomb accurately. The wireless location system was essentially useless, as well as being dangerous as it was far more useful to the defences than the Zeppelins. The German weather forecasting system was fairly reliable at low altitudes, but consistently failed to predict the weather at extreme height, and Zeppelins were caught in gale-force winds and crashed as a result. Eventually, fighter aircraft could simply fly higher and faster than Zeppelins, and the era of the airship was over.

The last of the line

After the various types based on the 'R' series, the Zeppelin Company produced only four more airships during the war. There were two of the 'W' types, often called the Africa Ships because they were constructed to fly from their bases in Bulgaria to supply the army of General Paul von Lettow-Vorbeck in East Africa. The *L.57* and *L.59* were basically 'R' type ships lengthened to 743 feet to add two extra gas cells to increase the capacity to $2,418,700\text{ft}^3$. There were numerous modifications made because they were designed for a one-way mission. The ship would be stripped to allow the supply of extra war materials to the forces in East Africa, and the crew would stay with the Army or return overland. However, the mission did not go ahead because of the changing military situation and the airships returned to normal duties.

The last Zeppelins constructed for war were the 'X' type, started in July 1918. Only one saw action, the *L.70*, which was 693ft long with a diameter of 78ft. It was built for speed as well as height, with seven MB1Va engines of 245hp. It had a gas capacity of $2,195,800\text{ft}^3$ and a top speed of 81 mph. It was to be the last Zeppelin to raid England and was shot down in flames.

The Zeppelin Company also completed *L.71* but it did not see service and was handed over to Britain as part of war reparations. The company did not complete a third 'X' type, *L.72*, until after the war, and it was handed over to France under war reparations.

Schutte-Lanz airships

Like the Zeppelin Company, the Schutte-Lanz Company developed its ships as the war went on. The first to see active service was the *SL.2*, which was a 'B' type. The company produced only one of these, in May 1914, for the Army. It was quite active, engaged in bombing missions on the Western and Eastern Fronts. It was 472ft long with a diameter of 60ft. When it was produced in February 1915, the 'C' type was the largest airship in the world.

Three of these - *SL.3*, *SL.4* and *SL.V* - were produced from February 1915, two for the Navy and one, *SL.V*, for the Army. At 513ft long with a diameter of 64ft, they were generally seen as more advanced than the Zeppelins at the time, with four C-X 210hp engines, a gas capacity of 1,147,575ft³ and covered gondolas. They were capable of a top speed of about 53mph and had a ceiling of about 8,000ft. The best Schutte-Lanz was the 'E' type, of which twelve were produced, eight for the Army and four for the Navy. They were very similar to the 'Q' type Zeppelin, 570ft long with a diameter of 65ft, giving a gas capacity of 1,369,000ft³. They were fitted with four HSLu 240hp engines, and could reach 55mph and operate at about 8,000ft. The last Schutte-Lanz to be produced, the 'F' type, was similar to 'R' type Zeppelins, with almost the same length of 651ft, a diameter of 75ft and a gas capacity of 1,989,700ft³. With five HSLu engines, it had a top speed of about 60mph and a useful lift of about 83,000lb, similar to a 'V' type Zeppelin. The 'F' type built for the Navy in September 1917 served in the Baltic late in 1917 and was destroyed in the Ahlhorn fire in early 1918.

The Navy Airship Service, particularly Peter Strasser, was bitterly opposed to taking any Schutte-Lanz ships, his argument based on the wooden airframe which he thought not only made new SL ships inferior to Zeppelins, but inevitably made them much less durable, as the wooden frame would gain weight and weaken as it absorbed moisture. When forced to take Schutte-Lanz airships, Strasser tended to use them in the East, where they were subject to less opposition. It is difficult to separate prejudice from wanting the best for his crews; he claimed they were 'useless for combat'. The Schutte-Lanz Company was favoured by the War Ministry, as a counter to a Zeppelin monopoly, while Strasser had a close relationship with the Zeppelin Company. It is difficult to find any opinion in post-war memoirs by Zeppelin men about the value of Schutte-Lanz ships, though they recognize Strasser was bitterly opposed. After the war, Strasser and Count Zeppelin tended to be referred to in almost saint-like terms, so it is not surprising that little is said about the squeeze on Schutte-Lanz products.

It is the case that fewer Schutte-Lanz ships were lost in combat than Zeppelins, but they were deliberately kept from the more difficult operations, so this is to be expected. In the early days of the war, there is no doubt that Zeppelin used Schutte-Lanz design features to build the very successful 'P' and 'Q' type Zeppelins. After that, it seems Schutte-Lanz followed the lead set by Zeppelin. They were working on an experimental aluminium framed airship in 1918, but this was halted by the end of the war.

Chapter Two

Operations in 1914

In the West in 1914, Zeppelins were involved in a war of movement. Acting on the Schlieffen Plan, the Germans moved rapidly across France and Belgium. There were fierce battles at the German frontier in August and then on the Marne in September, which slowed the Germans, but by November most of the fighting took place in Flanders and led to both sides digging in with the massive trench system from Nieuport in Belgium to the Swiss frontier: the Western Front. For the next four years, neither side could make a decisive breakthrough and the war was a slow process of attrition.

On the Eastern Front, there was also an initial war of movement. In early August, the Russians invaded East Prussia, at first advancing quickly, but when the Germans became organized they suffered a massive defeat at the Battle of Tannenberg in late August. The German advance continued into the Masurian Lakes in September, but was held up by Austro-Hungarian defeats in Galacia. By the end of the year, the Russians had suffered a series of massive defeats but the front line was roughly where it had been before the outbreak of war. However, it was a fluid line, with the opposing armies holding their positions around fortresses. Germany was no longer under threat from Russian forces, though some of Austria-Hungary was.

Airships operated on both fronts. Most were Army machines. The Zeppelins were used in the early months for daylight reconnaissance, which rapidly proved impractical. The early model Zeppelins flew at about 2,000ft and provided excellent reports of enemy positions and movements, which with radio could be reported quickly to regimental commanders. However, there was a serious problem: if the Zeppelin could see infantry or cavalry, then they could also see it. And a lot of soldiers with a lot of rifles were certain to hit anything as big as an airship. There were a number of losses because of this. Bullets would generally not bring the Zeppelin down immediately when it was hit, but the punctures in gas cells made by bullets led to a loss of hydrogen, forcing the airship to land. If the Zeppelin was near its base, this was not a major problem, and the gas cells would be repaired. The problem was if the airship couldn't make it back to base. Obviously if it landed behind enemy lines the crew would be captured, but there were also examples of ships that landed in German territory but were lost because the ship couldn't be safely recovered. The crew would use anchor ropes to hold the Zeppelin, but without a storage shed and a trained crew to walk it in there, windy conditions could easily destroy a Zeppelin.

After a month or so, the Army stopped using Zeppelins for daylight operations and switched to tactical bombing, usually of enemy supply dumps or railway junctions. This was the main task of Army ships during the later months of 1914. It was very dangerous work, often carried out in moonlight for greater accuracy. The Army had a number of successes, mainly on the Eastern Front, but lost several airships.

The German Navy used its airships for joint work with warships, reconnaissance and minesweeping work. It also carried out a few night bombing raids on dock or shore installations on the Baltic coast of the Eastern Front. Both the Army and Navy saw a significant role for the airship as a strategic bomber, a weapon that could win the war by destroying the enemy's will to carry on by destroying its major cities. In December, German battle cruisers bombarded Hartlepool and Scarborough on the east coast of England. The Zeppelin Company had an order for thirty-eight modern airships, and terror bombing would begin in 1915.

In August 1914, the German Army was enthusiastic about the airship as a weapon. It had six Zeppelins and one Schutte-Lanze ship, as well as two non-rigid (blimp) craft. The Navy only had one, though some of the civilian craft mainly used for pleasure flights in the summer were requisitioned and fitted with bomb racks and radio. As we shall see, flying in them in 1914 was not a pleasure.

5/6 August 1914

'L' type Army Zeppelin *LZ.VI*: Oberleutnant Kleinschmidt commanded the first Zeppelin raid of the war, flying from Cologne to bomb Liege with 420lb of artillery shells with tails made from blankets to act as stabilizing fins. He attacked from low altitude because of cloud, and anti-aircraft and rifle fire punctured the gas cells. He crash-landed in a forest near Bonn, a few miles from his hanger in Cologne.

16 August 1914

'L' type Army Zeppelin *Z.VII*: Hauptman Otto Jacobi was probably the first Zeppelin commander to be shot down. *Z.VII* attacked units of the retreating French Army in Lorraine, in daylight, and had all its gas cells punctured by rifle fire. It was destroyed when it crashed near St Quirin, Lorraine, and many of the crew were captured.

23 August 1914

'H' type Army Zeppelin *Z.VIII*: Hauptmann Andree was shot down by French bullets and shell splinters. His first problem was friendly fire; as he crossed the front line, he was fired on by German troops. He climbed away to continue his mission, but it is not clear whether this fire punctured any gas cells, because when he saw French troops he was only a few hundred feet high. The steering gear was shot away and the gas cells splintered by thousands of bullets and shell splinters. He landed between the lines at Badonvilliers, in a wooded and mountainous region, trying to set fire to the Zeppelin, but it wouldn't burn because most of the hydrogen was gone. A squadron of French cavalry attempted to capture them, but the crew fought them off before marching eastward to meet an advance troop of the German Army eleven hours later.

25 August 1914

'M' type Army Zeppelin *Z.IX*: Hauptmann Alfred Horn bombed Antwerp, dropping ten 100kg bombs near the Royal Palace of King Albert. The bombs killed ten people and injured eight more.

28 August 1914

'H' type Army Zeppelin *Z.V*: On the Eastern Front, Zeppelins provided useful reconnaissance around Novogeorgievsk. During the Battle of Tannenberg, *Z.V*, piloted by Hauptmann Ernest Gruner, was sent out in daylight to bomb a railway station at Mlawa (now in Poland). It was shot down by gun fire from Russian infantry and machine-gunners, and the crew of ten were captured by Cossacks. Most of the captured men died in Siberia during the war.

1/2 September 1914

'H' type Army Zeppelin *Sachsen*: Oberleutnant zur See Ernst Lehmann, with Baron Max von Gemmingen as his second officer, took off to bomb

Antwerp. *Sachsen* was a civilian machine which had been taken over by the Army at the outbreak of war. Lehmann had worked for the Zeppelin Company before being commissioned into the Navy. Von Gemmingen was the nephew of Count Zeppelin. *Sachsen* took off from Cologne at 23.00 and followed the railways to Aachen and then over the Belgian border to Antwerp. They crossed the city at almost 6,000ft and the crew threw bombs over the side of the gondola. It appears no one was killed, though considerable damage was done. The Zeppelin was caught by a searchlight and fired on by anti-aircraft gun, but appears to have been undamaged. They got back to Cologne at about 11.00 the next day.

'M' type Army Zeppelin Z. *IX*: Hauptmann Alfred Horn was unable to reach his bombing target of Ostend, but made a detailed reconnaissance of Ghent before returning safely.

24 September 1914

'M' type Army Zeppelin *Z.IX*: Hauptmann Alfred Horn, this time attacked Ostend. His bombs did some damage at the railway station but there were no casualties. He also is reported to have carried out a reconnaissance mission along the French coast two days later.

8 October 1914

Attack on a Zeppelin shed at Dusseldorf: The British also carried out anti-Zeppelin missions. A Zeppelin shed in Dusseldorf was bombed by a Sopwith Tabloid flown by Flight Lieutenant Reginald Matrix RNAS (Royal Naval Air Service), flying from Antwerp. Inside was Zeppelin *Z.IX*, the airship commanded by Alfred Horn which had bombed Antwerp in August and Ostend in September. It was destroyed in the raid.

21 November 1914

Attack on Zeppelin works at Friedrichshafen: Three Avro 504 aircraft took off from a French airship base at Belfort to bomb the Zeppelin ring shed at Friedrichshafen on Lake Constance. They were Squadron Commander Edward Briggs, Flight Commander John Babington and Lieutenant Sidney Sippe, all from the Royal Naval Air Service. It is said that Noel Pemberton-Billing took part in a spying mission in a fishing boat on the lake as Zeppelin *L.7* was being completed. Though heralded as a major success by the British press, in fact little damage was done. No Zeppelins were destroyed. Two pilots got back to France: Babington and Sippe. Briggs was shot down and captured.

25 December 1914

'M' type Navy Zeppelin *L.6*: The young aristocrat Oberleutnant zur See Horst Treusch von Buttlar-Brandenfels, who was born on 14 June 1888, was one of the first Zeppelin commanders. Recently promoted, he was in combat on Christmas Day 1914, when truces were taking place all over the Western Front. On that day, British seaplanes attacked the Nordholz base, dropping a few bombs but causing little damage. Buttlar, in the 'M' type Zeppelin *L.6*, spotted HMS *Empress*, a British seaplane carrier, and attacked it. He dropped a bomb, which missed the target, but then engaged in a gun fight with the ship. He was fired on by rifles, replying with machine-gun fire. When he returned to Nordholtz there were a number of bullet holes in his gas bags.

Chapter Three

Terror bomber: the raids of 1915

At the beginning of 1915, the Western Front was static, the Germans generally taking a defensive posture against Allied attacks. Almost every attack led to severe losses and a continuation of the stalemate. The names of the battles of Neuve Chapelle, Second Ypres and Loos present a picture of massive loss of life for little gain. The casualty figures show the Germans lost 612,000 men, the French 1,092,000 and the British 279,000.

Army Zeppelins continued their tactical support raids against railways and supply dumps. This was still a very dangerous activity, although the ships generally bombed from a much greater altitude. It is often not appreciated that Zeppelins avoided the Western Front if at all possible. Zeppelin pilot Horst von Buttlar wrote, in his autobiography, probably the best description of the Western Front at night, as he flew towards England:

> It was not pleasant to have that glowing white streak behind one – the bleeding wound. For that huge gleaming gash across the night-covered world was the Western Front! Thousands of simultaneous shots, explosions, star-shells and light rockets kept that terrible streak constantly glowing. It knew no night for years and years. To fly over that streak of fire meant certain death.

Though at times Zeppelins did fly over the Western Front, it was only in emergency situations, usually when gale-force winds prevented a return to base over the North Sea or Belgium. It was usually done in cloud, at maximum altitude and often with the engines stopped. As we shall see when we look at the Silent Raid in 1917, it was a death trap for many.

The German Army transferred troops and a number of airships to the Eastern Front. The German Army, commanded by Hindenburg and Ludendorff, were much more successful in the East, defeating the Russians in several battles and capturing Warsaw by August 1915. Once again, there was a pattern of German success and Austrian defeat, though by the summer of 1915, German support for the Austrians had largely stabilized the front. By the end of 1915, the Eastern Front ran from near Riga in the Baltic to the Carpathian Mountains. Army Zeppelins operated mainly in the north and centre of the front in tactical bombing attacks. It was dangerous work, though airships generally operated at higher altitude, learning the lessons of 1914. What was probably the most effective Zeppelin attack of the entire war took place in Russia in August 1915, when Zeppelin *LZ.XII*, commanded by Ernest Lehmann, bombed railway yards in Bialystok (now in Poland) and hit an ammunition train, the resulting explosions destroying the entire railway junction and much of the town. Airships were very active on the Eastern Front from June-September 1915. The German 12th Army under General Max von Gallwirz captured Warsaw between 4-7 August, Brest-Litovsk was captured on 25 August, Grodas on 2 September and Vilna (now Vilnus in Lithuania) on 19 September.

The German Navy continued its work with surface ships in the North Sea, but concentrated many of its resources on bombing England. East Anglia and the North-East were initially the main targets, with Hull, in particular, suffering civilian casualties, though London was soon seen as the major prestige target. The Army also put considerable resources into strategic bombing, with the South-East and London as targets, but there was little co-ordination between Army and Navy raids.

At first the Kaiser insisted that bombing of England be restricted to military targets such as shipyards, arsenals, docks and military installations. But cities were soon seen as military targets, both as the concept of total war developed and as military professionals realized that the ability of high-flying airships to engage in precision bombing was limited – although it took a long time for them to understand just how limited. The first Zeppelin attack on England was on 15 January 1915, when two Navy Zeppelins bombed Great Yarmouth, Snettisham and King's Lynn, killing four people and injuring sixteen. By May 1915, the Kaiser agreed that attacks could be made on London, but insisted the Royal palaces be spared. The changing orders of the Kaiser were very difficult to keep up with, and seemed to be based on some degree of humanity and regard for his British cousins. It was agreed on 9 July 1915 that the City of London could be bombed, but only between Saturday afternoon and Monday morning. Presumably, British bankers would not then be at their desks, and only a cynic would ask whether this aided or hindered the war effort. By 20 July, the Kaiser agreed that the City along with the rest of London could be bombed, so long as buildings of historic interest such as St Paul's Cathedral and the Tower of London were spared.

The first raid on London took place on 31 May 1915, utilizing two Army Zeppelins. During 1915 there were nineteen airship raids on England, killing about 182 people. The largest raid was the last attack of 1915 on London on 13/14 October, killing seventy-one people and causing £80,000 worth of damage. During 1915, all raids were either on London or the East Coast, which led to a concentration of anti-aircraft defences on the coast or around London.

19/20 January 1915

'M' type Navy Zeppelin *L.3*: In the first raid on England, carried out by Zeppelins from the German Navy, Kapitänleutnant Hans Fritz took off from Fuhlsbuettel, near Hamburg (now the site of Hamburg airport) with orders to attack targets in the Humber Estuary. He reached the British coast further south than anticipated, but after dropping a parachute flare he was fully aware of his position. Crossing the coast near Haisborough in Norfolk, he decided to attack Great Yarmouth, which he reached about 20.20. He used another parachute flare and dropped six HE and seven incendiary bombs on the town. Several buildings were destroyed in the vicinity of St Peter's Church. Two people were killed: Martha Mary Taylor and Samuel Alfred Smith, a bookmaker, the first to die in a Zeppelin attack. Returning to Fuhlsbuettel, *L.3* was badly affected by icing but got back to base at 08.40 the next day.

'M' type Navy Zeppelin *L.4*: Kapitänleutnant Magnus Graf von Platen-Hallermund, flying out of Fuhlsbuettel, was also affected by the weather. He thought he was in the Humber area, but had crossed the coast close to *L.3*, at Bacton in Norfolk, at about 20.30. He was totally lost all the time he was over England. He is recorded as dropping one HE bomb on the village of Snettisham, and he then flew towards Kings Lynn. He reported seeing a 'twinkling light' and said he was fired on by anti-aircraft guns, although there were in fact no guns, then dropped seven HE and six incendiary bombs on Kings Lynn. The bombs severely injured two people, who later died: a boy called Percy Goate and a widow, Alice Maud Gazley. Platen reported back to base by radio at about 23.45 that he had successfully bombed fortified places between the Tyne and Humber. *L.4* landed just after *L.3* the next morning at Fuhlsbuettel at 08.45, after more than twenty-two hours in the air.

'M' type Navy Zeppelin *L.6*: Oberleutnant zur See Horst von Buttlar left Nordholz in *L.6* at 08.38. He had the commander of the Naval Airship Service, Korvettenkapitan Peter Strasser, as a passenger. After some hours in

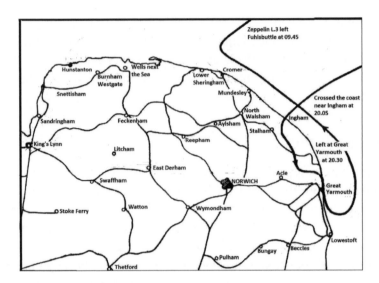

Map 3: The route of Zeppelin L.3 on the first raid on Britain. 19/20 January 1915.

Zeppelin L.3 took off from Fuhlsbüttel at 09.45 am. It crossed the coast at Ingham at 20.05 and dropped seven bombs on Great Yarmouth, at about 20.25, killing two people and injuring three more. It went out to sea at about 20.30, returning to Fuhlsbüttel at 08.40 the next morning.

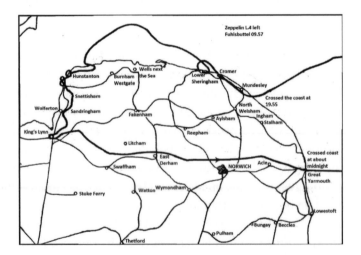

Map 4: The route of Zeppelin L.4 on the first raid on Britain. 19/20 January 1915.

Zeppelin L.4 took off from Fuhlsbüttel at 09.57 am. It crossed the coast near Ingham at 19.55. It then flew west, bombing Sheringham, Hunstanton, Snettisham and King's Lynn. It killed two people, and injured thirteen more, in King's Lynn at about 22.50. It flew back north of Norwich, crossing the coast at Great Yarmouth at about midnight. It returned to Fuhlsbüttel at 08.45.

the air near the Dutch island of Terschelling, the crankshaft of the port engine of *L.6* broke, which combined with the weather led Buttlar and Strasser to return to base. *L.6* landed at Nordholz at 17.30 after almost nine hours in the air. Buttlar was to become the only Zeppelin commander to remain in service right through the war. Both Fritz and Platen were soon out of it.

25 January 1915

Navy Parseval *PL.19*: Oberleutnant Meier's airship was the first of the German Navy to be lost to enemy action. The Parseval *PL.19* was a small non-rigid 'blimp'-like airship. It had been built by the Parseval Company for the British Army, but the outbreak of war left it in German hands. She had a crew of seven, including volunteer civilian airship pilot Dr Rotzell. She was ordered to bomb the Russian Baltic naval base at Libau (now Liepaja in Latvia). She took off from Konigsberg (now Kalingrad in Russia) loaded with seven 50kg bombs. The problems started early in the flight, the covering envelope starting to ice up. Even worse, there was a build-up of ice on one of the propellers, which was thrown off, damaging the envelope and causing a gas leak. By this time the ship was down to about 1,500ft. Meier saw through the clouds a factory near Libau, and dropped all their bombs on it, but didn't see the results. At low altitude and descending all the time, the airship was fired on by Russian troops. It seems their bullets hit the envelope but did little further damage as it was already leaking. Things got worse when both engines failed and the Parseval ditched in the Baltic about 7 miles off shore. The wreck was seen by a Russian minesweeper and the crew surrendered.

16 February 1915

(Zeppelins *L.3* and *L.4* were sent out on a scouting mission to look for British shipping off the Norwegian coast. Both had engine trouble and were caught in a gale, forcing them to make emergency landings near the Danish coast.)

'M' type Navy Zeppelin *L.3*: Kapitänleutnant Hans Fritz, out from Fuhlsbuettel, made an emergency landing on the Danish island of Fano. His crew were interned in neutral Denmark.

'M' type Navy Zeppelin *L.4*: Kapitänleutnant Magnus Graf von Platen-Hallermund, also operating from Fuhlsbuettel, crash landed just off the Danish coast. Eleven members of the crew were able to scramble out of the open gondola – they were the lucky ones. Lightened by the loss of eleven men, *L.4* lifted off from the sea with five crew members still in the rear gondola, was blown out to sea and was never seen again. The surviving eleven crew members were also interned in Denmark.

Platen escaped from Denmark in 1917 and was later reported to have served with White forces against the Bolsheviks. He died in Hamburg in 1943 from natural causes.

4 March 1915

'M' type Navy Zeppelin *L.8*: Kapitänleutnant Helmut Beelitz left the Army base at Gontrode near Ghent, the main reason for his flight being to return to his home airfield at Dusseldorf, but he decided to bomb London on the way. Due to low cloud, he flew low to locate his position, which at the time was near Ostend. He then flew at low altitude over Nieuport at the northern end of the Western Front where the Belgian trenches reached the sea. He was fired on by rifles and machine guns. Though this did not bring the ship down, the gas cells were punctured and Beelitz tried to get back to Dusseldorf. On the way back, he had engine trouble, and the combination of that and gas leakage caused him to crash land at Tirlemont in Belgium. The Zeppelin broke up in high winds after this.

Beelitz did not command an airship again. He survived the war and worked in the German Admiralty Archives after the war. It is said that in doing this he removed many of the records about his less than successful mission.

17 March 1915

'N' type Army Zeppelin *Z.XII*: Oberleutnant der Reserve Ernst Lehmann, according to his autobiography, left his base at Maubeuge in France and crossed the English coast at about 21.00. He was unable to locate the River Thames because of cloud cover, so turned back. Crossing the English Channel, he could see the lights of Calais, so used his invention, the cloud car, for the first time, with his second officer Baron Max von Gremmingen as observer. Suspended on a steel cable about 2,500ft below the Zeppelin, Gremmingen was able to see the town perfectly from 2,500ft, and telephoned the location of targets to the airship. They circled for 45 minutes and bombed storehouses in the docks, the railway station and arsenal. Though searchlights were operated, they did not see Grimmingen or the Zeppelin above the clouds. *Z.XII* returned to base but made a poor landing on a railway at Maubeuge, just outside the base, and damaged the tail. Repairs took about fourteen days.

21 March 1915

This was the first of only two airship raids on Paris. It is likely the main reason for this was that to bomb the city, an airship had to cross the Western Front, at considerable risk. Unlike London, Paris remained well lit. Although there was considerable damage caused, casualties were fairly light. Seven HE and 14 incendiary bombs were dropped. One person was killed and eight injured.

'M' type Army Zeppelin *Z.X*: Hauptmann Alfred Horn was hit by anti-aircraft fire near Noyon and came down near St Quinton, where the airship broke up.

'M' type Army Zeppelin *LZ.35*: Hauptmann Masius was hit by anti-aircraft fire, the guns and searchlights mounted on lorries and pursuing the airship across the city. There was considerable damage to the gas cells, but the airship returned safely.

'B' type Army Schutte-Lanz *SL.2*: Hauptmann Richard von Wobeser had been transferred from the Eastern Front on 26 September 1914, where he had been supporting Austrian forces in Galacia. Taking off from his base in Trier, he did not reach Paris as he was hit by anti-aircraft fire crossing the Western Front and suffered damage. Wobeser dropped his bombs near Compiegne and returned to base.

13 April 1915

'M' type Army Zeppelin *LZ.35*: Hauptmann Masius, back from the Paris raid, suffered one of the best examples of the crazy nature of the war at this stage. He was given orders to bomb supply dumps at Cassel, St Omer and Hasbrouck, but was handed a decoded urgent telegram sent by the Kaiser, who had received intelligence that the kings of England and Belgium were to attend a meeting in St Omer that day, so any attack was forbidden. The fact that about half the generals in the Allied armies were likely to be there as well didn't seem to count. Poperinghe was the alternative target, inhabited presumably by the lower classes. Masius' chivalry towards enemy royalty didn't help him, as he was shot down at Thielt near Ypres.

14/15 April 1915

'O' type Navy Zeppelin *L.9*: Kapitänleutnant Heinrich Mathy was regarded as the best and bravest Zeppelin commander, both by Peter Strasser, the Commander of the Airship Force, and the small group of British intelligence officers in the GHQ with an encyclopaedic knowledge of the personnel and methodology of the German airship service. Mathy was born on 4 April 1883 at Mannheim. He joined the Navy when he was 15 and was described as an exceptional cadet. He became a destroyer captain when still quite young, and was selected for a naval staff role. He went to the *Marine Akademie* in 1913 and 1914, and while there learned to fly in the DELAG Zeppelins. He was personally selected for the airship service by Strasser, and joined in 1915.

Mathy had a reputation for boldness, determination and superb navigational skills. He became known in Germany and Britain as the man who had been responsible for the fires causing some half million pounds worth of damage in London. As a Zeppelin commander, he was regarded as by far the best navigator, pressing on and finding targets long after his colleagues had given up. His combat reports provide some idea of his methods: on a flight over England, he tended to stop and hover every thirty to sixty minutes, often dropping a parachute flare to find his position; that established, he would plot a direct course and fly straight to his next waypoint, where he would drop another flare as he went towards his objective.

He first raided England on 14 April 1915 in Zeppelin *L.9*. He took off from Hage in the morning on a scouting mission off the coast near Terschelling Island; he failed to see any enemy ships, but radioed to seek permission to raid England as the weather was unusually favourable. He decided to attack the Tyneside shipyards, and reported bombing Jarrow, Hebburn, Carville and Newcastle. British reports show he crossed the coast at Blyth at 20.45 and actually bombed mining villages north of the Tyne: Sleekburn, Choppington, Bedlington, Cramlington and Wallsend, near Newcastle, injuring two people and causing minor damage. He crossed the coast near Marsden, returning to Hage the next morning.

15/16 April 1915

Following favourable reports from Mathy, Strasser ordered three Zeppelins to attack the Humber the next day. Strasser himself travelled with Peterson in *L.7*. None of the ships reached the Humber; the bombs fell in Norfolk and Essex.

'M' type Navy Zeppelin *L.5*: This was Kapitänleutnant Alois Bocker's first raid on England. He was a very experienced naval officer, who had previously been a merchant seaman: a captain with the Hamburg-Amerika shipping line. He was born on 12 May 1879 and survived the war. He left Fuhlsbuettel at about midday and was reported off Southwold at 21.40. He spent some time looking for targets before bombing Henham Hall, Reydon, and seeing the lights of a large town at about 23.30. This was Lowestoft, where he dropped HE and incendiary bombs on a timber yard, setting it on fire and damaging several houses, without causing any casualties. Bombing from about 5,200ft, he reported he could hear the sound of sirens and the bells of fire engines below.

'M' type Navy Zeppelin *L.6*: Oberleutnant zur See Horst von Buttlar left Fuhlsbuettel at about midday in *L.6*. He crossed the coast near the Naze at 23.30. Becoming completely lost, he was reported by British observers over Clacton, dropping his bombs near Malden in Essex. He reported being caught in a searchlight and fired on by cannon and machine guns. Though there were no searchlights in the area, it seems he was fired on by troops at Brightlingsea and by pom-pom guns at Landguard Fort. When he returned to base, one of his gas bags was completely empty; he counted two large and six smaller holes, and 17 bullet holes in other gas bags.

It is interesting to look at Buttlar's own version of events from his autobiography *Zeppelins over England*. He freely admits to being totally lost; he says he saw a single searchlight beam and only then realized he was over England. He then saw a myriad of faint lights beneath the gondola, then whitish-green beams came through the mist and suddenly covered the envelope in a blinding glare. Little red dots of fire appeared below - they were anti-aircraft guns. He climbed to the maximum height *L.6* could reach, 4,500ft. Leutnant zur See Hans Schiller then started dropping bombs, with three 50kg bombs and a large number of incendiary bombs which had to be armed by the removal of a pin and thrown over the side of the open gondola. The chief engineer helped the *Wachoffizer* do this. The HE bombs landed in a formation looking like the number six from the air: Buttlar says they had 'branded the number of the ship indelibly on English soil'. By that time the space between the Zeppelin and the ground had become a perfect inferno of gunfire and bursting shells - 'shrapnel meant for us'. Buttlar and *L.6* eventually got back to Fuhlsbuettel with only a few pints of petrol left in the tanks. When he got back he was questioned about where he had bombed, but didn't know so couldn't put it into his report. He prevaricated all day until the evening, when he bought an evening newspaper containing a report from the German Admiralty which said an airship had attacked certain fortified places in England. At the end it quoted a Dutch newspaper, the *Nieuwe Rotterdamsche Courant*, which said the London correspondent of the paper had reported an airship carried out a bombing raid at 01.15 over the English town of Maldon. He immediately telephoned his base to have the town included in his report, and a week or so later received a communication 'which stated the accurate navigation of the airship and location of the place raided were worthy of the highest praise'.

'M' type Navy Zeppelin *L.7*: Oberleutnant zur See Werner Peterson, born on 24 July 1887, was a young professional naval officer who had joined the Navy as a 19-year-old in 1906 and served as an Ensign on a destroyer. He transferred to the Airship Service in 1913, first as a student and then as second officer. He was rapidly promoted, taking command of Zeppelin *L.7* in November 1914. He had been at Friedrichshafen to take over *L.7* during the British raid on 21 November 1914, a few days before the ship was commissioned. He described the British pilots as very skilful. He was described by Douglas Robinson as popular with his fellow officers and renowned as the best ship-handler. In his first raid on England he was accompanied by Peter Strasser. Hampered by strong headwinds, it seems he reached the English coast at Brancaster at 01.40, but didn't realize it because of the blackout. British observers reported he crossed the coast and flew south-east near Cromer towards Yarmouth, crossing the coast again at Gorleston at 02.35. Unable to see any targets, he didn't drop any bombs on land and so went back to base.

29/30 April 1915

'P' type Army Zeppelin *LZ.38*: Hauptmann Erich Linnarz commanded the first raid by an Army airship to reach England. Linnarz left his base at Evere, near Brussels, in *LZ.38*, the first of the larger 'P' type Zeppelins to enter service. He crossed the coast near Old Felixstowe and flew westward over Ipswich to Bury St Edmunds, dropping bombs as he went. He circled over the town for ten minutes, dropping three HE and 40 incendiary bombs. He set two houses on fire in Ipswich and four at Bury St Edmunds, but there were no casualties.

9/10 May 1915

'P' type Army Zeppelin *LZ.38*: Hauptmann Erich Linnarz raided again a few days later. Zeppelin *LZ.38* was spotted over Southend at 02.45 when he dropped an incendiary bomb close to a ship holding German prisoners of war. He was still over Southend at 02.50 and dropped a number of incendiary and four HE bombs. Linnarz then turned up the Thames Estuary, probably heading for London, but was fired on by anti-aircraft guns at Cliffe. He turned back and again flew over Southend, dropping the rest of his bombs. It is estimated between ninety and 100 incendiary bombs fell on the town, causing much damage with a house and a timber yard burnt out and 60-year-old Agnes Whitwell, of North Road, Prittlewell, killed, and two other people injured. A crew member on the Zeppelin dropped a note written on a piece of cardboard: 'You English. We have come and will come again soon. Kill or cure. German.'

16/17 May 1915

'P' type Army Zeppelin *LZ.38*: Hauptmann Erich Linnarz was soon involved in another attack. He was sighted over Margate at 01.40 and flew via Thanet to Ramsgate. He dropped twenty bombs on Ramsgate, one hitting a pub, the Bull and George Hotel, killing two people and injuring another. The victims were John Smith and Florence Lamont, aged 43, both of whom had been outside the Bull and George when the bombs fell. *L.38* appeared over Dover at 02.25, when it was caught in a searchlight beam and fired on by anti-aircraft guns. Linnarz dropped all of his remaining bombs; about thirty-three fell without causing damage at Oxney.

20 May 1915

'M' type Army Zeppelin *Z.XI*: Hauptman Gaissert's airship caught fire after being damaged colliding with the doors, in windy conditions, while leaving its shed at Posen (now Poznan in Poland). *Z.XI* was destroyed but the crew escaped.

21 May 1915

'M' type Army Zeppelin *LZ.34*: Hauptmann Otto Jacob is recorded as making a number of raids on Russian positions in Grodno (now Hrodna, Belarus), Kovno (now Kaunas, Lithuania) and Warsaw. He was shot down by anti-aircraft fire and crash-landed near Insterburg (now Chernyakovsk, Russia), the airship being burnt out.

26/27 May 1915

'P' type Army Zeppelin *LZ.38*: Hauptmann Erich Linnarz made his second attack on Southend. He dropped about seventy bombs on the town, killing three people and injuring three others. The dead were: May Fairs (35) of Bow, London, who died in Westcliffe Grove, Westcliffe; Marion Pateman, (7) of 3 Broadway Market, Southend, who died when an incendiary bomb went through the roof of the house and set fire to her bed; and Florence Smith of Westminster Drive, Westcliffe, whom it appears was killed by shrapnel from a falling anti-aircraft shell.

31 May/1 June 1915

'P' type Army Zeppelin *LZ.38*: Hauptmann Erich Linnarz made the first attack on London. in *LZ.38*, which was first spotted near Margate at 21.42. He crossed the coast at Shoeburyness and arrived over London at 23.20, flying over Hoxton, Shoreditch, Whitechapel, Stepney, West Ham and Leytonstone. The first house bombed in London was 16 Alkham Road, Hackney, where there were no casualties. The killing started at 33 Cowper Road, Lambeth, where an incendiary fell into the bedrooms of five children, all of whom suffered serious burns. Three-year-old Elsie Leggatt, was killed outright, while May Leggatt, aged 11, died in hospital from her burns. The next casualties were at Balls Pond Road, Hackney, where Henry and Caroline Good were also killed by incendiary bombs. The charred bodies of the Goods, a married couple living as lodgers, were found in their burnt-out bedroom, kneeling as if in prayer. Linnarz then flew over Stepney and on to Whitechapel. Another two people died in Christian Street, St Georges: Leah Leahmann, aged 30, and 10-year-old Samuel Reuben were killed outside a cinema, the Greenburg Picture Palace. Twelve people were injured in the street, Samuel Reuben was killed outright and Leah Leahmann died a few hours later in hospital. A number of British aircraft tried to intercept the Zeppelin, but none got near. Linnarz crossed the coast north of the Crouch, receiving machine-gun fire from Burnham and anti-aircraft fire from Southminster. In all, seven people were killed in this first London raid and thirty-five injured, with damage caused worth £18,596.

The known names of the victims were: Elsie Leggatt (3) of 33 Cowper Road, Lambeth; May Leggatt (11) of 33 Cowper Road, Lambeth; Henry Thomas Good (49) of 187 Balls Pond Road, Hackney; Caroline Good (46) of 187 Balls Pond Road, Hackney; Leah Leahmann (30); and Samuel Reuben (10).

'M' type Army Zeppelin *LZ.37*: The commander for this raid is not known. It seems *LZ.37*, an earlier 'M' type Zeppelin, set out for London but was attacked by aeroplanes near Dunkirk. It appears the airship crossed the English coast south of the Swale, but returned to base after being fired at by anti-aircraft guns.

4/5 June 1915

This was the first raid by the Navy for several months. Hisrch in *L.10* had orders to attack London while Boemack in *SL.3* was on a reconnaissance mission and if the weather was favourable had permission to attack the Humber.

'P' type Navy Zeppelin *L.10*: Kapitänleutnant Klaus Hirsch took off from Nordholz at 12.20 with orders to attack London. He reached the Thames Estuary at about 21.15, thinking he was over Harwich. He was actually near Gravesend and dropped nine HE and eleven incendiary bombs on the yacht club, then being used as a military hospital. The hospital was destroyed by fire, but all the patients were successfully evacuated.

'C' type Navy Schutte-Lanz *SL.3*: Kapitänleutnant Fritz Boemack, also from Nordholz, crossed the coast at 23.30 just south of Flamborough Head in Yorkshire. He intended to bomb Hull, but was held back by a headwind and made slow progress. He saw the lights of a railway train below him and dropped three bombs on a railway junction, which fell on open country. Only two bombs were recorded by the British: one in a garden at Great Driffield and another in a field.

6/7 June 1915

This was to be one of the most important raids in our story. The Germans lost two Zeppelins, including the first to be destroyed by a British pilot. There were major casualties in Hull, where twenty-four people were killed.

'O' type Navy Zeppelin *L.9*: Kapitänleutnant Heinrich Mathy entered the public eye when he bombed Hull in *L.9*. Nineteen people - five men, nine women and five children - were killed that night, and twenty-four more were seriously wounded. GHQ recorded that nineteen people died in the raid, although the war memorial in Hull records twenty-four who were killed or died of their injuries. There was damage to the tune of £44,795. Zeppelin *L.9*, flying from Hage, was first reported crossing the coast at Mundesley after 20.00. Mathy was then reported as flying over Bridlington, before reaching Hull at about midnight. He dropped a parachute flare to illuminate the city and bombed the area around the docks. There were no anti-aircraft guns in Hull; the only gunfire came from HMS *Adventure*, which was under repair in Earle's Yard. Mathy then flew east to Grimsby, where he dropped his remaining incendiary bombs, which did little damage. He was fired on by pompom guns at Immingham and Waltham before flying out to sea.

They next day there were riots in Hull, targetting businesses that had apparently German names or connections. We have details of many of the casualties in Hull that night. They were: Maurice Richardson (11) of 50 South Parade, Hull; Violet Richardson (8) of 50 South Parade, Hull; Tom Stamford (46) of 5 Blanket Row, Hull; Ellen Temple (5) of 20 St James Square, St James Street, Hull; Elizabeth Picard Foreman (39) of 37 Walker Street, Hull; Sarah Ann Smith (86) of The Poplars, Durham Street, Hull; Johanna Harman (67) of 93 Arundel Street, Hull; Jane Hill (45) of 12 East Street, Hull; George Hill (48) of 12 East Street, Hull; Eliza Slade (54) of 4 Walker Terrace, Waller Street, Hull; Florence White (30) of 3 Waller Street, Hull; George Isaac White (3) of 3 Waller Street, Hull; Alfred Mathews (60) of 11 Waller Street, Hull; William Walker (62) of 2 St Thomas Terrace, Campbell Street, Hull; Alice Pricilla Walker (30) of 2 St Thomas Terrace, Campbell Street, Hull; Millicent Walker (17) of 2 St Thomas Terrace, Campbell Street, Hull; Norman Mullins (10) of 39 Blanket Row, Hull; George Mullins (15) of 39 Blanket Row, Hull; William Watson (67) of 21 Edwin's Place, Porter Street, Hull; Anne Watson (58) of 21 Edwin's Place, Porter Street, Hull; Georgina Cunningham (27) of 22 Edwin's Place, Porter Street, Hull; Emma Pickering (68) of Sarah's Terrace, Porter Street, Hull; Edwin Jordan (10) of 11 East Street, Hull; and Hannah Mitchell (42) of 5 Alexander Terrace, Woodhouse Street, Hull.

'M' type Army Zeppelin *LZ.37*: The first Zeppelin to be destroyed by a British airman was brought down by bombing. This was the *LZ.37*, commanded by Oberleutnant Otto van der Haegen, brought down by Flight Sub-Lieutenant Reginald Warneford of the RNAS. His was not a planned attack, as Warneford was flying a French Morane parasol monoplane on a mission to bomb Zeppelin sheds in Belgium. He was flying at about 11,000ft when he saw the Zeppelin about 4,000ft below him over Ostend, gave chase and after about an hour caught up with it over Ghent. He flew about 150ft above *LZ.37* and dropped six 20lb bombs on it. The Zeppelin immediately exploded, the blast throwing the Morane on its back, but Warneford managed to regain control and saw the blazing Zeppelin fall like a stone, crashing to earth around a Belgian convent. The commander and most of the crew were burnt to death. However, in one of the strangest escapes of the war, helmsman Oberleutnant Alfred Muhler fell over a mile from the front gondola as the blazing Zeppelin fell to earth, went straight through the roof of the Convent of St Elisabeth and landed on a bed, surviving with fairly serious injuries. A number of nuns were killed when the burning Zeppelin hit the convent.

Because Muhler survived we have a unique report of what happened. Zeppelin *LZ.37* had set out from Brussels-Etterbeek with orders to bomb Calais. It seems the airship crossed the British coast and was fired on by warships at Dover, then flew in a large circle and bombed Calais. With the bombs gone, Van der Haegan steered for Ostend and then Brussels. As dawn was breaking, the ship was over Ghent, at 2,000 metres (about 7,000ft) when Muhler heard 'three tremendous explosions'. In the front gondola, most of the crew seemed to be unconscious, and looking back at the rear gondola he saw the ship was on fire. He was looking at the roaring flames, thinking of jumping out, when the airship broke up. The next thing he knew he woke up on a bed with a nun standing by him, and the room was on fire. He got out and ran into the convent garden, where he lost consciousness again.

When he returned to base, Flight Sub-Lieutenant Warneford made a full report of his attack. He said he had sighted a Zeppelin above Ostend at about 01.00. It took him about an hour to catch up with the airship, and as he got near he was met with spirited fire from the Zeppelin crew. At about 02.15, he was over Ghent at about 11,000ft and the Zeppelin was at about 7,000ft. He cut his engine to drop to the airship's height, and flew over, dropping his bombs. He saw a massive explosion in the hull of the Zeppelin, and the Morane was blown upside down by the blast. He could not restart the engine of the Morane and was forced to land in a field behind German lines. He mended a broken fuel pipe and got the engine going, having to swing the propeller then run to get in the cockpit as the aeroplane moved forward. He said he took off just as the 'Boche' ran out of the woods firing at him. He crossed the Allied lines and had to refuel again, before getting back to base at about 10.30. He wrote a brief report and went to his bunk, exhausted. When he woke up he was a national hero. Within a day he was awarded the Victoria Cross and taken to Paris on a propaganda mission, also receiving the French Legion of Honour. Plans were made for him to go to

Buckingham Palace to receive his VC from the King, But sadly his story was to end in tragedy.

Warneford was ordered to pick up a new Henry Farman biplane and deliver it to his squadron at St Pol. The Farman was a pusher biplane, with the engine behind the pilot and passenger, who sat in a bathtub-like fuselage in front of it. The tail unit was carried on a cage-like structure of wooden booms. As part of the celebrations, he was to take American journalist Robert Needham on a short flight over Paris. It appears neither Warneford nor Needham strapped themselves into the aeroplane. They took off and reached 2,000 feet, and were banking, when a loud crack was heard above the noise of the engine. It seems one of the tail booms had broken and the others were shattered by the propeller. Both pilot and passenger then fell some 700ft into a corn field. Needham died immediately, and Warneford soon after in hospital.

There were lessons to be learned from the shooting down of *LZ.37*. The first was that a relatively high performance, not particularly stable, aeroplane like the Morane could be flown at night by a competent, experienced pilot. The RNAS knew this, but it took more than a year for the RFC (Royal Flying Corps) to grasp it. The second lesson was even more serious. It had to be recognized that Warneford's victory was the result of a number of favourable coincidences: he was already in the air and higher than the Zeppelin when he saw it and did not have to climb to catch it. Therefore the bombing was effective. The failure to recognize the limitations of bombing led to the introduction of the Ranken Dart, which proved useless as it had to be dropped from above and the Zeppelins could climb faster than British night-fighters, so its use almost certainly held back RFC anti-Zeppelin operations until September 1916.

'P' type Army Zeppelin *LZ.38*: Hauptmann Erich Linnarz had engine trouble shortly after leaving Brussels-Evere. He returned *LZ.38* to base and it was put back in its shed. Just before dawn, two Henri Farman HF27 aeroplanes flown by Flight Lieutenant John Phillip Wilson and Flight Sub-Lieutenant John Stanley Mills from the RNAS station at Dunkirk dropped bombs on the airship shed at Evere. According to reports, Wilson dropped three bombs, which caused a large explosion, and Mill dropped twelve bombs into the shed, which totally destroyed Zeppelin *LZ.38*. The machine that had brought such carnage to London just a few days previously was no more. There are no reports of human casualties in this raid.

15/16 June 1915

This was the first raid on England by the German Navy in the more advanced 'P' type Zeppelins: the target was the North of England.

'P' type Navy Zeppelin *L.10*: Kapitänleutnant Klaus Hirsch left Nordholz at 12.30. He crossed the English coast at Blyth at 23.30 before turning south for the Tyne. He found Wallsend well lit and dropped bombs, damaging houses and the Eastern marine engineering works. He went on to bomb collieries at Wallsend and Hebburn. He then flew to Jarrow, bombing Palmers Engineering Works with seven HE and five incendiary bombs. Hirsch caused serious damage, seventeen men were killed and seventy-two injured. After this, he dropped further bombs on Wellington quay, East Howden, Cookson's antimony works and Pochin's chemical works. He went back out to sea near South Shields, returning to Nordholz at 08.27 the next day.

We have a record of most of the Jarrow victims, the majority of whom were killed at about 23.45 in the Palmers shipyard: Albert Bramley (54), colliery labourer; Mathew Carter (66), ship fitter; John Cuthbert Davison (31), fitter (he died later in hospital from his injuries); Carl Karling (24); Joseph Lane (67), mechanical engineer; Robert Thomas Nixon (32), mechanic turner and fitter; Frederick Pinnock (31); Laurence Fraser Sanderson (16); Thomas Henry Smith, apprentice engineer; Ralph Snaith(48), turner; William Stamford (40), colliery fitter; Joseph Beckworth Thornycroft (31), sea-going engineer; William Grieves Turner (20), apprentice fitter; George Ward (22), apprentice fitter (died later in hospital from his injuries); John George Windle (22), screwing machine fitter; William Ernest Cook Young (16); and Ann Isabella Laughlin (62), who died of shock.

'P' type Navy Zeppelin *L.11*: Oberleutnant zur See Horst von Buttlar was assigned a new ship, Zeppelin *L.11*, in June 1915. He seems to have been developing the sense of caution that meant he was the only airship commander to serve right through the war. He set out to raid England from Nordholz at 13.04 but had to return because of engine trouble. He landed at 23.20 after just over ten hours in the air.

5 July 1915

'C' type Army Schutte-Lanz *SL.V*: Hauptman Von Watcher, out from Darmstadt, crash-landed at Giessen in Germany due to bad weather. The airship was damaged beyond repair.

6 August 1915

'M' type Navy Zeppelin *L.5*: Kapitänleutnant Herbert Ehrlich seems to have been the commander with the least public attention. He was born on 20 March 1884 in Dresden. The son of Admiral Alfred Ehrlich, he was a senior teacher at the Navy officers training school in Cuxhaven and won the Iron Cross 2nd class in 1914. He was a cautious and competent commander who survived the war. He seems to have been well respected by Peter Strasser, who recommended him for technically difficult missions or experimental work. On 14 July, *L.5* was transferred to the Baltic, based at Seddin in East Prussia (now near Slupsk in Poland). *L.5* was one of the 'M' type ships, replaced by a more modern ship in the West, but still seen as useful in the East. It was lost in a rash daylight raid on Dunamuade (now Daugavgriva, Latvia). Ehrlich was hit by anti-aircraft fire but managed to make it back to German lines at Plungiany in Russia. The airship was wrecked in the crash landing, but the crew escaped, with just one man injured.

9/10 August 1915

This was intended as a major raid by the Navy on England. The older Zeppelin *L.9* was to raid the North, with the more modern 'P' types attacking London. The airships targeting London failed completely, but *L.9* bombed Goole, causing significant casualties.

'O' type Navy Zeppelin *L.9*: Kapitänleutnant Odo Loewe took off from Hage at 10.50. This was Odo Loewe's first raid on England in Zeppelin *L.9*. He had taken over the ship from Heinrich Mathy in June. The policy was that less experienced commanders got older ships, with the more experienced promoted to the newer models. He had been involved in a naval action on 3 July 1915. At 13.19 on 9 August, Strasser radioed all the Zeppelins, ordering them to assemble north of Borkum Island. The target for the 'P' class airships was London. Loewe, in *L.9*, was detached to make a solo attack on the Humber.

Loewe first crossed the coast off Flamborough Head at 20.15, and as he flew over the RNAS aerodrome at Atwick, near Hornsea, two aeroplanes took off and Loewe went back out to sea to avoid them in the twilight. The RNAS pilots – Flight Sub-Lieutenant R.G. Mack, in a Bleriot, and the commander of the Atwick Station, Flight Commander Christopher Draper, in a Bristol TB 8 – lost the Zeppelin in the mist. Mack crashed on landing.

L.9 was seen over Hornsea once more at 21.10, and Draper took off again and pursued Loewe for thirty-five minutes when he went out to sea again, until he lost the Zeppelin in the fog. Loewe crossed the coast for a third time at 22.15, with Hull as his target. He had a problem with his rudder control and circled out of control for some time. With the rudder cables repaired, he saw the lights of a town, which he believed was Hull: it was in fact Goole. He dropped all his bombs, destroying warehouses and houses and killing sixteen people. Most of the bombs fell in Sotherton Street, North Street and Aire Street. Loewe returned to Hage at 06.35 the next day. A memorial in the town cemetery identifies most of the Goole victims: Sarah Acaster (65), of 2 Sotherton Street, Goole; Sarah Ann Acaster (34), of 2 Sotherton Street, Goole; Kezia Acaster (32), of 2 Sotherton Street, Goole; Hannah Goodall (73); Florence Harrison (4); Beatrice A. Harrison (6); Margaret Selina Pratt (8 months); Agnes Pratt (35); Alice Elizabeth Woodall (9 months); Grace Woodall (31); Mary Carroll (30); James Carroll (31); Alice Carroll (3); Gladys Mary Caroll (2); and Alice Smith (17).

'P' type Navy Zeppelin *L10*: Oberleutnant zur See Friedrich Wenke left Nordholz at about11.52. His target was London; he reported he had bombed the city through thick rain clouds. British reports show he crossed the coast near Adleburgh, flew towards Chelmsford and dropped twelve bombs on the landing ground of the Eastchurch naval air station on the Isle of Sheppey. The only damage was broken windows in Eastchurch. He returned to Nordholz at 07.38 the next day.

'P' type Navy Zeppelin *L.11*: Oberleutnant zur See Horst von Buttlar left Nordholz at 11.28. British reports show he crossed the coast near Lowestoft, was fired on by anti-aircraft guns and quickly dropped his bombs: some fell in the sea, some on land. The streets affected were The Avenue, Lovewell Street, Lorne Park Road, Wellington Esplanade and Wellington Road. One person was killed – Kate Crawford, aged 18, of 12 Lovewell Street, Lowestoft – and seven others injured, with several houses destroyed. Buttlar returned to Nordholz at 04.14 the next morning. Because of his very cautious methods, it is difficult to attribute many casualties to Buttlar; the unfortunate Kate Crawford is the only victim I can identify as being killed by his bombs.

'P' type Navy Zeppelin *L.12*: Oberleutnant zur See Werner Peterson left Hage at 11.05 and reported passing Yarmouth, Lowestoft and finally Orfordness Lighthouse. Flying south, he then claimed to have bombed

Harwich harbour. British reports show he crossed the Kent coast, and the port he identified as Harwich was actually Dover. He dropped two 100kg HE bombs and twenty 50kg bombs, injuring three men and damaging some buildings. He was fired on by a 3in anti-aircraft gun, which fired ten rounds, and one was seen to hit *L.12*. Luckily for Peterson it didn't cause a fire, but severely damaged two gas bags. Because of the substantial loss of lift, *L.12* lost height. At 01.40, he had all moveable spare parts, machine guns and provisions thrown overboard to try and gain height. At 02.40 the Zeppelin sank into the English Channel, but was rescued by a German torpedo boat which towed it into Ostend harbour. The wreck of the *L.12* was bombed by British aircraft in Ostend harbour but was not hit. The Germans were able to salvage some parts but the Zeppelin was written off.

'P' type Navy Zeppelin *L.13*: Kapitänleutnant Heinrich Mathy took over Zeppelin *L.13*, which he would call his lucky ship, on 25 July 1915. On 9 August, he left Hage at 11.30. This was to be the first of three unsuccessful missions; he set out three times to bomb England in August, on the 9th, 12th and 17th, but each time he had to turn back due to engine trouble. After his first mission, he returned to Hage at 03.45 on August 10.

10/11 August 1915

'M' type Army Zeppelin *Z.IX*: In June, Oberleutnant zur See Ernst Lehmann was transferred to the Eastern Front, based at Allenstein (now Olsztyn in Poland). He began operations along the Russian lines between Warsaw and Rovno (Rivne). While we don't have exact dates, Lehmann described bombing Pultusk and railway lines between Warsaw and Petrograd. Later in August, Lehmann set out from Allenstein to bomb a railway shunting terminal near Bialystok. One of the trains was carrying munitions and a bomb detonated them all, destroying the entire railway junction. On his way back, Lehmann was fired on by Russian troops at Ossoverts (now Osowiec in Poland). His ship was hit by shrapnel, which caused a loss of gas and prevented *Z.IX* reaching its base. It landed in a lake a few miles from Allenstein, and after a crewman telephoned the base, the airship was walked with its guide ropes to the base by a troop of Russian PoWs.

'O' type Army Zeppelin *LZ.79*: Hauptman Gaissart was based at Posen (now Poznan in Poland), and according to Lehmann was aided in his navigation by the fires started by the retreating Russian Army. He flew over the fortress and railway junction at Brest-Litovsk and then on to Kovel (now in Ukraine). In a mission lasting seventeen hours, he had flown more than 1,000 miles and dropped about 3,000lb of bombs.

12/13 August 1915

'O' type Navy Zeppelin *L.9*: Kapitänleutnant Odo Loewe flew *L.9* out from Hage, but had engine problems and did not cross the coast.

'P' type Navy Zeppelin *L.10*: Oberleutnant zur See Friedrich Wenke, flying from Nordholz, had Harwich as his target and, fairly unusually, was able to find it. He correctly identified Woodbridge, Ipswich and Harwich. He was fired on by troops stationed in Woodbridge, and at 23.15, according to British reports, replied with four HE and twenty incendiary bombs which destroyed five houses and damaged sixty-four others. He caused considerable casualties when a bomb landed on a pavement in St John's Hill, with seven people killed and six injured. Among the dead were: Roger Tyler (31), a boot maker, of 4 St John's Hill, Woodbridge; Dora Tyler (40), his wife, of 4 St John's Hill, Woodbridge; Edward Turner (50); Dennis Harris; Eliza Bunn (67), of 14 New Street, Woodbridge; and James Marshall (16), of 27 New Street, Woodbridge.

Upon leaving Woodbridge, Wenke flew towards Ipswich and dropped six bombs at Kesgrave without damage. *L.10* was attacked by machine guns mounted on a lorry at Rushmere. Wenke dropped two bombs in reply, which again caused no casualties. He then went on to Harwich, where he dropped the rest of his bombs on Parkestone. Eight HE and four incendiary bombs damaged two houses there and injured 17 people. Zeppelin *L.10* then went out to sea at Aldeburgh.

'P' type Navy Zeppelin *L.11*: Oberleutnant zur See Horst von Buttlar appeared briefly over the coast at North Foreland but did not drop any bombs. On the way back to Nordholz, *L.11* was caught in a heavy thunder storm. Showing a degree of piloting skill, Buttlar attempted to steer around it but was forced down to 300ft by heavy rain squalls. In his autobiography, Buttlar describes flying home in perfect conditions, with all engines working well, when at about 23.30 he saw thick black cloud and flashes of lightning. Because of a headwind it wasn't possible to fly around the storm, so he forged ahead at 12,000ft. There were sheets of lightning ahead, with flashes every few seconds. He received a message from one of the lookouts on the top platform that 'the machine-gun sights are burning': it was St Elmo's fire forming a sort of halo of blue flames. The whole airship seemed to be surrounded by a violet cloud of radiating electricity. When Buttlar touched the metal compasses on his map table, he got an electric shock from the static. Because of the heavy rain the Zeppelin was gaining weight and was being thrown about in the wind, at times flying only 600ft above the sea. After a few hours, as dawn broke, *L.11* flew out of the storm and the sun dried the wet outer cover. Buttlar then made a perfect landing at Nordholz. A few weeks later, he fully realized the danger he had been in when he saw Zeppelin *L.10* enter a thunder cloud and burst into flames.

'P' type Navy Zeppelin *L.13*: Kapitänleutnant Heinrich Mathy once again had to return to Hage when *L.13* suffered engine trouble.

17/18 August 1915

'P' type Navy Zeppelin *L10*: Oberleutnant zur See Friedrich Wenke was the first Naval airship commander to bomb London. Flying from Nordholz, he crossed the coast at Shingle Street at 20.56, and it seems followed the River Stour to Manningtree in Essex. He then followed the railway to Colchester before flying near Chelmsford. He was fired at by anti-aircraft guns at Waltham Abbey as he reached London. He dropped three bombs at Walthamstow at about 22.34. Over Leyton, he dropped sixteen HE and ten incendiary bombs, killing nine people and injuring forty-eight. A considerable number of houses were wrecked or damaged and the railway station was damaged, as was the tram depot. Wenke went on to Leytonstone, where he dropped four bombs, killing another man, and then to Wanstead. He turned around and returned to the coast, dropping two more bombs at Chelmsford. It seems that in all ten people killed and damage of £30,750 was caused in this raid by Wenke and *L.10*.

'P' type Navy Zeppelin *L.11*: Oberleutnant zur See Horst von Buttlar and *L.11*, according to British reports, crossed the English coast at Herne Bay at 21.30 and bombed Ashford and Faversham in Kent. Although he dropped sixty-two bombs, no casualties were reported. It appears that after the raid, Buttlar claimed to have bombed London. Douglas Robinson, following discussions with Zeppelin crews many years after the events, says that Buttlar made false claims on occasions, which was one of the reasons he was unpopular in the Airship Service.

'P' type Navy Zeppelin *L.13*: Kapitänleutnant Heinrich Mathy, flying from Hage, again had mechanical trouble and had to turn back.

'P' type Navy Zeppelin *L.14*: Kapitänleutnant Alois Bocker took command of Zeppelin *L.14* on 10 August 1915, and set out for England a week later. Leaving Nordhotz in the afternoon, he was sighted off the Would Lightship at about 20.20, and heard off the East Coast until about 23.00. According to British records, Bocker did not cross the coast and dropped his bombs in the sea off Yarmouth. Bocker reported he gave up his attempt to reach London because of mechanical trouble, but dropped fifty incendiary and twenty HE bombs on blast furnaces and factory premises in the vicinity of Ipswich and Woodbridge.

26 August 1915

'P' type Army Zeppelin *LZ.79*: Hauptman Gaissert, based at Posen (Poznan, Poland), dropped 1,000kg of bombs on a railway junction at Luminetz near Brest-Litovsk. He had been ordered to bomb Brest, but could see when he got there that the Russians were setting it on fire before evacuating, so instead he bombed the railway junction at Luminetz (now in Belarus).

3 September 1915

'P' type Navy Zeppelin *L.10*: Kapitänleutnant Klaus Hirsch, with second officer Oberleutnant der Reserve August Sticker, set out from Nordholz on a scouting mission. At the end of the patrol, *L.10* sent a wireless message to Nordholz to say it would land at about 14.30. The ground crew kept a lookout, and at about 14.20 saw a large flash of flame, like an explosion, near Neuwerk Island. Observers on shore at Cuxhaven had a better view: the Zeppelin entered a large dark cloud, and then they saw a flash of lightning and a red glow in the hull of the airship. It burst into flames and landed in the shallow water. All nineteen members of the crew were killed.

7/8 September 1915

This raid by three Army airships had London as its target.

'P' type Army Zeppelin *LZ.74*: Hauptmann Friedrich George left *LZ.74*'s shed in Belgium and crossed the coast near Broxbourne. He flew towards

London, passing over Cheshunt, where he dropped eighteen HE and twenty-seven incendiary bombs, damaging several houses and many glasshouses. He was fired on by guns at Waltham Abbey, but *LZ.74* reached London, flying directly across the city from north to south. George dropped his only remaining incendiary bomb, which landed in Fenchurch Street at 00.20. He then flew on to Harwich, in company with *SL.2*. They were fired on by the guns at Purfleet, but returned safely to base.

'P' type Army Zeppelin *LZ.77*: Hauptmann Alfred Horn crossed the coast at Clacton at 22.40. He flew an erratic course to Hatfield Broad Oak, but turned back to Lowestoft where he dropped seven bombs, only causing little damage. Horn crossed back over the coast at Lowestoft and returned safely to base.

'B' type Army Schutte-Lanz *SL.2*: Hauptmann Richard von Wobeser, who had set out to bomb Paris in March, this time successfully bombed London. His second officer was Oberleutnant Wilhelm Schramm. Using the oldest surviving Shutte-Lanz airship, his raid caused considerable damage, mainly to working-class housing. He crossed the coast at the mouth of the River Crouch at 22.50 and made for London, reaching Leytonstone at about midnight. Wobeser flew over Millwall, Deptford, Southwark, New Cross, Greenwich, Charlton and Woolwich. He dropped eighteen HE and twenty-seven incendiary bombs, killing eighteen 18 people – six men, six women and six children – and injuring thirty-eight more. The victims included: William J. Beechey (56) of 34 Hughes Fields, Deptford; Elizabeth Beechey (47) of 34 Hughes Fields, Deptford; William Beechey (11) of 34 Hughes Fields, Deptford; Margaret Beechey (7) of 34 Hughes Fields, Deptford; Helena Beechey (3) of 34 Hughes Fields, Deptford; Arthur Suckling (30) of 32 Childeric Road, Deptford; Emily Suckling (29) of 32 Childeric Road, Deptford; Dorie Suckling (3) of 32 Childeric Road, Deptford; Frederick Dann (44) of 66 Clifton Hill; and Mary E. Dann (45) of 66 Clifton Hill.

SL.2 went back out to sea with *LZ.74* at Harwich, aiming to return to his shed after flying over Holland with only one engine working, but crash-landed at Berchem in Belgium. This was Richard von Wobeser's last raid on London. He did not survive the war. Transferred to the Easern Front, on 27 July 1916 he left Jamboli (now Yambol), Bulgaria, in Schutte-Lanze *SL.10* to bomb Sevastopol. He did not bomb the city or return to base. His fate was unknown, but presumably *SL.10* crashed into the Black Sea.

8/9 September 1915

This was a raid by three Navy airships. Zeppelin *L.9* had the Humber as its target, while the larger *L.13 and L.14* headed for London.

'O' type Navy Zeppelin *L.9*: Kapitänleutnant Odo Loewe flew out from Hage, his target the Skinningrove Chemical Works near Loftus on the North Yorkshire coast. A benzol plant had been built at the site before the war by German engineers, so detailed maps were available to him. He crossed the coast at Port Mulgrave, between Whitby and Kettleness, at about 21.15, and dropped six bombs which caused no damage. He arrived at the Skinningrove site at 21.35, dropping nine HE and twelve incendiary bombs on the iron works. In his report, he said he could not find the benzol works, but according to the British one incendiary bomb actually hit the benzyl house but failed to penetrate the concrete, while another HE bomb landed within 10ft of it. The latter caused some damage, but failed to damage the tank which held 45,000 gallons of benzyl. If it had, it is likely the whole works would have been destroyed. Another of Loewe's bombs hit the TNT store but failed to explode. Potentially, the attack by *L.9* could have done massive damage, but in fact damage was only slight and there were no casualties. Such is the luck of war. Zeppelin *L.9* re-crossed the coast at Sandsend at 21.45. Three RNAS aeroplanes were scrambled to look for the airship, but to no avail.

'P' type Navy Zeppelin *L.13*: Kapitänleutnant Heinrich Mathy, out from Hage, crossed the coast over the Wash near Kings Lynn at 20.45, flying over Cambridge, from where he could see the lights of London. He dropped his first bombs on Golders Green at 22.40, probably to check his bomb sight. They landed in fields and did no damage. He then flew right over the City of London. Mathy had visited London in 1909 and had a good mental picture of the city. He headed right for the centre, flying over Euston Station and dropping his first bombs - two incendiaries - near Bedford Place. He then dropped a HE bomb in Queen Square, Bloomsbury, a park surrounded by hospitals. Travelling east, another HE bomb badly damaged the offices of the National Penny Bank. His next HE bomb landed at the corner of Lamb's conduit and Red Lion Street at about 22.49, damaging the front of the Dolphin pub and killing Henry Coombes, aged 23, who was standing outside. Mathy then followed Grays Inn Road, dropping one HE and two incendiary bombs on tenements at Portpool Lane, killing three children and injuring twenty-five other people. He also bombed a printing works at

Farrington Road, and at Bartholomew Close, near St Bartholomew's hospital, he dropped a 300kg bomb, making an 8ft-deep crater. He then flew over and bombed a number of textile warehouses, starting serious fires. He caused the most damage near Liverpool Street Station at the end of his bomb run, killing fifteen people. A HE bomb hit a No. 35A bus, killing or injuring most of the passengers, while another bomb hit a No. 8 bus, killing the driver and eight passengers.

During his raid, Mathy had been under fire from London's twenty-six anti-aircraft guns. Flying between 8,500-11,200ft, he used cloud cover to avoid searchlights, and only one gun came close to hitting him. By 23.15, he was near St Albans at 11,150ft, and had reached Norwich by 01.00. He landed back at Hage at 08.10 the next day. The raid had demonstrated to the world the power of the Zeppelin as a terror weapon. Mathy killed twenty-two people in London, eighty-seven were injured and damage of £530,787 caused. On the day after the raid, someone in Barnet found a small bag with a parachute, in which was a scraped ham bone, with a cartoon on it. It showed an image of an elderly Edward Grey, the Liberal statesman, with a Zeppelin dropping a bomb on his head, saying *Was fang ich, armer Teufal, an?* ('What shall I poor devil to do?'). On the back was '*Zum Adebkan an das ausgehungerte Deutschland*' ('A memento from starved out Germany'). Questioned after the raid, Mathy would never reveal who was responsible for this prank.

Mathy had more questions to answer after the raid. He was summoned to Berlin on 18 September 1915 to meet Admiral von Muller, the Chief of the Kaiser's Naval Cabinet. The subject of the meeting shows what a strange society Germany was at the time. The admiral said the Kaiser and Kaiserin (his wife) had been alarmed by reports of bomb damage in central London, and wanted to be assured that no harm had been done to Buckingham Palace, churches or historic buildings. Mathy informed von Muller all bombs had been correctly aimed, and was told: 'Their Majesties would be greatly relieved.'

'P' type Navy Zeppelin *L.14*: Kapitänleutnant Alois Bocker, flying from Nordholz, had London as his target. As he approached the coast, he was fired on by the armed trawler *Conway*. He crossed the coast near Cromer, but had engine trouble so decided to abandon his attack on London and instead bomb Norwich. He actually dropped fifteen bombs on Bylaugh, thirty-one on East Durham and nine on Scarning. He caused many casualties, with four people killed in East Durham and seven injured. Those killed in

East Durham, who were in or near the White Lion pub, were: James Taylor (61); Harry Patterson (44), a jeweller; Lance Corporal Alfred Pomeroy; and Private Leslie McDonald.

The 8 September raid was the most destructive so far. In total, twenty-six people had been killed and damage caused to the tune of £534,287. But worse was to come.

11/12 September 1915

'P' type Army Zeppelin *LZ.77*: Hauptmann Alfred Horn, operating from Belgium, crossed the coast over the River Blackwater at 23.15 and made for London. He got lost in the fog in the Epping Forest area and dropped all his bombs – eight HE and fifty-two incendiary – on the Royal Artillery Camp at North Weald Bassett. While this was a genuine military target, even if found accidentally, the raid was a total failure as the safety pins had not been taken out of the HE bombs, so none of them exploded. There were no casualties or damage.

12/13 September 1915

'P' type Army Zeppelin *LZ.74*: Hauptmann Friedrich George ran into fog over much of East Anglia. He bombed between Colchester and Woodbridge, possibly responding to machine-gun fire from the ground, but there were no casualties and the only damage was broken windows.

13/14 September 1915

The target for the airships was London. The weather was very difficult, thunderstorms and headwinds forcing two of the ships to turn back.

'P' type Navy Zeppelin *L.11*: Oberleutnant zur See Horst von Buttlar, flying from Hage, turned back about 30 nautical miles from the coast.

'P' type Navy Zeppelin *L.13*: Kapitänleutnant Heinrich Mathy, also flying from Hage, crossed the coast near Orfordness at 23.10. He attempted to reach London, but at midnight was over Harwich and was picked up by several searchlights. At about 00.05, *L.13* was hit by a 6-pdr anti–aircraft gun in Felixstowe, damaging several gas cells. Mathy immediately jettisoned his bombs. His problems worsened when one of his engines failed. He took the shortest possible route home over neutral Holland and was able to reach Hage at 04.20, but damaged the ship in a crash-landing. The airship was repaired in four days.

'P' type Navy Zeppelin *L.14*: Kapitänleutnant Alois Bocker, from Nordholz, turned back before he crossed the coast.

Various dates in October 1915.

Both these Zeppelins were transferred to the Eastern Front, first to Schneideidemuhl (now Pila in Poland) and then to Allenstein (Olsztyn, Poland) and Konigsberg (Kaliningrad, Russia).

'P' type Zeppelin *LZ.85*: We know that Oberleutnanr Scherzer's *LZ.85* carried out raids from Allenstein, dropping about 12 tons of bombs on railways and bridges in the area of Dunaburg (Daugupils in Latvia), Riga and Minsk. The airship was transferred in January 1916 to Szentandras near Temesver in Hungary (now Timisoara, Romania).

'P' type Army Zeppelin *LZ.86*: Hauptman Erich Linnarz, the London bomber who lost his ship, *LZ.38*, in the bombing of the shed at Evere, took over *LZ.86*. He made two attacks on Dvinsk (now Daugupils, Latvia) before moving to a new base at Kovno (Kaunas, Lithuania) early in 1916. The airship was moved to Szentandras near Temesvar in Hungary in mid-1916 to attack Rumania.

8 October 1915

'P' type Army Zeppelin *LZ.74*: Hauptmann Friedrich George crashed in the Eifel mountains in Germany, and the airship's gondolas were torn off. As often happened in airship crashes, due to the loss of weight, the rest of the airship floated off, and with several members of crew still aboard came down in Mezieres, France.

13/14 October 1915

Five Zeppelins set out, with London again their target. It seems the attack was co-ordinated, as four of the airships came over the coast at Bacton at much the same time. The raid was to be the heaviest on Britain of the entire war: seventy-one people were killed, 128 injured and damage caused to the value of £50,250.

'P' type Navy Zeppelin *L.11*: Oberleutnant zur See Horst von Buttlar left Nordholz at 11.22. In his combat report, Buttlar claimed to have bombed London. He said he crossed the coast at Southend and claimed to have hit West Ham, the docks and Woolwich. The British report is very different. They say *L.11* crossed the coast at Bacton at about 22.25, long after the other airships. As the airship crossed the coast, it came under machine-gun fire from troops at Bacton, and Buttlar jettisoned his bombs on the villages of Horstead, Coltishall and Great Hautbois in Norfolk. No casualties were recorded. *L.11* went back out to sea north of Yarmouth and was fired on by a gun at Mousehold Heath on the way. Buttlat returned to Nordholz at 07.02.

'P' type Navy Zeppelin *L.13*: Kapitänleutnant Heinrich Mathy left Hage at 12.40, crossing the coast at Bacton at 19.15 as he lead a loose formation of four airships. In the moonlight he navigated easily to London. He was fired on by anti-aircraft guns at Hatfield, dropping four 50kg bombs in reply, and reached the River Thames at Staines at 21.30. He then got lost while attempting to reach the water works at Hampton, but was over the village of Shalford at 22.30. Thinking it was Hampton, he dropped twelve 50kg HE bombs, reporting hits on the pumping and power stations. In fact, only minor damage was done to housing and a golf course. He then flew over Bromley, coming close to Bocker in Zeppelin *L.14*. At 23.45, he dropped all his remaining bombs on Woolwich Arsenal without causing much damage to the works but killing four men in the barracks and nine in the works. Mathy got back to Hage at 09.30.

'P' type Navy Zeppelin *L.14*: Kapitänleutnant Alois Bocker took off from Nordholz at 11.40, crossed the coast at Bacton with the other ships, but then it seems he too got lost on the way to London. He flew near Norwich and Thetford, but then flew south-east over the Isle of Sheppey and reached the sea near Hythe. In his report, Bocker said he attacked Woolwich Arsenal with nine HE bombs, but in fact bombed the Otterpool Army Camp near Hythe, killing fourteen soldiers, injuring twelve more and killing sixteen horses. He eventually reached Croydon at 23.20, destroying a number of houses, killing nine people and injuring fifteen more. He got back to Nordholz, but had to wait for several hours for the fog to lift before he could land at 13.20 the next day.

'P' type Navy Zeppelin *L.15*: Kapitänleutnant Joachim Breithaupt was an experienced professional naval officer. He was 32 at the time of this raid, born on 28 January 1883. Like most airship commanders, he had previously served in an older ship, the *L.6*, which he took over from von Buttlar. He was promoted to Zeppelin *L.15* in September 1915; this was the first ship to be fitted with the new Maybach HSLu High compression 240hp engines. These engine had been introduced with little testing and were very unreliable.

This was his first raid on England. He left Nordholz at 11.50 and crossed the coast at Bacton. He saw the lights of London at about 20.10. At Broxbourne, he was fired on by a 13-pdr gun and dropped three HE bombs which landed very close to the gun, injuring the gunners. He crossed London at about 8,500ft and was caught by searchlights and fired on by guns from Green Park. He tried to bomb the Bank of England, but his aim was slightly out and he actually attacked Central London in the so-called 'Theatreland' raid, bombing around the Strand in the theatre district. His first bomb landed in Exeter Street near the Lyceum Theatre, killing one person and injuring two more. The next bomb landed in Wellington Street, where it shattered and set fire to a gas main, killing seventeen people and injuring twenty-one others. A third bomb hit Catherine Street near the Strand Theatre. At Aldwych, two more bombs killed three people and injured fifteen. He then bombed the Inns of Court, bombs falling on Lincolns Inn, Chancery Lane and Grays Inn. He went on to bomb Aldgate, a bomb hitting the Minories, damaging a bank, restaurant and hotel. In all, Breithaupt killed twenty-eight people and injured seventy.

Breithaupt had problems on his return journey, navigating by radio bearings because of fog, and arrived at Nordholz at 09.00 but could not see the ground. A captive balloon was sent up to mark the base. Breithaupt used it to try and land, but the fog was too thick to see the ground, even at 250ft. He dropped his landing ropes, hoping the ground crew would find them, but they didn't. With the engines running out of fuel, he had to land quickly, so made a blind crash-landing. He landed about 3 miles from the base, and the ground crew had to walk *L.15*, pulling her landing ropes, into a shed. Repairs to the Zeppelin took several days to complete before it transferred to Hage about a week later.

'P' type Navy Zeppelin *L.16*: Oberleutnant zur See Werner Peterson, after the loss of Zeppelin *L.12*, was given command of *L.16* at the end of September 1915. He took off from Hage at 12.30 and crossed the coast at Bacton. He flew near Norwich and Cambridge. He saw the *L.15* lit up by searchlights over London. He thought he was over London and claimed to have bombed Stratford, East Ham and West Ham, but in fact was over Hertford, where he dropped eighteen HE and thirty incendiary bombs, killing nine people and injuring fifteen. Like most of the other Zeppelins, Peterson had problems with fog on the return journey. He was fired on by Dutch guns over Vlieland Island, but got back to Hage at 06.25.

17 November 1915

'P' type Navy Zeppelin *L.18*: This ship flew for the first time on 3 November 1915. Kapitänleutnant Max Dietrich was assigned to it on 6 November but was unable to take part in any operations due to adverse weather conditions. He took the airship to its shed at Tondern on 16 November. The next morning, the crew and maintenance engineer were topping up the gas cell with hydrogen when there was a fire followed by an explosion. One crew member and six maintenance workers were killed, with seven others injured. It was another reminder of just how inflammable hydrogen could be: a fatal lesson Max Dietrich would learn a year later.

18 November 1915

'D' type Navy Schutte-Lanz *SL.6*: Kapitänleutnant Fritz Boemack, with Leutnant zur See Hans Schaper as second officer, was operating in the Baltic. The airship exploded in the air, north of Seddin, probably as a result of being struck by lightning. All twenty crew members were killed.

11 December 1915

'C' type Navy Schutte-Lanz *SL.4*: Kapitänleutnant Richard Wolff's airship was involved in another weather-related accident. The door of the Selim shed at Sedden was opened in gale-force winds, and *SL.4* was blown out of the shed on to the airfield and damaged beyond repair.

18 December 1915

'P' type Army Zeppelin *LZ.39*: Kapitänleutnant der Reserve Eberhardt Laempertz was another naval officer in an Army ship. The airship had been transferred from the West to the Russian Front in June 1915, as the Army grew increasingly concerned about the vulnerability of Zeppelins. Laempertz set off from Allenstein (now Olsztyn in Poland) to bomb Rovno in Russia (Rivne, Ukraine). Accurate anti-aircraft fire destroyed a number of gas cells and hit the control gondola, causing two mechanics to fall to their deaths. The ship made an emergency landing on the German side of the front line at Lyck (also quoted as Luck, it is now Elk in Poland). The second officer on the flight was Hauptmann Wilhelm Schramm, whose luck would soon run out. Dr Eberhardt Laempertz survived the war and later worked for the Zeppelin Company at Friedrichshafen.

Chapter Four

The raids of January and February 1916

The stalemate on the Western Front continued, both sides engaged in costly and futile attempts to break through. The Germans attacked first at the French fortress of Verdun on 21 February, which turned into a battle of attrition lasting until 18 December.. The only way for supplies to reach Verdun was along a road to Bar-le-Duc which became known to the French as *La Voie Sacree* (the Sacred Way). In the weeks before the first assault and during the early part of the battle, Army airships bombed supply lines, in particular railways. The German Army Airship Service started a much more aggressive bombing policy at the end of 1915, establishing radio location stations at Cologne, Metz, Strasbourg, Charleville and Friedrichshafen in preparation for this.

They also made a serious mistake, thinking airships could bomb from height on moonlit nights and remain unseen from the ground. Zeppelin *LZ.77*, commanded by Hauptmann Alfred Horn, had made a few test flights over Cologne at about 10,000ft on moonlit nights. Observers said they could not see the Zeppelin. The Navy correctly saw this as plainly stupid. The Naval Leader of Airships, Peter Strasser, was convinced that operating in moonlight was very dangerous; observers had failed to take into account slightly misty conditions over Cologne that night. Oberleutnant zur See Werner Peterson was ordered to conduct tests with Zeppelin *L.16* over Hage. The Zeppelin was clearly visible from the ground at 10,000ft; it was also clearly visible to an aeroplane, as a silhouette against the moon or as a light shape away from it. The aeroplane could not be seen from the Zeppelin, even when it fired signal flares. Strasser was to be proven right in the next month.

The Army took the decision to carry out tactical bombing, flying over the Western Front, all through the month, in preparation for the attack on Verdun. Casualty rates were high and virtually ended the use of the airship over the battlefield by the Army. They continued strategic bombing throughout the year, and in 1915 had established a base in Hungary and some tactical and strategic bombing on the Eastern Front and the Balkans, but significant losses led to a reduction of airship operations and the end of Army airship operations in 1917.

The Navy, and very enthusiastically Strasser in the Zeppelin Force, saw an increased role for itself and its modern weapons as a way to end the stalemate of the Western Front. It couldn't break the British blockade, but it could reduce the capacity of the English to make war, by hitting the civilian population, destroying both morale and industrial capacity.

In January, command of the German High Seas Fleet was taken over by *Vizadmiral* Reinhard Scheer, whose operational brief was to pursue an aggressive strategy of total war against Britain's industrial capacity. The main thrust of the campaign was to be the introduction of unrestricted submarine warfare against merchant shipping, although because of concerns about America entering the war this didn't come into effect until 1917. Along with this, battle cruisers were to bombard British East Coast towns and the Airship Division was to intensify its campaign of bombing industrial cities.

Peter Strasser developed the details of the strategic bombing campaign. He had long been an enthusiast for the role of the Zeppelin as a bomber, able to significantly alter the course of the war. Clearly an intelligent man, he faced up to, and justified, the moral dilemma of terror bombing in a letter written to his mother:

> We who strike at the enemy where his heart beats have been slandered as 'baby-killers' and 'murderers of women' … What we do is repugnant to us too, but necessary, very necessary. Nowadays there is no such animal as a non-combatant: modern warfare is total warfare. A soldier cannot function at the front without the factory worker, the farmer, and all the other providers behind him. You and I, Mother, have discussed this subject, and I know you understand what I say. My men are brave and honourable. Their cause is holy, so how can they sin while doing their duty? If what we do is frightful, then may frightfulness be Germany's salvation.

A complex man with a strong sense of duty, Strasser thought it was necessary to go on combat operations with his crews to maintain morale and maintain his tactical skills. He tried to fly on missions at least once a month. It is certainly the case he didn't have to go on operations, and it did not always endear him to the crew chosen to take him as a passenger. Nevertheless, his willingness to put his life on the line made him a popular figurehead and charismatic commander.

Strasser met with Admiral Scheer in January 1916 to agree the details of his 'frightful' strategy. There were three attack zones: England North, from the River Tyne to Edinburgh; England Middle, from Liverpool across to the River Humber; and England South, London and East Anglia. The raid of 31 January 1916 was the first conducted according to the new strategy. The plan was for nine Navy Zeppelins to bomb industrial targets, mainly in 'Middle England': Liverpool was to be their primary target.

29 January 1916

This was the last Zeppelin raid on Paris. It demonstrated both the effectiveness of the defences around the city and the dangers of operating near the Western Front.

'P' Type Army Zeppelin *LZ.77*: Hauptmann Alfred Horn had engine trouble and was forced to return to base.

'P' Type Army Zeppelin *LZ.79*: Hauptmann Gasseirt left his base at Namur to bomb Paris. Over the French capital, he was attacked by a Maurice Farman MF7 plane flown by Sergeant Denneboude and Corporal Louis Vallin, who fired incendiary bullets from an army rifle, claiming to have hit the ship. Gasseirt bombed Paris from about 10,000ft, aiming to hit railway stations, but most of his bombs landed in the Belleville Quarter, killing eighteen people. The airship was hit by anti-aircraft fire over Paris, which caused it to lose hydrogen. It did not catch fire, but lost height and was forced to crash-land at Ath in Belgium, about 50 miles from its base, and was scrapped.

31 January 1916

'P' Type Army Zeppelin *LZ.85*: Oberleutnant Scherzer's airship took part in a bombing raid on Salonika (now Thessalonica, Greece), which was a major supply depot for Allied troops on the Macedonian Front. On the first raid it was well lit and the harbour installations were damaged. Scherzer left Temesvar, Hungary, with 4,400lb of bombs, and returned safely after an 885-mile round trip.

31 January/1 February 1916

This was probably the most significant raid of the War. The Zeppelins flew over an almost completely undefended part of the country, the English

Midlands. The main target was Liverpool. None of the airships got there, mainly due to fog, but major damage was done to industrial towns previously untouched by air raids. This led to political pressure for a country-wide air defence strategy. Seventy people were killed, 113 injured and damage caused to the tune of £53,832.

'P' Type Navy Zeppelin L.11: Oberleutnant zur See Horst von Buttlar-Brandenfels was assigned a new ship, Zeppelin *L.11*, in June 1915. He seems to have been developing the sense of caution that meant he was the only airship commander to serve right through the war

Zeppelin *L.11* left Nordholz in good weather before noon. While Buttlar was nominally in command, he was accompanied by the Commander of the Navy Airship Division, Korvettenkapitain Peter Strasser. It must have been difficult for Buttlar to command with his boss looking over his shoulder. It seems Strasser was an unpopular passenger, however much he was otherwise admired by Zeppelin crews. He had a reputation as a Jonah, many of the missions carrying him going wrong. He didn't bring *L.11* much luck that day.

Less is known about the route of *L.11* than most other Zeppelins, as it operated further north, and the fog which hampered its operation also hampered ground observations. There is no doubt that the GHQ report confuses part of the route of *L.11* with that of *L.13*. The GHQ report seems accurate for the first part of the flight of *L.11*. It crossed the coast in the company of Zeppelin *L.20* near Sutton Bridge at about 19.10; it had been slowed down and had been unable to climb because of a build-up of ice on the hull, as it had flown through fog, snow and rain. In his combat report, Buttlar said he had about two tons of rain and ice on the hull as he reached England. This cleared as he moved inland, but Buttlar could see very little because of the remaining fog. At 20.15, *L.11* passed a big city, which Buttlar thought was Lincoln, and then headed directly west until about 23.00. His report indicated he thought he had reached the west coast, but it seems more likely he flew over the sparsely populated Peak District between Sheffield and Manchester.

The GHQ report indicates that *L.11* took a separate route from *L.20* at the coast. The report says Buttlar dropped one incendiary bomb at Holbeach at 19.40, and then turned north-west, in the direction of South Yorkshire. The report says *L.11* dropped one incendiary and three HE bombs on Digby in Lincolnshire, and then four HE bombs on nearby Bloxholm Hall at about 20.00, without causing any casualties. The main problem with this account is that it is widely believed that the most remarkable feature of the cruise of *L.11* is that it did not drop any bombs. Buttlar wrote in his combat report that because he failed to find any military targets, he and Strasser decided to bring their bombs home. This caused British historian H.A. Jones, writing after the war, to comment on his 'high conception of his duty'. Ground observers certainly lost *L.11*. GHQ said that a Zeppelin they believed to be *L.13* was credibly reported in the Peak District; it was heard at about 21.50, but not seen. The GHQ map shows *L.13* just west of Buxton in Derbyshire. After that, the GHQ reports seem to get more accurate, albeit still believing they were tracking *L.13*. Zeppelin *L.11* was finally spotted again over Horncastle, north of Lincoln, at 22.50, and crossed the coast near Ingoldmells at 23.15. *L.11* returned to Nordholz at 09.50 the next day.

'P' Type Navy Zeppelin *L.13*: Kapitänleutnant Heinrich Mathy left his base at Hage in Zeppelin *L.13* with a crew of sixteen at about 11.45. We have good records of the early part of the flight: *L.13* crossed the English coast, accompanied by *L.21*, at 16.50, north of Mundesley, Norfolk. The two Zeppelins then separated at Foulsham, Mathy taking *L.13* directly west, being spotted at East Dereham. He was then seen at Sporle at 17.15, and was north of Swaffham at 17.30. He then turned north-west and went out to sea over the Wash north of Lynn, then back over land at Fosdyke at 18.30. Mathy flew directly west over Grantham, then was seen at 19.30 south of Nottingham. Hhe was over Derby at 19.45, and then went south of Cheadle to Stoke-on-Trent, witnesses in the town describing seeing and hearing the Zeppelin approaching from the direction of Trentham. *L.13* bombed Fenton Colliery near Stoke-on-Trent at about 20.15, dropping six HE bombs in a cluster of 70 yards, doing some damage but without causing any casualties. This demonstrates how Zeppelins bombed: to do this, *L.13* must have been virtually stationary when the bomb aimer, Oberleutnant zur See Kurt Friemel, dropped his bombs. Mathy then turned towards Newcastle-under-Lyme, dropping a flare at Madeley at 20.20. It seems Mathy had lost his way, as he then circled northward over Alsager, Woolstanton, Basford and back to Stoke.

British observers then lost *L.13*. It seems Mathy flew north-west, probably looking for Manchester but failing to find it because of the blackout and fog. He then flew east, trying to reach the Humber. He was spotted again over Retford, circling for some time, at 21.50. He then went north near Gainsborough, then south-east towards Lincoln, dropping another flare over Hackthorne at 22.30. The airship then went at high speed north towards Hull.

In his combat report, Mathy claimed to have bombed Goole, but in fact had found the brightly lit blast furnaces of the Frodingham Iron and Steel Works near Scunthorpe. The Zeppelin was heard at about 22.45. It seemed to be approaching at speed, making a noise like a 'heavy goods train'. Newspaper reports suggest the Zeppelin was clearly seen right above the town. The authorities in Scunthorpe had been warned that they were likely to be bombed, and lighting had been reduced as much as possible in the various works, with all the street lights turned off. It seems likely that because nearby Hull had been bombed, the authorities had plans in force for an air raid. The first bombs fell on workers' housing on Ravendale Street. They did considerable damage to the back of four houses, partly demolishing the washhouses and coal houses, shattering all the windows within hundreds of yards. There were newspaper reports that a pig kept in the yard of one of the houses was decapitated by a bomb. A well-known local woman, Mrs Sabina Markham, aged 86, of Trent Cottages, widow of the founder of the Scunthorpe Co-operative Society, displayed courage and fortitude. It appears an incendiary bomb fell through the roof of her house, but without any panic she threw a bucket of water on the flaring object, which was then thrown through a window by a plucky neighbour. The bombing didn't seem to have done any lasting harm to Sabina, who died in 1924 at the ripe old age of 94.

It appears the airship was moving slowly after this, as it bombed the nearby Glebe pit and the Trafford Street area, again breaking many windows. Mathy then circled over a number of different steel works covering an area of several square miles. A local historian, Harold Dudley, wrote that two HE bombs fell in the vicinity of the North Lincolnshire Works, and then a single bomb hit the closed Redbourne Hill Steelworks, killing two men. The men were Cyril J. Wright, a 24-year-old laboratory attendant, of 43 Ashby High Street, Ashby, and Thomas W. Danson, 29, an engine tender, of 2 Park Street, Scunthorpe. The latter was a noted footballer, the goalkeeper for Scunthorpe and Lindsey, the forerunners of Scunthorpe United FC. Mathy then turned *L.13* back towards the town, towards the chemical works. He flew in a northerly direction over the old Lindsey Iron Works, dropping several more HE bombs near Dawes Lane, where another man was killed and a number injured by a bomb which fell in the road. The man who was killed was Ernest Wilkinson Benson, 31, a steel worker, of 3 Ethel Terrace, Scunthorpe. The Zeppelin turned and flew off in a southerly direction. It had been over Scunthorpe for eight or nine minutes and dropped about twenty HE and 50 incendiary bombs. According to the GHQ Intelligence report, three men were killed and seven people injured, five men and two women.

L.13 was again spotted again at Humberston at 23.35 and fired on by the
1-pdr pom-pom gun at Waltham Wireless Station, without suffering any
damage. Mathy crossed back over the coast at about 23.40, north of North
Somercoates, returning to Hage by 08.30.

'P' Type Navy Zeppelin *L.14*: We once again have quite a lot of information about the route of Kapitänleutnant der Reserve Alois Bocker's Zeppelin
L.14 after it left Nordholz at 11.40. Bocker crossed the English coast north
of Holkham, Norfolk, at about 18.15. He was sighted over Burnham Market
at 18.20 and Sandringham at 18.35. He bombed Knipton, south-west of
Grantham, at about 20.00, without any casualties. *L.14* then headed west
for the Midlands, passing south of Nottingham and Derby and north of
Stafford, being spotted over Shrewsbury at 22.05. It then passed over
Wellington, Oakengates and Gnosal. It appears that Bocker thought darkened rural Shropshire to the west was the sea and he had reached the west
coast. He then turned east and flew over Cannock, Lichfield and Tamworth.
At 23.35, he saw the light of furnaces at Ashby Wolds, near Ashby de la
Zouch. He dropped one HE and one incendiary bomb, which fell on a cinder
heap and caused no damage. He reached Overseal in Derbyshire at about
midnight, where he dropped four HE bombs: three fell in open fields and
one in a canal, again with no damage. A few minutes later, at Swadlincote
in Derbyshire, he dropped three HE bombs which did a little damage, but
caused no casualties. *L.14* reached Derby, which was showing many lights,
some four hours after the start of the raid.

We have very good reports about what happened in Derby, which reveal
why the town was bombed when it was, and illustrate the chaotic lack of
planning and communication so apparent in every place bombed that night.
Derby certainly did better than any other place when the authorities were
first warned of a possible Zeppelin raid. The police had been alerted at
about 19.00 and had arranged for precautions to be taken. Works sirens were
sounded, special constables reported for duty, trams stopped running and
some works shut down. This almost certainly resulted in Derby not being
bombed earlier that evening. Four Zeppelins had flown close to the town,
which must have been dark and not seen. *L.21* passed north at about 18.55,
L.13 passed over at about 19.45 and *L.20* passed close at about 21.00, while
Bocker in *L.14* flew just south at about 21.00. In his combat report, Bocker
claimed to have seen Derby but had decided not to bomb it as his main target
was Liverpool. He returned three hours later. Telephone calls to police in
other towns seemed to confirm that the raids had ended and the danger was

over. At some time between 22.00 and 23.00, a decision was made that the crisis was over. The special constables were sent home, the trams returned to their depots and most works with a night shift turned their lights back on. Some of the street lights were also put back on.

After a long night, *L.14*, unlike most other Zeppelins, still had an almost full bomb load. Although Bocker did not realize he was over Derby, it was a glittering prize. We have very full reports from the ground of the bombing. According to the GHQ report, Bocker reached Derby at about 00.10, ten minutes after he bombed Swadlincote. He was travelling almost due north when he left Swadlincote, so as he approached Derby from the south he would have crossed the Birmingham–Derby railway line and probably followed it into the city. If there were any lights showing, he would have seen a mass of railway lines between the Osmaston and London roads to the south of the city. In 1916, Derby was one of the principal railway towns in the country. The factories building railway engines and carriages were obviously connected by railway lines, but the whole area was like a huge goods yard, with numerous branch line and sidings to shunt and store the railway stock being built. It is unlikely Bocker would fail to see it from 9,000ft. Witnesses on the ground said that the Zeppelin was over Derby for about ten minutes, dropping bombs in salvos of two or three every minute or two. No one reported that the Zeppelin was circling, so it seems likely he was flying slowly above the railway, slowing down to a hover when he dropped his bombs. In Derby, all the bombs were dropped in fairly small groups, the targets being railways, factories or workers' housing. It seems certain Bocker could see his targets, first from lights and then possibly from fires he had started. It is likely the Zeppelin was stationary when the bombs were dropped.

If Bocker flew north over the city, the first bombs landed about a mile south of the city centre. The first targets of *L.14* were factories around the Rolls-Royce Works on Nightingale Road, just west of the Osmaston Road. Bocker dropped a salvo of six HE bombs aimed at targets in the area. Two HE bombs obviously aimed at factory buildings hit waste land near the Rolls-Royce factory. Another hit the motor-car test track at the end of the Rolls-Royce factory, which did some damage to the workshops but caused no casualties. The next target was the nearby Metalite Works of the Derby Lamp Company in Gresham Road, where bomb aimer Oberleutnant zur See Kurt Frankenburg dropped three HE bombs, causing considerable damage to goods awaiting dispatch and almost demolishing a building, but causing no causalities.

Bocker continued a few hundred yards further north, bombing the Midland Railway Carriage and Wagon Works, dropping five more HE bombs, doing some damage but again causing no casualties. The next salvo was another few hundred yards north, where it seems the Zeppelin next bombed the T.W. Fletcher Lace factory in Osmaston Road with two incendiary bombs; they landed in the factory yard and did little damage. Probably still hovering, Bocker then bombed some working–class housing with four incendiary bombs; a house in Horton Street was set on fire by one such bomb which went through the roof. It seems here that Bocker and Frankenburg could see enough to decide the type of bomb to use: incendiaries were dropped on housing, where they were more effective.

Still following the Osmaston Road, Bocker went a little further north. Frankenburg dropped one HE bomb on a large house, the Rolls-Royce Foreman's Club on the corner of Bateman Street and Osmaston Road. Bocker then turned east across the London Road and over the railway yards. These were almost certainly well lit. He bombed the Midland Railway Locomotive Works off the London Road: this was the target where the most damage was done. *L.14* dropped nine HE bombs which killed three men outright and injured one so severely he died in hospital three days later. The GHQ Intelligence report says that most of the bombs seemed to be aimed at trains in Chaddesden Sidings, and a bomb hit the side of an engine tender. The men killed, all employed by the railway works, were: William Barcroft (32), a fitter, of 34 Strutt Street, Derby; Harry Hithersay (23) of 73 Devonshire Street, Derby; James Gibbs Hardy (56), an engine driver, of 11 Strutt Street, Derby; and Charles Henry Champion (41), an electrician, of 33 Fleet Street, Derby.

It seems the four men were killed by a single bomb. The coroner's report gives more detail. There were a number of witnesses who had been working with the victims when the bomb fell. One said he and the victims had clearly heard the engines of the Zeppelin, and it also seems Bocker was using a searchlight to look for targets. (He would have seen a train but not individuals at 9,000ft.) The witness said he ran in one direction and the victims another; the men who died had sheltered under the engine tender, but the bomb landed a few yards from them. The witness was blown off his feet but not injured. Another witness was the departmental foreman, who said he had turned up the lights in his department, as he seen another department do the same, and thought they had been given the authority to do so. When he heard the bombs, he turned the lights off again, but obviously too late. It is likely the last bombs to be dropped hit the works of the Derby Gas Company, south-east of the engine works. Two HE bombs hit the gas works and one incendiary bomb hit a coal heap, which failed to ignite. According to the GHQ report, these bombs had no effect.

L.14 then left Derby and flew east. It was spotted south-east of Nottingham at 00.35, and near Newark and south of Lincoln, before leaving our shores north of the Wash at about 02.10 on 1 February, after almost eight hours in enemy territory. It had penetrated the furthest west of any Zeppelin on the raid. The raid on Derby showed the chaotic nature of decision-making, but in another way the town was lucky. Had the lights been on earlier, there would have been more casualties as people would have been out on the streets, as they were in other towns. The victims were shift workers; most people in the bombed area were tucked up safely in bed. Statistically they were much safer there.

There was a great deal of criticism of the actions of the local authorities and railway companies in putting the lights back on before midnight. While this was deserved, the real failure was at national level in the War Office. The route of *L.14* from Shrewsbury to Derby was very well recorded, which meant that ground observers could see it and were sending accurate information by telephone to the War Office. The chaotic organization and lack of an effective communication system meant there was no way to collate the intelligence and warn the authorities in the East Midlands that a Zeppelin was on its way back.

L.14 arrived back at Nordholz at about noon on 1 February. The Germans said in a press release the next day that Liverpool was the main target and had been hit by a number of Zeppelins. The story does not end there, as on Saturday, 23 September 1916. Bocker and many of the crew of *L.14* were shot down in Zeppelin *L.33*. The airship was hit by anti-aircraft fire over London. Luckily for them, the ship did not catch fire but it crash-landed. The twenty-two-man crew was captured and intensively interrogated. Bocker refused to say much, but many crew members talked openly. They all maintained that *L.14* had bombed Liverpool, as had been claimed in the press communiqué. There seems no doubt that most of the crew genuinely believed this. The GHQ report says they all believed the claims made by their commanding officer and navigator, on which they believed the communiqué was based. However, it is unlikely many had much idea of the course of the ship; a man working in an engine gondola would have little clue as to the location of the Zeppelin. Along with Bocker, there was one man who did: he was the Steuermann, a warrant officer, responsible for navigation. After prolonged cross-examination, he said he knew *L.14* had not been to Liverpool, but he had seen the lights of Manchester and Sheffield. It may be that Bocker believed at the time he had been over the west coast; Steuermann, who was an equally experienced seaman, responsible only for navigation, probably had a better idea of the route, but certainly didn't know the ship had bombed Derby. He said during his interrogation that by compass readings and dead reckoning he was certain *L.14* had bombed ironworks between Birmingham and Nottingham. The GHQ report says that this could only be the pipe furnaces at Ashby Wolds. This indicates he had a better idea of the position of *L.14* than Bocker, though neither correctly identified Derby as the target.

'P' Type Navy Zeppelin *L.15*: Kapitänleutnant Joachim Breithaupt, with Leutnant zur See Otto Kuhne as his executive officer, had taken off from Hage at noon. *L.15* had engine trouble over the North Sea, with two out of four engines out of action. By the time it reached England they had been repaired in flight by the mechanics, and the airship then made good time. Though *L.15*'s flight was poorly recorded by British ground observers, it seems to have crossed the coast north of Maundsley at about 17.50. Breithaupt then cruised directly westwards, reaching Burton-on-Trent with a full bomb load at about 20.30. The combat report of Breithaupt was very full and is worth quoting in some detail. He identified his target as Liverpool. He reported that he was over the west coast at about 20.30 when he recognized a large city complex divided by a large sheet of water running north and south, joined by a lighted bridge. He identified this as Liverpool and Birkenhead. He dropped a parachute flare and most of the lights in the city went out. From a height of 8,200ft he dropped 3,100lb of HE and 660lb of incendiary bombs, mostly along the waterfront, in four bomb runs. All the HE bombs burst, but fires did not result. On the other hand, the incendiaries worked well and a huge glow of fire could be seen over the city from a great distance.

After this, Breithaupt flew east to return to base. There are poor records of his course as his magnetic compass was faulty, and the ship was steered by the stars. This gives a good indication of the weather on the night over the Midlands: while patchy ground fog often obscured the ground, at height the sky was clear and bright. British records were very unreliable; they reported *L.15* dumped forty bombs in the Fens district north-east of Cambridge. These were almost certainly the bombs dropped by *L.16*. It seems they got it right, however, when the airship was spotted south of Skegness at 22.00.

It is possible *L.15* dropped nine incendiary bombs at Welbourne Hill Top, north of Sleaford, at 21.30, and then went on towards Skegness. It seems that it then turned south and dropped a single incendiary bomb on Holland Fen, near Boston, at 22.30. Breithaupt went out to sea over the Wash and crossed the coast again near Kings Lynn. He was spotted at Swaffham at 23.20 and over Wymondham at 23.50, then left our shores at Corton at about 00.35.

L.15 arrived back at Hage at about 10.05 on 1 February. Like many of the Zeppelins fitted with the 240hp engines, it was out of action for some time as they were returned for modification to the Maybach factory at Fredrichshafen, where modified engines were fitted and the ship was readied for action in March 1916.

While it is not certain that bombs from *L.15* killed all the Burton-on-Trent victims, it certainly was responsible for most, so it is fitting to record them here: Margaret Anderson (60) of 195 Scalpcliffe Road, Burton; Ada Brittain (15) of 5 Slaters Yard, Burton; Berty Geary (13) of 89 Blackpool Road, Burton; Charles Gilson (52) of 34 Wellington Street, Burton; Edith Measham (10) of 32 Wellington Road, Burton; Mary Rose Morris (55) of 32 Eaton Place, Brighton, a vicar's wife who was on a speaking tour; Lucy Simnett (15) of 150 Branstone Road, Burton; Elizabeth Smith (45) of 73 Park Street, Burton; George Stephens (16) of 332 Blackpool Road, Burton; Rachel Wait (78) of 72 New Street, Burton; Flora L. Warden (16) of 206 Uxbridge Street, Burton; George Warrington (6) of 108 Shobnall Street, Burton; Mary Warrington (11) of 108 Shobnall Street, Burton; and Florence Jane Wilson (23) of 8 Casey Lane, Burton.

'P' Type Navy Zeppelin *L.16*: Oberleutnant zur See Werner Peterson lifted off from Hage at 12.15. Like most of the Zeppelins fitted with newer 240hp HSLu engines, *L.16* suffered from engine trouble. Peterson made slow progress as an engine failed before he reached the British coast. The airship was also covered with snow and ice, and unable to climb above 7,000ft. It was spotted when it crossed the coast at Hunstanton at 18.10. Because of the engine problems, Peterson decided to abandon the mission to bomb Liverpool, and to target Great Yarmouth instead. There is some confusion in the British reports about *L.16*'s movements. It was reported as wandering about Norfolk, dropping two bombs near Swaffham, one of which did not explode, until it crossed back over the coast at 21.05 at Lowestoft. Peterson's combat report contradicts this, as he claimed to have dropped all his bombs on various factories and industrial works at Yarmouth. While we know Yarmouth was not bombed that night, and he was lost in the fog, he would certainly know if he had dropped all his bombs. It seems likely that British ground observers, watching Zeppelins sliding in and out of view in the mist, confused his bombing and attributed it to another airship. It is probable the bombs dropped in the Fens district attributed to *L.15* actually came from

Peterson in *L.16*.

If this is the case, we can confirm much of his route from where the bombs landed. A Zeppelin was spotted over Mildenhall at 19.10, which dropped three HE and fifteen incendiary bombs at West Row Fen at 19.15. The Zeppelin then flew west to Isleham Fen, where it dropped twenty-two HE bombs at 19.35; probably because of the marshy ground, only fifteen exploded, a hen house was destroyed and sixteen chickens killed. The Zeppelin was again spotted over Pulham at 20.30 and Bungay at 20.40, and it went out to sea north of Lowestoft at 21.05

'P' Type Navy Zeppelin *L.17*: Kapitänleutnant Herbert Ehrlich was assigned to *L.17* on 27 October 1915, following service in Russia on *L.5*. After taking off from Nordholz at 11.17, Zeppelin *L.17* suffered from engine trouble. Two of its engines seized before reaching the English coast. Ehrlich's mechanics had spent much of the afternoon repairing the forward engine. His starboard engine also failed repeatedly. This led to Ehrlich making very slow progress. Ground observers spotted *L.17* as it crossed the coast at Sheringham at 18.40. In his combat report, Ehrlich said he could not determine his position due to thick cloud, but saw the glow of blast furnaces to the starboard and steered towards them. He was then caught by a searchlight beam, and said he was fired on by small-calibre guns. He said he made two runs over the industrial area, and that the battery was silenced and all lights were out by the end of his attack. He later calculated his position by dead reckoning, and thought he had bombed Immingham. But he had not: the British, in their GHQ report, said *L.17* was the only Zeppelin to be troubled by British defence forces, being caught in a searchlight beam operated by the Royal Naval Air Service at Holt. This caused it to drop its bombs at Bayfield and Letheringsett, missing the searchlight and landing mainly in fields, damaging a barn and a house but causing no casualties. The airship left British airspace, south of Yarmouth, at 20.30. *L.17* made slow progress back to Nordholz, taking over twelve hours to cross the North Sea and land safely.

'P' Type Navy Zeppelin *L.19*: Kapitänleutnant Odo Lowe's Zeppelin *L.19*, carrying a crew of sixteen, left its base at Tondern in Schleswig Holstein at 11.15 for a rendezvous with the rest of the attack force over Borkum Island. It crossed the English coast over Sheringham, Norfolk, at about 18.20. It seems to have been travelling more slowly than the other airships, though it is impossible to be precise, as the combat log was lost. The rather slow progress also caused problems for ground observers charting its movements. It was spotted over Swaffham at 19.05, Stamford at 20.10 and Loughborough at 21.30. From Loughborough, Loewe seems to have seen the fires caused by other Zeppelins at Burton-on-Trent. He dropped a few incendiary bombs there at about 21.45. From Burton, *L.19* moved in a south-westerly direction, passing near Wolverhampton. Between 22.30 and 23.30, it was reported 'wandering' about south of Birmingham, being seen or heard near Enville, Kinver, Wolverley, Bewdley, Bromsgrove, Reddich and Stourbridge.

In July 1939, an unexploded Great War German bomb was found on a river bank near Kidderminster by men of the Worcestershire Highways Department who were erecting a coffer dam to repair the Old Iron Bridge. It was reported to weigh about 50lb, and was about 2ft long, with fins. It was 13ft down below the river bank, was live but hadn't exploded because it fell into soft ground. In early 1915, ground observers did not note the fall of a bomb in the Kidderminster area, but this may well indeed have been one from *L.19*. They did record *L.19* as it passed over Wythall at 23.00 going towards Birmingham. Loewe failed to find Birmingham, which was in total darkness, and started his attack on Wednesbury at about midnight, possibly attracted by fires started by *L.21*. The official GHQ Home Forces report states he dropped a single HE bomb on the axle department of the Monway Works, doing slight damage to the building and machinery.

From Wednesbury, Loewe turned towards Dudley. He dropped five HE bombs on Ocker Hill Colliery, damaging the engine house and one dwelling house. He reached Dudley at 00.15, dropping seventeen incendiary bombs, most of which fell in the castle grounds or open fields. One fell on a grain shed at the railway station, causing only £5 worth of damage. The site is now part of Dudley Zoo. He caused much more damage when he flew north to Tipton, bombing almost the same area as *L.21* a few hours earlier. He was probably able to see the still-burning gas mains. The GHQ report states that Loewe dropped eleven HE bombs at about 00.20, mainly in the western part of the town between the L&NW railway station and Bloomfield. He caused considerable damage to a number of houses, but caused no casualties. As well as damage to houses, there was damage to the railway, with rails and sleepers blown some distance.

We can work out what happened in more detail by combining GHQ information, with newspaper reports. One bomb fell in Union Street a few yards from the crater caused by *L.21*, and another in the Waterloo Street area. Two more HE bombs fell near the Bush Inn at 127 Park Lane West, Tipton. The newspapers described in graphic detail the destruction caused by one of these bombs. It hit the roof of a house without exploding, and then bounced into the roadway, where it detonated 5ft in front of the Bush Inn. The pub was completely wrecked by the explosion; every door and window was smashed, the whole place rendered a ruin. From Tipton, Loewe seems to have followed the railway to Walsall. As with *L.21*, we have more details of what happened when *L.19* reached Walsall. At about 00.25, Loewe dropped two HE bombs on Dora Street and Pleck Road in Pleck.

We have an interesting witness account of this from Gilbert Bromley, who was just a boy at the time. His father asked him to go outside and put a street lamp out, and he climbed the lamppost to extinguish the gaslight. Shortly after, he heard a whirring noise and looked up, seeing a Zeppelin in the sky. Suddenly, it seemed a door opened on the machine and 'a light flashed down like someone with a big torch'. Gilbert darted back into the house to tell his mum and dad. All of a sudden 'there was a crash, bang and then two more'. From the noise, they assumed a nearby house had tumbled down, but in fact it was their stable. The bomb had killed their horse, four pigs and about 100 fowl. In a rather unusual display of dry humour, the *Walsall Pioneer* newspaper commented in its report of the raid: 'With a fellow feeling for the rest of their kind, the Germans no doubt, would have spared the pigs if they had known.'

Loewe then turned north and moved over Birchills, in Walsall, where he dropped another HE bomb, damaging St Andrews Church and vicarage in Hollyhedge Lane. The buildings were severely damaged, but there were no further deaths or injuries. In all, Loewe seems to have dropped twenty HE and seventeen incendiary bombs on the Black Country.

After leaving Walsall, Loewe steered a course eastward for home. *L.19* made very slow progress, spending almost nine hours over England. Engine trouble seems to be the main reason for this, though the airship seems to have pursued a very curious route to and from its targets. On the journey to the coast, it was spotted over Sutton Coldfield at 00.30 and Coleshill at 00.40. It then passed north of Coventry and south of Bedworth at 00.50, then north of Rugby at 1.00. After this it made much slower progress.

At 02.23, Loewe radioed his base for a navigation bearing. He was located between Kings Lynn and Norwich. Loewe again radioed his base at 04.37 to give his attack report:

> At 12 midnight (23.00 GMT) I was over the West Coast. Orientation and attack there were impossible due to thick fog; dropped incendiaries. 1,600Kg (3,500 Pounds) of bombs dropped on several big factories in Sheffield.

This shows very well the navigational problems he was having. He seems to have bombed Burton-on-Trent thinking it was Liverpool, and the Black Country thinking it was Sheffield. As for bombing factories, most of his victims were killed in a stable.

L.19 finally crossed the English coast at Martham, Norfolk, at 05.25, some hours after the other Zeppelins. It was spotted by a British observer, who reported seeing a Zeppelin travelling very slowly and in difficulties. By this time, it seems *L.19* had three out of four engines operating on reduced power. British naval vessels were sent to look for it, but they found nothing.

Loewe requested another navigational bearing at 05.41, and the German Navy ordered three flotillas of destroyers to raise steam to search for him. It took *L.19* another ten hours to cross the North Sea. At 15.05 on the afternoon of 1 February, Loewe radioed to say he was over the German North Sea coast. His signal, again decoded by British Naval Intelligence, read:

> Radio equipment at times out of order, three engines out of order. Approximate position Borkum Island. Wind is favourable.

As a result of this, the searching destroyers were called back to base, even though the bearings on Loewe's signal indicated he was further west than he thought. *L.19* was in fact about 20 miles north of Ameland, one of the Dutch Friesian Islands. This was radioed to Loewe, but it is not known whether he received the message. It was to be a costly navigational error. Hardly able to steer or maintain forward speed because three engines were out of action, Loewe had probably given up hope of reaching Tondern. He almost certainly intended to land at Hage or crash-land when he reached German territory. Though only a few miles from the German coast, luck was running out for Loewe and the crew of *L.19*. The crippled Zeppelin was pushed by the wind over Ameland, about 30 miles south of Borkum, at 16.00. Ameland was part of the territory of neutral Holland, and heavily garrisoned. When *L.19* appeared out of the fog, a number of Dutch soldiers fired repeatedly at it. The rifle fire punctured the hydrogen gas cells. It is probable that if its engines had been working properly, *L.19* could have reached German soil. However, the combination of engine trouble and gas leakage meant Loewe could not maintain speed or height. Virtually out of control, *L.19* sank towards the cold North Sea. Its crew had long before discharged all ballast, and then thrown overboard heavy objects, first the machine guns and then the useless petrol tanks. Finally, anything not fixed to the structure of the Zeppelin was discarded. This was all in vain, as sometime during the night of 1/2 February, perhaps thirty-six hours after leaving base at Tondern, *L.19* splashed into the North Sea.

The German Navy sent out destroyers and seaplanes to try and find *L.19*, without success. Two seaplanes operating out of Borkum Island were lost, their crews - a pilot and observer in each - adding four more casualties to the toll of the raid. Nothing more was heard until 3 February, when a British fishing boat reported seeing *L.19* and became embroiled in a war crime controversy. The trawler *King Stephen*, out of Grimsby, had been fishing in a prohibited area. At 07.00 on Wednesday, 2 February, its crew spotted a large white object in the water. They sailed close to it and found the *L.19* looking 'like a great White Mountain in the sea'. A group of men were in a roughly constructed shelter on top of the envelope, and more seemed to be inside the hull. The crew of the *King Stephen* heard a knocking sound; probably the crew of *L.19* trying to caulk leaks inside the hull. Loewe hailed the skipper, Captain William Martin, and asked to be taken aboard. After consultation with his crew, Martin refused. The *King Stephen* had a crew of nine, and he thought the Zeppelin had a crew of thirty; in fact it was sixteen. Captain Martin feared, probably correctly, that if he took the Germans aboard, then they would take over his ship and take her to Germany. Martin later told the press that 'it went to a seaman's heart not to take them off', but he had to think of his crew and their families. Even though he reported that a German speaking perfect English had offered the crew £5 to rescue them, Captain Martin sailed away. He promised to report the position of the *L.19* to the first warship he saw, but unfortunately the *King Stephen* didn't come across any other vessels until it reached the Humber on 3 February. By then it was too late: the *L.19* had gone down with all hands.

Once the fate of *L.19* became known, the propaganda changed. The German press promptly accused the skipper of the *King Stephen* of a war crime, the atrocity of leaving the crew of *L.19* to perish in the North Sea. While this can be seen as typical propaganda, countering criticism of the sinking of the *Lusitania* by a German U-boat, as well as the bombing of civilians, the British position was not helped by the Bishop of London, who, the press reported, supported leaving of the Zeppelin 'baby killers to drown in the cold North Sea'. To be fair to the bishop, it seems what he actually said was that the whole of the British people ought to stand by the skipper of the trawler who came upon the ruined Zeppelin, and you could not trust the word of the Germans. Had Martin taken aboard the Germans, it was probable they might have turned on the crew and the whole German press would have applauded this as a clever piece of strategy. Any English sailor would have risked his life to save human life, but the sad thing was that the chivalry of war had been killed by the Germans and their word could not be trusted. The bishop probably disagreed with the German who said he 'acted less as an apostle of Christian charity than as a jingoistic hatemonger', though to the press on both sides 'jingoistic hatemonger' was probably seen as a compliment.

The end of the story of *L.19* took another six months to come to light. Kapitänleutnant Odo Loewe wrote a last report, which he put in a bottle. A Swedish yacht picked it up several months later. Loewe had written:

> With 15 men on the top platform and backbone girder of the *L.19*, floating without gondolas in approximately 3 degrees east longitude. I am attempting to send a last report. Engine trouble three times repeated, a light head wind on the return journey delayed our return and in the mist carried us over Holland where I received heavy rifle fire; the ship became heavy and simultaneously three engines failed.
>
> February 2nd 1916, towards 1.00 PM, will apparently be our last hour.
>
> Loewe.

'Q' Type Navy Zeppelin *L.20*: This was Kapitänleutnant Franz Stabbert's first raid on England. A regular naval officer, born on 13 February 1881, he was an inexperienced airship commander. His first command was Zeppelin *L.7* in November 1915, which he 'inherited' from Max Dietrich. He took over *L.20* on 22 December 1915; this was a new airship, the first of the longer 'Q' type Zeppelins. It had a better bomb load than the smaller 'P' type, but still had the problems caused by the HSLu engines.

The route of *L.20* was well monitored by the British. It left its base at Tondern at about 11.06, but was slowed down by engine trouble, the forward engine being out of action for much of the flight over the North Sea and the starboard running irregularly. Stabbert also had to fly low at 6,500ft because of heavy rain and snow, which caused icing on the hull. This further slowed *L.20*, but did not stop it reaching the English Midlands. The icing reduced as *L.20* flew overland and it was able to climb to about 9,000ft. The airship was spotted crossing the coast at about 19.10 near Sutton Bridge, in the company of Zeppelin *L.11*, and was seen over Peakirk at 19.40. Travelling west, it bombed Uffington at 19.45, dropping one HE bomb, just breaking a few windows. It then passed north of Oakham and Leicester. Both nearby Nottingham and Leicester had a full blackout, but Loughborough did not.

At about 20.00, Stabbert spotted the lights of Loughborough. The bomb aimer and Second Officer, Leutnant zur See Ernst Wilhelm Schirlitz, dropped four HE bombs at 20.05, killing ten people and causing a considerable amount of damage. In his combat report, Stabbert claimed he bombed and silenced an anti-aircraft battery which fired at him. It is difficult to understand why he said this unless he believed it was true. He made the report when he returned to Tondern, and was not under pressure to claim he only hit military targets, as he may have been as a prisoner of war.

The most likely explanation for Stabbert's report is that as he approached Loughborough he saw, through the ground mist, flashing lights which he took to be gun fire. The Empress Crane Works was operating a night shift, and other factories probably also did. An explanation for flashing lights could be welding flashes or intermittent light. Add to that the airmen'sanxiety, tiredness and restricted vision, and the imagination takes over.

The British Intelligence report on the raid is quite explicit about the order in which the bombs were dropped, and from this we can work out what happened. It seems *L.20* passed over Loughborough from east to west, and then cut its engines and slowed down looking for targets. We know the first bomb dropped in the garden of the Crown and Cushion pub in Orchard Street, the next a few seconds later nearby in The Rushes, a main thoroughfare. It seems Stabbert then circled and headed east, the last two bombs landing close together in the Empress Road area, several hundred yards east of the first two, according to witnesses about three minutes later. They were also dropped in quick succession. The third bomb dropped on an orchard in Thomas Street, causing no casualties but breaking many windows in the area, and the fourth, seconds later, in front of the Empress Crane Works. It was noted in the British Intelligence report that the Crane Works did not put its lights out until the first bomb had dropped. Ten people – four men and six women – were killed. About twelve people were injured. After dropping the bombs, Stabbert opened the throttles on the engines and sped away to the north. Several witnesses noted the roar of the engines, but nobody saw the Zeppelin. Those killed at Loughborough were: Annie Adcock (42) of 13 The Rushes, Loughborough; Alice Elizabeth Adkin (29) of Kingthorp Street, Loughborough; Joseph Williamson Adkin (27) of Kingthorp Street, Loughborough; Ethel Higgs (25) of 104 Station Street, Loughborough; Joseph Gilbert (49) of Empress Road, Loughborough; Elsie Page (16) of 87 Empress Road, Loughborough; Joseph Page (18) of 87 Empress Road, Loughborough; Mary Ann Page (44) of 87 Empress Road, Loughborough;

Martha Shipman (49) of 5 Orchard Street, Loughborough; and Arthur Christian Turnill (50) of 83 Station Street, Loughborough.

Stabbert claimed that after bombing the battery in Loughborough, he made the decision not to go on to Liverpool, because of his engine trouble, but to bomb Sheffield, which he calculated was near. He turned north to do this, but was much further south than he thought he was. *L.20* flew north at high speed, Schirlitz dropping one more bomb as he left the town, which landed in soft ground and didn't explode. Stabbert next saw lights at Ilkeston; he probably took Ilkeston for Sheffield, which he claimed to have bombed in his combat report. He dropped seven HE bombs on the railway at Bennerley and Trowell at 20.27, damaging a signal box and the Bennerley railway viaduct on the Derbyshire-Nottinghamshire border, at Awsworth, but causing no casualties. The signalman in the Bennerley signal box was very lucky. He had been telephoned a few minutes before and told to stop all the trains, and was walking along the track towards a waiting train to tell the driver to extinguish all his lamps when the bomb hit his signal box.

Stabbert continued west to Hallam Fields near Ilkeston, where he dropped fifteen HE bombs on the Stanton Ironworks at 20.30. He caused considerable damage to buildings and killed two men: James Hall (56) of Homer Cottage, 12 Frederick Street, Stapleford, and Walter Wilson (41) of 2 Albert Villas, Station Road, Ilkeston. We have reasonably good information about what happened, and can reconstruct much of the events of that night. There were two coroner's inquests on the victims, that on James Hall on the Thursday, 3 February, and the one on Walter Wilson the next day. There seem to have been a number of common facts remembered by all the witnesses. It was a clear night – there was no mist in the area at the time of the raid – so almost everyone saw as well as heard the Zeppelin. The explosions on the railway were heard and people saw the Zeppelin coming from the Bennerley area. There is also agreement that the Zeppelin spent a few minutes over the works, probably circling looking for targets. Several witnesses who were standing in the tram terminus with Walter Wilson, one of the victims, said it dropped a few bombs, went away where they heard more explosions, then returned and dropped a few more before it flew off again.

From this it seems likely that the first bombs were dropped near the works offices and workers' housing a few hundred yards or so from St Bartholomew's Church. A number of the offices, houses, a rifle range and a pub were damaged. It is certain Stabbert didn't know he was bombing offices and housing, but from 9,000ft over a clear target, Schirlitz, the bomb aimer, probably saw lights and signs of activity. It seems he dropped five bombs in the first cluster. They damaged houses, offices and two pubs. We have a description of what happened at one of the pubs, the Stanton Hotel in Crompton Street. The local newspapers, one of which may have been a supporter of the teetotal movement, reported what happened next with some glee. The drinkers had a terrible fright when a bomb dropped in the pub garden, blowing out all the windows on that side. Bottles were thrown from the shelves and some of the beer barrels in the cellar lost their plugs and spilled their contents. The pub immediately cleared after the explosion, with not many finishing their drinks. Stabbert then turned away to the manufacturing area of the works, a witness many years later saying the bombs were dropped near the 'Old Works' furnaces. The GHQ reports say the moulding shop was damaged. The first death occurred here. We have some fairly confused reports from the inquest of James Hall, an assistant furnace keeper, but it seems the bomb hit a pile of pig iron, which added to the effect of the shrapnel from the bomb. Hall was killed instantly, his body badly mutilated and the top of his head blown off.

We know more about what happened to the second victim, Walter Wilson. He was waiting at the tram terminus opposite the church with three workmates; he had finished work and was waiting to go home. The Zeppelin had bombed in the vicinity a few minutes before. It seems likely the men knew the trams had been cancelled and were getting ready to walk back to Ilkeston when *L.20* returned and dropped two more bombs. The first landed near the men, and they ran away to find shelter, Wilson by the wall of St Bartholomew's Church. A few seconds later, in what seems like a frightening cat and mouse game, another bomb landed near them, the witness then describing hearing a shrill whistle, an ear-splitting crash and a blinding flash. The bomb hit the parish room, completely destroying it and breaking a stained glass window in the church. Wilson was found lying against a wall near the demolished parish room. He was taken to Ilkeston Hospital, where he saw his wife and told her he was too badly injured to survive. He was operated on. The doctor who attended to him said he was in a collapsed condition, and part of his intestine was protruding through a 3in wound in his back. He never recovered from the operation and died on Tuesday afternoon, the day after the raid.

Stabbert then flew to Burton-on-Trent, bombing the town at 20.45, the second of the three Zeppelins to do so. By this time he had used all his HE bombs, so he dropped only incendiaries. As three airships bombed Burton in a one-hour period, with fifteen people killed and a great deal of damage done, it is impossible to determine which airship was responsible for individual casualties. However, as Stabbert only had incendiary bombs left, it seems likely he only caused fires and most of the casualties were caused by *L.15*, which arrived before him. It is interesting to note that the commander of *L.15*, Breithaupt, stated in his combat report that he saw a huge glow of fire as *L.15* left Burton. As far as we know, there were no major fires in Burton, so it may be that he saw the incendiary bombs dropped by Stabbert but did not see the Zeppelin. Certainly neither commander reported seeing the other airship, though they must have been over Burton at much the same time.

After bombing Burton, *L.20* suffered from more engine trouble and made slow progress. It was spotted travelling in a north-easterly direction, passing north of Derby and Nottingham, and then went south-east to the vicinity of Stamford. The airship was spotted at Thornley at 22.30 and near Swaffham at 23.15, crossed the coast near Blakeney at 23.45 and was last seen from Cromer going out to sea at 23.52. It seems it had more engine trouble because it took twelve hours to cross the North Sea, arriving at Tondern at noon the next day.

'Q' Type Navy Zeppelin *L.21*: This was also the first raid on England by Kapitänleutnant der Reserve Max Dietrich, about whom we know quite a lot. He was born on 27 November 1870 at Angermunde, north of Berlin. At 45, he was old for a combat officer. His background was different from most other Zeppelin commanders. He came from a solidly middle-class family. One of sixteen children, he went to sea at the age of 17. He did well as a merchant seaman, becoming the youngest captain in the North German Lloyd shipping line. He commanded a number of ocean liners before the outbreak of war. He was regarded as a war hero early in the conflict when he broke through the British blockade, sailing from America in the SS *Brandenburg*, getting the Iron Cross Second Class for the exploit. As an officer in the merchant service, he was also a reserve officer in the Imperial German Navy. It is said his exceptional skill as a navigator led him to the Zeppelin Service. He had commanded two Zeppelins before *L.21*, gaining the Iron Cross First Class in the process. His first airship was Zeppelin *L.7*, in which he had been involved in a daylight naval action against a British minelayer on 9 August 1915. In November 1915, he had been given command of Zeppelin *L.18*, but she was destroyed in her shed at Tondern when being topped up with hydrogen. On a more personal note he was the uncle of the actress Marlene Dietrich, though she was an unknown teenager when he set out on 31 January 1916.

L.21 left its base at Nordholz at about 11.00. Max Dietrich's orders were to bomb Liverpool. The Zeppelin crossed the English coast near Mundesley, Norfolk, at about 16.50 as dusk fell. Observers on the ground noted *L.21* over Narborough at 17.20 and Kings Lynn at 17.25. It passed south of Grantham at 18.30, and then flew south of Nottingham and north of Derby just before 19.00. From Derby, *L.21* flew south-west, passing over Rugeley before reaching Stafford at 19.25. Observers reported that the airship then suddenly turned south, heading for Wolverhampton at high speed. Dietrich passed over Wolverhampton, then subject to a partial blackout, at 19.45, reaching Netherton at 19.55 and hovering over the town for about three minutes. It is probable that Dietrich then spotted the lights and furnaces of the Black Country, which was not subject to any blackout restrictions. He turned north, passing over Dudley and reaching Tipton just after 20.00.

In his combat report, Deitrich said he thought he was over the Irish Sea when he saw the bright lights of two towns, separated by a river, which he took to be Liverpool and Birkenhead. The lights were actually those of the Black Country. The 'river' must have been one of the many canals. He aimed his bombs at the glow from the foundries he glimpsed through the clouds. Dietrich reported bombing docks, harbour works and factories, with thirty-five 50kg HE and twenty incendiary bombs. He claimed to have seen the explosions of all the bombs and wrote that good results were clearly seen from onboard.

Tipton is where the killing started. The bomb aimer was the second in command, Leutnant zur See Christian von Nathusius. He dropped three HE bombs on Waterloo Street and Union Street, quickly followed by three incendiary bombs on Bloomfield Road and Barnfield Road. In Waterloo Street, outbuildings at the rear of houses were destroyed and one person was killed. In Union Street, two houses were completely demolished and others damaged, the gas main under the road being set alight. Thirteen people were killed here. The incendiary bombs fell in yards and gardens and failed to ignite. Walking around the Union Street area today, it is easy to see why Dietrich thought he was bombing docks: the area is between two levels of the Birmingham Canal and the street lights probably glittered on the water, making it a tempting if misleading target. According to GHQ records, the five men, five women and four children killed in Tipton were: Thomas Henry Church (57) of 111 Dudley Road, Tipton; Elizabeth Cartwright (27) of 1 Coppice Street, Tipton; Arthur Edwards (26) of 69 Union Street, Tipton; Mary Greensill (67) of 1 Court, 8 Union Street, Tipton; William Greensill (64) of 1 Court, 8 Union Street, Tipton; Benjamin Goldie (43) of

58 Queens Road, Tipton; Martin Morris (11) of 10 Union Street, Tipton; Nellie Morris (8) of 10 Union Street, Tipton; Sarah Jane Morris (44) of 10 Union Street, Tipton; George Henry Onions (12) of 66 New Road, Great Bridge, Tipton; Daniel Whitehouse (34) of 31 Union Street, Tipton; Annie Wilkinson (44) of 18 Union Street, Tipton; Frederick N. Yates (9) of 66 Union Street, Tipton; and Louisa Yorke(30) of 15 Waterloo Street, Tipton.

L.21 then dropped three incendiary bombs on Bloomfield Brickworks. Two of the three bombs failed to ignite and no damage was done. The Zeppelin then reached Lower Bradley and dropped five HE bombs which exploded between Potlatch Bridge and the Bradley Pumping Station. One landed on the canal bank, killing a courting couple, Maud Fellows (24) of 45 Daisy Street, Bradley, and William Fellows (23), of 33 Castle Street, Coseley. The bomb blast damaged the canal bank and pumping station, as well as breaking a considerable number of windows in the area.

Dietrich then turned *L.21* east, bombing Wednesbury at about 20.15. He killed fourteen people in the area of King Street, near the Crown tube works. Other bombs fell at the back of the Crown and Cushion Inn in High Bullen and along Brunswick Park Road. Damage was done to the Hickman and Pullen brewery, railway wagons and buildings in Mesty Croft goods yard, where one person was killed. Slight damage was also done to Old Park Colliery. From GHQ records, we know four men, six women and five children were killed in Wednesbury. The known victims were: Matilda May Birt (10) of Dale Street, Wednesbury; Mary Emma Evans (57) of 32 High Bullen, Wednesbury; Rachel Higgs (36) of 13 King Street, Wednesbury; Susan Howells (50) of 12 King Street, Wednesbury; Mary Ann Lee (59) of 13 King Street, Wednesbury; Gordon Madeley (21) of 48 Great Western Street, Wednesbury; Ina Smith (7) of 14 King Street, Wednesbury; Joseph Horton Smith (37) of 14 King Street, Wednesbury; Nellie Smith (13) of 14 King Street, Wednesbury; Thomas Horton Smith (11) of 14 King Street, Wednesbury; Betsy Shilton (39) of 13 King Street, Wednesbury; Edward Shilton (33) of 13 King Street, Wednesbury; and Rebecca Sutton (51) of 28 King Street, Wednesbury.

From Wednesbury, Dietrich flew on to Walsall. Reaching the town at 20.25, he dropped seven HE and four incendiary bombs. One bomb hit the Wednesbury Road Congregational Church. A few hundred yards further on, incendiary bombs landed in the grounds of the General Hospital. Others landed in Montrath Street, damaging houses and the Elijah Jeffries Saddlery Works. The last bomb landed in Bradford Place, outside the Art and Science Institute. A number of people were killed in the Bradford

Place area, and the public toilets were completely demolished. The dead included Mary Julia Slater, the Mayoress of Walsall. According to GHQ records, four people – three men and one woman – were killed in Walsall. They were: Charles Cope (34) of 84 Crankhall Lane, Wednesbury; Frank Thomas Linney (36) of Perry Street, Wednesbury; Thomas Merrylees (28) of 58 Hillary Street, Walsall; and Mary Julia Slater (55) of The Elms, Bescot Road, Walsall.

Dietrich's combat report shows that he dropped a total of thirty-five HE and twenty incendiary bombs. War Office GHQ records show that he killed thirty-five people in the Black Country and injured twenty-nine. The bomb in Bradford Place was the last dropped by *L.21* on the Black Country. It is fitting that Walsall Cenotaph now stands on the spot where the bomb landed.

With the killing over, Dietrich turned *L.21* for home, travelling at high speed. He was reported over Sutton Coldfield at 20.35 and Nuneaton at 20.45. The last attack took place at about 21.15 at Thrapston, Northamptonshire, where Dietrich ordered his six remaining incendiary bombs to be dropped on a blast furnace. They missed, landing in fields and causing no damage. *L.21* was then spotted over Ely at 22.00 and Thetford at 22.35. It crossed the coast south of Lowestoft, between Pakefield and Kessingland, at 23.35. The crew spent another exhausting eleven hours crossing the North Sea, arriving back at their base at Nordholz at about 10.45 the next day. *L.21* was one of the last Zeppelins to return, having covered an estimated 1,056 miles in just over twenty-three hours.

Britain had a month of respite from Zeppelin attacks in February 1916. The German Navy continued its maritime reconnaissance operations, though these were limited by the need to send the HLSu engines back to the Maybach factory in Friedrichshafen for proper testing and development work

21 February 1916

As the Verdun offensive started, Army Zeppelins were ordered to attack railway junctions supplying the forts. Four Zeppelins attacked on the moonlit night of 21 February. Because of the short range of the mission, the airships carried heavy bomb loads as they needed less petrol for the trip. Zeppelin *LZ.95* attacked the railway junction at Vitry-le-Francois with 8,800lb of bombs, and was shot down by anti-aircraft fire. During the bombing campaign on Verdun, the Army only had one success, when Zeppelin *LZ.90*, commanded by naval officer Oberleutnant zur See Ernst Lehmann, bombed Bar-le-Duc with 6,700lb of bombs.

'P' Type Army Zeppelin *LZ.77*: Hauptman Alfred Horn failed to reach his target. After crossing the Western Front, he was shot down in flames by incendiary shells near Revigny-sur-Ornain, crashing into the ground at Brabant-le-Roi. Because of the short distance to be covered on the raid, he was carrying a reduced crew of eleven, all of whom were killed.

'P' Type Army Zeppelin *LZ.88*: This airship was unable to reach its target at Chalons-du-Marne because of snow squalls, but landed safely at Maubeuge. The Zeppelin was transferred to the Russian Front in May 1916, and later transferred to the Navy, becoming Zeppelin *L.25*.

'Q' Type Army Zeppelin *LZ.95*: Hauptman Friedrich George, with a very heavy bomb load of 8,800lb, could only climb to 10,500ft. His target was Vitry-le-Francois. The airship was hit by anti-aircraft fire and crash landed, with major damage, at Namur in Belgium.

'D' type Army Schutte-Lanz *SL.7*: This airship dropped 3,500lb of bombs on Le-Neuville before returning to base at Mannheim. The airship was later transferred to East Prussia.

Chapter Five

Blinker's Boys: Radio location and the tracking of airships

The Zeppelin raid of 31 January 1916 was the first in the industrial heartland of Britain. As people worked on the cold Tuesday morning to aid survivors and dig bodies out of the rubble, there was anger and fear. The anger was shown in numerous attacks on foreign-owned shops and growing criticism of the Asquith Government, the Northcliffe press using it as another stick to beat it down. The press, censored as it was, recognized the raid as a defeat and did little to calm public fear, the newspapers full of atrocity stories and politicians issuing statements calling for reprisals. There was far more public and political concern following the January raid than after the 1915 raids on London. The capital was protected, surrounded by a ring of searchlight sites and anti-aircraft gun batteries, as well as fighter airfields. Though this had not prevented the bombing, the public could see something was happening. In the Midlands, Zeppelins had roamed unmolested over England for up to twelve hours. British defence forces were almost totally ineffective: only one Zeppelin, *L.17*, was troubled, dropping its bombs on the coast after being caught in a searchlight. The only searchlights and anti-aircraft guns were on the East Coast or around London. The raiders had been tracked as they crossed the coast, but an assumption was made that they would attack London, and aircraft took off in the fog to be ready for them. Twenty-two aircraft took off, but because of the fog two very experienced pilots were killed, six aircraft completely destroyed and seven more damaged. The main cause of the failure was the lack of an effective system to share intelligence between the Army and Navy.

Within days, local councils in the affected areas held emergency meetings. They made ad hoc plans and criticized the Government for its lack of defence measures. A major political initiative came on 8 February 1916, when a conference to which all Midlands mayors were invited was held at Birmingham Council House. The meeting was chaired by a man who would become much better known for his role in another war, the Lord Mayor of Birmingham, Neville Chamberlain. People who attended the Birmingham conference included the Earl of Dartmouth, the mayors of most West Midland boroughs, as well as their town clerks and chief constables. The meeting took place in private, but a press statement was issued. Neville Chamberlain said he had expressed in strong terms his opinion that the arrangements for warnings were inadequate on the night of the raid; however, it was important to improve the system rather than apportion blame. The conference then agreed a uniform system of lighting regulations and discussed ways in which telephone warnings could be given to the local police forces.

The conference also elected a committee to meet with the military authorities to discuss an effective air-raid warning system. This group included Chamberlain, the Earl of Dartmouth and the mayors of Coventry, Dudley and Walsall. The Mayor of Walsall, Alderman Samuel Mills Slater, was one of the most vocal critics of the Government. The press gave no hint of the strong personal interest he had in this, his wife Mary having died in a Walsall hospital from septicaemia cased by the shrapnel from a bomb dropped by Zeppelin *L.21* as she sat on a tram in the town centre.

With the benefit of hindsight, it is easy to underestimate the importance of Neville Chamberlain. He is almost universally seen as the nervous funny little man with the umbrella, standing at the bottom of the steps of the aeroplane that had brought him and his delegation back from meeting with Hitler in Munich in 1938, promising 'peace in our time'. It has always been interesting to speculate to what extent his experience of the Zeppelin raids affected his policy of appeasement. One of the ideas behind appeasement was the concept that 'the bomber will always get through', and that civilian morale would quickly collapse following the destruction caused by large-scale bombing of cities. He certainly saw signs of that in February 1916. In early 1916, Chamberlain was one of the most powerful men outside of government. He was essentially a conservative, a Liberal Unionist. He was the son of Joseph Chamberlain, one of the richest and almost certainly the most powerful politician in Birmingham history. Joseph was connected to the Nettlefold family, owners of the Smethwick-based metal screw manufacturer which later became GKN. He started his political life as a radical liberal, using the City Council to improve the lot of the poor. The city still has pride in many of his achievements, from public parks to the town hall. Joseph used city money to establish municipal gas and water companies: a policy often called 'municipal socialism'. He was in fact anything but a socialist. He moved to the right in later life and became an enthusiast for the Empire. He still, however, supported measures to alleviate the lot of the working class, such as old age pensions and city loans so working men could buy their own houses. He became the MP for Ladywood in Birmingham in 1876, becoming a Liberal Unionist, a party that would eventually merge with the Conservative Party.

Neville Chamberlain was born in Edgesbaston, Birmingham, in 1869, and was educated at Rugby School and Birmingham University. For many years he avoided going into politics, unlike his younger brother, Austin, and various cousins. He managed a sisal plantation in the Bahamas for his father, managing to lose £50,000. His father then helped him become the managing director of Hoskins and Company, a substantial manufacturing firm which became very successful. He was asked many times to stand for parliament. In 1911, he was elected to Birmingham City Council as a Liberal Unionist in a council ward in his father's parliamentary constituency. By 1915 he was Lord Mayor of Birmingham. He was powerful and popular, pursuing a hard-line nationalist agenda and support for the war, while also supporting liberal welfare and employment policies at home. Today he would probably be called a 'One Nation Conservative'. In 1916, he was appointed by new Prime Minister Lloyd George as the Director of National Service, with responsibility for co-ordinating conscription and ensuring essential industries had sufficient workforces. Though this failed and left Chamberlain and Lloyd George as bitter enemies, his appointment did show his calibre and political weight. He was seen as an expert on manufacturing, civilian morale and being able to negotiate with the military, civil powers and trade unions.

The Midlands delegation travelled to London to meet Field Marshal Sir John French. The result of his meeting was an improved air defence system. If Neville Chamberlain was a rising political star, the man on the other side of the table was a man watching his power fall away and was desperate to hold on to it. John Denton French was born in 1852, like so many military men from an Anglo-Irish family. He joined the military as a midshipman in the Royal Navy in 1866. He served at sea but was unable to continue in the Navy because he suffered from chronic seasickness and acrophobia (a fear of heights). He then joined the Army and was commissioned into the 8th Kings Royal Irish Hussars in 1874. He made rapid progress and served in Sudan with General Gordon. After service in India, he was promoted to Major General in 1899. He served in South Africa throughout the Boer War and finished the war with an enhanced reputation. In 1911, he was Aide-de-Camp General to the King and by 1912 Chief of the Imperial General Staff. He was an enthusiast for greater Army–Navy co-operation and promoted to Field Marshal in 1913. French was able to avoid taking sides in the Curragh Incident (the proto-mutiny involving British Army officers who said they would not fire on the Ulster Volunteer Force in March 1914), and was one of the few generals sympathetic to and trusted by the Asquith Government.

When the Great War started in 1914, French became commander of the British Expeditionary Force. One of the odd things about French is that despite his talent to climb the greasy pole of Army politics, he was often described – both by friends and enemies – as nervous and not particularly intelligent. King George V wrote: 'I don't think he is particularly clever, and he has an awful temper.' He was blamed for the poor performance of the BEF in 1915. He lost a degree of political support by claiming the cause of the failure of the Neuve Chapelle offensive was a shell shortage, and after the debacle of the Battle of Loos he was effectively sacked, replaced by his bitter rival and former protégé Douglas Haig. Because of his prestige and remaining political support, French was allowed to resign and as a sop to his feelings he was made a Viscount and given what seemed to be a 'non-job', Head of Home Defence. Determined and bitter, considering himself to be a scapegoat, the now Viscount French, Earl of Ypres was probably the only man with the background, contacts and clout to produce a workable system of air defence out of the existing system, where inter-service rivalry and poor communication with the civil powers had led to an operation on the night of 31 January 1916 described as 'a disaster for the defences, producing the highest proportion of aircraft losses, casualties and accidents per sortie of any home defence operation of the entire war'. Moreover, none of the air defence casualties were as a result of enemy action, just poor equipment, leadership and communication.

The meeting with the Midlands delegation was the second he had attended in February 1916. A few days before, he had met a delegation of councillors from London boroughs who had complained about inadequate defences and lack of an efficient warning system. He also took into account a 12 February 1916 report by the Ministry of Munitions that there was a complete lack of faith in official warning arrangements, and that 'Workmen are refusing to work at night at all unless guaranteed that warnings will be given in sufficient time for them to disperse.' As he learned more about the anti-Zeppelin strategy, French was not a happy man. The air defence system was in a state of chaos. Much of 1915 had been spent in bickering between the Army and Navy about the role of each service. Broadly, it was agreed that defence of the coast was the responsibility of the Navy, and inland defence that of the Army. The 31 January raid had taken place at a particularly difficult time; the organization of air defence was transferring from the Navy to the Army in February 1916. Responsibility for London was due to transfer on 16 February and responsibility for the rest of the country on 22 February. Most importantly, there was no proper system of communication between the intelligence systems of the Navy at the Admiralty and GHQ at the War Office. There was plenty of intelligence coming in; the

Navy had a very sophisticated system of monitoring and decoding radio signals from Zeppelins, and the Army had thousands of soldiers reporting sightings and telephoning them to the War Office. The problem was there was no system to collate all this information and issue air-raid warnings and deploy fighter aircraft. To say the defence system did badly on 31 January 1916 is being generous. In reality, there was no defence system, just a series of ad hoc measures resulting from inter-service rivalry and poor communication. It is very much to their credit that the British were willing and able to accept this and build an effective air defence system which led to the complete defeat of the Zeppelins.

To be fair to Field Marshal French, he remained as Head of Home Defence until 1918 and seems to have done a reasonably good job. He let competent officers get on with developing the air defence system, and during the later Gotha attacks on London successfully argued that modern fighters be transferred from France to Home Defence squadrons. The fact that he did this against the opposition of his former friend and bitter enemy, Douglas Haig, he probably regarded as no more than his duty.

The only parts of the air defence strategy that worked well on the day of the 31 January raid were the tracking of the Zeppelins and decoding of their signals by British Naval Intelligence, which knew at about noon that there was to be an attack in strength. Zeppelins were fitted with powerful radio transmitters and, in the early days of radio communication, their slack radio discipline was another technique where lessons needed to be learned. All signals were monitored by Naval Intelligence. The Royal Navy had a series of radio stations all down the East Coast, from Lerwick in the Shetland Isles to Lowestoft. They had been erected to monitor all radio signals from the German High Seas Fleet, which were then instantly transmitted by telephone cable to the Admiralty in London, which monitored all radio communications. Zeppelin commanders were initially probably not aware of the range their signals could be picked up from. The British radio receivers were very sensitive: they had been developed to intercept signals from ships, and even a low-power transmission from a Zeppelin at altitude on the other side of the North Sea could be picked up. Though Admiralty Intelligence knew at noon there was to be a raid on 31 January, they did not know where it was to take place. The police across the country were told an air-raid was possible. However, no public air-raid warnings were given. Ground observers were also alerted that a raid was likely, and good observations and excellent records were kept. The main problem seems to have been that there was no satisfactory system to cope with all the intelligence coming in. It seems to have been communicated on an ad hoc basis, which did not help in any decision-making.

The Germans at first regarded the 31 January raid as a major victory. The combat reports of many of the Zeppelin commanders indicated most had hit Liverpool or important secondary targets. They claimed they had done considerable damage, with reports of large sections of these towns or cities on fire. The positions established by the radio location stations seemed to confirm the combat reports. German and neutral newspapers told of a significant raid with major damage. The fact that Zeppelin *L.19* had been lost was used to their advantage by the Germans, as the crew had been found by the British trawler the *King Stephen*, which had refused to rescue them for fear of being overpowered. This was reported as a war crime, and was certainly a propaganda victory. It did not seem to have a negative effect on crew morale, though Zeppelins were afterwards fitted with canvas lifeboats in case of a landing at sea.

The Germans kept secret their main problem: the failure of the Maybach HLSu 240hp engines. These engine problems prevented any more raids until March 1916 whilst the engines were sent back to the Maybach works at Friedrichshafen, along with some crew members. When they returned, the engines were adequately reliable and bombing raids resumed.

The real Achilles heel of the Zeppelins was the radio location system, the navigation tool the commanders were reliant on. The Leader of Airships, Korvettenkapitan Peter Strasser, realized it could be used by Britain to locate airships, but this seemed unimportant because of the lack of opposition: it was to be a fatal mistake. Although radio had been used to a limited extent in the Balkan Wars, the Great War was the first electronic war. Guglielmo Marconi, the man probably most significant in the development of radio, demonstrated his radio equipment to senior officers in the British Army and Royal Navy by sending a wireless signal almost 2 miles across Salisbury Plain in 1896. Marconi, an Italian physicist, did not invent radio – it was a German physicist, Heinrich Hertz, who first demonstrated in a laboratory that electromagnetic waves could be transmitted and received in 1887 – but he was undoubtedly the most significant player in the development of wireless as a practical method of communication. By 1901, Marconi had transmitted radio waves across the Atlantic, and by 1907, the Marconi Company was running a commercial transatlantic wireless service.

The Army was interested in wireless, the Navy positively enthusiastic, and the latter almost immediately collaborated with Marconi to develop the system. The Navy claimed to be the more forward-looking and technically adept service, and while this is probably true, it is also the case that early radio sets were very heavy and needed a lot of power to operate: this was not a problem in a ship, but much more difficult on land, in an Army largely reliant on horse-drawn transport. The Marconi Company signed an exclusive deal with the Admiralty. Marconi was very open with them about technical developments, and Marconi employees worked closely with Navy personnel to equip all of its ships. The Navy was particularly interested in a radio interception system that could listen in to German communications. The Marconi Company built wireless stations along the coast of Britain and across the Mediterranean. By the time the war started, 5,000 Marconi wireless operators served in the Royal Navy, and Marconi had built thirteen long-range wireless stations around the world.

Of course in any arms race the other side responds, and in Germany the Telefunken Company worked closely with the military, and all German ships, U-boats and Zeppelins had Telefunken wireless sets. All its ships had up-to-date radio and skilled personnel to operate them. On both sides of the North Sea, tall radio towers were built to intercept signals and check the movement of ships, submarines and airships. The first British station was at Lowestoft; by May 1915, there were stations on the East Coast at Lerwick in the Shetland Islands, Aberdeen, York, Flamborough Head and Birchington. The German Navy had stations at Tondern, List, Nordholz and Bruges in Belgium.

The Germans formed a bureau to decipher signals: the Entzifferungs dienst, or E-Dienst. The Royal Navy had the Naval Cryptography and code-breaking section, usually known as 'Room 40' from its initial location in the Old Admiralty Building in Whitehall. Though by 1916 the section had several buildings and a staff of hundreds, it was always universally known as Room 40. It had been set up by a scientist and inventor Sir Alfred Ewing, who was the Director of Naval Education at the Royal Naval College in Dartmouth, Devon. Ewing said: 'It is educated men the Navy wants today when appliances – appliances too of an extremely complicated nature – are multiplying so rapidly in every department.' Ewing developed much of the organizational structure and wireless interception equipment used by Room 40. He retired late in 1914, exhausted, it is said, by several years' work. He was replaced by a man generally regarded as the supreme intellect in British military intelligence, Captain Reginald Hall, almost universally known, if not to his face, by his rather cruel nickname 'Blinker' Hall as a result of a persistent facial twitch.

Reginald Hall (26 June 1870 – 22 October 1943) was the son of the first head of Naval Intelligence, William Henry Hall. He joined the Navy as a midshipman at the age of 14 in 1884, and had risen fairly rapidly through the ranks of the peacetime Navy, which to an extent promoted on merit because of the pressures of the 'Naval Race' with Germany. He gained the reputation of being a 'modernizer', keen to investigate and use new technology. This probably made him more enemies than friends among traditionalists, but his reputation as a man of principle and intellect got him noticed by men of influence. These included a man soon to become First Lord of the Admiralty, Winston Churchill. He was promoted to captain in 1905 and appointed Inspector-Captain of the Mechanical Training Establishment. Always a man into intrigue and politics, Hall became involved in intelligence work. It seems his first exploit was when, as part of a Navy delegation to the Kiel Regatta, with all the German High Seas Fleet present, he was ordered to spy on the Kiel harbour fortifications. Unable to get near the well-guarded ships and sites, he devised a cunning plan: he borrowed a high-speed motor boat from the Duke of Westminster, a personal guest of the Kaiser, and with some of his officers dressed as ordinary sailors, he took them for a joy ride through the harbour and massed ships of the German Navy. He had a hidden camera and was able to photograph ships and secret installations. One of the officers on the boat was a man who captured Zeppelin crews were to know only too well a few years later: Major Bernard Trench.

Bernard Trench was a Royal Marine officer, fluent in French and German, who had worked mainly as an interpreter before the war. In 1908 and 1910, he and a fellow Marine officer, Lieutenant Vivian Brandon, were recruited by Naval Intelligence for ad hoc spying missions. In 1908, he received an official commendation for his useful report on coastal defences around Kiel. His next mission planned by Hall was to be less successful. In 1910, he was recruited to prepare a report on defences on the Friesian Islands. In what appears to be a very amateurish operation, Trench and Brandon were given the cover story that they were officers on leave going on a walking tour of Borkum Island. A day or so after the start of the mission, in August 1910, Brandon was arrested taking photographs of a restricted area. Trench tried to get to Holland, but was also arrested.

The men were held in custody and interrogated. The story Brandon told, that he had photographed defences to write a newspaper article, was seen as less than the whole truth by the cynical Germans. Intelligence material with details of military sites at Kiel, Wilhelmshaven, Borkum and the Kaiser Wilhelm Canal was found in Trench's hotel room under his bolster. Trench and Brandon were put on trial in Leipzig, and unsurprisingly found guilty. They were both sentenced to four years' imprisonment in a fortress. Trench was sent to Glatz in Silesia. Along with some other British spies, the men were released in 1913 after the Kaiser granted an amnesty following the marriage of his daughter, Victoria Louise, to the Duke of Cumberland. It is said the two-and-a-half years in Germany had left Trench with 'a fluent command of the language and a thorough dislike of anyone who spoke it'. It was a quality he put to use as head of the German section of Naval Intelligence, interrogating captured Zeppelin crews.

When the men were in prison, the Admiralty denied any knowledge of their operation, which was fair enough in the pre-war period. However, upon their release, the Admiralty refused to pay them. As soon as he became head of Naval Intelligence, Hall ensured they were well compensated. This was typical of Hall: he demanded dedication and loyalty from his men, but recognized it was a two-way thing.

In 1913, Hall was given command of one of the Navy's latest warships, the *Queen Mary*, a battle cruiser. He came to public notice because of the introduction of a surprising piece of new equipment: washing machines. One vital but unpleasant aspect of naval life was 'coaling up'. Most large warships were steam-powered and coal-burning. Before going to sea, the coal bunkers had to be filled from the shore or supply. Traditionally, all hands were involved. It was a hard and very dirty task shovelling tons of coal into the bunkers. After doing it, sailors were expected to wash their clothes by hand, while petty officers sent them to be laundered ashore. To Hall, this was unacceptable both in terms of efficiency and the welfare of his men. The answer was a contract with a washing machine company. This was viewed with scorn by old school traditionalists, but was insisted on and done. Hall usually got what he wanted.

The *Queen Mary* took part in one naval engagement under Hall, the first full-scale naval engagement of the war, off the Heligoland Bight, on 28 August 1914. However, Hall, never a physically strong man, became seriously ill because of bronchial problems around this time, and was diagnosed not to have the strength to command a warship at sea during wartime. Strings were pulled to get him a shore posting. He became Director of Naval Intelligence in 1914, based at the Admiralty in London. Once in command of Room 40, he had a virtually free hand to recruit his staff, and took a radical approach. He recruited civilians, particularly academics: men who could think outside the box. Men, and later women, who proved particularly useful were people with backgrounds in ancient languages. An example is a fellow of King's College, Cambridge, Alfred Dillwyn Knox, a man with degrees in mathematics and ancient Greek. He had spent much of his life deciphering, reconstructing and translating an incomplete ancient manuscript of ancient Greek satirical poetry, Herodas' *The Mimes*. The manuscript consisted of faded papyrus in fragments, incomplete and poorly translated. Getting the fragments in the right order and making educated guesses about what was missing was an ideal background for a codebreaker. Another academic recruited was a specialist on medieval German theology; he had translated obscure religious texts into English. We know something of how Knox worked. He would find mundane German coded communications, such as weather reports, and look for errors made by wireless operators in transmission, spelling mistakes or short cuts, anything that might provide clues to the cipher keys to complex messages. Perhaps the best way to understand the civilian staff of Room 40 is as men who could do *The Times* crossword in ten minutes, very clever, eager to solve puzzles, often not very worldly. Hall had a particular talent for building teams, adding to the mix very worldly Navy men. They were sailors who understood naval technology, structures and methods of operation. He recruited men who knew how the German Navy worked. One of them was Major Trench RM. Their work was helped by the rigid and disciplined structure of the German Navy; it was very methodical and made a lot of routine signals, repeated every day. For example, before a raid it was the practice for headquarters to hold a sort of roll call with Zeppelins which had taken off: a signal was sent to all the airship commanders and acknowledged by each in turn. This enabled Room 40 to establish patterns and decode signals.

We need to look at the nature and technology of Zeppelin radio signals to understand how Room 40 worked. Zeppelins were large enough to be fitted with powerful radios operating with Morse code by a skilled wireless operator, usually a petty officer (Funkentelegrafiesmaat). The 'P' and 'Q' class ships operating in the early part of 1916 had two radio sets, the largest a 1Kw Telefunken set driven by a generator operated by one of the engines; this had a range of several hundred miles, using a long retractable aerial which could be wound in and out when needed. The smaller radio set, powered by batteries, was to be used if the main set was inoperable, for example if the engine driving the generator failed; this had a much shorter range. The radio had two basic functions. The first function was transmitting and receiving orders from the shore bases, or communicating with other airships. Almost all communication was in code; up to the middle of 1916, Zeppelins used the HVB code, which was also used by U-boats. The usual pattern was for the Second Officer to code and decode messages and pass them to the wireless operator for transmission. What the Germans didn't know - and it took them an inordinate amount of time to find out - was that from early 1914, the British, via Room 40, were reading their codes. On 11 August, the Royal Australian Navy interned a German merchant ship in Melbourne. They captured the *Handelsschiffs Verkbuch* (HVB), the merchant-to-warship code-book. It was based on four letter codes. It was, until mid-1916, the main code used by Zeppelins and U-boats. The Admiralty had another lucky break on 26 August 1914 when the *Magdeburg*, a German battle cruiser, ran aground in the Baltic. Its capitain ordered the destruction of two out of the three cop-ies of his codebooks, the *Signalbuch der Kaiserlichen Marine* (SKM), the main cipher book of the High Seas Fleet. However, before he could scuttle the ship, it was boarded by Russian forces, and one of the codebooks sent to the Admiralty in London by 30 October. It contained 300,000 three-letter codes, each one referring to a word or phrase. In November 1914, a British trawler recovered from a sunken destroyer the *Verkhrsbuch* (VB) used for correspon-dence with naval attachés abroad. It was a five-number code.

In May 1916, the Germans worked out that British Intelligence had decoded their HVB system and introduced another for U-boats and Zeppelins, the *Allemeines Funkpruchbuch* (AFB). Knox was given the job of decoding it, which took several months to be done. He started by looking for a pattern, and noticed several word endings of 'en' regularly appeared in sim-ilar places. He guessed that a wireless operator was using a poem to code his signature. A colleague, an expert on German literature, worked out that this was from a poem by Schiller. From this, Knox was able to identify a num-ber of code words and was on the way to reconstructing the whole thing. It was estimated it would take him several more months to complete the work. This was unnecessary, because on 24 September 1916, Zeppelin *L.32* was shot down. Hall and a team from Room 40 arrived while the wreckage was still smoking. Amid the hot wreckage and burned bodies of the crew they found the AFB codebook, charred but usable. It seems likely that some of the staff in Room 40 would have seen the irony in the connection between the poetry of Schiller – a Romantic poet lauded as a liberal intellectual – and men burned alive in a Zeppelin, or indeed children buried in bombed buildings.

The second and most important use of radio for the Zeppelin commanders was as their main navigational aid. Though all commanders were skilled and trained navigators, flying on moonless nights, in or above the clouds, made normal navigation methods very difficult. The answer was radio location. The science of radio location was fairly simple in principle. For most of the war, Zeppelins used a method devised by an employee of the Marconi Company, the Bellini-Tosi system. The moving object, in this case the Zeppelin, trans-mitted a Morse signal with the airship's identification code. This was picked up by at least two shore stations. Using a system of triangulation, each station would find the direction of the strongest signal and draw a line on a map at that angle. The point where the lines intersected would be the position of the Zeppelin. This would then be sent, in code, to the Zeppelin. There were a number of problems with this system. It was not very accurate; in the early days of radio, the effect of atmospheric conditions on the apparent direction of a radio signal was not understood. The triangulated position of the Zeppelin over England could be as much as 50 miles out. Zeppelin commanders almost always overestimated the accuracy of the position they were given by radio, and became overly reliant on it. The main problem was that if a German shore base could triangulate the position of a Zeppelin, then so could the British. Though the position was sent in code, the Zeppelin's identification signal was easily read, which allowed the ship to be recognized. Even if the identification code was changed between raids, a skilled wireless operator could often identify the Morse code signature of a German operator. It is like if two people you know are speaking a foreign language, even if you can't understand what they are saying, you can recognize the different people by the tone of their voice. The same is true of Morse code. As Zeppelin crews tended to stay together, knowing a particular operator was in a Zeppelin could usually identify it. Of course the British didn't have to wait for the German position to be sent to the Zeppelin: they could find its location by triangulation. It is likely that operators in Room 40 could work out the position of a Zeppelin before the commander knew it. British direction-finding stations were directly connected by telephone cable to Room 40, and they had the resources and manpower to do the necessary calculations very quickly. In 1916, speed probably wasn't very important, but with the use of flying boats on anti-Zeppelin operations in 1917, it was quite literally a matter of life and death.

Room 40 worked throughout the war on all aspects of intelligence-gathering. It was responsible for the capture of Sir Roger Casement, who landed off the west coast of Ireland with a supply of weapons and ammunition on 20 April 1916, just before the Easter Rising on 24 April. It is said Hall circulated copies of Casement's diaries with details of his homosexual encounters, to counter the considerable political pressure to save him from execution for treason. Another triumph for Room 40 was the decoding of the Zimmerman telegram, in which Arthur Zimmerman, the German Secretary of Foreign Affairs, promised German support for Mexico if it attacked the USA, a move that helped bring the USA into the war in 1917. Room 40 had spying operations all over the world. Its anti-Zeppelin ring was very efficient. The main factory of the Zeppelin Company was (and still is) at Friedrichshafen on Lake Constance, which was only a short ferry ride across the lake to neutral Switzerland. Using the safety of Switzerland, intelligence about the technical details of the Zeppelins and the Airship Service was easily gathered by spies based across the border. There are many reports of captured Zeppelin crews, interrogated by Major Trench and his team, being amazed when questioned how much the interrogators knew about their missions, ships and even service gossip. All of this enabled Room 40 to accurately report when Zeppelins set out, crossed the coast and returned home.

In February 1916, the lead responsibility passed from the Admiralty to the Army. The Royal Naval Air Service (RNAS) was to concentrate on Zeppelins while they were over the sea, and the Royal Flying Corps (RFC) while they were over the United Kingdom. This meant the task of tracking airships once they were over the coast was the primary responsibility of the Army. There was, however, a real need for Army-Navy co-operation, as only Room 40 had the technical capacity to plot the position of the Zeppelins by radio location triangulation. The Army formed a special section of Military Intelligence, MI.1(e), to decode and collate radio signals from airships. A special aerial was erected on the roof of the War Office to intercept signals; the information was then passed to GHQ Home Forces Control. The information from Room 40 was also sent there, and formed the basis of air defence. It was a system designed to avoid the disastrous failings of the 31 January 1916 raid. Though there were occasional problems due to inter-service rivalry, it was made to work efficiently. Perhaps the influence of Sir John French helped. The Army system was based on soldiers on the ground acting as spotters. At the end of 1916, there were up to 17,000 men out on nights when there was intelligence from Room 40 that an attack was likely to take place. A group of soldiers with an officer would be sent to designated locations, both along the coast and inland. They had a field telephone or access to a telephone, and would watch and wait. A Zeppelin could be heard from several miles away – the sound was described as like a 'heavy goods train'. If they saw or heard a Zeppelin, they would telephone the information to an Army sub-control section of GHQ, giving their location, the time they saw or heard the airship and its estimated height and direction. All these reports would be collated and telephoned to GHQ from the sub-sections. Though the ground observers couldn't identify the airship they had seen, a series of observations often could.

There is a good description of the process which dates from 1918. It describes the operations room of the London Air Defence Area (LADA), but it shows how the system worked in 1916. The main feature of the central operations room was the large table displaying a map with numbered and lettered squares, surrounded by ten plotters. This showed an area showing all of southeast England from Portsmouth to Harwich. A dais provided a grandstand view for Major General Edward Ashmore, commander of LADA, Brigadier General Charles Higgins, commander of 6th Brigade RFC, a police representative and a few senior operations officers. Plotters received information through telephone headsets from twenty-six sub-control centres and transferred it to the map, a disc for a single enemy aircraft and a rectangle for a formation, with arrows indicating courses if known. Fighters were represented by aircraft-shaped counters. The counters were pushed across the map by women with croupier-style rakes, following instructions from the plotters. The sub-control centres received their reports from gun and searchlight sites, sound locators and the observation posts. Ashmore had a switchboard enabling him to cut into plotters' lines should he require further information or to issue instructions to a sub-commander, and Higgins had direct lines to his fighter wings.

The system described was a development of the anti-Zeppelin system and can be seen to be in embryo the basis of the fighter control system so successful a quarter of a century later in the Battle of Britain. In the 1916 system, a Zeppelin could usually be identified by Room 40 before it crossed the coast. When it reached the coast, it would be given a counter with its identification number - e.g. *L.15* or *L.34* - and tracked across the map. As the spotters' reports came in, it was usually possible to identify which Zeppelin they had seen and the counter be moved. If it sent a signal to its base in Germany asking for a radio location position, that would be picked up by Room 40 and the information used to update its position. As the counter progressed across the map, fighter stations would be alerted and pilots could be given an approximate direction to search and ordered to take off. The police in towns likely to be bombed would be alerted, and air-raid warnings and all-clear signals could be given when necessary. It was sometimes the case when there was a big raid that spotters' reports could be misinterpreted and the wrong airship identification recorded on the counter. We know for example that when Schutte-Lanz *SL.11* was shot down by William Leef Robinson, it was at first wrongly identified as Zeppelin *L.21* and not corrected until the wreckage and bodies of the crew had been examined. During a raid, this didn't really matter so much. So long as the defence forces were able to track an airship, it didn't matter which one they shot down.

The 2/3 September 1916 raid was particularly difficult to track because fourteen airships were involved, and there was much confusion. GHQ came up with an interesting method to make things clearer, which was used from then on. Rather than being given the Zeppelin number, each counter was given a name: Navy airships a girl's name and Army ships a boy's name. In practice, after the destruction of *SL.11*, the German Army stopped raiding

England, so only girls' names were used. At first the names were made up, so for most of September there was Mary, Rose, Lily, Kate, Jane, Hilda and Sally prowling across the GHQ map. This was found to be very successful, as it not only reduced confusion but seemed to give each Zeppelin a personality, which added interest and relaxed tension. During the night of 27 November 1916, Zeppelin *L.21* was given the name Mary and tracked all across the country to Stoke-on-Trent, which it bombed. It was tracked all the way back to the coast, and one of the last messages by GHQ before *L.21* was shot down in flames a few miles out to sea from Lowestoft was 'Mary is going home'. After about a month, the Army changed the rules so that later raiders were named alphabetically according to when they crossed the coast. So we had Ada, Betty, Chloe, Dinah, etc.

The air defence system developed in 1916 was certainly the most important factor in the defeat of the Zeppelins. They could be tracked virtually in real time, and a decision made to launch fighters to attack them made their defeat inevitable. The irony of it all is that the Zeppelins were the authors of their own downfall. The radio location signals they sent asking for a position made it certain the British knew where they were, and once they were traced they could be caught and shot down.

The French Army also had a radio direction-finding network, under the command of General Gustave Ferrie. It did not work in conjunction with the British, though the allies co-operated and shared intelligence. It had a series of wireless interception stations, including one on the Eiffel Tower. When Zeppelins returned home after a raid on England, over France and Belgium rather than the North Sea, the French tended to jam RDF signals from Zeppelins. This had a definite effect during the 'Silent Raid' in October 1917, which is covered in detail in Chapter 12. It has been claimed that French Intelligence operators would transmit false positions to Zeppelins sending a signal for a radio location, seeking to draw them on to searchlights and guns. This seems unlikely, as the genuine radio location positions were so inaccurate that false ones would have little effect.

In early 1918, the German Airship Service stopped using the Bellini-Tosi radio location system and moved to the much safer Telefunken *Kompass* system. In this new system, the ground station transmitted the directional signal, not the Zeppelin. We have a good description of the working of the system in *The Zeppelin in Combat* by Douglas H. Robinson. The transmitting station had sixteen pairs of aerials, positioned at the thirty-two points of the compass. A rotating contact turning every thirty-two seconds transmitted signals from each set of directional wires. The *Kompass* station transmitted every thirty minutes: quarter past and quarter to the hour. The commander or watch officer in the Zeppelin had a special stopwatch with a compass face, which rotated every thirty-two seconds. The operator started the watch when the *Kompass* station sent a special signal indicating the north aerial wire; he stopped the watch when he heard the weakest signal indicating the bearing of the Zeppelin. When reception conditions allowed, the commander took five separate readings from different stations and drew the compass directions on a map, triangulating them, basing his final position on the average calculation. Though the system was probably less accurate than the Bellini-Tosi system, as the calculation had to be done in the cold, noisy and stressful environment of a Zeppelin, it was much safer as wireless operators in Britain couldn't pick it up. Despite this, Zeppelins continued to transmit signals well into 1918. We have a combat report from Kapitänleutnant Walter Dose, commander of Zeppelin *L.65*, who wrote about what happened when the Leader of Airships, Fregattenkapitan Peter Strasser, was shot down on the night of 5 August 1918: 'First there was a long radio signal from Strasser, which was surely plotted by the English direction finding stations.' Minutes later, Strasser, in Zeppelin *L.70*, and all his crew were shot down in flames. It is ironic that in his last order before the attack, Strasser had emphasized the need to 'preserve careful wireless discipline'.

Sir William Reginald Hall was knighted in 1917 for his work on the Zimmermann telegram affair. He was promoted to Rear Admiral in 1917. He retired from active service in 1919, but was twice promoted on the retired list, becoming an Admiral in 1926. On his retirement, he found a new enemy: Bolshevism. He moved into politics, becoming the Conservative MP for Liverpool West Derby in March 1919 when the sitting MP, Sir Frederick Smith, went to the House of Lords. Smith eventually became the Earl of Birkenhead. It seems strings must have been pulled, because Smith had been the Crown Prosecutor in the trial of Sir Roger Casement. Hall lost in the general election of 1923 to a Liberal. He was again elected, at a by-election in 1925, as Conservative MP for Eastbourne. He did not stand in 1929, in the first democratic general election by universal suffrage in the UK.

Like a number of former intelligence officers, probably because of his passion for intrigue, he engaged in anti-democratic extreme right-wing politics. He founded a society called National Propaganda, financed by many leading industrialists, and became its first chairman. It opposed universal suffrage and the Labour Party. Hall is believed to have had a significant part in the Zinoviev letter affair (a forgery that was blamed for Labour losing the 1924 general election). National Propaganda later became the Economic

League, which financed itself by spying and recording information on trade union activists, information that could be bought by employers to 'blacklist' workers. The organization existed until 1993; when it was wound up it was found to have files on 22,000 individuals, including a certain Gordon Brown MP. We have to hope 'Blinker' would have known better.

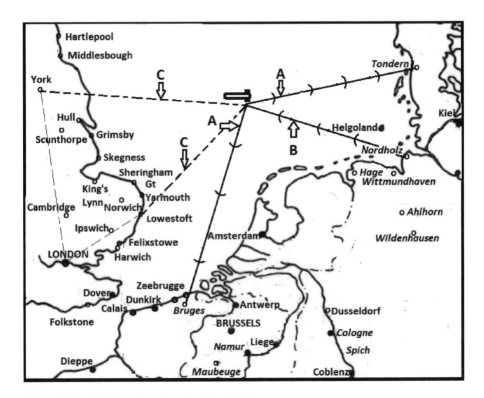

Map 5: Radio locations in the North Sea

'A' The Zeppelin sent a signal with its code number to the German shore stations. They would then workout its position by drawing the direction of the radio signals received at different stations, on a map.

'B' using the system of triangulation they would send the Zeppelin its position in a coded message.

'C' The main problem was that the British could also receive the signal. They did not need to decode the message to locate the position of the Zeppelin. They would measure the direction of the signals and send the signals by telephone cable to the Admiralty, and GHQ in London. They would then calculate the position of the Zeppelin, by triangulation, and send the information to the defence commander. As Britain had radio location stations from the Shetland Islands to Lowestoft, their triangle had a longer base than the Germans. So their locations were usually more accurate. Locations sent to radio-equipped flying boats probably made them the most effective anti-Zeppelin weapon. They were stationed on the coast of East Anglia, at Felixstowe, Killingholme and Yarmouth. The locations were equally useful for fighters operating inland.

Chapter Six

Fokker Fodder: the development of night fighter aircraft

L ike Count Zeppelin, British military observers to the American Civil War were very impressed by the use of observation balloons by the Federal armies. Finance was made available for the British Army to carry out a few flights using a hired balloon. In 1878, the Army purchased its first balloon, called by some imaginative soul the 'Pioneer'. This led to the use of balloons in colonial adventures, and a school of bal-looning was set up in Aldershot. By 1890 there was a Balloon section of the Royal Engineers.

A Balloon Factory was set up, which produced observation balloons during the Boer War. This expanded and the Government decided the Army should have an airship. To enable this, the Balloon Factory was moved to a more rural location at Farnborough. Along with this, it had the task of evalu-ating other forms of aerial activity following the work of the Wright Brothers in the USA. The American showman and aviation pioneer Samuel Cody was employed as the Chief Kite Instructor to the British Army, at the not incon-siderable salary of £1,000 per year, following experiments with man-carry-ing kites. Cody developed the British Army aeroplane No. 1, a 50hp pusher biplane. It flew a quarter of a mile over Farnborough Common, reaching a height of 30ft, before crashing. It was the first powered flight in Britain. Interest in aviation grew, and the Balloon Factory was instructed to conduct experiments with aeroplanes bought from private industry. Politics played a role even at this stage, as the Balloon Factory – a state enterprise – was not to be allowed to take business from private industry. In 1910, it purchased a pusher biplane from Geoffrey de Havilland for £400. It named it the F.E.1, and offered de Havilland a job as designer and test pilot. The F.E.1 flew for over an hour in January 1911, 'without repair or adjustment', although de Havilland was allowed to land twice to warm up, 'the January day being very cold'. By April 1912, the Farnborough site was very busy testing British and foreign aeroplanes and training mechanics. It changed its name to the Royal Aircraft Factory.

It is useful to understand the system the Royal Aircraft Factory used to name its products:

> B.E. was Bleriot Experimental, the standard tractor biplane, with the engine at the front, such as the B.E.2c.
> F.E. was Farman Experimental, a pusher biplane with the engine at the back of the fuselage nacelle, such as the F.E.2b.
> R.E. was Reconnaissance Experimental, larger tractor biplanes, such as the R.E.8.
> S.E. was Santos Experimental, canard aeroplanes with the engine at the back and a small plane or elevator at the front. As no canards were actually successfully built and flown, the S.E. designation was changed to Scout Experimental, producing fighter biplanes like the S.E.5a.

The first Royal Aircraft Factory-designed aeroplane built in any number was the B.E.2, designed by Geoffrey de Havilland. The first B.E.2 flew in February 1912. The various prototypes were subject to considerable development, and following the competitive military trial at Larkhill in the summer of 1912, the B.E.2 was adopted as the main Army observation aircraft and the order given to a number of manufacturers for production. When Geoffrey de Havilland left the factory, the development of the B.E.2 passed to Edward Busk, the assistant engineer at the factory. His design speciality was inherent stability; his R.E.1 was regarded as the world's first inherently stable aeroplane. This was not put into production, but many of its features were adopted for the B.E.2c. In comparison to earlier B.E.2 versions, the B.E.2c had a number of modern features. Most versions of the B.E.2c were powered by the 90hp RAF 1a engine, also designed by the Royal Aeroplane Factory. This was an air-cooled V.8 engine of about 9 litres. It had ailerons rather than wing warping for lateral control, and because of this had a new deeper aerofoil section and a stronger wing. It had staggered wings with pronounced dihedral, these features giving it a high degree of stability. Pilots at first liked the machine, because it would fly hands-off, and recover to fly straight and level from most manoeuvres; it was particularly easy to recover from a spin, the real fear of many early pilots. In its early days, it was given the nickname 'stability Jane', one of the few positive epithets used to describe it.

Cecil Lewis wrote of the first time he saw a B.E.2c while he was training as a pilot: 'While I was training at Brooklands one came over, and to our unaccustomed eyes it was wonderful, elegant, beautiful. Rumour which exaggerated said it actually touched eighty on the level.' A few months later he was flying one in active service at St Omer: 'Actually she was as docile and dull as a motor bus - and about as heavy to handle.'

When war broke out, the B.E.2c was put into mass production. It had a significant advantage over its privately designed rivals. It had been designed in a drawing office and was built using engineering drawings, rather than chalk lines on the floor. All its components had detailed engineering drawings, which meant they could be manufactured by non-specialist producers, like furniture makers and car manufacturers, rather than only specialist aeroplane factories. This meant it was produced in significant numbers and many people had an interest in its continued production.

It was perhaps not the best auger for the future of the B.E.2c when its designer Edward Busk was killed test-flying one. The aircraft developed a petrol leak and burst into flames, killing Busk, in November 1915. To be fair to the B.E.2c, it did exactly what it was designed to do, which was to provide (by the standards of the time) a reliable stable observation platform, that was easy to fly and could be piloted by young men with a few hours' tuition. While they look very old-fashioned, completely unstreamlined, wire-braced biplanes, they were by the standards of the time sturdy and reliable aircraft. The problem was they were built to a design specification which made them inherently stable. In ordinary language this seems to be a good thing; however, in aeronautical terms 'inherently stable' has a more precise meaning: that the plane will naturally fly straight and level unless the pilot moves the controls. The down side of this was that the B.E.2c was stable but very difficult to manoeuvre. It was so slow and clumsy that it was a death-trap when used during the day in its original role as a reconnaissance aeroplane over the Western Front, easy prey for German fighter planes.

When it was designed, pre-war military aircraft were seen as basically observation posts. They would fly over enemy positions to gather intelligence, to map what the enemy was doing. What was needed was a stable aeroplane that would virtually fly itself so the observer could add details to his maps, and the pilot could take photographs. As the observer was the most important, he had the seat with the best view in the front cockpit. The pilot sat behind. For the first few months of the war, this seemed a reasonable arrangement, as observation aircraft from either side waved at each other as they flew missions over the front. It wasn't long before observers used rifles to take largely ineffective pot shots at enemy aircraft. They soon began to take machine guns. With this the Germans had a built-in advantage, as their observation aircraft were built by more traditional methods and the design was modified more easily in the light of experience. The first German observation aeroplanes had the observer's seat in the front, like the B.E.2c, but by mid-1915 German two-seaters had the observer in the back with a machine gun and a wide field of fire sidewards and to the rear. As the B.E.2c was mass produced, such changes were more difficult to do as it would require a major redesign. So the B.E.2c was stuck with the dangerous situation of having the observer sitting in front of the pilot. Sitting in the front of a B.E.2c, with a machine gun, the observer had a difficult job. If he fired forwards, he was likely to hit the propeller; if he fired upwards, he would hit the wing; if he fired sideways, he would hit the wing struts; and if he fired towards the rear, he would shoot the pilot. It wasn't impossible to use the machine gun, and a number of different mountings were designed, but it was difficult, and the B.E.2c was very much the hunted rather than the hunter.

Things got much worse in 1915 with the evolution of the single-seat fighter aircraft. The first true fighter aircraft was the result of an unofficial venture by Roland Garros, a pre-war French aviation pioneer. He took various Morane-Saulnier monoplanes and fixed a standard French Hotchkiss machine gun to the fuselage, so it fired forward through the propeller. To aim, the pilot flew at the target, aiming the machine gun with the aeroplane. To avoid shooting off the propeller, Garros fixed a hardened steel deflector plate on each propeller blade. Most bullets missed the rotating propeller blades; those that didn't, hit the deflector plates and bounced off without breaking the propeller. It was a crude but simple device that shot down several German aircraft in early 1915. Garros was shot down by ground fire in April 1915 and the deflector mechanism was captured by the Germans. It is often thought that the deflector system was a crude device, because no one had come up with an effective system to enable a machine gun to fire through a propeller disc. This is not the case, as for several years there had been patents for different sorts of interrupter gear. Details of a mechanism had even been published in the magazine *Scientific American*. Swiss engineer Franz Schneider had patented a system not unlike the one used by Fokker, and after the war attempted to sue Fokker for infringing his patent.

The Germans asked different aircraft companies if they could copy the device. Anthony Fokker, a Dutch aviation pioneer, said he would. They didn't know that Fokker had already been working on a synchronization mechanism to enable a machine gun to fire though the propeller. The deflector system wouldn't work with standard German bullets, which were steel-jacketed rather than copper-jacketed like French bullets. The harder steel jacket would crack the steel deflector plates. There was also a good engineering reason not to use the deflector system, as roughly 5 per cent of bullets would hit the deflector plates. In effect, that would mean in any burst of fire, on average, at least one bullet would hit a deflector plate; this would always cause a vibration, and in the long run would certainly damage the engine. The rotary engine where the cylinders revolved with the propeller was a precision machine, and hitting the deflector with a bullet was like hitting the crankcase with a sledgehammer: eventually something would break.

It is often thought that Fokker invented the synchronization system, but in fact by 1915 there were various patents for mechanisms to enable a gun to fire through the propeller. It is also often believed that Fokker merely copied other people's ideas, but again this is not really the case. Fokker was an excellent development engineer. He might not come up with the original idea, but he had the common-sense engineering skills to see if it could work and find a practical way to make it. In a little more than a month, Fokker had fitted a synchronized machine gun to one of his own aircraft, the Fokker M.1, a shoulder wing monoplane, based on, but not copied from, the pre-war Morane-Saulnier racing monoplane, a type that had been used by Roland Garros. Fokker demonstrated the synchronized machine gun to members of the German High Command, who were unimpressed by the ground demonstration so Fokker took to the air and shot up a series of ground targets. He was then given the contract to produce his fighter for the German air force. In military service it was produced in various types, from the E.I to the E.IV. It was almost universally known as the Fokker Monoplane, or by its German title, the *Eindecker*.

The Fokker *Eindecker* was not a particularly good machine. It was quite primitive, having lateral control by wing warping, was not very manoeuvrable and the model produced in the greatest numbers – the E.III, powered by an Oberursal rotary engine – had a top speed of only about 90mph and a poor rate of climb. However, compared to the B.E.2c it was fast and manoeuvrable. The *Eindecker* went into squadron service from August 1915, and the period known as the Fokker Scourge began. Allied observation aircraft were shot out of the sky, but the B.E.2c continued as the standard RFC observation aircraft as it was virtually all they had. Almost all German fighter pilots who later became aces started their career as fighter pilots on the *Eindecker*.

In 1915, no two-seat observation aircraft was a match for a single-seat fighter. While German two-seater observation aircraft by mid-1915 had the observer in the back with a machine gun and a wide field of fire, even they had very little chance against a single-seat fighter with the gun firing through the propeller. Roland Garros had proven with his deflector system how vulnerable observation aircraft were. In time, it became apparent that the only way to combat the single-seat fighter was with another single-seat fighter, so observation aircraft were routinely protected either by fighter escorts or more usually fighter sweeps to drive away enemy fighters.

Germany only produced about 400 *Eindeckers* between 1915 and 1916, but they caused a major crisis in the RFC. They shot down dozens of British observation aircraft, most of them B.E.2s. The training squadrons could hardly turn out enough pilots to make up the numbers killed. The newspapers described RFC pilots and observers as 'Fokker Fodder', and the cause was taken up by probably the strangest character in British aviation history, Noel Pemberton Billings MP. He said in a debate in Parliament that pilots on the Western Front had been murdered rather than killed, being sent to fight in aircraft so outdated and outclassed.

Noel Pemberton Billings (3 January 1881 – 11 November 1948) was born in London, the son of an iron founder. He was a notable self-publicist with strange and extreme right-wing views. He served in the Army in the Boer War, and then made money in a garage business. He saw himself as an inventor and was an aviation pioneer. He got his pilot's licence after a bet with Frederick Handley Page that he could go solo in a day. He did, winning £500 and his pilot's licence one day in 1913. He started an aviation company in 1913, making flying boats; the flying boats are little remembered, but the name of the company is: Supermarine, Southampton.

When war broke out, he joined the Royal Naval Air Service and claimed to have planned the raids on the Zeppelin works at Friedrichshafen in November 1914. Like much about Pemberton Billings, it is difficult to decide the extent to which this was true or spin. Pemberton Billings started his political career in 1916, when he published a weekly journal called the *Imperialist*, with some support from Lord Beaverbrook. It was not the finest exemplar of journalism, publishing anti-Semitic conspiracy theories and stories about homosexual plots. It claimed to be against Jews, pacifism, Fabianism, aliens, feminism and internationalism. Billings entered Parliament in 1916 as MP for Hertford, with support from powerful sections of the British press. He also wrote a book, *Air war: how to wage it*. Once in the House of Commons he called himself the 'Member for air', and launched a vigorous campaign against the state-owned Royal Aircraft Factory, in particular the B.E.2c.

As a well known and surprisingly popular public figure, Pemberton Billings was used by members of the RFC as an unofficial conduit for criticism of their equipment. They had their own nickname for the B.E.2: the 'Quirk'. One pilot described it, not unfairly, as 'underpowered, under armed and un-manoeuvrable'. Pemberton Billing made a speech in the House of Commons, soon after his election, in which he criticized the Government and High Command of sending poorly trained pilots to war in inadequate aeroplanes. He went on to say that 'pilots are being murdered rather than killed', and called for a public inquiry.

To see what was happening we have to understand that the position of the Royal Aircraft Factory, as a state enterprise, was highly political. There were those who used the 'Fokker scourge' as a stick to beat the Asquith Government. It was deeply unpopular with the aviation manufacturing lobby, who saw it as having a monopoly on the purchasing of aeroplanes by the Army, and hence an attack on their profits. The conflict was played out in the pages of the two aviation trade journals, *Flight* and *The Aeroplane*. *Flight* broadly supported the factory, while the editor of *The Aeroplane*, Charles Grey, was bitterly opposed. Perhaps the fact that the aviation trade advertised in *The Aeroplane*, while the Factory did not, was a factor in this. There was the ironic situation that because of rivalry between the Army and Navy, the RNAS was able to buy what aircraft it wanted, while the RFC was restricted to designs approved by the Factory. This is why the RNAS was able to use effective aircraft like the Morane Parasol and Sopwith Pup earlier than the RFC in anti-Zeppelin operations; we should not forget that the first Zeppelin to be bought down was by a RNAS pilot in a Morane.

The result of the 'murder' speech was the setting up of two separate committees of inquiry. The first was into the operation of the Factory, under the chairmanship of Richard Burbridge, a man whose grasp of the science of aerodynamics can be judged by his more normal role as general manager and later managing director of Harrods. The second committee of inquiry was into the operation of the RFC, under chairmanship of a High Court Judge, Mr Justice Bailhache. Both broadly supported the status quo and made minor recommendations. The most telling observation about the Factory was made in the Bailhache Report in July 1916, which said: 'The Royal Aircraft Factory should be judged by its greatest achievement, the B.E.2c, which was aerodynamically sound and capable of being built by companies that had never built aeroplanes before.'

Noel Pemberton Billings MP was not amused. His real claim to fame was in May 1918 when in his journal, the *Vigilante*, which had replaced the *Imperialist*, probably not for reasons of political correctness, he claimed that American exotic dancer Maud Adam was one of a high society coterie of sexual perverts, susceptible to German blackmail and so actively or potentially disloyal. Maud and her theatre impresario, J.T. Grien, decided, as it turned out unwisely, to sue for libel. The trial made headlines. The evidence, such as it was, produced in his defence by Pemberton Billing was a 'Black Book' according to him in the possession of a German prince, containing the names of 47,000 British men and women with records of their alleged moral and sexual weaknesses. It was said for months afterwards that the supposed 'Black Book' was the main subject of gossip in high society, people jokingly asking each other 'are you in the Black Book?' More worryingly, Pemberton Billing managed to convince a jury in London of this nonsense, and he was acquitted, to jubilation inside and outside the courtroom.

After the different committees of inquiry, the B.E.2c remained the main aeroplane of the RFC, although it was accepted that it was vulnerable and could only be used with significant fighter protection. It was largely super-seded by the end of 1916 by the Factory-designed R.E.8 as the main RFC observation aircraft on the Western Front. This was only slightly better than the B.E.2, but at least it had the observer gunner in the back seat.

It took some time for the Allies to develop synchronization gear, but by mid-1916 they were able to counter the Fokker using pusher fighters like the British D.H.2, with the engine behind the pilot, or the French Nieuport, with a machine gun on top of the wing firing over the propeller. The Germans then brought into service much better bi-plane fighters with two synchronized machine guns, such as the Albatross. By 1917, the RFC had fighters such as the Sopwith Camel which had two synchronized guns and were at least a match for the Germans. The Royal Aircraft Factory produced a superb fighter, the S.E.5a.

With 3,500 B.E.2 aeroplanes built or on order, the RFC was stuck with the 'Quirk' in 1916. It continued working as an observation machine and light bomber. While it was phased out over the Western Front, it contin-ued in service until the end of the war in Macedonia and Mesopotamia. It was used as a test bed for various innovations, including the very reliable Constaninesco synchronizing gear, used in most British fighters after 1917. It was a test bed for relatively lightweight radio transmitters used to send artillery observations back to the guns. It was even used as a test bed for armour plate, although this was a failure as the weight further reduced the already abysmal rate of climb.

After the B.E.2c, other models were produced. The B.E.2d was a dual-control model used for training and the B.E.2e a slightly more aero-dynamically advanced version. A fighter version, the B.E.12 – basically a B.E.2 with a larger 140hp RAF 4a engine – was produced, a single-seater with a synchronized Vickers machine gun firing forwards and a Lewis gun mounted on top of the wing. This was a total failure on the Western Front, but had some success on other fronts and as a night fighter.

It wasn't until 1917 and 1918 that efficient two-seater aircraft were designed, able to survive in combat with single-seat fighters. The British had the Bristol Fighter, the French the Salmson and Breguet, and the Germans the Hanover.

There was one duty in which the B.E.2 was a major success: as a night fighter. Nine airships were shot down over England, two of these – *L.15* and *L.33* – by anti-aircraft fire. One Zeppelin, *L.70*, was shot down by a D.H.4 aeroplane, and all the rest by B.E. type aeroplanes. Zeppelin *L.48* was shot down by a B.E.12, and the remainder – *S.L.11*, *L.21*, *L.31*, *L.32* and *L.34* – by B.E.2c aeroplanes. The irony about the B.E.2 series of aircraft is that their various weaknesses led to their success as night fighters. The poor rate of climb meant that there was only one way to attack a Zeppelin, and that was with an upward-pointing gun from underneath. The inherent stability made the B.E.2c relatively easy to fly at night, its top speed of about 85 mph making it faster than the Zeppelin, though as it took sixteen minutes to reach 6,000ft its rate of climb was much less. The usual armament of Lewis guns angled to fire upwards over the wings was a necessary result of this. The usual method of attack was to fly under the Zeppelin and fire at a small area in the belly, which was very effective. As higher performance aeroplanes were introduced later in the war, most kept the upward-firing Lewis gun as their main armament.

The stability and lack of manoeuvrability was no real handicap at night, and was a positive advantage in changing the magazine of the Lewis gun. The time most pilots mentioned manoeuvrability was when they had to get out of the way quickly when they shot a Zeppelin down. Though experiments did take place to fit a synchronized machine gun to a B.E.2c, it was never seen as practical. This meant they had to be armed with a Lewis gun mounted on top of the wing. The design with the pilot in the back and observer in the front worked well in a single-seat fighter; the pilot could reach the gun and pull it towards himself. The observer's position was just covered with an aluminium cover. To change the magazine there had to be a mounting to enable the gun to be pulled towards the pilot so he could reach it. This led to the development of various mountings, with the Foster and Strange mounts probably the most used. These not only allowed the gun to be loaded, but enabled it to be clamped to fire upwards and forwards at any angle. Most pilots set the gun at about 45 degrees from the horizontal.

The Lewis gun was the ideal weapon for this type of operation, its round magazine holding forty-seven or ninety-seven rounds, which enabled different combinations of incendiary ammunition to be experimented with. After a successful interception, pilots almost always reported what combination of bullets they had used: William Leefe Robinson used alternate New Brock and Pomeroy, while Frederick Sowery used Brock, Pomeroy and tracer ammunition.

By March 1916, Britain had an effective system of fighter control and air-raid warnings, but it took several months before the first Zeppelin was shot down. There were a number of reasons the B.E.2c become Britain's most successful night fighter, changing from Fokker fodder to Zeppelin killer. The first was simply availability. Being the standard military aircraft of the Army, the B.E.2 was produced in much greater numbers – 3,500 were built – and while other machines might have done a better job, they were simply unavailable. Another reason was the belief that only an inherently stable aeroplane could be safely flown at night, which ruled out faster, more efficient fighters. However, it needs to be said the Morane Parasol of Lieutenant Werneford of the RNAS, which brought down the first Zeppelin at night, was certainly not inherently stable. It took the RFC over a year to use effective single-seat fighters at night; they were used when the Gotha raids on London started, as the B.E.2 had little chance of getting near to a Gotha.

The most important reason it took so long before a Zeppelin was shot down was the totally erroneous idea that Zeppelins had a system of circulating inert exhaust gas from the engines around the gas cells, thus preventing the ignition of the highly inflammable hydrogen gas. Though there was never any inert gas system, pure hydrogen is not easy to ignite, and tracer bullets passed through Zeppelin gas bags without causing a fire. The gas only became really inflammable when mixed with air, and it needed a combination of incendiary and explosive bullets. The explosive bullets would cause the gas bags to tear and leak hydrogen, and the incendiary bullet would ignite the mixture. It took several months to work this out and develop suitable incendiary ammunition, and during much of 1915 and 1916 bombing was seen as the way to destroy Zeppelins over Britain.

The first Zeppelin destroyed by a British aircraft was brought down by bombing, and this led to a delay in the development of the upward-firing machine gun. This was the Army Zeppelin *LZ.37*, commanded by Oberleutnant van der Haegen, brought down on 7 June 1915 by RNAS Flight Sub-Lieutenant Reginald Warneford. Yet it was not a planned attack. *LZ.37* was returning from an aborted raid on England, having been forced to return because of poor weather. Warneford was flying a French Morane parasol monoplane on a mission to bomb Zeppelin sheds in Belgium. He was flying at about 11,000ft when he saw the Zeppelin about 4,000ft below him over Ostend, gave chase, and with the Zeppelin crew firing at him, after about an hour caught the airship over Ghent. He flew about 150 feet above *LZ.37* and dropped six 20lb bombs on it. The Zeppelin immediately exploded, the blast throwing the Morane on its back, but Warneford managed to regain control and saw the blazing Zeppelin fall like a stone around a Belgian convent. The Zeppelin commander and most of the crew were burned to death. Warneford was awarded the VC for the action, but died ten days later in a flying accident. Warneford's victory had been the result of a number of favourable coincidences; he was already in the air, was armed with bombs and was higher than the Zeppelin when he saw it.

The idea that bombing was the way to defeat the Zeppelin led to the development of a technological blind alley, the 'Ranken Dart', which was essentially a small bomb, with vanes at the tail that would spread out in the airflow on release and stick in the envelope of the Zeppelin, giving time for its incendiary charge to set the airship on fire. The pilot had a box of twenty-four darts, and was expected to drop them on the Zeppelin, three at a time, a very difficult feat in 1916 as Zeppelins could easily outclimb the cumbersome aircraft used as night fighters. The only example of an attack on a Zeppelin with Ranken Darts seems to have been when Lieutenant Barth-Brandon, in a B.E.2c, attacked *L.15*, commanded by Joachim Breithaupt, on 31 March 1916. He was able to attack the Zeppelin from above as it had been hit by anti-aircraft fire and was losing height when he found it. The darts did not have any effect; we don't know whether they missed or failed to ignite. Zeppelin *L.15* landed in the English Channel, with most of the crew captured, due to loss of hydrogen caused by the anti-aircraft fire.

The spring and summer of 1916, after a long period of development, saw the mass production of effective incendiary and explosive ammunition for aircraft machine guns. Buckingham incendiary bullets, and Pomeroy and Brock explosive bullets were reliable enough for use in night fighters and spelled doom for the highly inflammable hydrogen-filled Zeppelins. There was the ludicrous situation in the summer of 1916 where pilots in B.E.2cs were ordered to carry a box of Ranken Darts as well as a Lewis gun in anti-Zeppelin operations. In time, even the High Command came to understand you had to be above a Zeppelin to bomb it, and if you were weighed down with useless weapons it made a poor rate of climb even worse. By September 1916, squadron commanders were given tacit approval to leave behind the Ranken Darts, and the B.E.2c armed with an upward-firing Lewis gun was the aeroplane to take on the Zeppelins.

The upward-firing gun was a British invention, basically making a virtue out of necessity, allowing fighters with very little performance advantage over the Zeppelins to shoot them down. It was a very successful weapon in the Second World War, used not by the RAF but the German Luftwaffe in all their twin-engine night fighters from 1943. They called it *Schrage Musik*, literally oblique music or colloquially jazz music. A fighter would attack from underneath and slightly behind a bomber, usually unseen until the cannon shells hit their target.

The last Zeppelin to be shot down was *L.53*, commanded by Kapitänleutnant Edward Prolss, dispatched by a Sopwith Camel flown by Lieutenant S.D. Cully off the coast of Holland on 11 August 1918. The aircraft, which can still be seen at the Imperial War Museum, had the forward-firing synchronized Lewis guns removed and replaced by a pair of upward-firing Lewis guns. The Zeppelin was at 19,000ft when it was shot down.

The major advantage of the B.E.2c at night was its reliability, slow landing speed of about 40mph and robust construction. In 1916, the B.E.2c was probably the best that Britain had. It is a tribute to the pilots' bravery that they were able to shoot down the airships with such a limited performance advantage.

Chapter Seven

The Belgian Rattlesnake: the Lewis Gun

T he machine gun is probably the weapon that defines the First World War. Along with poison gas, massive artillery bombardments and Zeppelins, the machine gun seems to symbolize the horror of flesh against steel and the soldier as a victim rather than a conqueror. The first militarily useful machine gun was used in the American Civil War, the Gatling gun. But it and similar weapons such as the Nordfelt gun needed the operator to turn a handle to manually operate the mechanism. The first fully automatic weapon was the Maxim gun, which used the energy of the firing to load and eject the cartridges.

The Maxim gun was invented by an American, Hiram Maxim (1840-1916), who described it in as a great peace preserver. He was probably most influenced by a man he described in his biography: 'In 1882 when I was in Vienna, I met an American who said "Hang your chemistry and electricity, if you want to make a pile of money invent something that will enable those Europeans to cut each other's throats with greater facility".' And he certainly did that.

The Maxim gun was invented in 1883, it was a recoil-operated weapon, as the cartridge fired the recoil and would force the breech back, this force ejecting the spent cartridge, loading another cartridge, locking the breech and then firing the round. The process would repeat as long as the trigger was pressed. Maxim was financed by Albert Vickers and the company became part of the large Vickers armaments empire. The Maxim gun was first used in anger by the British Army during the first Matabele War in Rhodesia in 1893/4, where it is said 700 soldiers with four Maxim guns fought off 5,000 attackers. The use in colonial warfare was famously summed up by Hiliare Belloc, who wrote:

> Whatever happens we have got.
> The Maxim gun and they have not.

Over the next few years, the Vickers Company licensed armaments manufacturers in other countries to produce the Maxim gun. With the exception of the French, who had the Hotchkiss gun, most of the combatants in 1914 had versions of the Maxim gun as their main machine gun. The British had the Vickers gun, the Germans the *Maschinengewhr 08*, the Russians the *Pulemyt Maxima*. All were slightly modified versions of the Maxim gun, made to fire each army's standard rifle cartridge.

The Vickers Company made some improvements to the basic Maxim design before the war, and in 1912 the Gun, Machine, Vickers, 0.303in, Mk 1 was introduced, manufactured at the Vickers factory in Crayford, Kent. It was lighter and more reliable than the original. At first it was only used at the rate of two per battalion, but as the war progressed it was soon understood that the Army needed many more. It was also recognized that the Vickers was a complex weapon and needed soldiers trained to use it. In 1915, the Machine Gun Corps was established. Many years ago I had the privilege of interviewing one of the last survivors of the Machine Gun Corps in the Great War. He was about 90 but was articulate, with a marvellous memory, and said he was trained as a gunner and that the men of the corps saw themselves as a bit of an elite, but above all were pleased not to be in the infantry. He was conscripted in 1916, and when he reported to be inducted he told the recruiting sergeant he was a bicycle mechanic by trade and was immediately signed up for the Machine Gun Corps. It seems bicycle mechanics were actively recruited, because they were used to assembling, adjusting and keeping clean complex machinery. While they were attached to an infantry battalion, in his case the local South Staffordshire Regiment, they had privileges and did not have to do fatigue duties out of the line. They spent much of their time out of the line working on the guns and assembling ammunition belts, which certainly beat digging trenches. He served in Ireland just after the Easter Rising, which he said he enjoyed; it was just camping on Phoenix Park. Then it was on to Palestine, which he said was interesting, but the flies were terrible, and Passchendaele, which he didn't like talking about.

By 1917, the Vickers was mostly used for indirect fire. A typical mission would be to go out at night to a prepared position, often a shell hole in no man's land, and set up the gun in a way the muzzle flash couldn't be seen by the enemy. One way of doing this was firing through an army blanket on a frame in front of the gun. The gun would then be fired for long periods at a pre-directed zone, the beaten ground, with the target being communications trenches behind the front - latrines were a favoured target. If well hidden, the gun was hard to find, and the Germans would not want to draw counter-fire. If the position was targeted by the Germans, the gun would be moved to another surveyed position.

The Vickers gun was a heavy weapon; the gun itself weighed about 40lb, and the tripod – which was always used – about 48lb. Added to this were the water condenser and thousands of rounds of ammunition. The gun was fed by canvas ammunition belts, each containing 250 rounds. Supplied with ammunition and cooling water, a Vickers gun could fire thousands of rounds non-stop. After 10,000 rounds the barrel had to be changed because of wear, but set up as an indirect fire weapon the Vickers could fire many thousands of rounds. Moving and setting up a Vickers gun was a task that needed quite a lot of men from an infantry platoon or Machine Gun Corps. It was found early in the war that an infantry platoon needed a lighter, more easily moved machine gun, which is where the Lewis gun was introduced.

The Vickers gun was used in massive numbers by the armies of the British Empire, and was also supplied to the French and American military. The main problem with the Vickers gun was simply availability: it couldn't be produced quickly enough for everyone who wanted it. The answer was the Lewis gun, a very different weapon to the Vickers. It was a much lighter, gas-operated machine gun. Although it had a rate of fire similar to that of the Vickers – 450 to 500 rounds per minute – it couldn't be fired in long continuous bursts, just short bursts of a few shots at a time. It was gas-operated, some of the gases produced when the gun was fired diverted through a hole at the bottom of the barrel near the muzzle, which drove a piston which extracted the spent cartridge and loaded and fired the next one. The best thing about the Lewis gun was that it could be produced much more quickly than the Vickers, so was able to meet the demands of the Army.

The Lewis gun was designed by an American, Samuel McLean, though much of the development and selling was done by another American, Colonel Isaac Lewis. Like the British Army before the war, the American Army was not too enthusiastic about machine guns in general, and light machine guns in particular. Lewis toured Europe to sell it and was given an order by a Belgian syndicate, Armes Automatique Lewis Societe Anonyme Belge, to mass-produce under licence. This, along with the short burst of fire generally used, gave the gun its nickname of the 'Belgian rattlesnake'. With the outbreak of war and the occupation of Belgium, the manufacturing licence went to the Birmingham Small Arms Company (BSA), who produced hundreds of thousands of Lewis guns for the British Empire, with many also going to the USA, France and Russia.

As for the use of machine guns in aeroplanes, the first true fighter plane, the Morane-Saulnier of Roland Garros, used a French Hotchkiss gun, a gas-operated gun introduced as the main French Army machine gun, but much less efficient than the Vickers which was imported in large numbers. When Anthony Fokker produced his *Eindecker* he used a *Maschinengewhr 08*, generally known as the Spandau, the German development of the Maxim gun, for his synchronization mechanism. The Maxim pattern was the basis of all synchronized weapons in the war, as a gas-operated gun does not have the stable firing cycle that a synchronized system needs. By 1917, most German fighters had two forward-firing machine guns, using a synchronizing mechanism considerably more reliable than the original Fokker system, and fed by an ammunition belt. When they had developed their synchronizing system, the British and French followed suit, using belt-fed Vickers guns. Both the Vickers and Spandau guns had the water jackets lightened so cooling air could circulate, but remained heavy belt-fed weapons, capable of firing long bursts. For the British, the best synchronization system of the war was the *Constantinesco* hydraulic system developed by George Constantinesco, a Rumanian mining engineer, and used in most British fighters from mid-1917.

The Lewis gun had been introduced early in the war, first as an observer's weapon and then, as the need for a fixed forward-firing gun was recognized during the Fokker Scourge, either fitted to pusher biplanes or fitted on top of the wing so they could fire over the propeller. The French Nieuport biplane was effective against the Fokker using the wing-mounted gun. Though the gun was not as good, the Nieuport 11 was stronger, faster and more manoeuvrable than the Fokker, so matters were evened out in combat. In the early part of the war, wing-mounted Lewis guns were fitted to many different aeroplanes, including the B.E.2c. The Lewis gun on the top wing of a biplane was fired by a simple mechanism, using a Bowden cable (like the brake cable on a bike) to operate the trigger on the gun from a firing lever on the control column in the cockpit. The pilot needed to be able to get to the gun to change the ammunition drum or clear jams. All Lewis guns had forty-seven or ninety-seven cartridge magazine, in a round drum on top of the breech. To change the magazine, the pilot needed to be able to pull the breech of the gun towards him. There were a number of mechanisms designed to do this, the best being the Foster mount, a quarter circle of rail that enabled the gun to be pulled back into the cockpit area and pushed back on to the wing. The B.E.2c had the 'Strange mount', basically just a steel tube in front of the cockpit, with a pivot in the centre, so the gun could be pulled back for reloading and forwards for firing over the wing. The gun was horizontal in the firing position over the wing, and vertical – with the barrel pointing up at 90 degrees – when it was in the loading position. All the mounts had a clamp mechanism to hold the gun horizontal or vertical. They could also hold the gun in any position the pilot wanted, and it was soon worked out that the best position was with the gun firing upwards and forwards, at about 45 degrees to the wing. This way the fighter could fly under the Zeppelin and fire upwards into its undefended belly, by far the best way to bring one down with an aeroplane without a significant advantage in ceiling or rate of climb. Though the Lewis gun was far less efficient than the belt-fed Vickers guns fitted to most day fighters – which could fire longer bursts and carry more ammunition – its drum magazine was much safer to use with incendiary and explosive bullets.

Essential to the defeat of the Zeppelin was incendiary and explosive ammunition. At the beginning of the war, there were concerns about the legality of incendiary ammunition under the terms of the St Petersburg Declaration and The Hague Convention. The St Petersburg Declaration banned bullet weighing less than 400g being explosive or filled with fulminating or inflammable substances. The basis of this was to avoid unnecessary suffering to individual soldiers. The argument used by the British was that the tracer, incendiary or explosive bullet was intended to destroy aircraft, not cause unnecessary suffering to the occupants. In practice, the British at first only used these bullets against Zeppelins or bombers over Britain, and only later in the war was incendiary ammunition used extensively by both sides on the Western Front. The Germans did threaten to try in courts British airmen captured and found to have used incendiary bullets, but they never did, and by 1917 were using them themselves.

SPK Mark V11.T

At the beginning of the war, the RFC was issued with tracer ammunition so the pilot or observer could see the path of the bullet towards the target. This was especially important at night. The first tracers were ineffective and development was switched to ammunition made by Aerators Ltd; this company made the 'Sparklet' soda siphon, so not surprisingly the ammunition was called the 'Sparklet'. A lot of development work took place, and by June 1916 a tracer mixture of one part magnesium to eight parts barium peroxide was found to give a bright clear trace. The ammunition was issued to the RFC in July 1916, being replaced in 1917 by a better tracer, the SPG Mark VII.G.

The Buckingham 0.303 bullet

John Buckingham, the owner of a Coventry engineering company, took out a patent in April 1915 for a phosphorus-based incendiary bullet. The bullet was filled with phosphorus held in place with a solder, and when the gun was fired the solder would melt and the phosphorus ignite in the air. The Admiralty placed an order, and the RNAS started using it from December 1915 and the RFC in April 1916. At first the nose of the bullet was pointed, which was largely ineffective against Zeppelins as it would go straight through the gas cell, making only a small hole which didn't let enough gas escape to easily ignite. In June 1916, Buckingham introduced a flat-nosed version which made a bigger hole and let out a lot more gas. Though it was less accurate, the bullet was much more effective and used until the end of the war. By 1918, it was also used by France and the USA. By the end of the war, some 26,000,000 rounds had been produced.

The Brock Bullet

The Brock Company produced fireworks before 1914 – 100 years later it still does. A member of the Brock family was in charge of the Air Intelligence Department at the Admiralty. At the time it was thought that Zeppelins had a system of using inert exhaust gas around the gas cells to stop the ignition of hydrogen. The explosive bullet produced by Commander Frank Arthur Brock (1888-1918) was seen as the answer to this. It was filled with potassium chlorate and was designed to ignite when it hit a solid object. It was not particularly successful. The RFC initially ordered a batch of 500,000, but did not renew it. It was, however, used by the RNAS for anti-Zeppelin patrols over the North Sea. Brock was a serving Naval officer and was killed during the raid on Zeebrugge on 22/23 April 1918.

The PSA bullet

John Pomeroy, an Australian engineer, submitted his design for an explosive bullet to the War Office in August 1914. He was initially ignored. It wasn't until December 1915 that the Munitions Inventions Unit carried out tests, and the bullet was introduced into service as the PSA in July 1916, though pilots usually called it the Pomeroy. The bullet was filled with a mixture of 73 per cent nitroglycerine and 27 per cent kieseguhr. It was not without its problems: it would not detonate except at high striking speed, nor on soft surfaces like rubber, not ideal for an anti-Zeppelin weapon. This explains why pilots often had to fire several drums of Lewis gun ammunition to bring down an airship. An improved version, the PSA Mark II, was introduced in February 1917; this had a small steel ball at the base of the explosive mixture which would move forward when the bullet decelerated, making it much more sensitive. This new model PSA Mark II was supplied in large number to RFC home defence units.

The RTS bullet.

This was a particularly nasty weapon, invented by Sir Richard Threlfall (1861-1932), a consulting engineer at the Allbright and Wilson chemical company in Oldbury, and put into production in November 1917. It was both explosive and incendiary, and very sensitive, the front of the bullet filled with a mixture of nitroglycerine and sawdust and the back with white phosphorus and tungsten powder. The Ministry of Munitions ensured it was produced in secret, and a special factory was set up to do this. In 1918, 200,000 bullets were delivered each week. Up to September 1918, it was only used in Britain against raiding aeroplanes, probably more to keep it secret than because of its doubtful legality. It is noticeable that when Zeppelins were shot down in 1918, they caught fire quickly when hit; it seems likely the RTS bullet was the main cause of this.

Vickers machine guns were only ever loaded with standard ball ammunition and tracer, usually in a combination of four balls to one tracer cartridge. Looking at the various anti-Zeppelin bullets, another advantage of the Lewis gun becomes apparent. The mixtures inside the projectiles were unpleasant and often unstable. The round magazines of the Lewis, open to the airflow, made them safer to carry and allowed pilots to experiment with different combinations of bullets. It is noticeable that in pilot reports made after the shooting down of a Zeppelin, they almost always describe the particular combination used. William Leefe Robinson, who shot down *SL.XI* on 3 September 1916, said he used one drum of 'alternative new Brock and Pomeroy'; Frederick Sowery shot down *L.32* on 24 September 1916 and said his drums were loaded with 'a mixture of Brock, Pomeroy and tracer'; when he shot down *L.70* on 5 August 1918, Egbert Cadbury said he saw the Pomeroy explosive bullets 'blow a great hole in the fabric'.

Chapter Eight

March to August 1916

The German Navy remained enthusiastic about the role of the Zeppelin for strategic bombing and co-operation with surface ships in operations like minesweeping. The Army, however, was becoming disillusioned. Army airship commanders were ordered not to operate over the Western Front as it was just too dangerous. A number of Army airships were transferred to the East, where they remained useful.

There were attempts by the Russians to recover some of the ground they had lost in 1915. In March, their attack at the Battle of Lake Naroch, in the north of the Eastern Front, failed utterly. In June, the Brusilov offensive - mainly against the Austrians in the south - was initially very successful, but was halted by the transfer of German troops from Verdun. Army Zeppelins were engaged in tactical bombing missions in support of German and Austrian forces; losses were high but the operations seemed militarily useful.

The major offensive for the British was the Battle of the Somme, from 24 June to 13 November. Little was achieved, despite or because of massive casualty rates. There was no substantial role for the Zeppelins, though the strategic bombing campaign had some effect on industrial output. It is doubtful whether increased output would have had much effect; the real problem was manifest incompetence by the British High Command.

Things were much better in the air defence campaign. One Zeppelin had been shot down by anti-aircraft fire, but the air defence system was being developed and would show results in the autumn. Airships were tracked virtually all the way from their bases to the coast, then across Britain. The missing ingredient, incendiary ammunition, was in production and would go on to defeat the Zeppelin.

Navy Zeppelins were involved in a reconnaissance role in the Battle of Jutland on 31 May/1 June, although because of the weather their support was limited. The battle did not produce a clear result for either side. Though the Germans sank more ships, they never again set out in force to attack the British Fleet, so in a tactical sense it was a British victory.

5/6 March 1916

The Navy made its next raid on Britain on 5 March 1916, when three Zeppelins set out to bomb England North; the main target was to be the Firth of Forth and Rosyth in Scotland. The Zeppelins were the only airships available still having the older but more reliable C-X engines. They were *L.11* commanded by Korvettenkapitan Victor Schutze, who had taken it from von Buttlar – who was destined for the new series 'R' Zeppelin *L.30* – Heinrich Mathy in *L.13* and Alois Bocker in *L.14*. Radio signals from the Zeppelins were picked up by Room 40 at about midday, and radio location indicated a north-westerly course. There was a severe decline in the weather as the Zeppelins approached the coast, and the target was changed to England Middle.

'P' type Navy Zeppelin *L.11*: Korvettenkapitan Viktor Schutze left Nordholz and crossed the British coast at Tunstall just north of Spurn Head, much farther south than he had estimated, his intended target being Middlesbrough. The British thought he was heading for Lincoln, though it seems likely he was lost. He flew through heavy snow, sighting Hull at about midnight, which he recognized, the snow on the ground making navigation easier. He saw bombs from another Zeppelin exploding in the city. He turned to attack Hull, but lost sight of the city in more clouds. Clear sky returned at about 01.00, and he returned to bomb Hull, dropping 3,600lb of bombs. He said that the streets of the city showed up clearly under the starlit sky, like a drawing, with blocks of houses, quays and dock basins easily visible. His bombs damaged a vessel being built in Earle's shipyard, set fire to the Mariners Almshouses and destroyed a number of houses. *L.11* then turned for the coast. Schutze was fired on by an anti-aircraft gun over Killingholme. He used the last of his bombs, dropping four on the battery, killing one man. He crossed the coast over Spurn Head at 01.40.

'P' type Navy Zeppelin *L.13*: Kapitänleutnant Heinrich Mathy in *L.13*, which he regarded as his lucky ship, had more problems. After leaving Hage, he had engine trouble over the North Sea and then met very poor weather, being covered in snow when he was over the Dogger Bank. He had to dump fuel to lighten the ship. Because of this he decided to attack the Tyne region rather than the Forth. He saw lights at 22.00 and thought he was over Sunderland, but he had actually been driven further south and crossed the coast at North Coates. *L.13* was spotted near Nottingham, and after another engine failure he had to jettison fifteen HE bombs and all his incendiaries. British records show L.13 dropped bombs from Newark to Sheerness, but it seemed the commander was unable to properly aim them. Thirty-two incendiaries fell in fields near Sproxton and fourteen HE bombs in fields near Thistleton. It is said the explosions could be heard in Norwich, some 85 miles away.

Mathy was pushed further south by the wind. He saw a number of warships in the Thames Estuary at 01.10 but could not attack them because of the strong wind. He crossed the coast near Dover, and at 3.00 had a radio direction 'fix' which showed L.13 was 20 miles north-east of Calais. He crossed the Belgian coast at Ostend at 04.15. Shortly after this, a second engine failed and he was forced to land at Namur at 07.30. Later that day, Mathy set out for his base at Hage on the two working engines. Two hours into the journey, a third C-X engine failed and he had to return to Namur. Substitute engines had to be sent by train to Namur, and L.13 didn't get back to base until 10 March.

'P' type Navy Zeppelin L.14: Kapitänleutnant Alois Bocker, after leaving Nordholz, crossed the coast north of Flamborough Head. He bombed Beverley with six HE bombs and reached Hull just after midnight, bombing working-class housing near the docks. Both L.11 and L.14 bombed the docks and surrounding areas, Schutze in L.11 about 45 minutes after Bocker. There is a record of most of the causalities, but as two airships bombed Hull that night it is not possible to determine what damage each Zeppelin did. A list of most of the people killed that night in Hull shows, like most Zeppelin victims, the random nature of the bombing. The oldest victim was 89 and the youngest just 4. They were: Robert Cattle (48) of Little Humber Street, Hull; Frank Cattle (8) of Little Humber Street, Hull; Edward Cook (38) of 33 Lukes Street, Hull; James William Collinson of 14 Johns Place, Regent Street, Hull; Charlotte Naylor (30) of 32 Collier Street, Hull; Ethel Mary Ingamells (33) of The Avenue, Linnaeus Street, Hull; Lotte Ingamells (28) of The Avenue, Linnaeus Street, Hull; Mary Rebecca Ingamells (35) of The Avenue, Linnaeus Street, Hull; Ruby Naylor (8) of 32 Collier Street, Hull; Annie Naylor (6) of 32 Collier Street, Hull; Edward Naylor (4) of 32 Collier Street, Hull; Edward Ledner (89) of Trinity House, Carr Lane, Hull (now the Admiral pub); John Longstaff (71) of 6 Williams Place, Upper Union Street, Hull; James Patterson (68) of 33 Regent Street, Hull; Edward Slip (45) of 23 Queen Street, Hull; and John Smith (30) of 2 Queen Alley, Blackfriersgate, Hull.

Bocker then turned towards Grimsby, but couldn't find it because of cloud, so turned north and dropped seven more bombs near Tunstall.

In all, eighteen people were killed and fifty-two injured in the bombing that night in Hull. The morning after the raid, a RFC vehicle was stoned by the enraged population in the centre of Hull. The main cause of the anger was the lack of anti-aircraft guns, which had been promised after the raid of June 1915 but had not arrived. Major General Lawson, in command of the northern sector, met with the Lord Mayor and other leading citizens, and temporary mobile anti-aircraft guns were delivered the next day. A full battery system, including guns at Immingham, Killingholme, Waltham, Spurn and Hornsea, was installed in the next few weeks.

6 March 1916

'P' type Army Zeppelin *LZ.90*: The debate in the Army High Command about the ability of Zeppelins to operate near the front in moonlight was over. The Army completely changed its attitude, deciding it was impractical to operate over the Western Front at all, moonlit or not. The Army would carry out a few more raids over England, but most of its Zeppelins were to be sent to other fronts: Russia, Salonika and from Bulgaria, where air defences were much weaker. By the end of 1916, the Army had realized that the Zeppelin was finished as a weapon of war, but quite a few more soldiers would die proving them right.

During the Verdun campaign, the Army only had one success, when Zeppelin *LZ.90*, commanded by naval officer Oberleutnant zur Reserve Ernst Lehmann, bombed Bar-le-Duc with 6,700lb of bombs. Because of the relatively short distance, he only left Trier in the afternoon. When he got to Bar-le-Duc, he crossed the line at 10,000ft to avoid attracting fire, using cloud for cover and slowing down the engines to cut the noise. When they got to the railway station it was in darkness, but they managed to find it. Lehmann dropped most of the bombs on the first run and saw fire and smoke rising from the railway yards. They circled to bomb again and were fired at by anti-aircraft artillery, Lehmann seeing objects like 'big yellow sky-rockets' which went high above the ship to an altitude of about two miles. He immediately turned away and climbed as high as possible, but the shells still followed him, and looking down he saw that the guns were mounted on trucks that were tracking the Zeppelin. He found a cloud bank and crossed back over the lines, returning safely to Trier.

7 March 1916

'N' type Army Zeppelin *LZ.XII*: The Army continued to operate airships on the Eastern Fronts. On the Russian Front, the older Zeppelin *LZ.XII* based in Warsaw made a successful attack on a railway station at Stolpce (now Stowbtsy, Belarus).

17 March 1916

'Q' type Army Zeppelin *LZ.85*: Oberleutnant Scherzer, who had previously bombed Salonika on 31 January, took off from Temesvar on 17 March with a new plan of attack. He intended to fly directly to Salonika, but on the way back land at Sofia in Bulgaria to refuel, so he could carry more bombs. When he got to Salonika, the city was better defended and shrapnel damaged a propeller and gas cells. He landed at Sofia to refuel, but the base didn't have enough hydrogen for him to top up the leaking gas cells. He had two engines removed and, with a skeleton crew, flew the much lighter ship back to base. The rest of the crew returned to Temesvar by train.

31 March/1 April 1916

The next night of the new moon was 31 March, the start of an intensive operation by Strasser, where Zeppelins would bomb England almost every day for a week. The HSLu high compression engines were back from being modified at Freidrichshafen. The main target for the Navy Zeppelins in the first raid was to be London.

'O' type Navy Zeppelin *L.9*: Hauptmann August Stelling flew from Hage but returned early with engine trouble.

'P' type Navy Zeppelin *L.11*: Korvettenkapitan Viktor Schutze flew from Nordholz but also had to return early with engine trouble.

'P' type Navy Zeppelin *L.13*: Kapitänleutnant Heinrich Mathy, after leaving Hage, found the temperature of 37.5°F too high to reach a safe altitude over London, with his heavy bomb load of 5,300lb. He crossed the coast north of Aldeburgh at about 20.00 and decided to bomb the New Explosive Works at Stowmarket, but had problems finding the factory because of mist. He circled and dropped a flare when he was over the town, looking for the works. He came under anti-aircraft fire, but continued to look for the works; his bombs did land near the factory but failed to do much damage, only breaking windows. Demonstrating the bravery which made him admired by both sides, Mathy then flew towards the gun battery and aimed twelve bombs, which the British reported did little damage. The anti-aircraft gun then hit the Zeppelin and damaged some gas cells. The British had an interesting piece of intelligence about exactly what happened. A German Navy message blank was found in Stowmarket the next day. Mathy had scribbled a note to the Executive Officer and wireless operator, ordering a radio message to be sent to the Commander in Chief High Seas Fleet: '10.00pm (21.00 GMT) Have attacked and hit a battery at Stowmarket with 12 bombs. Am hit, have turned back, hope to land in Hage towards 4.00 am. L.13.' The message must have found its way out of the command gondola in the chaos following the damage. Flying home with the ship losing height, Mathy dropped the rest of his bombs near Lowestoft as he crossed the coast. British reports show seven HE and twenty incendiary bombs exploded at Wangford and the aerodrome at Covehithe. L.13 got back to Hage safely, but needed repairs.

It is interesting to note that Mathy got back home despite being hit by at least one anti-aircraft shell. This was surprisingly common in raids over England. The cause of this was the relatively weak structure of a Zeppelin. The best analogy is a house and a garden shed. If a shell hit a house, it would explode and wreck the house. If it hit a garden shed, it would go through one wooden wall and out of the other, and unless it hit something solid inside, the only damage would be the hole where it went in and the hole where it went out. British anti-aircraft shells had two fuses. One was a time fuse; a calculation was made on how long it would take for the shell to reach the height of the target, and the fuse set. It would explode in shrapnel burst, hopefully near the target. It was particularly important the unexploded shell did not return to earth in a populated area. The second fuse was an impact fuse, designed to explode when it hit a solid object; fortunately for Mathy and his crew, L.13 wasn't solid enough.

Lehmann, in his autobiography, wrote that during his attack on railway junctions at Verdun, he had noticed the French were using a different type of incendiary artillery shell. He described them as looking like 'big yellow sky-rockets, moving rather slowly but continuing rising until they had passed our ship … far beyond our altitude of nearly two miles'. We know that LZ.77, commanded by Hauptmann Horn, was shot down in flames by one of these shells near Verdun, as was Kapitänleutnant Stabbert in L.44 a year later over France.

'P' type Navy Zeppelin *L.14*: Kapitänleutnant Alois Bocker, flying from Nordholz, had the Leader of Airships, Peter Strasser, on board as he set out to bomb London. In his combat report, Bocker claimed he hit the city, but British reports show he bombed Sudbury, where five people were killed, and Braintree, where four more died. *L.14* also flew over Brentwood and Thameshaven. As this was a major raid, with seven Zeppelins killing forty-eight people and injuring sixty-four, causing £19,431 of damage, it is not possible to determine what further damage Bocker did. However, he certainly was responsible for many of the deaths. We have a record of people killed in Sudbury, Suffolk, probably by *L.14*. They were: Ellen Wheeler (64) of 34 East Street, Sudbury; Thomas Ambrose (48) of 35 East Street, Sudbury; Ellen Ambrose (35) of 35 East Street, Sudbury; John Edward Smith (50) of East Street, Sudbury; Rifleman Edward Hill, Army billet, Constitution Hill, Sudbury; and Rifleman Robert Valentine Wilson (42).

'P' type Navy Zeppelin *L.15*: *L.15* had been out of action for some time. Like many of the Zeppelins fitted with the 240hp engines, *L.15*'s engines had been removed and returned for modification to the Maybach factory at Fredrichshafen, and the mechanics in its crew trained to deal with them. It had modified engines fitted and was readied for action in March 1916. Flying from Nordholz, Kapitänleutnant Joachim Breithaupt crossed the coast at Dunwich, Suffolk, at 19.45 and flew towards the Thames, via Ipswich and Chelmsford. While London was a difficult target because of effective defence, the city was easy to find: the Thames was an excellent signpost. He was over north-east London at 22.30 and dropped fourteen HE bombs near Dartford. At about the same time, he was picked up by searchlights, manoeuvred to avoid them but was caught again. At about 22.45, he was hit by two shells from the Woolwich anti-aircraft battery. The shells destroyed a number of gas cells and punctured others. Breithaupt dropped the rest of his bombs to lighten the ship. Lucky not to catch fire, *L.15* rapidly lost height as it lost hydrogen. To add to Breithaupt's problems, he was seen and attacked by an aeroplane. The pilot, Second Lieutenant Alfred de Barthe Brandon, from Hainault Farm RFC station, climbed above *L.15* in his B.E.2c and attacked with Ranken Darts. For once the Zeppelin was not a sitting duck, as machine-gunners stationed on the top of the hull fired to some effect. Upon landing, Brandon found a number of bullet holes in his plane, one of the few cases of damage caused to a fighter by a Zeppelin. All the darts missed, and *L.15* was able to evade Brandon.

Breithaupt knew he was in deep trouble. He radioed his base to say he intended to try to reach the Belgian coast near Ostend. He jettisoned most of his fuel, keeping just enough to reach German-occupied territory. After the fuel, the machine guns were thrown overboard, yet all this was in vain, as at about 23.15 the Zeppelin ditched into the sea about 15 miles from Margate, near the Kentish Knock lightship. After several hours, seventeen members of the crew, standing on top of the floating hull, were rescued by British armed trawlers. One crew member drowned. Breithaupt had a number of complaints about his treatment; the first was that the crew of the trawler, obviously thinking about the *King Stephen* affair, forced the Zeppelin crew to strip naked before taking them aboard. They were then taken to Chatham and were subject to intense interrogation by the formidable Major Trench. It is said that Breithaupt never lost his deep sense of grievance of his treatment during interrogation. There is no doubt much useful material was collected, including the fact that most of the crew were convinced they had bombed Liverpool on 31 January. When they had given as much information as Major Trench calculated he was going to get, they were treated as prisoners of war. Breithaupt and the executive officer went to Donington Hall. Leutnant Kuhne was repatriated on the condition he would not participate in combat operations; he spent the rest of the war on Strasser's staff. Breithaupt and his men spent the rest of the war as PoWs.

'P' type Navy Zeppelin *L.16*: Oberleutnant zur See Werner Peterson, flying from Hage, crossed the coast at Great Yarmouth at 22.10. He claimed to have bombed Hornsey in London, but British observers recorded that he bombed Bury St Edmunds, killing seven people and injuring five. The damage occurred mainly in Mill Road and Chalk Road. He finally dropped a single bomb on Lowestoft as he crossed the coast just after midnight.

We have the names of some of the Bury St Edmunds victims: Harry Frost (44) of 74 Mill Road, Bury St Edmunds; Annie Dureall (29) of 75 Mill Road, Bury St Edmunds; Catherine Dureall (3) of 75 Mill Road, Bury St Edmunds; and James Dureall (5) of 75 Mill Road, Bury St Edmunds.

'Q' type Navy Zeppelin *L.22*: Kapitänleutnant Martin Dietrich, flying from Nordholz, was held up by strong winds and engine trouble, so decided not to attack London but steered north to the Humber Estuary, intending to bomb Grimsby. He crossed the coast at Mablethorpe at about 01.00. In his combat report he said he bombed Grimsby, but in fact was a few miles away over Cleethorpes. It seems he made two bomb runs over the town, in the first of which he dropped most of his bombs, all of which fell harmlessly in fields. He went back out to sea, but turned back to bomb again. Dietrich had only three bombs left: the first hit Sea View Street, causing minor damage to housing and breaking windows over a wide area; the second destroyed the council offices; while the third struck a Baptist chapel in Alexander Road, which completely by accident turned out to be a military target. Men of the 3rd Special Reserve Battalion of the Manchester Regiment were billeted in the chapel awaiting deployment to France. It seems likely that they were ordered to do what was generally the safest thing to do in an air raid, and stay indoors if there were no air-raid shelters. Twenty-nine soldiers were killed by the single bomb – with two more victims dying later – and forty-eight injured. Many were buried in Cleethorpes Cemetery and there is a memorial. We have a record of the men killed: Private Ernest Ball; Private Joseph Beardsley; Private Louis Archie Beaumont (born 1882); Private Samuel Bell; Private William Robert Bodsworth; Private Thomas Brierley (born 1892); Private William Henry Brown; Private Ernest Budding (born 1897); Private Joseph Chandler; Private Frank Chandley; Private Job Clowes (born 1897); Private John Henry Corfield (born 1897); Private Harry Cuthbert; Private Thomas Deviney (born 1879); Private Frederick Dimelow; Private Albert Edward Downs (born 1896); Private Robert Fox; Private William Francis (born 1897); Private Thomas Hannon; Private Percy Harrison (born 1895); Lance Corporal Alfred Haynes; Private William Hetherington; Private Tom Pierce (born 1891); Private Joseph Radford (born 1897); Private Henry Ramsden (born 1895); Private James Russell (born 1895); Lance Corporal Jack Smith (born 1893); Private Thomas Tomkinson (born 1892); Private John Wheeler; Private William Wild; and Private Robert Wood (born 1894).

After bombing Cleethorpes, *L.22* went out to sea south of Spurn Head, coming under fire from a paddle minesweeper on the Humber, but returned safely to Nordholz.

The raid of 31 March was damaging for the British and the Germans. The Germans lost Zeppelin *L.15*, whilst the bombs killed forty-eight people and injured another sixty-four, causing damage worth £19,431. Most of the casualties occurred in Cleethorpes.

1/2 April 1916

This was a small but very costly raid by two Navy Zeppelins, in which twenty-two people were killed in Sunderland.

'P' type Navy Zeppelin *L.11*: Korvettenkapitan Viktor Schutze took off from Nordholz, crossed the coast at Seaham and went on to bomb Eppleton Colliery with two bombs, Hellon Downs with two bombs and Philadelphia with one bomb. He then flew to Sunderland, where he dropped 22 bombs, killing twenty-two people, with twenty-five seriously injured and 103 less seriously hurt, causing £25,568 worth of damage. We have limited information on the casualties in Sunderland, many of which occurred when a bomb hit a tram, where one of the people killed was the tram inspector. Two of the Sunderland victims were Harry Patrick (16) and Mary Patrick (18). Schutze dropped more bombs as he made for the coast: one at Port Clarence and two at Brotton. As he crossed the coast over the River Tees he dropped a final bomb, but missed his target of shipping.

'P' Type Navy Zeppelin *L.17*:. Kapitänleutnant Herbert Ehrlich took off from Nordholz and was first seen at dusk off the coast near Flamborough, where he waited for the dark. Ehrlich had engine problems, with a broken propeller on the aft engine, as he crossed the coast, and to maintain height while the mechanics made repairs he had to jettison bombs into the sea. He returned to Nordholz safely.

2 April 1916

'P' type Army Zeppelin *LZ.93*: Hauptman Wilhelm Schramm took over *LZ.93* on 23 February. We have few details, but it seems Schramm bombed Dunkirk. Casualty figures are not recorded.

2 April to 3 May 1916

'P' type Army Zeppelin *LZ.86*: Sent to Kovno (now Kaunas in Lithuania), *LZ.86* bombed railway stations in Minsk, Ruezyea and Wyschki between 2 April and 3 May 1916.

2/3 April 1916

This was a raid by four Navy Zeppelins and two Army Zeppelins. It was the first time Scotland was bombed.

'P' type Navy Zeppelin *L.13*: Kapitänleutnant Heinrich Mathy, flying from Hage, was forced to return to base with engine trouble.

'P' type Navy Zeppelin *L.14*: Kapitänleutnant Alois Bocker, flying out of Nordholz, was the first Zeppelin commander to bomb Scotland. He knew Edinburgh and Leith well, having often docked there as the captain of a passenger liner with the Hamburg-Amerika shipping line. He dropped nine HE and eleven incendiary bombs on Leith, killing one man and a baby and causing £44,000 worth of damage when he destroyed a whisky warehouse. Bocker reached Edinburgh at about 00.15, where he dropped eighteen HE and six incendiary bombs. He caused severe damage in the city centre, damaging many houses and Princes Street Station, killing eleven people and injuring twenty-four. There is an inscribed paving stone commemorating the raid at the place one of the bombs fell in the Grassmarket.

'P' type Navy Zeppelin *L.16*: Oberleutnant zur See Werner Peterson, flying out of Hage, is reported to have bombed Ponteland north of Newcastle with twenty-three bombs, nearby Cramlington with eleven bombs and Broomshill Colliery with seven bombs. It appears he was attracted to Cramlington by airfield flares. None of his forty-one bombs caused any damage.

'Q' type Navy Zeppelin *L.22*: Kapitänleutnant Martin Dietrich, flying from Nordholz, crossed the coast north of Berwick-upon-Tweed at 21.00. In his combat report he said he had bombed Newcastle, but the British report most of his bombs fell in fields inland of Berwick. After this, he flew northward along the coast towards Edinburgh, dropping three bombs near Colington and Liberton, which only broke windows.

'P' type Army Zeppelin *LZ.88*: Both Army airships came over Belgium. Their target was London. Hauptmann Falck in *LZ.88* seems to have crossed the coast south of Orford Ness in Suffolk, then flew over Ipswich, circling above the town, but it seems he didn't see it because British records only show that seventy-four bombs were dropped at nearby Alderton, Ramsholt and Hollesley.

'P' type Army Zeppelin *LZ.90*: Oberleutnant Ernst Lehmann, a sailor in an Army Zeppelin, bombed the Waltham Abbey area with ninety bombs, damaging several houses. *L.90* crossed the coast at Clacton, and we have a good report of this mission from Lehmann himself. He wrote that he intended to attack London from the north. He left his base at Trier and then spent an hour over Ghent waiting for darkness to fall before going out to sea at Ostend. He crossed the coast over the Thames Estuary, and was fired on by surface vessels while searchlights 'commenced their relentless search'. He decided not to reply and thought he went inland towards the Albert Docks. He was caught by a searchlight and saw anti–aircraft shells burst all around him. He managed to evade the searchlight and believed he dropped all his bombs on docks to the east of London, crossing back over the coast at the mouth of the Thames. He returned to Trier after nineteen hours in the air.

3/4 April 1916

'P' type Navy Zeppelin *L.11*: It seems both Zeppelins left Nordholz at about 14.00 and had London as their objective. Korvettenkapitan Viktor Schutze crossed the coast at Sheringham in *L.11* at 01.30. As visibility was poor, he abandoned the plan to attack London and decided to target Norwich, Yarmouth and Lowestoft. He failed to find any of these, and turned back over the sea near Caister. In his combat report he said he saw flashing lights near Yarmouth, which he thought was a gun battery. He attacked these and dropped all his bombs on the lights. The British have no record of these bombs; H.A. Jones, in *The War in the Air*, said it was possible the lights were from the funnels of destroyers that had been sent out of Harwich that night, though the destroyers made no report of bombs. Four incendiary bombs fell on land but did no damage.

'P' type Navy Zeppelin *L.17*: Kapitänleutnant Herbert Ehrlich, flying from Nordholz, got near the Norfolk coast at Haisborough but could make little headway, mainly due to engine trouble.

5/6 April 1916

This was a raid by three Navy Zeppelins on the North of England.

'P' type Navy Zeppelin *L.11*: Korvettenkapitan Viktor Schutze, flying out of Nordholz, had intended to bomb the Firth of Forth, but because of heavy rain, went south and crossed the coast at Hornsea Mere at 21.10. He intended to bomb Sheffield, but failed to find it so bombed Hull again. One bomb damaged a house in Portobello, where it seems one person, Jessie Mathews, died of shock. This may be the same Jessie Mathews, aged 1, of 11 Cotton Terrace, Barnsley Street, Hull, named as one of the August 1916 victims.

By this time Hull had significant anti-aircraft defences, and Schutze was picked up by a searchlight and fired on by anti-aircraft guns. He left the city and followed the coast north, intending to bomb Hartlepool, but suffered an engine failure. He was about to return home when he saw more lights from the brightly lit furnaces of the Skinningrove Ironworks. He dropped nine HE and twenty incendiary bombs, destroying the works laboratory.

'P' type Navy Zeppelin L.13: Kapitänleutnant Heinrich Mathy, flying from Hage, returned early with engine trouble.

'P' type Navy Zeppelin L.16: Oberleutnant zur See Werner Peterson, also flying out of Hage, crossed the coast north of Hartlepool and flew over Bishop Auckland, then on to Evenwood, where he destroyed fifteen miners' cottages and damaged Ramshaw School. He then moved to the Bishop Auckland area and dropped sixteen bombs in Gurney Valley, killing one person, schoolboy Robert Moyle, aged 9, of 21 Halls Row, Elden, who is buried in the churchyard of St Mark's, Eldon. In this raid L.16 also injured nine others and caused £7,883 worth of damage.

24/25 April 1916

This was a raid by six Navy Zeppelins and one Army Zeppelin, but it seems the Army and Navy operations were not coordinated. The British report that all the Naval Zeppelins crossed the coast between 22.15 and 01.35, most between Cromer in Norfolk and Southwold in Suffolk. It seems the initial target was London, but strong winds kept all the Zeppelins in East Anglia. It was difficult to know which airship bombed different targets, as most bombs fell in open country and little damage was done. The raid had been timed to coincide with the bombardment by the German Navy of Lowestoft, which in turn was to coincide with the Easter Rising in Dublin. The bombardment of Lowestoft took place in the early hours of 25 April All the Zeppelins had left England by 02.30, while the German battle cruisers *Lutzow*, *Derfflinger*, *Moltke* and *von der Tann* did not begin to shell Lowestoft until just after 04.00.

'P' type Zeppelin L.11: Korvettenkapitan Viktor Schutze flew out of Nordholz. British records show that Schutze struck Honing Hall in Norfolk with four bombs and Dilham with forty-five bombs. This caused the only casualty of the night, with an elderly lady dying of shock in Dilham.

'P' type Zeppelin *L.13*: Kapitänleutnant Eduard Prolss, a reasonably experienced officer, had taken over *L.13* from Mathy in April 1916. He had been a reserve officer since 1889, but unlike most of his fellow commanders he was not a professional sailor: he had been the head of the fire brigade in Magdeburg. Flying from Hage, he reported that he found a strong southwest wind over England and gave up the attempt to reach London. He was fired on by an anti-aircraft gun and sustained damage to the front gondola, but returned home safely.

'P' type Zeppelin *L.16*: Oberleutnant zur See Werner Peterson, flying out from Hage, dropped a parachute with propaganda-filled German illustrated newspapers at Kimberley, Norfolk, and then went to Newmarket, where he was fired on by machine guns and dropped one incendiary and eighteen HE bombs which wrecked five houses and damaged 100 others. He dropped two more bombs on the outskirts of Newmarket and five at Honingham. His combat report claimed he had bombed Cambridge and Norwich. It seems he thought Newmarket was Cambridge and Honington was Norwich. *L.16* crossed back over the coast at Mundesley at 01.35.

'P' type Zeppelin *L.17*: It seems Kapitänleutnant Herbert Ehrlich, operating from Nordholz, crossed the coast further north than the other Zeppelins. He is recorded as bombing in Lincolnshire. Three bombs were recorded at Alford and one at Anderby.

'Q' type Zeppelin *L.21*: Kapitänleutnant Max Dietrich flew out of Tondern. Records are sparse about his activities. We know he had Peter Strasser as a passenger and is recorded as dropping two bombs in the sea off Kessingland in Suffolk, nine at Old Newton and one at Wilton.

'Q' type Zeppelin *L.23*: Kapitänleutnant Otto von Schubert, out from Tondern, is recorded as dropping three bombs at Caister in Norfolk, nine at Ridlington and six at Backton.

'P' type Army Zeppelin *LZ 93*: It appears Hauptmann Wilhelm Schramm's attack was not coordinated with the day's naval attacks on England. Schramm, who was a very active raider, bombed Fort Mardyck, near Gravelines, in France.

25/26 April 1916

This raid by five Army Zeppelins was the last major attempt by the Army Airship Service to raid London. It was a total failure, causing no casualties and only £568 worth of damage. It seems headwinds were a major problem. All the Zeppelins came in over the English Channel, rather than the North Sea.

'P' type Army Zeppelin *LZ.81*: There is little information about Hauptmann Otto Jacobi's mission. It seems his airship did not cross the English coast and bombed Etaples in France.

'P/Q' type Army Zeppelin *LZ.87*: Oberleutnant Barth approached the Kent coast at Deal and dropped eight bombs on the steamer *Argus* without hitting it. *LZ.87* was targeted by anti-aircraft guns at Walmer and turned away. Barth cruised off the coast to Ramsgate, and then returned home via Belgium.

'P/Q' type Army Zeppelin *LZ.88*: Hauptmann Falck crossed the coast near Whitstable, Kent, and flew over Canterbury. He dropped nine incendiary bombs near Preston, thirteen more on Chislet March and Sarre, then another fifteen as the airship crossed the coast at Minnis Bay. None of them caused any damage.

'P/Q' type Army Zeppelin *LZ.93*: Hauptman Wilhelm Schramm potentially had the most difficult target, bombing Harwich. Most of his bombs fell on the Royal Navy training barracks, but did little damage. The GHQ report indicates several of the HE bombs did not explode.

'Q' type Army Zeppelin *LZ.97*: Hauptmann Erich Linnarz was certainly the most successful and well-known Army Zeppelin commander. He was the first Zeppelin commander to bomb London on 31 May/1 June 1915. On this raid he had some limited success. He crossed the Essex coast over West Mersea at about 22.00. It seems he then followed the Blackwater River, possibly mistaking it for the Thames. He dropped forty-seven incendiary bombs in a line from Fyfield to Chipping Onger at about 22.45. Flying towards London, *LZ.97* was targeted by an anti-aircraft gun at Dog Kennel Hill at 23.08. Linnarz reached Barkingside in Essex, where he dropped twelve HE bombs, doing much of the damage caused that night. He flew towards

Newbury Park, where he dropped one HE bomb, and was targeted by anti-air-craft guns at Seven Kings. He dropped two more bombs at Goodmaynes and Chadwell Heath, before heading for the coast, crossing at Clacton at 00.35.

The most important event of this ineffectual raid was the action of the Royal Flying Corps. Captain Arthur Travers Harris, the Flight Commander of B Flight 39 Squadron, took off in a B.E.2c at 22.30. For the first time in any night fighter operation, Harris had a Lewis gun with the still exper-imental Brock explosive bullets. He spotted Zeppelin *LZ.97* caught in a searchlight and started firing when the Zeppelin was 2,000ft above him, but the Lewis gum jammed after six rounds. He cleared the jam and climbed to attack again, only for the Lewis gun to jam once more. As he cleared the jam, he lost the Zeppelin, which escaped. *LZ.97* was also attacked by a member of B Flight: Lieutenant William Leefe Robinson, armed with a Lewis gun with standard ammunition, fired at the Zeppelin with no effect, and suf-fered several jams with his Lewis gun. Harris wrote in his combat report that an aeroplane with better climbing ability would have had more chance of success. It may be that both the B.E.2cs were also loaded with Rankin Darts, which made the already poor rate of climb even worse. The action that night did show that the RFC was learning and that the development work on incendiary ammunition by ordinary pilots was paying off. We know now that Harris and Leefe Robinson would eventually succeed, and that Air Marshal Arthur 'Bomber' Harris would go on to learn from this and repay the Zeppelin raiders a thousand times over in the Second World War.

26/27 April 1916

'P' type Army Zeppelin *LZ.93*: Hauptman Wilhelm Schramm seemed keen to return to the city of his birth: he had been born in London when his father worked as an engineer for the Siemens Company. He was not to do it on this night, though, as *LZ.93* had engine trouble. He was able to cross the Kent coast at Kingsdown and drop three HE explosive bombs on shipping at Deal, but no damage was recorded.

1 May 1916

'C' type Navy Schutte-Lanz *SL.3*: Kapitänleutnant Von Wachter, with Oberleutnant zur See Dehn as his second officer, flew out from Seddin. They were operating in the Baltic between Gotland and Backofen, when they were forced to land in the sea. The crew were rescued but the airship destroyed.

2/3 May 1916

This was a raid by eight Navy Zeppelins and one Army Zeppelin. It seems there was some attempt to coordinate the Army and Navy operations. The Zeppelins were picked up by British wireless interception, and it was known by the middle of the afternoon there was to be a raid on the north of England or Scotland by seven or eight Zeppelins. The original target was England North, which included Scotland. Specific targets were Rosyth, the Forth Bridge and the north of England. When the airships were about 100 miles off the Firth of Forth, strong winds were encountered and most ships turned south to attack alternative targets in England Middle.

'P' type Navy Zeppelin *L.11*: Korvettenkapitan Victor Schutze took off from Nordholz. He was fired on by ships east of St Abbs Head before he reached the coast. He crossed the coast at Holy Island. Only two bombs were recorded as having been dropped before *L.11* returned home, crossing the coast at Amble.

'P' type Navy Zeppelin *L.13*: Kapitänleutnant Eduard Prolss from Hage was caught in severe snowstorms. His combat report says he intended to bomb Leeds, but became totally lost. He thought he saw Hartlepool and bombed the town, but it seems likely he was fooled by blazing heather on Danby High Moor, which had been started by Zeppelin *L.23*, and dropped all his bombs there. The British noted two bombs from *L.13* were dropped at Fridaythorpe and Seamer, but no damage was done.

'P' type Navy Zeppelin *L.14*: Kapitänleutnant Alois Bocker actually reached Scotland, having set off from Nordholz. In his combat report he said he had been over the Firth of Forth when he sighted two warships, which he bombed at 23.30. He then searched for Edinburgh and the Forth Bridge, which he could not find, so turned for home. British reports show why he couldn't find Edinburgh: he was not over the Forth but the Tay. It seems the warships he reported were probably trawlers or just lights on the shore. Some of his bombs landed in a field near Arbroath.

'P' type Navy Zeppelin *L.16*: Oberleutnant zur See Werner Peterson, flying from Hage, claimed in his combat report to have bombed Stockton-on-Tees, setting buildings on fire as well as clearly recognizable railway tracks and embankments. This seems to have been an honest mistake, as all the East Coast towns had blackouts and visibility was poor due to heavy snow clouds. In fact he was one of four Zeppelin commanders to have bombed Danby

High Moor. It seems he dropped most of his bombs there and caused no damage. He later dropped five bombs on Lealholm and five on Moorsholm, damaging a farmhouse.

'P' type Navy Zeppelin *L.17*: Kapitänleutnant Herbert Ehrlich, flying from Nordholz, crossed the North Yorkshire coast at Saltburn and made for Skinningrove Ironworks. He dropped thirteen HH and four incendiary bombs on Carlin How, which wrecked six houses and damaged others. He was also fooled by the fire on Danby High Moor, and dropped the rest of his bombs there. In his combat report, he claimed to have bombed a coastal town in the east, probably Saltburn. He went back out to sea north of Whitby.

'Q' type Navy Zeppelin *L.20*: Kapitänleutnant Franz Stabbert reached Scotland, though it is difficult to praise his navigational skills. The subsequent history of Franz Stabbert seems to confirm the RAF saying that 'you can have bold pilots, or old pilots: you never have an old, bold pilot'. Stabbert's story at times reads like a *Biggles* novel, without the happy ending. He was undoubtedly a brave man, though his skill as a Zeppelin commander is less obvious.

L.20, with a crew of eighteen, left Tondern in the early afternoon. The target was Dundee. It seems he reached the coast at about 19.00, but the weather changed – as it tends to do in Scotland – and a strong north-west wind had sprung up. By about 20.00, *L.20* was flying over dense cloud and in heavy rain and snow squalls. The hull began to ice up and Stabbert had to drop ballast and jettison fuel. The weather cleared by about 01.00, and Stabbert found he was over Loch Ness, far north in the Highlands. He dropped his bombs on Craig Castle, near Rhynie, which he took to be a pit head; six bombs broke windows but caused no casualties. He attempted to fly south, but was drifting in the strong wind. He crossed the coast near Peterhead at about 02.40, and was spotted by a British trawler at 05.00 about 95 miles east of Aberdeen. In his report, he said he had requested a radio position at about 06.00, and was told he was near the Orkney Islands. Later in the morning, he saw a neutral ship, the *Holland*, and descended to 60ft to get an exact position. It was 58 degrees north, 3 degrees east: he was in the middle of the North Sea, between the Orkneys and southern Norway. He realized he had no chance of getting back to Germany, so decided to land in northern Denmark. However, he failed to do so due to the strong south-easterly wind. To add to his troubles, his mechanic told him two engines were about to break down. By 11.00 he had reached the coast of Norway near Stavanger. In fierce winds, he made a crash-landing near the beach, destroying *L.20* but saving the crew. Some scrambled ashore and others were rescued by fishing boats. This led to a strange legal situation in neutral Norway, as the crew rescued by boat – including Leutnant zur See Schirlitz, the Executive Officer – were classed as shipwrecked mariners and returned home. Those, including Stabbert, who scrambled ashore were classed as combatants and interned.

The story then gets even more like *Biggles*, as after seven months in captivity Stabbert escaped and returned to Germany. He was soon returned to active service. He got the latest Zeppelin, the 'height climber' *L.44*, in April 1917, aboard which he was to die.

'Q' type Navy Zeppelin *L.21*: Kapitänleutnant Max Dietrich, flying from Nordholz, caused most of the damage and all of the casualties that night. The raid caused £12,030 worth of damage, killed nine people and injured thirty. Dietrich crossed the Yorkshire coast north of Scarborough and flew directly for York. He dropped eighteen bombs at Dringhouses, which damaged houses and injured two soldiers. He reached York at 22.40, dropping sixteen bombs which killed nine people and injured twenty-seven. The streets bombed included Nunthorpe Avenue and Upper Price Street. We can identify three of the people killed: George Avison (70) of 13 Upper Price Street, York; Sarah Avison (69) of 13 Upper Price Street, York; and Emily Chapman (28) of Nunthorpe Avenue, York.

'Q' type Navy Zeppelin *L.23*: Kapitänleutnant Otto von Schubert, flying on his first raid out of Nordholz, was probably the first airship commander to cross the coast. It seems he thought he was over Middlesbrough when he dropped all his bombs on Danby High Moor, where the incendiaries set fire to the heather on the heath. *L.23* caused no casualties, and in fact probably saved a lot of people as three more Zeppelins were attracted by the fire and bombed the open moor.

'Q' type Army Zeppelin *LZ.98*: We have little information about this raid by Oberleutnant Ernest Lehmann. It seems *LZ.98* was sighted off the Lincolnshire coast but never came over land. H.A. Jones suggests in *The War in the Air* that the initial target was Manchester, but Lehmann gave up because of the weather. Lehmann, in his autobiography, explains that he was returning from the East Coast where he said he had intended bombing Hull, when *LZ.98* was struck by lightning: 'there was a blinding flash. Our control car was as light as day.' The Zeppelin fell from an altitude of about a mile to only a few hundred feet. After safely returning to Hanover, he checked for damage: there were three small spots on the covering, the largest the size of a pea. He recorded that 'the metal girder below the spot had melted, but that was all'.

3 May 1916

'N' type Army Zeppelin *Z.XII*: On the Eastern Front, this airship made a successful attack on a railway station at Luninietz.

4 May 1916

'M' type Navy Zeppelin *L.7*: Kapitänleutnant Karl Hempel, with Oberleutnant zur See Friedrich Wenke as second officer, was in *L.7*, an obsolete airship no longer suitable for bombing raids. They had left Tondern on a scouting mission, sighting two British light cruisers, HMS *Galatea* and HMS *Phaeton*, just off the coast of Sylt near the Horns Reef lightship. Hempel, flying at low altitude, attempted to keep a safe distance, but anti-aircraft fire hit a fuel tank and the airship fell blazing into the sea. Seven members of the crew were lucky, being rescued by a British submarine, but eleven, including Hempel, were killed. Lehmann tells the story differently, saying that *L.7* was shot down but did not burn, and radioed for help; a British submarine then attacked the Zeppelin floating helplessly in the water, gunfire setting it ablaze, and nine of the crew were killed with the rest captured.

5 May 1916

'R' type Army Zeppelin *LZ.85*: Oberleutnant Scherzer had previously bombed Salonika in January and March. He once again took off from Temesvar. As the major supply port for the Macedonian campaign, Salonika was better defended and on his third raid on the city *LZ.85* was caught by searchlights and hit by anti-aircraft fire, which damaged many gas cells and caused the framework of the hull to buckle. The airship came down in the Vardar Marshes, not far from Salonika. The crew survived uninjured, but after attempting to walk to Bulgarian lines were all captured by French forces.

27 July 1916

'E' type Army Schutte-Lanz *SL.X*: Hauptman Richard von Wobester took off from Jamboli in Bulgaria to bomb Sevastopol. He did not bomb the city or return to base: the fate of Wobester, his crew and *SL.X* is unknown; presumably they all perished in the Black Sea. There is no more information, although fragments of burnt plywood were found months afterwards in the area, probably from the frame of the airship. It apparently burnt in the air, possibly struck by lightning.

29 July 1916

It seems that ten Navy Zeppelins set out, but only six reached the English coast. There was fog at sea and thick ground mist, and the Zeppelins who reached England only went a short distance inland into Yorkshire, Lincolnshire, Norfolk and Suffolk. Records show that sixty-nine bombs were dropped, but the only damage was a haystack set on fire and some cattle killed. There were no human injuries and only £257 worth of damage caused.

'P' type Navy Zeppelin *L.11*: Leutnant zur See Otto Mieth set out from Nordholz.

'P' type Navy Zeppelin *L.13*: The only information on individual airships is that of Kapitänleutnant Eduard Prolss, flying from Hage, which crossed the Lincolnshire coast at North Somercotes at 00.37. He then made for Lincoln and dropped two bombs at Fiskerton, east of the city. Prolss then turned towards Nottingham and circled east of Newark, dropping bombs on villages in the area without damage, and headed towards the coast. *L.13* went out to sea over the Wash and was heard to drop a bomb near Cromer Lighthouse.

'P' type Navy Zeppelin *L.16*: Kapitänleutnant Erich Sommerfeld flew from Hage.

'P' type Navy Zeppelin *L.17*: Kapitänleutnant Herbert Ehrlich took off from Nordholz.

'Q' type Navy Zeppelin *L.24*: Kapitänleutnant Robert Koch flew out of Tondern.

'R' type Navy Zeppelin *L.31*: Kapitänleutnant Heinrich Mathy flew from Nordholz.

31 July/1 August 1916

Ten naval Zeppelins set out from their bases in Germany, and a number were spotted over the Heligoland Bight in the afternoon. Peter Strasser had again planned an intensive campaign, with many raids over several days, but this raid was to be largely ineffective. When the airships set out against London and England South, low cloud and fog restricted their bombing. No injuries were caused and only £139 worth of damage. Two Zeppelins - *L.21* and *L.30* - turned back before they reached the coast. Four were spotted by the British trawler *Adelaide* at 20.30, about 50 miles from the mouth of the Humber. Weather conditions were very poor, and we have few records of individual airships. It seems most attacked Norfolk, Suffolk and the Isle of Ely. Fifty-seven HE and forty-six incendiary bombs were recorded.

'P' type Navy Zeppelin *L.11*: Korvettenkapitan Victor Schutze flew from Nordholz.

'P' type Navy Zeppelin *L.13*: Kapitänleutnant Eduard Prolss flew from Hage.

'P' type Navy Zeppelin *L.14*: Hauptmann Kuno Manger flew from Hage.

'P' type Navy Zeppelin *L.16*: Kapitänleutnant Erich Sommerfeld set out from Hage.

'P' type Navy Zeppelin *L.17*: Kapitänleutnant Herbert Ehrlich flew from Nordholz. It was recorded that L.17 bombed Mattishall near Norwich, causing no damage.

'Q' type Navy Zeppelin *L.21*: Hauptmann August Stelling, another Army officer in a naval airship, flew out from Nordholz but returned before reaching the coast.

'Q' type Navy Zeppelin *L.22*: Kapitänleutnant Martin Dietrich flew out from Tondern.

'Q' type Navy Zeppelin *L.23*: Kapitänleutnant Otto von Schubert set out from Nordholz.

'R' type Navy Zeppelin *L.30*: Kapitänleutnant Horst von Buttlar, flying out from Nordholz, returned without crossing the English coast.

'R' type Navy Zeppelin *L.31*: Kapitänleutnant Heinrich Mathy took off from Nordholz. He had taken command of the new 'R' type *L.31* on 14 July and was recorded as reaching the Kent coast, dropping bombs off Ramsgate and Sandwich.

2/3 August 1916

This was a raid by six Navy Zeppelins. All airships except *L.31* passed over the coast of East Anglia between 23.45 and 01.00. None ventured far inland. The raid was largely ineffective, with only one person injured and £796 worth of damage done.

'P' type Navy Zeppelin *L.11*: Korvettenkapitan Viktor Schutze took off from Nordholz. He was recorded as circling the defences of Harwich for twenty minutes while under fire. Thirteen of his bombs were traced; one injured a boy at Kirton, while others damaged some cottages.

'P' type Navy Zeppelin *L.13*: Kapitänleutnant Eduard Prolss, flying from Hage, got as far as Wymondham, south-west of Norwich.

'P' type Navy Zeppelin *L.16*: Kapitänleutnant Erich Sommerfeld flew from Hage.

'P' type Navy Zeppelin *L.17*: Kapitänleutnant Herbert Ehrlich, flying from Nordholz, is recorded as reaching Eye, near Diss, Suffolk.

'Q' type Navy Zeppelin *L.21*: Hauptmann August Stelling, flying out from Nordholz, was recorded over Thetford.

'R' type Navy Zeppelin *L.31*: Kapitänleutnant Heinrich Mathy, flying from Nordholz, set out to bomb London. Because of heavy cloud, it seems he thought he had done so, but British records show he only briefly crossed the coast of Kent, dropping all his bombs in the sea off Dover.

8/9 August 1916

This was a raid by ten Navy Zeppelins. It was a much more effective raid, resulting in ten people being killed, many injured and £13,196 worth of damage. Most of the damage occurred in Hull. It was difficult to identify many of the individual Zeppelins because of the foggy conditions.

'P' type Navy Zeppelin *L.11*: Korvettenkapitan Viktor Schutze flew out from Nordholz.

'P' type Navy Zeppelin *L.13*: Kapitänleutnant Eduard Prolss flew out from Hage.

'P' type Navy Zeppelin *L.14*: Hauptmann Kuno Manger, flying from Hage, was an Army officer who had spent most of his career in command of Navy airships, and had recently taken command of *L.14*, Bocker's old airship. He was recorded as crossing the coast south of Berwick-upon-Tweed at 00.25, then made a sweep inland, dropped his bombs, only eight of which were traced. Manger went back out to sea at Alnwick.

'P' type Navy Zeppelin *L.16*: Kapitänleutnant Erich Sommerfeld, flying from Hage, was apparently briefly spotted over Hunstanton in Norfolk at about 01.00. It appears it was difficult to identify other airships that made landfall between Tynemouth and Flamborough Head at different times between 00.15 and 02.00.

'P' type Navy Zeppelin *L.17*: Kapitänleutnant Herbert Ehrlich, flying from Nordholz, was attacked by British armed trawler HMS *Itonian* with a single 6-pdr gun. Ehrlich jettisoned all his bombs in the sea, but missed the trawler. It appears that he was flying with *L.23* at the time.

'Q' type Navy Zeppelin *L.24*: Kapitänleutnant Robert Koch flew out of Tondern. Most of the damage in the raid was caused by *L.24*, with ten people killed and eleven injured in Hull. We have the names of some of the August 1916 victims in Hull, in what was known locally as the Selby Street raid: Mary Louise Bearpark (44) of 35 Selby Street, Hull; Emmie Bearpark (14) of 35 Selby Street, Hull; John Charles Broadley (3) of 4 Rowlands Avenue, Hull; Rose Alma Hall (31) of 61 Selby Street, Hull; Elizabeth Hall (9) of 61 Selby Street, Hull; Mary Hall (7) of 61 Selby Street, Hull; Charles Lingard

(64) of 61 Walliker Street, Hull; Emma Louise Evers (46) of 25 Brunswick Avenue, Walliker Street, Hull; Esther Stobbart (31) of 13 Henry's Terrace, Wassand Street, Hull; and the Rev Arthur Wilcockson (86) of 32 Granville Street, Hull.

The following people are reported to have died of shock: June Booth (51) of 2 Alma Street, Hull; William Clarkson (62) of 2 Adderby Grove, Hull; William Jones (80) of The Almshouses, Posterngate, Hull; Sarah Masterman (58) of 9 Humber Avenue, Hull; and Jessie Mathews (11) of Cotton Terrace, Barnsley Street, Hull.

'R' type Navy Zeppelin *L.30*: Kapitanleutnamt Horst von Buttlar set out from Nordholz. The new 'R' type super Zeppelins *L.30* and *L.31* targeted London. Von Buttlar in *L.30* had been involved in some of the testing and development work on the 'R' series, taking part in scouting missions from 5 July. His first raid was on 8 August; we have few details of his flight, but it seems he turned back because of the weather.

'R' type Navy Zeppelin *L.31*: Kapitänleutnant Heinrich Mathy flew from Nordholz. This was Mathy's third raid in *L31* in just over a week. He turned back because of the weather in the first two raids, on 31 July and 2 August. Mathy claimed in his combat report to have bombed London, but realized his mistake. He wrote of the three raids that they show 'it is dangerous to fly for long periods at night, and over solid cloud ceilings, because winds that cannot be estimated and which are often very strong can produce significant and even serious drift errors unless wireless bearings are used freely'. The comment shows how Mathy was analyzing and passing on his experience. He knew how difficult it was to navigate over clouds, yet still overestimated the usefulness and underestimated the danger of wireless bearings.

23/24 August 1916

'Q' type Army Zeppelin *LZ.97*: British reports show *LZ.97* flew in over Belgium. The airship dropped thirty-four bombs near Trimley, Walton and Old Felixstowe in Suffolk, but they fell in open fields and caused no damage.

24/25 August 1916

This was a raid by eight Navy airships, although some again did not reach the coast. Using the longer period of daylight, the Royal Navy attempted to attack the Zeppelins before they reached the coast. They knew from radio signals that Zeppelins were in the air, and during the afternoon three light cruisers – HMS *Conquest*, HMS *Carysfort* and HMS *Canterbury* – accompanied by destroyers, steamed eastward to try and spot the Zeppelins in daylight.

'P' type Navy Zeppelin *L.13*: Kapitänleutnant Eduard Prolss, flying from Hage, was fired on by HMS *Conquest* and hit by an anti-aircraft shell. This passed through one gas bag, then exploded above the airship and damaged another gas bag. Luckily for Prolss and his crew, it did not cause a fire. He quickly turned back to Hage, dropping all his bombs and much of his fuel in the sea. He landed at Hage at 23.45.

'P' type Navy Zeppelin *L.14*: Hauptmann Kuno Manger, from Hage, encountered ships as early as 14.28, and because he was unable to outrun them, due to the wind, he turned back.

'P' type Navy Zeppelin L.16: Kapitänleutnant Erich Sommerfeld, flying from Hage, crossed the Suffolk coast very high above the clouds. He flew near Ipswich and dropped twenty bombs between Woodbridge and Bealing, causing no casualties.

'Q' type Navy Zeppelin L. 21: Oberleutnant zur See Kurt Frankenburg, flying from Nordholz, was previously Alois Bocker's executive officer but had command of his own ship, *L.21*, inherited from Max Dietrich. He claimed in his combat report to have bombed Harwich from 12,000ft in the face of heavy anti-aircraft fire. British records show he crossed the Essex coast at Frinton, and his bombs fell in the area of Great Oakley and Pewit Island. They narrowly missed the works of the Explosive and Chemical Company, only damaging some farm buildings.

'R' type Navy Zeppelin *L.31*: Kapitänleutnant Heinrich Mathy took off from Ahlhorn and reached London. Using mist to avoid searchlights, he reported bombing houses in south-east London. Records show he flew up the Thames to Canvey Island, then overland to Barking. He then went south to Millwall, where he bombed Deptford, Greenwich, Blackheath, Eltham and Plumstead. *L.31* dropped thirty-six HE and eight incendiary bombs, killing nine people and injuring forty, and damage was caused to the tune of £13,000. As he headed for home, *L.31* was caught by a searchlight at

Erith and fired on by anti-aircraft guns. Mathy crossed the Essex coast east of Shoeburyness. On the way home, the weather worsened and he made a heavy landing at Nordholz because of the weight of rain water on the envelope. *L.31* needed to have extensive repairs and was not airworthy again until 21 September 1916.

'R' type Navy Zeppelin *L.32*: Oberleutnant zur See Werner Peterson, flying from Nordholz, also had London as his target. He had been assigned to *L.32* on 7 August, And this was his first raid on England in the airship. He also had Korvettenkapitan Peter Strasser on board. Peterson got as far as Dover, came under anti-aircraft fire and dropped all his bombs in the sea. He claimed in his combat report to have bombed numerous ships, a hit on one causing a devastating explosion. The British Intelligence report does not bear this out; it says all his bombs fell in the sea off Dover, making a grand spectacle for watchers on the coast, throwing up fountains of water and spray. Peterson was followed out to sea by a fighter, but it lost him. He was later fired on by Dutch guns as he crossed the territory of neutral Holland, but got back to Nordholtz safely.

'E' type Navy Schutte-Lanz *SL.8*: Kapitänleutnant Guido Wolff, flying from Nordholz, reported he was fired on by two ships at 22.00. They did not use searchlights as the night was so clear. *SL.8* then had an engine failure, did not reach the coast and returned to base.

'E' type Navy Schutte-Lanz *SL.9*: Kapitänleutnant Richard Wolff, from Nordholz, reported that he had seen lights like those of a city through the clouds at 9,000ft. The British have no record of any bombs being dropped. *SL.9* suffered some damage in the raid, probably due to weather conditions. Upon its return to Nordholz, numerous breaks were found in the wooden hull girders and the airship was out of service until 5 September.

28 August 1916

'Q' type Army Zeppelin *LZ.101*: Army airships were active on the Rumanian Front after Rumania declared war on the Axis in August 1916. The Army erected another base at Jamboli, Bulgaria. Zeppelin *LZ.101* moved there early in August, and under Hauptman Gaissert attacked Bucharest from there on 28 August. He attacked the city again on 4 and 25 September 1916.

Chapter Nine

A dangerous Autumn: September to December 1916

In the West, the stalemate at Verdun and the Somme continued. Zeppelins had little involvement in these battles. In the East, Army airships continued to operate, and were increasingly used for tactical and strategic bombing of cities and supply lines in Russia and the Balkans. The German Army had airship sheds in Hungary and Bulgaria, from where Zeppelins went to bomb targets in Greece, Serbia, Italy and Rumania.

Over England, the air defence system worked magnificently. Five airships were shot down by aeroplanes, and another bought down by anti-aircraft fire. It was enough to end the use of Army airships in the strategic bombing of Britain, and forced the Navy to operate at much higher altitudes, where they were less effective. The cloud on the horizon was not a Zeppelin; on 28 November 1916, a LVG two-seat aeroplane bombed London, the first of many such attacks.

2/3 September 1916

This was a very large raid by twelve Navy airships and four Army airships. It seems there was a measure of coordination between the services. The target was England South, with London as the main target. As was normal, commanders had discretion to raid other nearer targets in the Midlands if prevented from reaching the main target. The GHQ report said weather conditions were favourable for an air raid. There was light rain over the north of England, with light winds. Four people were killed and more injured, but the raid was the beginning of the end for the Zeppelins. It is ironic that the first airship to be shot down over London was not a Zeppelin, but Schutte-Lanz *SL.11*.

'P' type Navy Zeppelin *L.11*: Korvettenkapitan Viktor Schutze left Hage at 13.25. The weather was bad over the North Sea, and Schutze was delayed by heavy rain and hail, with damage to the covering of the Zeppelin having to be repaired in-flight. *L.11* crossed the English coast at Yarmouth at 21.18,

ppelin *L.3*: We have reasonably good records of *L.3*, the first Zeppelin to bomb England on anuary 1915. This is a clear photograph, from a postcard. *L.3* was a very poor weapon as it s easy to shoot down and unable to cope with bad weather. (*Wikimedia*)

ppelin *L.3*: Note the open gondolas; this was soon rectified in later models, as during nbing raids crew spent up to twenty-four hours in the open, over the North Sea. It was not asant in January. (*Wikimedia*)

Marine Luftschiff L

(*Left*) **Terror bombing:** This is a postcard sold just after the Janua[?] 1915 raid, claiming to show the first house to be bombed at Grea[?] Yarmouth. The bombs were dropped by Zeppelin *L.3*. (*Postca[?] from 1915. Public domain*)

(*Below*) **Zeppelin *L.3*:** This was unable to cope with bad weather[?] The airship crashed in a gale at Fano Island, Denmark, and the crew were interned. (*Wikimedia*)

Ruiner af Zeppelineren. L.3. paa Fanø Strand.

Længde 160 M.
Diameter 17 M.
Egenvægt 28000 kg.
4 Benzinmotorer ialt 720 HK.
4 Mahognipropeller à 5 M. Diameter
Nedstyrtningsdato 17 Februar 1915.

(*above*) **Zeppelin LZ.39:**
Zeppelins operated in the East as well as the West. This crashed airship is probably the 'P' type Army machine LZ.39, which crashed at Lyck in German/Austrian-held Poland on 18 December 1915. The picture shows the internal structure in some detail. Also note that the soldiers around the wreck are not German but from the Austro-Hungarian Army. (*Wikimedia*)

(*right*) **Fregattenkapitän Peter Strasser:** The leader of the German Naval Airship Service. (*Wikimedia*)

A Zeppelin bomb release mechanism: The release mechanism, which holds the ring on t
tail of the bomb, can be seen. The bomb is released by the electrical mechanism on the to
opening the release when triggered by the bomb aimer in the command gondola in the fro
of the airship. (*Picture by Derek Powis, from example in RAF Museum*)

The receiving en
109 Shobnall Stre
Burton-on-Trent.
Three people
were killed here
on 31 January
1916. (*Picture fro*
Wolverhampton
Express and Star
originally appeare
in a number of
newspapers in 191

(*right*) **The Zeppelin Menace:**
In two consecutive air raids
on London, on 13/14 October
1915, and the Midlands, on
31 January/1 February 1916,
101 people were killed. The
Germans introduced an improved
type of Zeppelin, the 'Q' type,
which was 585ft long. In this house
in Tipton, near Dudley, three
generations of the Greensill family
were killed. Mary Greensill was
the mother of Sarah Jane Morris
and grandmother of Martin and
Nellie Morris. Along with William
Greensill, they were all killed at
3 Court, 8 Union Street, Tipton, the
Greensills' house. The oldest was
44 and the youngest just 8. (*Picture
from* Wolverhampton Express and
Star, *used in newspapers in 1916*)

(*below*) **London:** The centre of
London was not immune from
bombing. Though it was well
defended, the capital was easy to
find and bombed more often than
any other city. A bomb dropped
from Zeppelin *L.15* on 13 October
1915 hit Lincoln's Inn Chapel. The
shrapnel damage can be seen 100
years later. (*Picture by Derek Powis*)

THE ROUND STONE IN THE ROADWAY
OPPOSITE THIS POINT MARKS THE SPOT
WHERE, ON WEDNESDAY THE 13TH OCTOBER
1915, AT 9-25 P.M. A BOMB FROM A
GERMAN ZEPPELIN STRUCK THE GROUND
AND EXPLODED, SHATTERING THE
CHAPEL WINDOWS AND DOING OTHER
MATERIAL DAMAGE.

(*Left*) **The silent witness:** The Dolphin public house in Red Lion Street, Holborn, w
bombed by Zeppelin *L.13*, commanded by Heinrich Mathy, on 13 September 1915. The fro
was blown off the pub, and a man outside killed by shrapnel. This clock was the bar cloc
it stopped at 22.59, damaged by the bomb, and has been on display ever since, althoug
over the years the minutes hand has slipped. (*Picture by Derek Powis, courtesy of Dolphin In
Red Lion Street, Holborn, London*)

(*Right*) **Blinker Hall:** Admiral Sir Reginald Hall was probably the one man most responsible f
the defeat of the Zeppelins. An intelligent intelligence officer, he took over the Naval Intelligen
Service and built teams able to break German codes and build a workable radio location syste
A typical English eccentric with extreme right-wing views, he was still able to bring togeth
teams of people able to think outside the box, despite a stifling military hierarchy. (*Wikimedia*)

Zeppelin L.30: This was the first of the 'R' series Zeppelins. Commanded by Kapitänleutna
Horst von Buttlar, it went into service in May 1916. Parts of the engine gondola still survi
and can be seen at the Brussels Military Museum. Zeppelin development was very rapid
mid-1916. Called by the British the Super Zeppelin, the 'R' series were introduced just as tł
British perfected the techniques of tracking airships and developed incendiary ammuniti
to shoot them down. The Germans lost four 'R' type airships in the autumn of 1916: *L.32* a
L.33 on 22/23 September, *L.31* on 1 October and *L.34* on 27 November. (*Wikimedia*)

(*right*) **Kapitänleutnant Horst Treusch von Buttlar-Brandenfels (1888–1962):** Buttlar was the longest-serving Zeppelin commander. Described by the British as very cautious, he survived the war and was awarded the *Pour le Mérite* (Blue Max). He was the author of *Zeppeline gegen England*, translated in 1931 as *Zeppelins over England*. (*Picture public domain, on Tonder Zeppelin Museum website*)

(*below*) **Fokker Fodder:** This very new B.E.2c was unlikely to stay in that condition for long. The picture shows an unarmed observation aeroplane. Described by Pemberton Billings as 'Fokker Fodder', the B.E.2c was the standard RFC observation aircraft; it was virtually defenceless and was shot out of the sky over the Western Front. As a night fighter it was very successful, most airships shot down over England falling to pilots flying them. (*Wikimedia*)

The Lewis Gun on a Foster Mount: This picture shows how the pilot could pull the gun towards himself to change the magazine, and how the gun could be angled to fire forwards and upwards. The aeroplane is an S.E.5a, but Foster Mounts were also used on B.E.2 aircraft. The wire coming out of the gun is the Bowden cable (like a bicycle brake cable) which connects the trigger mechanism on the gun with the firing mechanism on the control stick. (*Wikimedia, taken by Second Lieutenant David McLennan in 1918*)

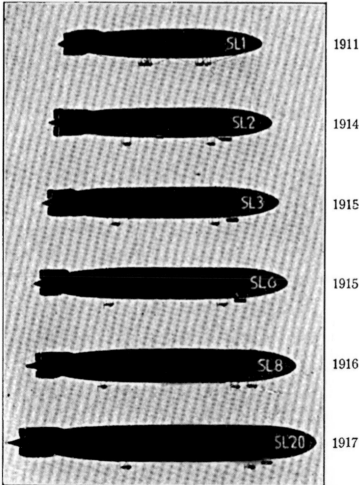

SL1 — 1911

SL2 — 1914

SL3 — 1915

SL6 — 1915

SL8 — 1916

SL20 — 1917

The Schutte Lanz Company: They produced wooden framed airships in competition with the Zeppelin Company. This drawing shows how they developed during the war (*Wikimedia*)

William Leefe Robinson: Robinson shot down the first airship over England. It was not a Zeppelin, but a Schutte Lanz, SL 11, flown by Hauptman Wilhelm Schramm of the German Army. Ironically, Schramm was born in London when his father worked for the Siemens company; he also died there, over Cuffley, on 3 September 1916, shot down by Lieutenant William Leefe Robinson of 39 Squadron RFC. Robinson was awarded the Victoria Cross and became a national hero. (*Wikimedia*)

Zeppelin *L.34*: It is unclear whether this widely circulated postcard was genuine, much retouched, or a complete fake. The latter is more likely, as the shape of the hull above the gondolas is like that of an early model Zeppelin. *L.34* was shot down over Hartlepool on 27 November 1916; its commander, Kapitänleutnant Max Dietrich, was killed on his 46th birthday. (*Wikimedia, from a postcard issued in 1916*)

LE RAID MALHEUREUX DES TREIZE SUPERZEPPELIN

13 ZEPPELINS SE SONT DIRIGÉS
SUR L'ANGLETERRE

3 SEULEMENT SONT RENTRÉS
DIRECTEMENT

ANGLETERRE

Norwich

Londres

Dunkerque

ALLEMAGNE

3 Seraient rentrés par l'Est de la France

Cherbourg

Le Hâvre

le L 44 abattu en flammes à Chenevières

Luneville

le L 50 a pris terre à Dammartin pour repartir

Paris

Brest

le L 49 descendu à Bourbonne-les-Bains

2 Seraient rentrés en Allemagne par Pontarlier

Nantes

SUISSE

Lyon

ITALIE

Bordeaux

Grenoble

Gap

le L 45 descendu à Mison près Sisteron son équipage l'incendie

Sisteron

Toulouse

Freju

Marseille

Toulon

ESPAGNE

le L.. désemparé perdu en Méditerranée

MER MEDITERRANÉ

The Silent Raid: By 1917, the British were able to shoot down most airships over Britain. T
Germans responded with a new type of Zeppelin, the 'Height Climber'. They could oper
at 20,000ft, but their use in a gale-force wind led to probably the worst night for the Germ
Naval Airship Service in the entire war, the so-called 'Silent raid' of 19/20 September 19
The French had a very different attitude to propaganda than Britain. Within a day or so
the raid, this front page not only gave details of the Zeppelins destroyed, but their routes a
where they landed. (*Wikimedia*)

CE QUI RESTE DU "L-45" QUI S'ÉCHOUA A MISON

— La carcasse du dirigeable qui s'abattit dans le lit desséché du Buech —

Parti de Tondern, dans le Schleswig-Holstein, mais privé d'essence, le "L-45", désemparé, suivit la vallée de la Saône, survola Lyon, traversa l'Isère et les Hautes-Alpes et vint s'abattre sur le territoire de Mison, dans le lit desséché d'un torrent appelé le Buech. L'équipage, composé de 17 hommes, mit le feu à l'enveloppe à l'aide de pistolets spéciaux chargés de balles incendiaires, puis se constitua prisonnier. Voici la carcasse du zeppelin que de très nombreux promeneurs sont venus visiter.

The Silent Raid: *L.45,* which was set on fire by its crew before capture at Sisteron in France. *(Wikimedia, taken from French newspaper* Le Miroir, *published 4 November 1917)*

(*Left*) **Zeppelin killer:** *L.34* was chased, a[nd] shot down, by a B.E.2c flown by this ma[n] Ian Vernon Pyott. (*Wikimedia*)

(*Below*) **Zeppelin L.49 Gondola:** This is an engine gondola from *L.49*, which crash-landed after the 'Silent Raid' at Bourbonne-Les-Baines, France. The crew of nineteen were all captured. (*Le Miroir* 4 November 1917)

ppelin L.49: French newspaper *Le Miroir* also published detailed pictures of other ppelins, including these of *L.49*. (Le Miroir, *4 November 1917*)

(*Above*) **Sopwith Camel No 6812:** This aeroplane flown by Lieutenant Stuart Cully, shot down Zeppelin *L.53*, having taken off from a lighter towed behind HMS *Redoubt*. The Sopwith Camel had to ditch in the sea but was undamaged. It has been preserved and can be seen at the Imperial War Museum in London. It is armed with the upward-firing Lewis guns used to shoot down Prloss and his crew. (*Photo Derek Powis*)

(*Left*) **Operations in the East:** German airships operated in the Baltic and the Mediterranean area. This is the airship shed at Jumboli, Bulgaria. (*Wikimedia*)

Zeppelin *L.59*: In November 1917, the German Navy planned a mission to East Africa to deliver supplies to the forces of General Lettow-Warbe. In the end the mission was recalled because the German's forces were in retreat, but the Zeppelin completed a flight of 4,200 miles, spending ninety-five hours in the air. This picture shows the crew. The commander, Kapitänleutnant Ludwig Bockholt, can be seen in the gondola window. All the men were killed during an attack on the British Fleet at Malta, when *L.59* exploded in the air near Brindisi, Italy. (*Wikimedia*)

Operation Albion: In October 1917, the German Army and Navy advanced through the Baltic States, taking advantage of the weakness of the Russian Army during the Revolution. This evocative picture shows a Zeppelin over a warship. (*Wikimedia, from Bundesarchiv Bild 146-1971-017-32*)

An important milestone in the defeat of the Zeppelin: This milestone in Victoria Park, Widnes, was damaged as a result of the last Zeppelin bombs to fall on Britain; they were dropped on 12 April 1918 from Zeppelin *L.61*, commanded by Kapitanleutnant Herbert Ehrlich. The milestone was on the Warrington to Prescott road at Bold near Widnes. Ehrlich dropped two bombs there, damaging the milestone. He then went north to Wigan, killing seven people, the last to die in a Zeppelin raid on England in the Great War. (*Picture courtesy Stephen Wainwright, Sutton Beauty & Heritage*)

The Ilkeston Memorial Plaqu
From 2015 many towns held ceremonies to commemorate the centenary of the Zeppelin raids. This plaque was erected by Steve Flinders of the Ilkest Local History Society to mark the bombing on the 31 Januar 1916. Steve is on the left, the man on the right is Fred Wils(the nephew of Walter Wilson, killed exactly 100 years before by Zeppelin L.20. There is a picture of Walter Wilson in m previous book *Zeppelins over t Midlands*. (*Picture courtesy of t Ilkeston Local History Society*)

(*Left*)**St Bartholomew's Church, Ilkeston:** This picture was taken in the same place exac 100 years before the plaque was erected. These gentlemen, with impressive mustach are inspecting damage to the church on the morning of 1 February 1916, after the ra (*Picture courtesy of the Ilkeston local History Society*)

(*Right*) **Monument in Nordholz:** This is a monument to Zeppelin crews lost in action Aeronauticam, the German Naval Air Service Museum at Nordholz. (*Photo Mick Powis*)

from where Schutze flew south and correctly identified Harwich. He moved off-shore and waited until 01.30 to attack the naval base. However, all his bombs missed and caused no damage. He had seen the demise of *SL.11* from near Harwich, and reported: '02.15 enormous flame over London, slowly sinking below cloud horizon, gradually diminishing. Burning airship.' He returned to Hage at 07.55.

'P' type Navy Zeppelin *L.13*: Kapitänleutnant Eduard Prolss left Hage at 13.30. Because of adverse winds he decided to go to the Midlands and raid Nottingham. He claimed to have bombed a brightly lit row of factories. Several fires broke out and the Zeppelin, at 9,500ft, was lit up as bright as day. While this sounds exaggerated, it may well be true. GHQ reports show *L.13* crossed the Lincolnshire coast at Cleethorpes at 22.56, bombing Humberstone at 00.10 with one incendiary and five HE bombs. At East Stockwith, two cottages were destroyed. The main attack was made on East Retford, 27 miles from Nottingham, at 00.56. Prolss dropped fifteen HE and four incendiary bombs. The town was blacked out but the railway well-lit. One of *L.13*'s bombs hit a gas holder at the town gas works, and a total of three gas holders were set alight, probably causing the biggest fire of any Zeppelin attack. One woman died of shock. Prolss then turned for home, dropping another bomb south of Gainsborough at 01.05 and crossing the coast at Donna Nook at 01.30. He returned to Hage at 07.30.

'P' type Navy Zeppelin *L.14*: Hauptmann Kuno Manger left Hage at 13.47. In his combat report, Manger claimed to have dropped six bombs on Boston at 21.45 and then turned south and bombed north London with sixteen HE and twenty incendiary bombs at 01.15. The British GHQ report said *L.14* had crossed the Norfolk coast at Wells-next-the-Sea at 20.50, then witnessed the fall of *SL.11* near Thaxted about 35 miles from London. It seems Manger dropped most of his bombs on Haughley, as he made for the coast and went out to sea over Bacton at 03.05, returning to Hage at 09.33.

'P' type Navy Zeppelin *L.16*: Kapitänleutnant Erich Sommerfeld left Hage at 14.00. He crossed the coast at Sheringham at 21.40, dropping bombs on a locomotive 10 miles south-west of Norwich. These fell on Kimberley Station, on the Great Eastern Railway. Sommerfeld said he saw the searchlights of London from more than 50 miles away, counted more than forty of them. He was targeted by the Essenden searchlights, 15 miles north of London, which he bombed at 02.20. The village was badly damaged. One woman - a telephone operator - and a child were killed. Sommerfeld said he saw the destruction of *SL.11* at 02.25; at that he headed full speed for the coast. He dropped one HE bomb at Aston in Hertfordshire at 02.35, was seen south of Baldock at 02.40 and near Cambridge at 02.50. As he neared the Norfolk coast at Raveningham, near Great Yarmouth, a blue navy cap was dropped or fell from the Zeppelin. *L.16* crossed the coast at Great Yarmouth at 04.20, returning to Hage at 08.34.

'**P**' **type Navy Zeppelin** *L.17*: Kapitänleutnant Hermann Kraushaar left Tondern at 12.00.Though Kraushaar claimed to have bombed Norwich and been hit by anti-aircraft fire, British reports indicate he turned back 30 miles off the Norfolk coast. As he returned to Tondern by 06.50, he obviously did not spend long over England, and the British found no sign of his bombs.

'**Q**' **type Navy Zeppelin** *L.21*: Oberleutnant zur See Kurt Frankenburg left Nordholz at 13.00. He crossed the coast at Mundsley in Norfolk at 22.20. He turned back to look for Norwich, but could not find it because of the efficient blackout. He was caught by four searchlights and fired on by guns, on which he dropped all his bombs. Frankenburg was over Sandringham, and the British thought he had deliberately tried to bomb the royal palace there. The British didn't realise the Kaiser had forbidden attacks on royal palaces, and Frankenburg bombed a decidedly military target. The anti-aircraft gunners claimed to have hit the Zeppelin, but there is no evidence they did. Frankenburg was near Hitchin when he too saw the destruction of *SL.11*, and described it as attacked by two clearly visible aeroplanes. He bombed Dodshill near Dersingham at 03.47, killing one woman and injuring two other people, with six houses seriously damaged. After this, Frankenburg had problems as *L.21* lost two engines, including one that powered the main radio, so he couldn't contact his base. He eventually returned to Nordholz at 15.52 after more than 26 hours in the air.

'**Q**' **type Navy Zeppelin** *L.22*: Kapitänleutnant Martin Dietrich left Tondern at 11.25. He had problems over the North Sea and had an engine faiure, and had to fly through snow squalls. This led him to abandon an attack on London and target Nottingham instead. Dietrich was totally lost when he crossed the English coast. He got contrary radio location positions from stations in Germany. Nordholz and Borkum told him he was near the Wash, but List informed him he was over the Humber. It seems in fact he was in the Humber area, as he was reported dropping seven HE and twenty incendiary bombs on Halton, on the south bank of the Humber Estuary. The British traced some bombs from him at Humberston. *L.22* returned to base at 10.40.

'Q' type Navy Zeppelin *L.23*: Kapitänleutnant Wilhelm Ganzel left Nordholz at 13.16. He also had problems with rain and hail, and couldn't reach a safe attack height for a raid on London. He decided to attack Norwich, and later claimed he did so, but the British reported that he bombed Boston in Lincolnshire, causing most of the casualties of the raid. He reached Boston at 22.54, where one man was killed and three people injured. He crossed the coast at Holbeach at 23.45, and then dropped the remainder of his bombs in the sea. He returned to Nordholz at 07.05.

'Q' type Navy Zeppelin *L.24*: Kapitänleutnant Robert Koch left Tondern at 11.45. He was slowed by heavy rain and snow; a heavy coating of snow on the Zeppelin caused him to decide not to attack London. He thought he had reached the Cambridge area before he turned back, aiming for Norwich. He reported he bombed a searchlight at Norwich at 23.40 and had reached Yarmouth when he again saw searchlights; he said he dropped the rest of his bombs on the lights, silenced a gun battery and hit the aerodrome, railway station and gas works. He returned to Tondern at 07.25.

'R' type Navy Zeppelin *L.30*: Kapitänleutnant Horst von Buttlar left Ahlhorn at 12.16. There is a distinct difference between Buttlar's combat report and British observations. Buttlar claimed to have bombed London. British observers spotted *L.30* crossing the coast near Lowestoft, then bombing villages and hamlets on the Norfolk-Suffolk border. Eight HE and twelve incendiary bombs fell on Bungay, nine HE and one incendiary bombs on Earsham, eight HE bombs on Ditchingham and four HE bombs on Broome. It seems Buttlar's bombs injured one man and badly damaged two farmhouses, killing two cows and injuring three others. Buttlar then turned for home near Lowestoft, and returned to Ahlhorn at about 07.13.

'R' type Navy Zeppelin *L.32*: Oberleutnant zur See Werner Peterson left Nordholz fairly late at 15.30. He crossed the Norfolk coast at Cromer and dropped a few bombs in Norfolk. He was over Tring in Hertfordshire at about 02.25 when he saw *SL.11* shot down about 20 miles away. He described the event: 'A great fire which shone out with a reddish–yellow light and lit the surroundings within a large radius and then fell to the ground slowly.'

After this his combat report and the British GHQ report differ substantially. Peterson claimed he went on to bomb London, but the GHQ report on him is very uncomplimentary. It seems a copy of Peterson's combat report was found intact in the wreckage of *L.32* after it was shot down on 23 September 1916. In it, Peterson claimed to have bombed Kensington, which the British knew was untrue. They say that after seeing the destruction of *SL.11*, Zeppelin *L.32* turned away from London. They infer that Peterson quite deliberately put misleading information in his report. He went on to bomb Hertford Heath in Hertfordshire, where he dropped five HE and eleven incendiary bombs, killing two horses, and at Great Amwell he dropped 16 HE and eight incendiary bombs, killing a pony. Peterson went to Ware, where he dropped his last two HE bombs, then headed for home, crossing the Suffolk coast at Corton. He arrived safely at Nordholz at about 09.40.

'E' type Navy Schutte-Lanz *SL.8*: Kapitänleutnant Guido Wolff, in the wooden framed Schutte-Lanz, left Nordholz at 13.00. He was flying over cloud near the maximum height of his airship at 8,200ft when he was observed by the British as crossing the Norfolk coast at Holkham at 22.05. It seems visibility improved as he saw the searchlights of London, and flew towards the capital. He reached Huntingdon when he saw the fall of *SL.11* and turned back, claiming to have dropped bombs on Norwich and Winterton. However, British records show he dropped his bombs over northern Norfolk. *SL.8* crossed the coast again near Holkham at 02.20 and reached Nordholz at 09.20.

'P-Q' type Army Zeppelin *LZ.90*: *LZ.90* left its base at Mannheim in the early afternoon and crossed the Essex coast at Frinton-on-Sea at 22.05. At 22.20 it was over Manningtree in Essex. The airship then started to deploy its sub-cloud car. This was a small streamlined bomb-shaped observation car, about 14ft long and 4ft deep, just big enough for an observer to lie in and report back to the commander by telephone. It was lowered by a winch on up to 5,000ft of cable below the Zeppelin. The idea was that the Zeppelin would remain above the clouds, while the car was lowered through the clouds to observe the target, being too small to be easily spotted. The car was found near Manningtree the next day; it appears that something went wrong with the winch, and the car, still attached to 5,000ft of cable, fell to earth. The winch was later jettisoned and had a mark which suggested the Zeppelin crew had tried to stop it by jamming an iron bar into the gears. There was no sign of any crew member. It seems likely no one was aboard when it fell, so it was probably being prepared for action and the fortunate observer was waiting to get in. The complete sub-cloud car still exists and can be seen at the Imperial War Museum in London. A sign describes its operation and states there was a lot of competition for the post of observer, as it was the only place on a Zeppelin that smoking was permitted. The health risks of smoking were probably the least of anyone's worries in a Zeppelin. *LZ.90* flew on to Haverhill, where it dropped six bombs, and went out to sea north of Yarmouth at 00.45.

'P-Q' type Army Zeppelin *LZ.97*: It appears *LZ.97*, most likely commanded by Hauptman Erich Linnarz, returned early to base at Darmstadt. British reports show it turned back about 20 miles off The Naze headland on the Essex coast because of heavy rain squalls.

'Q' type Army Zeppelin *LZ.98*: Oberleutnant der Reserve Ernst Lehmann took off from Wildeshausen at midday. He took a route over Belgium and crossed the English coast near Dungeness in Kent at about 23.00. He reached the Thames near Gravesend and came under heavy anti-aircraft fire from guns at Tilbury and Dartford. He dropped all his bombs on the guns, and flew north-east to the coast at 13,800ft. It appears he did this to escape the attention of a British aeroplane, a B.E.2c flown by Second Lieutenant William Leefe Robinson. Lehmann fled into the clouds before the pilot could attack. He may have had problems on the way back, because he landed at Ahlhorn at 10.00 the next day after twenty hours in the air.

'E' type Army Schutte-Lanz *SL.11*: (Note the Army service number of Hauptman Wilhelm Schramm's airship was *SL.XI*; the works number was *SL.11*.) It is ironic that the first airship shot down over England was not a Zeppelin but a Schutte-Lanz. *SL.11* was roughly the same size as a 'Q' class Zeppelin such as *L.21*, and it looked much the same, but the major difference was under the skin: it had a wooden rather than duralumin airframe. Wilhelm Schramm was 34 years old, a professional soldier. He had been born in London when his father worked there for the Siemens Company, and was to die at Cuffley, Hertfordshire, only a few miles from his birthplace. *SL.11* left its base at Spich near Cologne on the afternoon of 2 September with a crew of sixteen. The airships taking part in the raid were tracked when they left their bases and as they flew towards London. A number of fighter planes took off to intercept them, and the raiders were also met by searchlights and anti-aircraft fire. Lieutenant William Leefe Robinson, of 39 Squadron RFC, took off from Suttons Farm at about 23.08. He flew over London for more than three hours, sighting at least one other airship. He saw *SL.11* caught in a searchlight beam flying about 12,000ft over north-east London. Robinson flew between 500-800ft below the airship and fired three magazines loaded with Brock and Pomeroy ammunition into its belly. He reported that the hull started to glow, and within seconds the whole rear was blazing. Robinson then returned to base, almost out of petrol, at 02.45. The blazing *SL.11* was seen by thousands of people from all over London as it fell to earth near Cuffley. All crew members were killed. The wreckage became a major attraction, and in the next few days tens of thousands of people visited the crash site. Special trains were put on to cope with the numbers wishing to see the wreckage.

William Leefe Robinson was a national hero, and was awarded the Victoria Cross. In a macabre publicity stunt, he also received reward money of several thousand pounds mainly raised by national newspapers, promised to the first man to shoot down a Zeppelin. The same newspapers – who initially announced the downed airship was the *L.21*, as on the night the authorities had thought they had been tracking that Zeppelin – had headlines in the next few days campaigning against the 'Zeppelin baby killer' crew being given a military funeral. British pilots voiced their disgust at this attitude, and the crew were given a military escort at their funeral. In 1964, their bodies were moved and buried with other airship crews in a special plot at Cannock German Military Cemetery.

For some time after the destruction of *SL.11*, the British claimed it had been destroyed by bombs. This was both for military reasons, as they did not want to let the Germans know they had developed workable incendiary ammunition, and probably for political reasons, as there was still concern about the legality of incendiary bullets under the Hague Convention.

Much of the rest of the brief life of William Leefe Robinson was tragic. During the remainder of 1916 he was paraded on a string of official engagements. He returned to flying duty in February 1917, promoted to captain, and joined No. 48 Squadron equipped with the Bristol F2A, better known as the Bristol Fighter. Although he was a squadron commander and obviously a good pilot, his only experience on the Western Front had been two years previously as an observer. On his first operation on 5 April 1917, he was shot down by a member of the Von Richthofen Jasta and captured. He made a number of attempts to escape from a PoW camp at Friburg, on one occasion getting within a few miles of the Swiss border. He was convicted of bribing a guard and sentenced to a month in prison at Zorndorf, on the Oder. He was then returned to PoW camps, first at Clausthal and then Holzminden in the

Herz Mountains. The camps were commanded by twin brothers Henrich and Karl Niemeyer, who went out of their way to treat Robinson with great cruelty. When he was repatriated at the Armistice, Robinson was sick and

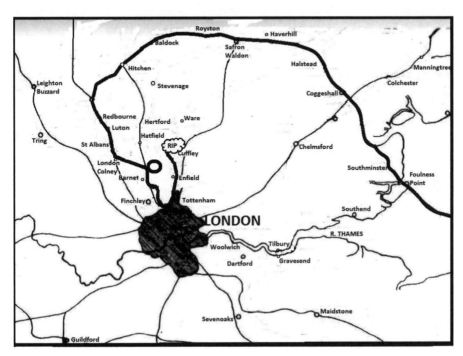

Map 6: The route of Schutte-Lanze Army Airship *S.L.11* (*S.L.XI*) commanded by Hauptman Wilhelm Schramm. Shot down 2/3 September 1916

22.10 Crossed coast at Foulness Point
22.20 Southminster
22.55 Crossed Blackwater River
23.05 Tiptree
23.10 Coggeshall
23.15 Halstead
22.20 Castle Hedlington
23.35 south of Haverhill
23.50 Near Saffron Waldon
00.30 Royston
00.35 Baldock
00.40 Hitchin
00.55 Luton
01.05 Redbourne
01.10 St Albans
01.20 London Colney
01.25 North Mimms

01.28 Littleheath
01.30 Northaw
01.35 Clayhill
01.40 Cockfosters
01.45 Hadley Wood
01.50 Southgate
01.58 Alexander Palace
02.00 Tottenham
02.12 Edmonton
02.14 Ponders End
02.17 Forty Hill and Turkey
02.23 Shot down near Cuffley
I take the times and place names from the GHQ report. Air Raids 2/3 Sept 1916. Some of the place names have changed as villages became suburbs and part of London Boroughs.

almost certainly suffering from post-traumatic stress because of his treatment by the twins. He only spent a few days with his fiancée and family in December 1918 before catching Spanish flu, one of the millions to die in the great pandemic. While he died from influenza, aged 23, it is possible he would have survived had he been treated properly as a PoW.

3/4 September 1917

'P-Q' type Army Zeppelin *LZ.86*: Oberleutnant Wolff bombed the city and oilfield at Ploesti in Romania on 3 September, then bombed Bucharest the next day. However, the airship crashed on landing back at Temesvar in high winds on 4 September, killing nine members of the crew including Wolff.

'Q' type Army Zeppelin LZ.101: Hauptmann Gaissert also bombed Bucharest from his base at Jamboli in Bulgaria. He went on to bomb the railway junction at Ploesti later in the month.

16 September 1916

The Navy lost two more Zeppelins in a maintenance accident. *L.6* and *L.9* had long since been relegated to training duties at Fuhlsbuttle. *L.6* was being topped up with hydrogen when there was an explosion and the Zeppelin burned rapidly, igniting L.9. Both airships were destroyed and the shed badly damaged. The cause of the fire remains unknown.

'M' type Navy Zeppelin *L.6*: Kapitänleutnant der Reserve Blew.

'M' type Navy Zeppelin *L.9*: Kapitänleutnant Hans Karl Gayer.

23/24 September 1916

This was a raid by twelve Navy Zeppelins. The smaller 'P' and 'Q' type ships were to raid England Middle, with the new 'R' class ships targeting London. The raid was very damaging for both sides: the Zeppelins killed forty people, injured 130 and caused £135,068 worth of damage, whilst the Germans lost two Zeppelins. Peterson in *L.32* was shot down and killed by a night fighter, but Bocker in *L.33* was more fortunate, being hit by anti-aircraft fire and captured.

GHQ reported that the weather was generally fair, with some mist or fog inland. There was just a light wind over the North Sea.

'P' type Navy Zeppelin *L.13*: Kapitänleutnant Franz Georg Eichler, who had recently taken command of *L.13*, left Hage at 13.23. He flew towards Sleaford in Lincolnshire, but was fired on by anti-aircraft guns and dropped all of his bombs. He returned at 07.08 the next day after more than eighteen hours airborne.

'P' type Navy Zeppelin L.14: Hauptmann Kuno Manger left Hage at 13.36. He bombed Lincoln and then the gun site at Cramwick, using forty-four bombs. He then turned back for the coast, and returned at 05.38 after more than sixteen hours in the air.

'P' type Navy Zeppelin *L.16*: Kapitänleutnant Erich Sommerfeld left Hage at 13.50, but appears to have had mechanical problems very early on in the mission as he returned to base at 00.52 after only eleven hours in the air.

'P' type Navy Zeppelin *L.17*: Kapitänleutnant Hermann Kraushaar left Tondern at 12.10. He had decided to bomb Sheffield, and thought he was near there when he saw fire belching from factory chimneys; he was in fact over Nottingham, and at about midnight he dropped eight HE and eleven incendiary bombs, damaging two railway stations and killing three people. There was considerable public anger at the failure of the rail companies to extinguish lights.

Kraushaar had taken over *L.17* from Herbert Ehrlich, and this was his second raid over England, his first having been on 2 September, when *SL.11* was shot down by William Leefe Robinson. On this occasion, on his way back home he was near Lincoln at about 01.00 when he reported seeing what he and his crew described as an evil omen: a burning airship. This must have been Zeppelin *L.32* with Werner Peterson and his crew. Kraushaar had seen the demise of *L.32* some 150 miles away above Billericay, where it crashed. Kraushaar got back to Tondern at 09.25 after almost twenty-two hours in the air. He was undoubtedly fearful of the future, and not without good reason as he too would die in a burning Zeppelin.

We have a record of the three people killed in Nottingham: Harold Taylor (1) of 3 Chancery Place, Broad March, Nottingham; Rosanna Rogers (43) of Newthorpe Street, Nottingham; and Alfred Taylor (59) of Newthorpe Street, Nottingham.

'Q' type Navy Zeppelin *L.21*: Oberleutnant zur See Kurt Frankenburg left Nordholz at 12.00. He had problems with *L.21* as he was unable to climb above 8,000ft. He was fired on by anti-aircraft guns near Stowmarket, dropped thirty-six bombs in open country in Suffolk and returned to Nordholz at 06.20.

'Q' type Navy Zeppelin *L.22*: Kapitänleutnant Martin Dietrich left Tondern at 12.25. Dietrich had trouble with radio bearings on this raid; he was unsure whether he was over the Wash, the Humber or Flamborough Head. He believed he had bombed Grimsby, and the British did find some bomb damage south-east of the town. He returned to Tondern at 06.15.

'Q' type Navy Zeppelin *L.23*: Kapitänleutnant Wilhelm Ganzel left Nordholz at 12.10. More than twelve hours later, at 00.20, *L.23* was near Lincoln. Ganzel recorded in his combat report that he saw a bright glow towards the mouth of the Thames and saw an airship falling in flames: it was Peterson in *L.32*, which Ganzel had seen burning from about 150 miles away. He turned for home, reaching Nordholz at 06.10.

'Q' type Navy Zeppelin *L.24*: Kapitänleutnant Robert Koch left Tondern fairly late, at 13.50. It seems he then had engine trouble over the sea, because he was back at Tondern by 21.35.

'R' type Navy Zeppelin *L.30*: Kapitanleutnat Horst von Buttlar left Ahlhorn at 12.40. Buttlar again claimed to have bombed London, though the British have no record of this. It is impossible to tell where *L.30* dropped its bombs, but it was almost certainly not near London. The GHQ Intelligence report says only that Zeppelin *L.30* reached Happisburgh in Norfolk and skirted the coast in its usual ineffective manner. Buttlar returned to Ahlhorn at 06.35 the next day.

'R' type Navy Zeppelin *L.31*: Kapitänleutnant Heinrich Mathy left Ahlhorn at 12.35 in his first raid since his heavy landing on 25 August. Mathy in *L.31* and Peterson in *L.32* flew towards London over occupied Belgium and the English Channel, rather than the normal North Sea route. Mathy reached London; there are detailed GHQ reports on the raid and the damage he did. The British thought Mathy was using a new technique; he was caught by searchlights over Croydon, but escaped them by dropping a parachute flare to dazzle the opposition. He bombed Brixton and Streatham, dropping a total of thirty-three HE and forty-one incendiary bombs, destroying a number of houses, shops and a tram. Six men and one woman were killed in Streatham, along with three men, three women and a child in Brixton, four men and one child in Leyton and two men and one woman in Lea Bridge. In all twenty-two people were killed and seventy-two injured. Mathy returned to Ahlhorn at 07.45 the next day.

Mathy witnessed the end of Peterson and *L.32*, believing he was shot down by anti-aircraft fire. His report, as quoted by D.H. Robinson in *The Zeppelin in Combat*, was unemotional: 'The ship was also heavily fired on, and after dropping her bombs appeared to have reached safety when additional searchlights opened up ahead of her and, after a brief very intense bombardment, the destruction followed, the ship fell in flames.'

Mathy returned to Ahlhorn at 07.45 the next morning.

'R' type Navy Zeppelin *L.32*: Oberleutnant zur See Werner Peterson left Ahlhorn at 13.10. Zeppelin *L.32* was spotted by the British when it crossed the Kent coast at Dungeness at 22.50, where it dropped six HE bombs. Peterson was also spotted at Tunbridge Wells at 00.10, reaching Ide Hill near Sevenoaks at 00.30 and dropping an incendiary bomb. He was caught by the searchlight at Crokenhall at 00.50 and dropped seven HE bombs, but only broke some windows. He crossed the Thames near Purfleet at about 01.00, and as he reached London he was fired on by a number of anti-aircraft guns – the battery at Tunnell Hill claimed definite hits. He dropped the rest of his bombs – twenty-three HE and twenty-one incendiary – over South Oakenden at about 01.05. As *L.32* crossed London it was much bothered by searchlights, which enabled Second Lieutenant Frederick Sowrey of 39 Squadron RFC to attack the airship in his B.E.2c at 01.10. Sowrey took off from Suttons Farm at 23.30, spotting a Zeppelin over Tilbury when he was flying at 13,000ft. With *L.32* well lit by searchlights, Sowrey used the tried and tested method of flying under the Zeppelin and firing upwards with his Lewis gun. It seems he sprayed bullets all along the hull, as it took three drums of ammunition loaded with a mixture of Brock, Pomeroy and tracer to set *L.32* on fire. He reported the first two drums seemed to have no effect, other than to cause the airship to wriggle and alter course, but the third drum made her envelope glow 'like a huge Chinese lantern' and catch fire. Sowrey watched the airship fall to the ground in flames. *L.32* crashed at Great Burstead, near Billericay in Essex. All twenty-two crew members were killed, and are now buried at Cannock Chase.

Peterson was one of the youngest commanders, but with more than sixty combat missions was regarded as one of the best ship handlers. The British in their GHQ Intelligence report described him as hesitant, but his loss along with that of Bocker on one night was a severe setback for the Airship Service.

Frederick Sowrey landed at 01.40. He and William Leefe Robinson drove to the wreckage of *L.32* in Robinson's Vauxhall Prince Henry car, bought with money donated by a national newspaper as a publicity stunt after Robinson shot down *SL.11*. Sowrey survived the war and served in the RAF during the Second World War, becoming a group captain. He was awarded the DSO and Military Cross, and died in 1968.

Among the first people at the crash site were members of the Naval Intelligence Service from Room 40, who found a copy of the still secret *Allgemeines Funkpruchbuch (AFB)* codebook, charred but readable, in the burned remains of the control gondola.

'R' type Navy Zeppelin *L.33*: Kapitänleutnant Alois Bocker left Nordholz at 12.24. Bocker had taken over the new Zeppelin *L.33* on 3 September. His first and last raid in the airship was on 23 September. As was normal, Bocker took most of the crew of *L.14* with him. However, the Executive Officer of *L.14*, Oberleutnant zur See Kurt Frankenburg, did not move with Bocker. He would soon be promoted to Kapitänleutnant, taking command of Zeppelin *L.21*, and had been replaced as Second Officer by Leutnant zur See Ernst Wilhelm Schirlitz, who had been Franz Stabbert's executive officer before the crash in Norway. Frankenburg would not live long to enjoy his promotion.

There are good records of the last flight of *L.33*. It had twenty-two crew members and left Nordholz at about 13.30. It was spotted flying above the Thames Estuary at 22.00 and was fired on by a destroyer at 22.12, but avoided damage. Bocker then went inland between Southminster and Burnham in Essex at 22.45, dropping an incendiary bomb at South Fombridge at 23.00 which caused no damage. He was spotted flying directly towards London, over Rayleigh at 23.05, south of Wickford at 23.20, west of Ingrave at 23.25 and over Billericay at 23.27. Now looking for targets, he dropped a flare south of Brentford at 23.35. Bocker dropped four incendiary bombs on Upminster Common at about 23.40, followed at about 23.50 by six HE bombs at South Hornchurch. Another flare was dropped at Chadwell Heath and *L.33* was picked up by a searchlight. Escaping its glare, the airship reached Wanstead at midnight. Heading towards East London, it came under steady anti-aircraft fire, being targeted by guns at West Ham, Victoria Park, Becton and Wanstead. A number of these batteries claimed to have hit *L.33*, but it is difficult to say which did so. It seems, however, that shrapnel damaged the Zeppelin, which began to lose gas.

It then flew over East London, dropping HE and incendiarybombs, killing six people in Bromley. The Black Swan public house in Bow was hit by a 100kg HE bomb which killed three women and two children. Bocker then turned towards Stratford, dropping more bombs. All this time he was still under anti-aircraft fire, and at about 00.15 witnesses on the ground said he appeared to be running badly and making a knocking noise. It seems that a shell had damaged one of the propellers, and *L.33* was also losing gas. The Zeppelin was again picked up by a searchlight at Kelvedon Common at 00.30, and attacked by an aeroplane, a B.E.2c piloted by Second Lieutenant Alfred de Bathe Brandon from Hainault Farm RFC field in Essex. The chase continued over Onger and south of Chelmsford. Bocker was very skilful, or lucky, as *L.33* was hit by several incendiary bullets; he managed to avoid the plane, but was in serious trouble because of loss of gas.

L.33's path became even easier to track as Bocker began to jettison cargo: Spare parts at Broomfield and machine guns at Boreham, Wickham Bishops and near Tiptree. He reached the Essex coast near West Mersea, but realizing he had only minutes left in the air, turned around and crash-landed at 01.20 in a field near Great Wigborough and Peldon. All the crew survived, but Bocker set the wreckage alight with a flare pistol. The crew were arrested by Special Constable Edgar Nicholas, and after a night guarded in Wigsborough Church Hall, were taken to London for days of interrogation by the redoubtable Major Trench and his team. Many captured Zeppelin crews seem to have held a lifelong resentment about their treatment during these interrogations, and a particular grudge about Major Trench, who was head of the German Section of Naval Intelligence. When as much intelligence as possible had been gathered by Trench, the crew went to PoW camps, with the officers sent to Donington Hall in Leicestershire, now the site of the Donington Park Motor Racing Circuit near East Midlands Airport. After two years in Donington Hall, Bocker was repatriated to Germany with the usual stipulation he would not serve in combat. He returned to Nordholz as Director of Airship Training, often flying his old ship *L.14*, which had been retained as a training machine. He saw out the war training airship crews, who no doubt appreciated the knowledge a very skilful and lucky commander could pass on to them.

25/26 September 1916

This was a raid by seven Navy Zeppelins. The Zeppelins attacked in two waves, the larger 'R' class ships raiding London and the south while the smaller 'P' and 'Q' class ships bombed the North. A number of places were attacked in the north of England: York, Bolton and Sheffield suffered heavy casualties, with forty-three killed and thirty-one injured, and £39,698 worth of damage. GHQ reported the weather was calm over the North Sea at the time of the raid. There was an increasing south-east wind on the east coast, but this died down to about 15mph after midnight.

'P' type Navy Zeppelin L.14: Hauptman Kuno Manger, flying out of Hage, claimed to have bombed Leeds, but he was in fact fired on by a gun at Collingham, 10 miles away. GHQ reports Manger flew near York and was caught by a searchlight at Acomb. He then turned north and dropped forty-three bombs without causing any casualties.

'Q' type Navy Zeppelin L.21: Oberleutnant zur See Kurt Frankenburg from Nordholz claimed to have bombed Derby, but British records show his main attack was on Bolton, 60 miles to the north-west. He crossed the Lincolnshire coast at Sutton-on-Sea at 21.45, flew over Lincoln at 22.30 and was seen north of Sheffield. He flew over Todmorden at 23.55, was seen at Bacup at midnight and then dropped two incendiary bombs near Newchurch. Frankenburg then sighted the railway at Rawtenstall and dropped two HE bombs. He followed the railway west and dropped five HE and two incendiary bombs at Ewood Bridge, which damaged the railway line. Still following the railway, he dropped seven HE bombs at Holcombe, killing one woman. He dropped two more HE bombs at Ramsbottom, followed by two incendiaries at Holcombe Brook. L.21 was seen from Bury at 00.19 and Atherton at 00.40. It seems Frankenburg then saw Bolton, which he described as well-lit, at 00.45. He dropped nine HE and eleven incendiary bombs on Astley Bridge, Sharples, Haliwell, Queens Park and the town centre, killing thirteen people: five men, six women and two children. Leaving Bolton, Frankenburg turned north, was seen south of Blackburn at 01.05 and then turned to fly near Burnley. He was next spotted near Skipton at 01.30 and at 01.35 dropped his final bomb at Bolton Abbey, a HE which failed to explode. L.21 was then seen near Ripon at 02.00 and Thirsk at 02.15. As he flew over the North Yorkshire Moors he seemed to be lost, but finally went back out to sea at Whitby at 03.05.

'Q' type Navy Zeppelin L.22: Kapitänleutnant Martin Dietrich set out from Tondern to bomb Sheffield. He crossed the Yorkshire coast at Mablethorpe at 21.40 and was seen over Gainsborough at 23.30. He reported seeing the lights of a city at 23.15 and initially thought he was over Lincoln, but later realized it was Sheffield. Most of his bombs landed on workers' housing among the Sheffield Armaments factories. He hit the John Brown engineering works, causing some damage and destroying houses: twenty-nine people were killed (nine men, ten women and ten children). Local historians have been able to identify all but one of the victims: Frederick Stratford (49) of 11 Court House, Danville Street, Sheffield; Ann Coogan (76) of 112 Grimsthorpe Street; Margaret Taylor (56) of 112 Grimsthorpe Street; William Guest (32) of Kilton Street; Thomas Wilson (59) of Petre Street; Elizabeth Bellamy (57) of 43 Writtle Street; Levi Hames (23) of 10 Cossey Road, Sheffield; Beatrice Hames (22) of 10 Cossey Road, Sheffield; Horace William Hames (1) of 10 Cossey Road, Sheffield; Nellie Rhodes (28) of 26 Cossey Road, Sheffield; Phyllis Rhodes (6) of 26 Cossey Road, Sheffield; Elsie Mary Rhodes (4) of 26 Cossey Road, Sheffield; George Harrison (59) of 26 Cossey Road, Sheffield; Elsie Ann Harrison (48) of 26 Cossey Road, Sheffield; Vera Harrison (13) of 26 Cossey Road, Sheffield; Albert Newton (28) of 28 Cossey Road, Sheffield; Alice Newton (27) of 28 Cossey Road, Sheffield; William Southerington (37) of 24 Cossey Road, Sheffield; Sarah Ann Southerington (41) of 24 Cossey Road, Sheffield; Martha Shakespeare (36) of 143 Corby Street, Sheffield (now Fred Mulley Street); Joseph Henry Tyler (45) of 136 Corby Street, Sheffield; Selina Tyler (41) of 136 Corby Street, Sheffield; Joseph Henry Tyler (14) of 136 Corby Street, Sheffield; Ernest Tyler (11) of 136 Corby Street, Sheffield; Albert Tyler (8) of 136 Corby Street, Sheffield; Amelia Tyler (5) of 136 Corby Street, Sheffield; John Tyler (2) of 136 Corby Street, Sheffield; and John Brewington (11) of 134 Corby Street, Sheffield.

L.22 was fired on by anti-aircraft guns outside Sheffield. It was seen over Mexborough at 00.45, flew between Tickhill and Doncaster and was then spotted north of Scunthorpe at 01.20 and near Barton-upon-Humber at 01.30. As Dietrich flew near the Humber Estuary, he was fired on by a number of anti-aircraft guns, including one on the warship HMS *Patrol*. He crossed the coast west of Grimston Hall at about 02.05.

'Q' type Navy Zeppelin *L.23*: Kapitänleutnant Wilhelm Ganzel, out from Nordholz, was recorded by the British as making three approaches to the Norfolk coast and three times reversing course, alleging that the forward engine had failed each time. It seems that Ganzel was in fact suffering from combat stress, and was moved from Zeppelin *L.23* to the light cruiser *Kolberg* a few weeks later. While we do not have all the facts of Ganzel's case, it is interesting to compare the action of Strasser in dealing with him with the cruel methods of the British Army in dealing with similar problems.

'R' type Navy Zeppelin *L.30*: Kapitänleutnant Horst von Buttlar claimed to have bombed Ramsgate and Margate, but the British have no record of any bombs falling in the area at this time. They say *L.30* was probably off Cromer at 20.15 and approached Yarmouth at about 20.50, wandering up and down the Norfolk coast for some time and dropping a large number of heavy bombs in the sea at about 22.25. The GHQ report further comments: 'Two airships L.23 and L.30 were becoming notorious for their pusillanimous conduct when near our shores.'

'R' type Navy Zeppelin *L.31*: Kapitänleutnant Heinrich Mathy was in action again two days after his last raid. Mathy again approached the English coast via Belgium and the English Channel, and because of the very clear night sky decided not to attack London, but targeted Portsmouth. He dropped most of his bombs on Portsmouth Harbour and dockyards, under heavy anti-aircraft fire, from about 11,000ft. None of the bombs were traced by the British, probably because they were aimed at ships and missed, falling harmlessly in the sea. It seems the main reasons for this were a combination of the altitude and being confused by searchlights and gun fire. The British, however, put it down to a failure of the bomb release gear on *L.31*. The GHQ report says of *L.31*: 'Her bold flight over Portsmouth Harbour on the 25th September fortunately had no results owing to the possible failure of her bomb releasing gear, but her success in flying over the Portsmouth defences remains. The decision of Kap Leut Mathy and the boldness of his navigation were alike remarkable.' Mathy flew back along the South Coast, dropping three further bombs which were recorded by the British, probably aimed at shipping near Dover. He returned home safely.

27 September 1916

'P/Q' type Army Zeppelin *LZ.81*: In November 1915 the German Army erected a base at Temesvar in Hungary. Zeppelin *LZ.81* was sent there in November 1915 and *LZ.85* in January 1916. Hauptmann Otto Jacobi in *LZ.81* bombed Bucharest on 27 September from Temesvar. Flying at 12,500ft, the Zeppelin was caught by searchlights over Bucherest and hit by anti-aircraft fire, which punctured several gas cells and he crash-landed in Timova, Bulgaria. There were no casualties, but the airship was damaged beyond repair.

October 1916.

'Q' type Army Zeppelin *LZ.97*: This airship replaced *LZ.81* at Temesvar in October, making a number of raids on other targets in Rumania, in particular the railway junctions at Ciulnita and Fetesti, and also made a final attack on Bucharest in late October.

1/2 October 1916

This was a raid by nine Navy Zeppelins. Heinrich Mathy in *L.31* set out on his last raid from Nordholz in the afternoon of Sunday, 1 October, along with ten other airships. Once again the smaller 'P' and 'Q' class Zeppelins were to raid the Midlands, the bigger 'R' class ships attacking London. The weather was poor, with strong winds over the German Bight and solid cloud over most of England, although GHQ had described conditions as highly favourable for an air raid, with light winds and lots of cloud, but no mist or fog.

'P' type Navy Zeppelin *L.13*: Kapitänleutnant Franz Georg Eichler embarked on the mission and got close to the English coast, but returned early to Hage.

'P' type Navy Zeppelin *L.14*: Hauptman Kuno Manger set out from Hage. According to GHQ reports, three Zeppelins raided Lincolnshire: *L.14* with Hauptmann Kuno Manger, *L.16* with Kapitänleutnant Erich Sommerfeld and *L.21* with Oberleutnant zur See Kurt Frankenburg. The three airships dropped fifty-eight bombs which killed a number of cattle, but did no further damage and caused no human casualities.

'P' type Navy Zeppelin *L.16*: Kapitänleutnant Erich Sommerfelt set out from Hage and raided Lincolnshire. It is not possible to identify where his bombs landed.

'P' type Navy Zeppelin *L.17*: Kapitänleutnant Hermann Kraushaar, flying from Tondern, was reported to have dropped two bombs west of Norwich, dropping the rest in the sea on his inward and outward journeys.

'Q' type Navy Zeppelin *L.21*: Oberleutnant zur See Kurt Frankenburg from Nordholz was lost over Lincolnshire for most of the raid. In his combat report, he said he saw a Zeppelin held by searchlights over London 70 miles away. It then started burning: it was Mathy in *L.31*.

'Q' type Navy Zeppelin *L.22*: Kapitänleutnant Martin Dietrich returned early to Nordholz.

'Q' type Navy Zeppelin *L.23*: Kapitänleutnant Wilhelm Ganzel also returned early to Nordholz.

'Q' type Navy Zeppelin *L.24*: Kapitänleutnant Robert Koch, flying from Tondern, had intended to bomb Manchester, but got completely lost. He finally determined his position by a star sighting. This showed he was much further south than he had estimated, near London. He decided to bomb the city, claiming to have hit Stoke Newington and Hackney. GHQ reports show he crossed the coast west of Sheringham in Norfolk and seemed to steer for Cambridge. He bombed Hitchin in Hertfordshire, killing one man, a soldier on guard duty. Koch had engine trouble on his return to Tondern, losing a propeller off his front engine, but made it back to base.

'R' type Navy Zeppelin *L.30*: Kapitänleutnant Horst von Buttlar took off from Ahlhorn and it appears returned early. The British in their GHQ reports were growing quite caustic about the commander of *L.30*; it appears they did not know who he was when the report was written, but said little needed to be reported other than that 'these ships habitually seem to avoid coming far inland'.

'R' type Navy Zeppelin *L.31*: Kapitänleutnant Heinrich Mathy, flying from Ahlhorn, was not to return that night. Despite or possibly because he was regarded by Strasser (and by the British) as the boldest and best Zeppelin commander, he was under terrible psychological pressure, with the destruction and burning of his comrades severely affecting him. He said: 'It is only a matter of time before we join the rest. Our nerves are ruined by this mistreatment. If anyone should say he was not haunted by visions of burning airships, then he would be a braggart.' He was asked by a newspaper reporter what he would do if his ship was on fire: would he jump or burn? He replid: 'I won't know until it happens.' He made his choice on that question over Potters Bar in Hertfordshire just before midnight on Sunday, 1 October.

   The route of *L.31* that night was well tracked by the British. It was seen by the Cross Sand Light Vessel at 19.45, then crossed the Suffolk coast at Corton and flew over Lowestoft, being spotted again at Wrentham at 20.05, Blythborough at 20.15, Framlingham at 20.30 and Needham Market at

20.50. Mathy continued in the same general direction, passing Hadleigh (21.00) south of Sudbury (21.10) and Halstead (21.15). He then seemed to stop his engines, as if he was checking his position. Mathy then changed course, flying more to the south. He was observed between Braintree and Terling at 21.25, then north of Chelsford (21.30) and above Writtle (21.35) and Blackmore (21.40). As she neared London, Mathy could see the searchlights, was caught in one near Klivedon Heath (21.45.) and changed to a north-easterly course. *L.31* was seen near Ongar at 22.00 and Harlow at 22.10. He stopped again to verify his position near Much Hadham (22.20), and then passed near Buntingford and turned north to attack London. Mathy flew north of Stevenage (22.55), and at 23.00 was west of Welwyn. He flew over Hatfield (23.05) and Hertford (23.10), then again stopped and drifted in the direction of Ware. It may be that Mathy was drifting without power to confuse the defenders, but if so it didn't work as he came under heavy fire from the guns at Newmans and Temple House. He then dropped most of his bombs at Cheshunt at about 23.40; thirty HE and twenty-six incendiary bombs destroyed four houses and slightly damaged about 300 buildings, including a large number of greenhouses. There was fortunately only one casualty, a woman, who was injured.

Mathy then seemed to give up the attack on central London and started weaving to avoid the searchlights. He was by this time being followed by a B.E.2c flown by Second Lieutenant Wulstan Tempest, who was, like William Leefe Robinson and Frederick Sowrey, a member of 39 Squadron RFC. Tempest took off from North Weald at 22.00, and spotted a Zeppelin coned in searchlight beams over Cheshunt about 15 miles away. He was at 14,500ft and flew flat out towards the Zeppelin, through British anti-aircraft fire. It seems Mathy saw the fighter as he dropped the last of his bombs at Potters Bar, just before Tempest attacked him. Tempest wrote in his combat report that the Zeppelin was at 15,000ft and climbing like a rocket. He dived to catch *L.31* and flew under it, then sat under the tail 'and pumped lead into her for all I was worth'. He could see tracer bullets from the airship's machine guns flying in all directions. As he fired, he noticed *L.31* begin to go red inside like a 'giant Chinese lantern', and a flame shot out of the front of the Zeppelin. The stricken airship shot up 200ft, and then began to fall straight at him. He put the B.E.2c into a spin and just managed to corkscrew out of the way as *L.31* shot past, 'roaring like a furnace'.

The red hot wreckage of *L.31* came to earth in a field just outside Potters Bar. People quickly reached the site, finding a man half-embedded in the soil. He was still alive, but soon died. It was Mathy: he knew what to do, and had jumped rather than be burned. The nineteen crew members of *L.31* are all now buried at Cannock Chase.

Wulstan Tempest crash-landed at North Weald at about 00.10; it seems he was still suffering from the effects of altitude sickness, which caused the crash. Awarded the DSO for shooting down *L.31*, he survived the war as commander of 100 Squadron RAF and retired as a major in 1922. He served in the Home Guard during the Second World War, and later in an Air Training Corps Squadron. He later moved to Canada and died there in 1966, aged 75.

'R' type Navy Zeppelin *L.34*: Kapitänleutnant Max Dietrich took over a new 'R' class Zeppelin on 27 September. This was his first raid in the new airship. He left Nordholz and was spotted crossing the coast at Overstrand, Norfolk, at 21.42. He reached the Corby area in Northamptonshire at about midnight. A searchlight and anti-aircraft gun based at Corby fired on *L.34*; the GHQ report says Dietrich turned towards the gun and dropped seventeen HE bombs on the railway near Corby tunnel, and thirteen incendiary bombs near the road from Rockingham to Gretton. He then turned for home and crossed the coast between Palling and Horsay at about 01.40, dropping his remaining HE bombs in the sea. The GHQ report was unsure whether Dietrich saw the fall of Mathy in *L.31*, which was probably 100 miles away, and dropped his bombs as a result of this, or because he was fired on from Corby. It may just be a coincidence that both events took part at about the same time.

7 November 1916

'P/Q' type Army Zeppelin *LZ.90*: The unmanned Zeppelin was swept away from its base at Wittmundhaven in a storm and destroyed.

27/28 November 1916

This raid by ten Navy Zeppelins was another disastrous night for the Germans. Max Dietrich in *L.34* and Kurt Frankenburg in *L.21* were both shot down. The Zeppelins attacked in two groups: *L.24*, *L.34*, *L.35* and *L.36* attacking the Tyne, the others the Midlands.

'P' type Navy Zeppelin *L.13*: It seems that Kapitänleutnant Franz Georg Eichler, flying from Hage, dropped twenty-four bombs at York and Barnaby Moor.

'P' type Navy Zeppelin *L.14*: Hauptmann Kuno Manger, flying from Hage, crossed the Yorkshire coast north of Spurn Head at 21.10. He is reported as wandering around the East Riding of Yorkshire for an hour, and it seems he approached Hull and was fired on by anti-aircraft guns. He then turned back, was fired on again and dropped forty-four bombs at Mappleton in answer to gun fire from Cowden.

'P' type Navy Zeppelin *L.16*: Kapitänleutnant Hans-Karl Gayer, flying out from Hage, was reported as being seen over Barnsley and Wakefield. Gayer dropped thirty-nine bombs in the area, which caused no damage. He was fired on by the anti-aircraft gun at Acomb, near York, where *L.16* ineffectually dropped its remaining bombs. Gayer was again fired on as he went out to sea south of Scarborough.

'Q' type Navy Zeppelin *L.21*: Kapitänleutnant Kurt Frankenburg, who had now been promoted, took off in *L.21* from Nordholz at about the same time as *L.34*. He crossed the coast near Atwick in Yorkshire at 21.20, and then spent several hours over England. He was fired on by the Brierlands gun and dropped one HE and two incendiary bombs in reply. He flew over Leeds at 23.34, and then over Wakefield and Barnsley, which were well darkened. Frankenburg dropped three bombs on Dodworth before reaching the Stoke-on-Trent area. Over the Potteries, he dropped bombs on Kitsgrove (one), Goldenhill (three) and Tunstall (three), then bombed burning ironstone hearths at Chesterton with sixteen HE and seven incendiary bombs. He finally bombed colliery waste tips between Fenton and Trentham. We know that a bomb dropped in the garden of a house at 8 Sun Street, Tunstall. The blast demolished the outhouses and sculleries of four houses, also damaging a church. One man, Mr Cantliff of 8 Sun Street, was injured, but recovered in hospital.

After leaving the Stoke area, Frankenburg headed back to the coast. On his way over the East Midlands, *L.21* made slow progress, probably experiencing engine trouble. He passed south of Nottingham, and was caught in an airfield searchlight at Buckminster. He was flying over dangerous territory here, as there was a concentration of home defence aerodromes in the Lincolnshire area at this time. He was attacked by two B.E.2c aircraft near Peterborough at about 03.00, but escaped. An hour later, near East Derham, he was attacked again, but the F.E.2b had an engine failure and crash-landed.

His luck ran out when he reached the coast near Lowestoft, Suffolk, at 06.05 in the early dawn. The system of air defence introduced after the 31 January raids was in operation, and working well. Given the codename 'Mary', *L.21* had been tracked on its nine-hour flight over the country. When it reached the Lowestoft area, three aeroplanes from the Royal Naval Air Service were in the air waiting for it. The pilots were Flight Lieutenant Egbert Cadbury, of the Birmingham chocolate family, Flight Sub Lieutenant Gerard Fane and Flight Sub Lieutenant Edward Laston Pulling. The first to attack was Cadbury, who had taken off from Burgh Castle Air Station at 06.18, spotting the Zeppelin a few minutes later. He attacked from 700ft below *L.21*, firing four drums from his Lewis gun without noticing any effect, though he was fired on by the airship. The second to attack was Fane, but his Lewis gun jammed after a few rounds. Pulling then made the final attack, taking off from Bacton at 04.45. Pulling flew 50ft under the Zeppelin and fired a few shots, but his Lewis gun jammed. As he turned away to clear the jam, he looked around and saw the Zeppelin burst into flames, and was so near he was scorched by the flames as the Zeppelin burned. He also had the grizzly experience of seeing the machine gunner, stationed on top of the airship's envelope, leave his platform and run straight off the nose of the Zeppelin to escape the flames. Pulling reported that the Zeppelin caught fire after a few shots and 'was in a few seconds a fiery furnace'. *L.21* fell into the sea about eight miles east of Lowestoft at 06.42 on 28 November; there were no survivors, all seventeen crew members being killed. Vessels searching the spot found only a broken propeller blade floating in a great pool of petrol and oil. The rest of *L.21* sank to the bottom of the North Sea, and as far as is known it is still there.

While all three pilots attacked *L.21*, Flight Sub Lieutenant Pulling received the credit for its destruction, as he fired the last shots. He received the DSO, while Cadbury and Fane got the DSC. Cadbury and Fane survived the war, and were engaged in further anti-Zeppelin operations. Pulling died a few weeks later, in March 1917; he was demonstrating aerobatics in the B.E.2c No.8626, in which he had shot down *L.21*, when the wing broke; both he and his passenger were killed. Cadbury and Gerard Fane went on to serve in the RAF and survived the war. Cadbury died in 1967 and Fane in 1979.

'Q' type Navy Zeppelin *L.22*: Kapitänleutnant Heinrich Hollander, flying out from Nordholz, was fired on by guns in the Howden area of Yorkshire and turned back. It seems he was hit by shrapnel; when the ship was examined, more than 150 holes were found in her envelope.

'Q' type Navy Zeppelin *L.24*: Oberleutnant zur See Kurt Friemel, it seems, turned back to Tondern before reaching the coast.

'R' type Navy Zeppelin *L.30*: Kapitänleutnant Horst von Buttlar set out from Ahlhorn and returned early. Buttlar apparently had a genuine reason for turning back, as two engines on *L.30* failed on the outward voyage. The British obviously did not know this, and the GHQ report commented that the commanders of Zeppelins *L.23* and *L.30* were timid to a degree. The commander of *L.23* at the time was Kapitänleutnant Ganzel.

It may be that Peter Strasser also had some concerns about the determination of Buttlar, because he didn't raid again for another year. On 11 January 1917, the command of *L.30* was transferred to Oberleutnant zur See Kurt Friemel, and von Buttlar wasn't assigned to another ship until 16 September 1917, when he received the much more advanced 'height climber' Zeppelin *L.54*.

'R' type Navy Zeppelin *L.34*: This was to be Kapitänleutnant Max Dietrich's last raid; and it was his 46th birthday. It is said that the officers' mess at Nordholz was decorated for his birthday celebration as the officers sat down for lunch at about noon. Peter Strasser's adjutant came in and said: 'Gentlemen we have attack orders, the industrial areas of Middle England, we have to be in the air by 1.00pm. (Noon GMT) We have excellent prospects.' It is said that the commander of *L.21*, Kurt Frankenburg, who had taken over the ship from Max Dietrich, said: 'Leave the birthday decorations, we can celebrate tomorrow.' But his Executive Officer, Hans-Werner Salzbrunn, said to a friend :'I know we won't come back from this flight.' Neither Max Dietrich nor Kurt Frankenburg returned for the party, but we can be sure those of his comrades who did, needed a drink after the raid.

L.34 left Nordholz, with a crew of twenty, on time at 13.00; its target was Newcastle. It reached England at 22.45, over Black Hall Rocks, north of Hartlepool. The airship was picked up by a searchlight near the Hutton Henry Lighthouse, and fired on by anti-aircraft guns. Dietrich dropped thirteen HE bombs on the searchlight battery, but failed to hit it, instead striking farm buildings and injuring two cows.

There are good records of what happened next. Dietrich then turned for home, heading over West Hartlepool, where he was again caught by searchlights. He dropped sixteen HE bombs on West Hartlepool, two falling in the Ward Jackson Park, where there is now a memorial stone plaque. He then bombed workers' housing in the Harley Street, Lowthian Road and Poplar Grove area, killing four people and injuring eleven, damaging a number of homes. He went on to bomb allotments and hit the grandstand of Hartlepool United Football Club, causing major damage. The bombing of Hartlepool was to be the last act of Max Dietrich. Zeppelin *L.34* had been spotted in the searchlight beams by a British night fighter. The pilot was Second Lieutenant Ian Vernon Pyatt, a member of 36 Home Defence Squadron of the RFC, flying a B.E.2c. He had taken off from Seaton Carew and chased *L.34* over Hartlepool. In his combat report, Pyatt said he caught up with *L.34* at about 23.42 over the mouth of the River Tees, and fired seventy-one rounds from his Lewis gun. He noticed a small patch on the airship's envelope become incandescent, where he had seen his tracer bullets entering: 'This patch rapidly spread and the next thing was that the whole Zepp was in flames.' He watched *L.34* fall into the sea, still burning, half a mile off-shore. The next day, only a patch of oil marked the spot where Dietrich and nineteen other crew members had died. A few parts of *L.34* were later washed up on the shore, along with two bodies on 11 January 1917. They had been in the sea too long to be identified, but were buried at Seaton Carew, then in 1962 reburied at Cannock Chase as unidentified German soldiers. Pyatt survived the war, dying in South Africa in 1972, aged 80.

'R' type Navy Zeppelin *L.35*: On 18 October 1916, Kapitänleutnant Herbert Ehrlich was assigned a new Zeppelin, *L.35*, taking Leutnant zur See Dietsch and his crew with him. This was his first raid in the new ship, flying from Ahlhorn and targeting Newcastle. Ehrlich had problems with the automatic gas pressure valves on some of his gas cells, and had to fly low at about 8,000ft. *L.35* had just crossed the coast near Seaham in County Durham when he saw Zeppelin *L.34*, commanded by Max Dietrich, caught in a searchlight near Hartlepool. More searchlights caught *L.34*, all holding it fast and brightly illuminated. Ehrlich saw an anti-aircraft gun fire at the Zeppelin. After about five minutes, a rocket or flare was fired and the gun stopped firing. A few minutes later, *L.34* became a brightly glowing ball of fire, tipped up vertically and was burning over its entire length. As the stricken airship fell, there was a bright ball of burning gas streaming behind it. Another rocket was fired and the searchlights went out. Lookouts in *L.35*'s gondola saw two aircraft in the vicinity, at which Ehrlich turned for home.

'R' type Navy Zeppelin *L.36*: Korvettenkapitan Viktor Schulz, flying from Nordholz, was commanding a new Zeppelin, *L.36*, and heading for Edinburgh. He reported he was preparing to cross the coast when he saw

L.34 shot down. He did not go in as it was too light. He described the weather as a clear bright night, with the Northern Lights visible. He could clearly see the burning *L.34*. Schulz attempted to fly north to his target, but had difficulty in climbing because of rising temperatures. Limited to 10,500ft, he decided to turn inland and attack Blyth, Newcastle or Sunderland. Just after 01.00, an engine failed and the Zeppelin became more difficult to control. He dropped fuel and bombs as ballast and turned for home. This was to be the last flight of Schulz in *L.36*; on 9 December he was promoted to commander of the Naval Airship Division. The command of *L.36* and its crew transferred to Franz Georg Eichler, who would not enjoy his next mission.

Returning to the destruction of *L.21*, it is interesting that when the Zeppelin had roamed over the Midlands on 31 January 1916, it did so without opposition, but when it journeyed across the Midlands again ten months later on 27/28 November, it was the hunted and not the hunter. The British had learned the lessons of the January raid, the Germans had not. At the time, the British had seen the earlier raid as a defeat. Zeppelins had roamed at will over the Midlands. The air defence operations were a total failure. It is much to their credit that those responsible for home defence were willing and able to accept this and build an effective air defence system. In a war where the biggest criticism of those in command is usually that they lacked the moral courage to acknowledge and learn from their mistakes, the development of the air defence system in 1916 deserves special credit. In some ways, the defeat of the Zeppelins was more to do with the efforts of failed generals, politicians and bureaucrats, than the bravery of pilots and the genius of scientists. It was developed by a system of trial and error, but above all it was based on a judgement of what worked.

December 1916

'Q' type Army Zeppelin *LZ.101*: In late December, Hauptmann Gaissert in *LZ.101* attacked the harbour and railway terminal at Galatz, a Rumanian port on the Black Sea.

28/29 December 1916

This was not a good day for the Navy Airship Service. Four of its airships were destroyed, in three separate missions. The cause of all the damage was the weather. The first mission was a raid on England. It appears that four airships were originally sent to attack England, but were called back because of the declining weather.

'E' type Navy Schutte-Lanze *SL 12*: Kapitänleutnant Waldemar Kolle, on his return from the abortive raid on England, crash-landed at Ahlhorn because of the weather, hitting the station gasometer and landing outside the airfield. The airship was wrecked in the storm.

The second mission of the day was a patrol in support of minesweepers in the German Bight.

'P' type Navy Zeppelin *L.16*: Kapitänleutnant Hans Karl Gayer took off from Hage to patrol in the German Bight. He was ordered back to base because of deteriorating weather conditions, and landed at 15.50 in strong winds.

'P' type Navy Zeppelin *L.17*: It seems Kapitänleutnant Herman Kraushaar's *L.17* was safely stowed in the Toska shed at Tondern, when *L.24* crashed on entering the shed and caught fire. Both Zeppelins were destroyed.

'Q' type Navy Zeppelin *L.24*: Oberleutnant zur See Kurt Friemel was sent out with *L.16* to patrol in the German Bight in support of minesweepers, but due to adverse weather was ordered back early. He returned to Tondern at 15.20, and as the airship was being walked into the Toska shed in strong winds, the after supporting tackle broke and the airship fell to the floor at the entrance to the shed, breaking its back. It immediately caught fire, and both *L.17* and *L.24* were destroyed.

The third mission was in preparation for a raid on Petrograd. In November 1916, the Navy Airship Service, pressed by Admiral Prince Henry, the Kaiser's brother, began planning for a raid on Petrograd. Two Zeppelins – *L.35* and *L.38* – were moved from Ahlhorn via Seddin to Wainoden, in Courland (now Vainode, Latvia).

'R' type Navy Zeppelin *L.35*: Kapitänleutnant Herbert Ehrlich set out from Wainoden in the early afternoon to raid Windau (now Ventspils, Latvia).

He was near Libau (Liepaja) when the weather worsened. The Zeppelin was buffeted by heavy snow squalls and iced up heavily, and could make little progress because of a strong headwind. Ehrlich gave up any hope of making an attack at midnight and turned for home. It was so cold that the engine oil congealed into a semi-solid form. One engine stopped and a propeller shaft broke. He landed back at Wainoden at about 08.10.

'R' type Navy Zeppelin *L.38*: Kapitänleutnant Martin Dietrich set out from Wainrode to bomb targets on Oesel Island (Saareman, Estonia). If anything, the weather conditions were even worse than for *L.35*. He had the same problems with congealed oil and engine trouble. He was over Arendsberg, on Oesel, at about midnight, but could not see anything because of heavy cloud. He crash-landed in a forest near Seemuppen in Russia (Ziemupe, Latvia) and the Zeppelin was destroyed, although the crew escaped uninjured.

Chapter Ten

The air raids of early 1917

In 1917, with the Allies slowly gaining in strength, Germany went on the offensive, introducing unrestricted submarine warfare in January. This and the Zimmerman telegram were significant factors in America entering the war. The USA declared war on Germany in April 1917.

On the Western Front, Germany withdrew to the Hindenburg Line between February to April, a much better defensive position, allowing it to transfer troops to the Russian Front against the weakened Russian Army. The French under General Neville launched a massive offensive in the Aisne in April: it was a disaster. It was quickly followed by a mutiny in the French armies. This revolt was put down by Petain with a mixture of ruthlessness and acceptance that the policy of attrition had to stop. The British continued as before, starting an offensive in Flanders in June, which quickly degenerated into the slaughter at Passchendaele, which Haig accepted as part of the tactic of attrition.

The real change in the political situation occurred in Russia. The February Revolution took place in March (Russia was then using the Orthodox calendar), the Tsar was forced to abdicate and a government promising parliamentary democracy and land reform took over. War Minister Alexander Kerensky also promised to continue the war, which was a big mistake. An attack on Austrian forces in July failed and led to a total breakdown of the Russian Army, with soldiers just heading home. The Germans advanced, meeting no opposition, but were limited by supply problems. In November, the October Revolution took place. Lenin immediately sued for peace and the Treaty of Brest-Litovsk ended the war on the Russian Front. Germany imposed very harsh peace terms in March 1918, which Lenin readily accepted, believing there would be further Communist revolutions. It didn't work out that way, but Germany would live to regret the Treaty of Brest-Litovsk for a very long time: the Allies said its terms had been even stricter than those imposed by the Versailles Treaty, so Germany could not complain about the latter's severity, and the border imposed on Russia by the Germans was used by the Allies after the war in creating the newly independent Baltic states of Latvia, Lithuania and Estonia.

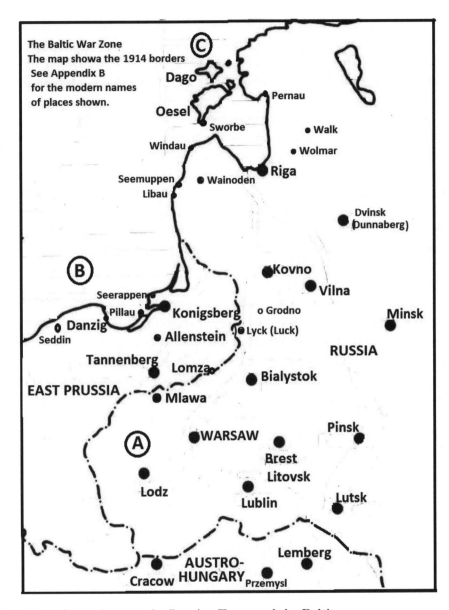

Map 7: Operations on the Russian Front and the Baltic

The map shows the 1914 borders.
'**A**' Much of the fighting in 1914 took place in East Prussia; after the Battle of Tannenberg the Germans pushed the Russians back through Russian Poland. By 1915, the Germans had captured Warsaw.
'**B**' The Naval Airships were active in the Baltic.
'**C**' Operation Albion took place in 1917 as the Germans took advantage of the Russian Revolution to take over the Baltic States.

Airship raids on England continued, but they were largely ineffective because of the high altitude the Zeppelins had to fly at to avoid fighters. Some anti-aircraft guns were transferred to the Western Front. The major British success was the use of flying boats and ship-borne fighters against airships near their home bases.

The real threat was when the Germans introduced the highly effective Gotha bomber. On 13 June, twenty Gothas bombed London, killing 162 people, and fifty-seven more were killed on 7 July. Squadrons of fighters were transferred to Home Defence and started to shoot down the Gothas. From September, the Gothas and larger four engine 'Giant' bombers attacked at night. This led to a very quick change of policy in the RFC regarding inherently stable night fighters: the B.E.2 didn't stand a chance against Gothas. High performance fighters such as Sopwith Camels, S.E.5s and Bristol Fighters began operating at night. Though they needed experienced pilots, they were highly successful.

The German Army had scrapped all its airships or transferred them to the Navy. The High Command considered stopping all airship production. It seems the crucial argument used by Peter Strasser to maintain some production was that aeroplanes could only bomb London or the South-East from their bases near Zeebrugge; only Zeppelins could bomb targets in the Midlands and North.

Airships continued to operate in the East, bombing targets in the Balkans, Italy and Russia. Zeppelins were involved in the last major operation in Russia, the amphibious Operation Albion, to capture Baltic islands and consolidate gains in Russia.

5 February 1917

'R' type Navy Zeppelin *L.36*: Kapitänleutnant der Reserve Franz Georg Eichler took over the ship from Viktor Schulze, who was promoted to command the Naval Airship Division. Shortly after Eichler took charge, *L.36* was taken out of service to be modified to operate at higher altitude. The modifications were basically to lose weight. One Maybach engine was taken out of the rear engine gondola, half the bomb shackles were removed and all the machine guns and fittings taken out. In all, this saved 3,380lb. On a test flight after the refit on 3 February 1917, the Zeppelin achieved an altitude of 16,400ft with a load of some 14,000lb.

The first operation of the modified *L.36* on 5 February was a night patrol. It left Nordholz at 22.14, but by midnight there were problems as the

Zeppelin was very tail heavy. A check found a fault in the number seven gas cell, which was only about 90 per cent full. This should not have been a major problem, but to compensate Eichler had ballast, bombs and fuel moved forward. This had some effect but did not solve the problem. It was probably the case that gas cell seven was full of air; as hydrogen had leaked out, air had taken its place, so the cell was empty, not 90 per cent full. This would account for the handling problems. Eichler decided to return to base. At 08.20, he was near Nordholz, which was covered with fog. He attempted to land but crashed into the estuary of the frozen River Waser. The control gondola at the front of the ship was torn off, and the rest of the Zeppelin shot up to 3,300ft. One member of the crew fell out of the control car, but survived to walk to the shore. Eichler and the rest of the crew in the control car managed to climb into the body of the airship. They had some control, but no compass, maps or radio. The seriously damaged ship flew on to land near Celle. All the crew survived, but the Zeppelin broke in two and was scrapped.

After the crash, a court of inquiry was held and the episode was found to be largely due to mistakes by Eichler. However, Strasser concluded that the commander should be absolved of blame because in airship operations slight mistakes can easily lead to serious consequences; lest a fear of responsibility should be engendered, one should not construe every mistake as a court-martial offence. Here we see again why Strasser was so respected by the Zeppelin crews; he was a good manager, far from the stereotypical Prussian officer.

8 February 1917

'E' type Army Schutte-Lanz *SL.13*: This was destroyed when a shed at its base in Leipzig collapsed on the airship due to accumulated snow on the roof.

16/17 February 1917

'Q' type Army Zeppelin *LZ.107*: This was the last raid in the West by an Army airship; Oberleutnant der Reserve Ernst Lehmann says the main target was Boulogne and the bombs were aimed using a cloud car. According to British intelligence, the Zeppelin was reported off Walmer at 01.45 and seen or heard later in east Kent. No bombs were dropped on British soil. After the destruction of *SL.11*, the German Army had ordered its airships not to go to England, or after the debacle at Verdun to cross the Western Front. This left few targets in the west: they included Rouen, Etaples and Boulogne.

March 1917

With the defeat of Rumania, Zeppelins remained in the Balkans with a wider range of strategic bombing missions. In late March 1917, the two Army Zeppelins still in the Balkans were *LZ.97* and *LZ.101*, but both were sent back to Germany in April. It was decided that the cost of keeping the airships there outweighed any military advantage.

'Q' type Army Zeppelin *LZ.97*: This airship was based at Temesvar. Its main task was to raid Italian ports, with attacks made on Valona, Brindisi and Imbros. In all, *LZ.97* made five flights to Italy, but according to Lehmann: 'Though they were successful from the viewpoint of piloting and navigation, they were without military results.' Which I suppose was the point of the exercise.

'Q' type Army Zeppelin *LZ.101*: Based at Jamboli, its task was to attack British bases in the Aegean Sea outside of the Dardanelles, and the bases on Greek islands, including Lesbos, Lemnos and Imbros. In late March, *LZ.101* bombed the British supply base on the island of Mudros.

16/17 March 1917

Five airships set out, with London their main target. Weather conditions were very poor, with high winds when the ships reached the English coast. Because of the weather, most dropped their bombs in open country, and according to GHQ reports there were no injuries and only £163 worth of damage. The raid was a disaster for the Germans, with one Zeppelin shot down over France and two damaged in crash-landings.

'R' type Navy Zeppelin *L.35*: Kapitänleutnant Herbert Ehrlich, returning from the cold of the Baltic, took off from Ahlhorn at 12.00 and reported he had bombed London. British observations showed *L.35* crossed the Kent coast at Broadstairs at 22.45, and flew to Ashford, where Ehrlich circled for about ten minutes. He dropped twenty bombs, including three 300kg bombs, but they landed in open country and did little damage. *L.35* crossed back over the coast at Dover at 00.15, reached the French coast near Calais and flew across Belgium in heavy snow, crossing the Western Front near Ypres. Because of the wind, Ehrlich was unable to return to Ahlhorn and made a forced landing near Dresden at about 12.30. The airship was damaged but repairable.

'R' type Navy Zeppelin *L.39*: Kapitänleutnant Robert Koch took off from Ahlhorn at 12.18. British observers spotted *L.39* over Margate at 22.20, and it then flew across Kent over Ashford to St Leonard's and Bexhill-on-Sea. Koch dropped six bombs on land, which damaged two houses. *L.39* crossed back over the coast near Pevensey at 23.50, and other bombs were heard exploding out to sea. Koch flew back over France because of the gale, and was seen at about 03.00 near Dieppe. He then flew towards Paris, but as dawn was breaking was seen over the Western Front, and at 05.30 was shot down by anti-aircraft fire near Compiegne. *L.39* came down near the German trenches, and all seventeen men on board were killed.

'R' type Navy Zeppelin *L.40*: Kapitänleutnant Erich Sommerfeldt took off from Ahlhorn at 11.30. He claimed to have bombed London, but British reports dispute this, showing L.40 crossed the coast at Herne Bay at 01.00 and flew over Kent to Romney Marsh, where it dropped thirty-one bombs in open country without causing any damage. Sommerfeldt went back out to sea at New Romney at 02.15. Driven by the gale, he had to return to base over the Western Front by way of St Omer and Bethune, crossed the trenches at Le Bassee at 03.20. He was very low on fuel when returning to Ahlhorn at 13.27 after almost twenty-six hours in the air.

'R' type Navy Zeppelin *L.41*: Hauptmann Kuno Manger took off from Ahlhorn at 12.00 and was seen over the coast at Winchelsea at 01.20, where he dropped ten bombs. Manger flew near Rye, dropping more bombs on Camber Marsh, and went out to sea at Dungeness at 02.05. He crossed the French coast at Boulogne, and because of the wind also had to go over the Western Front near Cambrai. *L.41* returned safely to Ahlhorn, landing at 14.53, after waiting until Sommerfeldt in *L.40* was safely down.

'S' type Navy Zeppelin *L.42*: Kapitänleutnant Martin Dietrich, with Fregattenkapitan Peter Strasser, recently promoted to Leader of Airships, as a passenger, took off from Nordholz at 12.30 but had engine trouble, and this combined with the wind pushed him south. At about midnight, near the Ostend Lighthouse, he turned back for Nordholz. Dietrich then got lost in heavy fog and, low on fuel, landed at Juterborg at 15.05 after more than twenty-six hours in the air. Dietrich and Strasser did at least live to fight another day.

This raid was a failure. It had cost the German Navy one Zeppelin and crew shot down, and two more airships temporally out of action due to damage from crash-landings. The damage in England was a grand total of just £163. The raid did worry the British defences, though: the Zeppelins over England had been very high, *L.35* reaching 18,500ft, *L.40* 19,000ft and *L.41* 17,100ft. The 'height climbers' were now active and would render obsolete many of the British tactics used in 1916.

30 March 1917

'E' type Navy Schutte-Lanz *SL.9*: Kapitänleutnant Hubert Johnke took off from Seerappen, and was returning to Seddin with Leutnant zur See Friedrich Martin as second officer when the airship was probably struck by lightning near Pillau. It caught fire and crashed, and the crew of twenty-three were all killed.

Chapter Eleven

The 'Large America' flying boat

The Zeppelins were to meet their greatest threat in the long range, radio-equipped flying boat. In April 1917, the RNAS took delivery of four Curtiss H.12 flying boats at Yarmouth and Felixstowe. With a wingspan of 92.7ft, and 46.5ft long, with two Rolls Royce Eagle 275hp engines, the H.12 – known for obvious reason as the 'Large America' – carried a crew of four with an armament of four Lewis guns and four 100lb bombs. Though only capable of a top speed of 85mph and a ceiling of 10,800ft, the H.12 had an endurance of six hours and, most importantly, had wireless. Despite the carnage of late 1916, radio discipline in the Airship Service had hardly improved. Zeppelin commanders were cavalier in the use of radio when on scouting missions, particularly when they were off the German or Dutch coast. The sector off Terschelling Island was to prove a good hunting ground for the H.12.

When a Zeppelin sent a radio message, its direction was logged and within minutes the British would determine its position by triangulation, using its radio location stations from Shetland to Lowestoft. The British used almost exactly the same system as the Germans when the Zeppelins asked for a radio location. On 26 April, the Admiralty issued a coded position chart for its flying boat crews. When a signal was picked up and the position of the Zeppelin determined, it would first be sent to the H.12 with the order to take off, and then was updated as new information was received during the mission.

Though the flying boats were large, the Zeppelins were much bigger and it was almost always the case that the men in flying boats saw the Zeppelin some time before they were sighted by the Zeppelin crew, and the airship commander realized he was being chased for his life. If a chase did take place, the 'Large America' boat was faster but had a much lower rate of climb and ceiling than a 'height climber' Zeppelin. Airships could and did escape when they were sighted, but even a large, slow and un manoeuvrable flying boat was more than a match for a Zeppelin when it got into machine-gun range.

9 May 1917

'E' type Navy Schutte-Lanz *SL.14*: Kapitänleutnant Von Wachter did not have much better luck with *SL.14* than with *SL.3*, his new airship badly damaged on the field at Wainoden and scrapped a week later.

14 May 1917

'Q' type Navy Zeppelin *L.22*: Kapitänleutnant Ulrich Lehmann was the first victim of a Curtiss H.12 flying boat. He had taken over *L.22* on 22 February, with Leutnant zur See Ewald Knobelsdorff as second officer. The old 'Q' type airship was no longer used for bombing missions over England because it had altitude limitations, but it was very useful for reconnaissance and minesweeping operations. *L.22* had previously taken part in eleven raids, and was the Zeppelin, commanded by Martin Dietrich, that had bombed Cleethorpes and Sheffield in 1916, killing sixty-one people.

At about 03.30 on 14 May, the Admiralty decoded a signal that *L.22* had taken off on a scouting mission from Wittmundhaven. The men in Room 40 knew its normal scouting area was in the area off the Terschelling Light Ship. A Curtiss H.12 commanded by Flight Lieutenant Christopher Galpin took off from Yarmouth to find the airship. The second pilot was Flight Sub-Lieutenant Robert Leckie, Chief Petty Officer Whatling was the navigator and Air Mechanic J.R. Laycock the wireless operator. The H.12 stopped sending radio signals when it was about 80 miles out from base, in case the Germans intercepted its signal, but received updated information on the position of the Zeppelin. At about 04.48, Galpin sighted a Zeppelin dead ahead about 10-15 miles away. His report contains detailed information. They were cruising at about 60 knots when they saw the airship, at 5,000ft, near the Terschelling Light Ship; they increased their speed to 65 knots and climbed to 6,000 feet, dropping three of their bombs to lighten the flying boat. Leckie took over the wheel of the ship while Galpin and Whatling manned the Lewis guns. It seems no one in the Zeppelin, by then flying at only 3,800ft, saw the H.12 until it was only about half a mile away. It then raised its nose and started to climb; Leckie dived to gain speed to attack and got to within about 50ft of the hull, when Galpin and Whatling fired the Lewis guns. One of the forward guns jammed, but both gunners fired a full magazine at the Zeppelin. They passed *L.22* and turned to make another attack, and saw a slight glow inside the envelope; as they completed the turn and flew alongside, the airship was in flames and hanging tail-down at an angle of 45 degrees. Whatling reported that he saw the number *L.22* painted on the nose. They saw two crew members jump out of the blazing machine, and a number of heavy objects – bombs or engines – fall from the airframe into the sea. It only took about 45 seconds from the first sign of ignition until the whole of the covering was burnt off, and the red hot bare framework fell into the sea. All that remained was a mass of black ash on the surface and a column of brown smoke. All twenty-one crew members of *L.22* were killed. While the Germans knew within hours that an airship was missing, they didn't know what had happened. They would a few days later.

23/24 May 1917

This was again a raid with London as the main target, but because of atrocious weather conditions little damage was done. There was snow and hail in the upper air and thick cloud obscuring the ground.

'R' type Navy Zeppelin *L.40*: Kapitänleutnant Erich Sommerfeldt, flying from Wittmundhaven, reported he gave up his attempt to bomb London because of low cloud and decided to bomb Norwich instead. British records show a single 300kg bomb fell at Little Plumstead about 4 miles east of Norwich, but no other bombs were reported. Sommerfeldt had a very lucky escape on his journey home, as a Curtiss 'Large America' flying boat had set out from Yarmouth to intercept Zeppelins on their way home.

At about 03.30, the pilot of flying boat H.12 No. 8666, Flight Lieutenant Galpin, had been ordered to steer a course towards Terschelling to look for Zeppelins returning from the raid. There was poor visibility when they got to the patrol area, and at about 05.40 they were about to return to Yarmouth. Quite unexpectedly, a Zeppelin appeared out of the clouds. Both the H.12 and Zeppelin were flying very low, the Curtiss at 1,200ft and the Zeppelin at 1,600ft. The two aircraft must have seen each other at much the same time, as the Zeppelin fired a white flare as a recognition signal, probably thinking the seaplane was German. Galpin opened the throttles on the H.12 and climbed towards the Zeppelin. He reported he was able to fire a half-magazine of Brock, Pomeroy and tracer ammunition, but when it had reached 3,000ft the Zeppelin put out a smoke screen and was able to climb into a cloud bank. The H.12 searched for some time without success and set off back for Yarmouth.

There is also a report of the encounter from Sommerfeldt. He said the attack took place about 10 miles north of Vlieland by a seaplane which took off from the water. When it did not respond to his recognition signal, he dropped his remaining bombs and ballast to lighten the ship and steered for the clouds. At all times the Zeppelin was 100 metres higher than the seaplane. The enemy aircraft hit the Zeppelin with machine-gun fire, and when Sommerfeldt returned to base he found twelve bullet holes in several gas cells. He said that after the attack he sent a radio warning to the other Zeppelins, alerting them of enemy aircraft. He returned to base safely.

The latter part of the story demonstrates the bravery and determination of Galpin and his crew. The flying boat flew towards Yarmouth without incident until it was near Cromer, when it ran out of petrol and ditched in the sea. Fortunately, it was soon found and taken in tow by a trawler.

'S' type Navy Zeppelin *L.42*: Kapitänleutnant Martin Dietrich, flying from Ahlhorn, was sighted near Braintree in Essex at about midnight, when it seems he could see the London searchlights but abandoned his mission because of engine trouble. *L.42* crossed the Norfolk coast near Sheringham at 03.25, its bombs landing in open country between Mildenhall and East Dereham, without causing any damage. The Zeppelin had a difficult trip back to base, flying through thunder clouds and hailstorms, and was several times struck by lightning. Upon landing, several holes were found in the envelope where the lightning had struck.

'S' type Navy Zeppelin *L.43*: Kapitänleutnant Hermann Kraushaar, flying out of Ahlhorn, was the only commander who claimed to have bombed London. He reported the heavy cloud layer had dissolved over the city and he could see the course of the Thames and position of the docks. He did not bomb the centre because of wind conditions, but hit the docks in Greenwich and the Isle of Dogs with all his bombs (1,850kg) from 20,000ft. The British have a totally different account of his raid. They say *L.43* crossed the Suffolk coast between Felixstowe and Orfordness at 02.20, dropping thirty-eight bombs between East Wrentham and Great Ryborough, with most falling on fields and villages, although one man was killed and several houses damaged. Kraushaar landed safely at Ahlhorn at 13.37 after some twenty-three hours in the air.

This was to be the last raid by Kapitänleutnant Kraushaar and L.43, as on 14 June they were shot down by a 'Large America' flying boat.

'T' type Navy Zeppelin *L.44*: The story of Kapitänleutnant Franz Stabbert gets more like *Biggles* as it goes on. We last heard of him in 1916 when he was interned in Norway. After seven months in captivity, Stabbert escaped and returned to Germany. He was soon returned to active service. He got the latest Zeppelin, the 'height climber' *L.44*, in April 1917. He raided England again on 23 May, flying from Nordholz. The raid, with Peter Strasser on

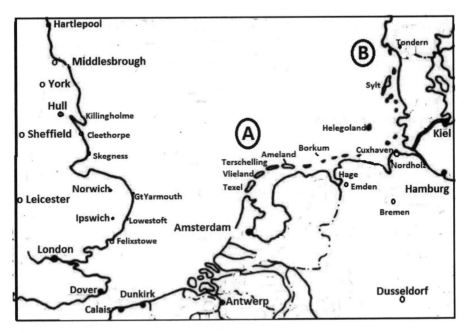

Map 8: Air-sea operations over the North Sea

'A' the majority of attacks on Zeppelins by flying boats took place close to the Dutch coast. The maps show why. Flying boats had just enough fuel to make the return journey, though occasionally it was a close run thing.

14 May 1917 *L.22* was shot down in flames, near Terschelling Light Ship, by an H. 12 'Large America' Flying Boat operating out of Yarmouth.

23/24 May 1917 *L.40* was attacked by a H.12 near Vlieland; the Zeppelin escaped.

5 June 1917 *L.40* was again attacked by a H.12, escaped.

14 June 1917 *L.43* shot down in flames by an H.12 operating out of Felixstowe, near Vlieland.

26 July 1917 *L.44*, *L.45*, *L.46* attacked by an H.12 from Yarmouth. All the Zeppelins escaped.

5 September 1917 *L.44* and *L.46* attacked by H.12 and D.H 4 of Teschelling, the Zeppelins escaped. The aeroplanes ditched in the sea and were only rescued days later.

11 August 1918 *L.53* shot down in flames near Teschelling by a Sopwith Camel from a lighter towed by HMS *Redoubt*.

'B' to attack Zeppelins and bases in the North needed ship-borne aircraft.

21 August 1917 *L.23* shot down near Tondern by a Sopwith Pup from HMS *Yarmouth*.

16 June 1918. *L.54* and *L.60* destroyed at their base at Tonden by Sopwith Camels from HMS *Furious*.

board, was not a success. *L.44* only briefly crossed the coast, coming over at Lowestoft and going back out a few minutes later at Great Yarmouth. In his combat report, Stabbert said he dropped all his bombs on Harwich, but as the British have no record of this they must have fallen in the sea. Stabbert and Strasser, however, had major problems. They had suffered from engine problems over the North Sea, and when they reached the coast all six engines failed. The mechanics managed to get one going again, and after a long, slow flight they got back to Nordholtz. Because of the difficulty of *L.44*'s flight home, Zeppelin *L.23* was sent out from Tondern to find and escort it back, or if it landed in the sea to rescue the crew or lead surface vessels to the airship. The ships sighted each other at 13.06. Stabbert did not land at Nordholz until 17.00, apparently mainly due to lack of experience in operating the new 'high altitude' Zeppelins, as they flew at 20,000ft, twice the height of the older ships. The crew suffered severely from altitude sickness, and it seems the cause of the engine problems was the loss of radiator water due to evaporation at high altitude. If the raid was a failure, it did at least demonstrate some of the problems that needed to be solved.

'R' type Navy Zeppelin *L.45*: Kapitänleutnant Waldemar Kolle flew out of Ahlhorn. There is little information of the flight: *L.45* was tracked across Suffolk and Norfolk, through an area of thunderstorms, and only two of its bombs were traced.

'R' type Navy Zeppelin *L.47*: Kapitänleutnant Richard Wolff operated out of Ahlhorn. In his combat report, Wolff said he flew at about 18,000ft, with a starlit sky above and solid cloud below. A wireless bearing indicated he crossed the Suffolk coast near Lowestoft; he dropped three bombs to bring the guns and searchlights into action. There was no response, so he abandoned his attack and took his remaining bombs home. The British had no record of any bombs, and believed *L.47* did not cross the coast and its bombs must have fallen in the sea.

5 June 1917

'R' type Navy Zeppelin *L.40*: On this day, Kapitänleutnant Erich Sommerfeldt's Zeppelin *L.40* and Curtiss H.12 No. 8666 were to renew their unfriendly relationship. On patrol off the coast of Terschelling, Flight Lieutenant Christopher Galpin reported seeing a Zeppelin at 2,000ft about 6 miles to the north-east. They lost sight of it in the mist, but saw it again at 4,000ft at 08.10. Sommerfeldt must have seen the H.12, because he fired a white Very pistol flare; this time Galpin replied with another white flare, which must have been the wrong reply because the Zeppelin started to climb fast and the H.12 had difficulty in following. With Leckie at the controls, Galpin, Whatling and Laycock fired ten magazines of Brock, Pomeroy and Buckingham ammunition without success. They were unable to get closer than 600 yards or higher than 1,000 feet below the Zeppelin.

There is also have a report of the encounter by Sommerfeldt. He saw the aeroplane about 12 miles away. When it did not respond to recognition signals, he flew east to try to draw it into range of the German seaplane station at Borkum Island. The aeroplane approached, firing tracer ammunition, and his crew fired back with tracer rounds which probably hit the target. By 08.48, the enemy aeroplane was at 10,500ft and *L.40* at 17,400ft. He remained on patrol and at 14.00 reported that the sky was clear and he could not see any vessels which could have transported the plane. Though Sommerfeldt had used the correct tactics, climbing to escape from the flying boat, the Germans still failed to understand the nature of the threat, unaware the enemy aeroplanes were operating from England.

14 June 1917

'S' type Navy Zeppelin *L.43*: Kapitänleutnant Hermann Kraushaar commanded the last raid by *L.43*. On 14 June, three Zeppelins – *L.23*, *L.42* and *L.43* – took off in the early morning on a scouting mission to support minesweepers in the U-boat blockade area off the Terschelling Bank. At 05.36, operating out of Ahlhorn, *L.43* radioed to say that it was starting to patrol near the Terschelling Bank lightship. A number of Zeppelin signals had been picked up by British wireless direction-finding stations, and a Curtiss H.12 flying boat, No. 8677, took off from RNAS Felixstowe in their direction. The Curtiss was flown by Flight Sub Lieutenant B.D. Hobbs and Flight Sub Lieutenant R.F.L. Dickey, with air mechanics H.M. Davis and A.W. Goody as wireless operators and gunners. They took off at about 05.15, and at 08.40 reported they sighted a Zeppelin off the Dutch coast at Vlieland: they were flying at about 500ft, with the Zeppelin at 1,500ft. It seems the crew of the Zeppelin did not see the flying boat approaching from its tail. During the attack, Hobbs flew the plane, Dickey operated the bow Lewis gun, Davies the midship gun and Goody the stern guns. During the attack, Goody noted the number of the Zeppelin, *L.43*. The 'Large America' got within about 100ft of the Zeppelin before opening fire; flying over the Zeppelin and firing downwards, using Brock and Pomeroy ammunition, the airship burst into flames. After the first pass, they turned to make a second firing run but saw the Zeppelin was completely enveloped in flames and falling very fast. Three men were observed to fall from the airship on the way down. Some of the wreckage, probably fabric, seemed to float on the water, as they saw flames and black smoke for some time after the wreckage crashed into the sea. Kapitänleutnant Kraushaar and his second officer, Leutnant zur See Ernst Zimmermann, were killed, along with twenty-two other crew members. Curtiss H.12 No. 8677 returned to Felixstowe at about 11.15.

The British put out a press report that day with brief details of the incident: 'Zeppelin *L.43* was destroyed this morning by our Naval Forces in the North Sea. Soon after being attacked she burst into flames fore and aft, broke into two and fell into the sea. No survivors were seen.'

The Germans had little idea what had happened to *L.43*, although they received a disturbing report at about 08.45 from Kapitänleutnant Heinrich Hollander in *L.46*, who said he was patrolling near the Hook of Holland when he was attacked by an enemy seaplane. Flight Lieutenant Galpin, in Curtiss H.12 No. 8660, had taken off from Yarmouth because of intercepted radio signals from Zeppelins. At around 08.30, Galpin saw a Zeppelin at about 10,500ft. He said Leckie, who was the pilot, turned to meet the airship. By 08.45, they had reached a height of 12,500ft and were under the Zeppelin. Galpin and the crew fired four magazines of Brock, Pomeroy and Buckingham ammunition upwards, but could not reach the climbing airship. Hollander's report says he was flying at 13,000ft when he saw a British seaplane, a bi-plane, with two occupants and one machine gun, coming up from astern. The plane came out of a cloud bank at 8,200ft and approached the Zeppelin very fast. Hollander dropped most of his ballast and started to climb. The seaplane reached a maximum of 13,000ft. The fight went on for almost an hour, with the aircraft under the Zeppelin so the crew could not fire back at it. *L.46* was able to climb away to safety, but whilst the airship was undamaged, it had dropped most of its ballast in getting away so Hollander had to cut short his mission and return to base.

When Fragettenkapitan Peter Strasser read Hollander's report, he ordered that in future all Zeppelins on scouting missions should fly at above 13,000ft. While this would keep them safe, it massively reduced their value as reconnaissance aircraft, making minesweeping and submarine spotting work impossible.

16/17 June 1917

This was not an ideal night for a raid, only a few days from the shortest night of the year. This would give the Zeppelins only about four hours of darkness over England, so GHQ only expected raids on coastal towns. Weather conditions were not favourable and all the Zeppelins experienced strong headwinds.

'S' type Navy Zeppelin *L.42*: Kapitänleutnant Martin Dietrich, flying from Nordholz, crossed the Kent coast over the North Foreland at 02.05, bombing Ramsgate, Manston and Gatlinge. One of the 300kg bombs from *L.42* hit a naval ammunition store near the clock tower in Ramsgate harbour, destroying many of the buildings in the base and killing two men and a woman. Seven men, seven women and two children were also injured in the fish market area. After he crossed the coast, Dietrich was chased by a number of aircraft from the RNAS. Flight Sub Lieutenant George Bittles, in a Sopwith Baby, got within 30 yards and fired a full drum from his Lewis gun at *L.42*. Dietrich was also chased by two of the men involved in shooting down Zeppelin *L.21*, Egbert Cadbury and Gerard Fane, both flying Sopwith Pups. Flight Lieutenant Cadbury got close to *L.42* but lost the airship at 16,000ft when the Pup had a petrol pipe fracture. At 03.35, Dietrich noted the burning of *L.48* from 70 miles away: 'A red ball of fire suddenly appeared' in the shape of a Zeppelin. The Curtiss H.12 No. 8666, flown by Flight Sub-Lieutenant Leckie, Flight Commander Nicholls and Leading Mechanics Farnie and Grant, took off from Yarmouth at 03.05 and spotted *L.42* at 8,000 feet. They followed Dietrich across the North Sea, reaching a position 10 miles north of Ameland Island off the Dutch coast, but could not catch him and returned to Yarmouth.

'T' type Navy Zeppelin *L.44*:. Kapitänleutnant Franz Stabbert, operating out of Ahlhorn, returned early due to engine trouble.

'R' type Navy Zeppelin *L.45*: Kapitänleutnant Waldemar Kolle, flying from Tondern, also had to return early with engine trouble.

'U' type Navy Zeppelin *L.48*: Kapitänleutnant Franz Georg Eichler had as a passenger Korvettenkapitan Viktor Schulze, recently promoted to commander of the Naval Airship Division. It is said the relationship between the two men on the raid was not good, Schulze finding fault with the way Eichler handled his old airship: the fact he had taken over Schlulze's old crew probably didn't help. Leaving Nordholz in the early afternoon, their target was the south of England, London if possible. *L.48* was first spotted north-east of Harwich at 23.34, spent some time off the coast and crossed south of Orford Ness at 02.00. It flew towards Harwich at 16,000ft and was fired on by anti-aircraft guns, then circled in the area and at 03.28 was attacked three aircraft. They were a D.H.2 flown by Captain Robert Saundby, a F.E.2b piloted by Lieutenant Frank Holder - with Sergeant Sydney Ashby as observer/gunner - and a B.E.12 flown by Lieutenant Louden Watkins of 37 Home Defence Squadron RFC. All three planes fired at *L.48*, but the credit for shooting it down was given to Lieutenant Watkins. The Zeppelin burst into flames and fell near Holly Tree Farm, Theberton, Suffolk. Sixteen members of the crew, including Eichler and Schulze, were killed, but three survived. Because of this there are very detailed reports of the attack, both from the Zeppelin crew and British pilots.

L.48 crossed the coast at 18,000ft, an engine having given trouble some time into the flight, and Eichler decided to attack Harwich. He thought he was over the port at 02.10, when he was caught in a number of searchlight beams and came under intense anti-aircraft fire. Leutnant zur See Otto Mieth, one of the surviving crew, said he counted twenty or thirty searchlights. Eichler dropped all his bombs, aiming for the gun battery; he was actually about 5 miles north of Harwich and most of the bombs fell in open fields near Kirton. With the bombs gone, *L.48* steered away from the guns, dropping to 13,000ft. By this time he was effectively lost, a frozen compass adding to his problems. As he flew across East Anglia, ground observers were updating GHQ on his position, and his reduction in altitude was to prove fatal.

At about 01.55, Lieutenant Holder and Sergeant Ashby of the RFC took off from Orford Ness Armament Experimental Station in a F.E.2b, a two-seat pusher biplane, armed with two Lewis guns. Holder found the Zeppelin and got below it just after dropping its bombs. He was at 14,200ft, but the Zeppelin was much higher. He and Ashby started firing with their Lewis guns, but without effect. At about 03.10, the Zeppelin started to descend and they were able to get much closer. Sergeant Ashby fired four drums of ammunition from his Lewis gun, and was about 300 yards from the airship when he fired a fifth drum, which jammed after about thirty rounds. Holder turned away so he could clear the jam, and when he looked back he saw the Zeppelin was on fire and beginning to fall.

At 02.55, Captain Robert Saundby of the RFC, in a D.H.2, a single-seat pusher fighter armed with a single forward-firing Lewis gun, also took off from Orford Ness. He was at a disadvantage as he had never previously been in action at night, and was glad it was near dawn so he could land in daylight. He performed very well though. He reported attacking the Zeppelin at 03.10. Getting behind it and climbing under its tail, he fired three drums of ammunition at a rapidly shortening range. Halfway through the third drum, a fire started on the *L.48* and spread rapidly along its hull.

The third aircraft, a B.E.12 flown by Canadian Loudon Pierce Watkins of 'A' Flight, 37 Squadron, RFC, took off from Goldhanger aerodrome at 02.06. He reported that he saw the Zeppelin at 13,000-14,000ft, making for the coast. He fired two drums from his Lewis gun when about 2,000ft below the airship without any effect. He climbed to 500ft below *L.48* before firing a third drum – two short bursts and one long burst – whereupon a fire started in the tail and quickly spread.

All three pilots thought they had shot down the Zeppelin. All had seen tracers from other machines, but Holder had not seen another aircraft. Both Saundby, who said he had seen a machine higher than him, and Watkins, who said he had seen an 'aircraft firing tracer early in the engagement but lost sight of it', had seen other aircraft, but could not identify them. We will never know who fired the fatal shot; the War Office arbitrarily awarded the victory to Watkins. It seems likely that all the bullets had some effect, ripping gas cells and allowing hydrogen to mix with the air, to be ignited by a tracer round.

Still burning, Zeppelin *L.48* crashed near Holly Tree Farm. The three members of the crew who survived were the second officer, Leutnant zur See Otto Mieth, Maschininistenmaat Heinrich Ellerkamm and Maschinistenmaat Wilhelm Uecker. There is a description of what it was like to be shot down in a Zeppelin from one of the very few survivors, Ellerkamm, who was an engine mechanic and was climbing up a ladder from his engine gondola into the hull to check the fuel supply when he heard a machine gun firing. He looked down and saw an English fighter firing its tracer bullets at *L.48*, and as he looked up into the hull he saw the bullets like fireflies in the dark shooting through the gas cells. There was an explosion, 'not loud but a dull woof as when you light a gas stove', then a burst of flame and more explosions as one gas cell after another caught fire. The Zeppelin fell very quickly as its hydrogen lifting gas burned. Luckily for Ellerkamm, the wind created by the fall kept the flames away from him, and he survived, badly burned, when the airship hit the ground. Otto Mieth had just come out of the radio cabin after sending a signal 'reporting the success of the raid' when the fire started. He and Eichler took off their fur-lined leather overcoats so they could swim if the ship landed in the sea. Viktor Schulze just stood calm and still, and said 'it is all over'.

Both Mieth and Ellerkamm survived the war, treated well by the British, and have greatly added to our understanding of Zeppelin operations. It is very difficult not to feel sorry for Uecker, who spent the rest of the war suffering from terrible burns and died on 11 November 1918 – Armistice Day. The crew of *L.48* – the last Zeppelin to be shot down over British soil – who died are now buried at Cannock Chase.

Of the four airmen who shot down *L.48*, Ashby and Watkins were killed in action in 1918. Sir Robert Saundby remained in the RAF, rising to Air Marshal, while Holder became a squadron leader.

17 June 1917

'R' type Navy Zeppelin *L.40*: Kapitänleutnant Erich Sommerfeldt crash-landed at Neuenwald, near the Nordholz base. The Zeppelin broke its back, was too badly damaged for repair and was scrapped, though some of its parts were used on other airships. There were no injuries in the crash.

26 July 1917

This was another significant anti-Zeppelin operation by Curtiss flying boats. On this occasion, however, all the Zeppelins escaped.

'T' type Navy Zeppelin *L.44*: Kapitänleutnant Franz Stabbert operated out of Ahlhorn.

'R' type Navy Zeppelin *L.45*: Kapitänleutnant Waldemar Kolle flew out of Tondern.

'T' type Navy Zeppelin *L.46*: Kapitänleutnant Heinrich Hollander operated from Ahlhorn.

The three Zeppelins took off on a scouting mission. Radio signals were picked up by the Admiralty, and Flight Lieutenant Galpin took off in H.12 No. 8666 from Yarmouth. The British had worked out another attack strategy: they would always approach the Zeppelin with the sun behind them. Galpin saw Zeppelin *L.46* at 10,000ft about 15 miles away. It seems Hollander did not see them until they were about a mile away, then dropped ballast and put his airship's nose up to an angle of 15-20 degrees and started climbing fast. Galpin reached 11,500ft, the maximum altitude that day, and fired four magazines of Brock, Pomeroy and Buckingham ammunition at *L.46* without effect. It seems *L.46* fired back, as bullet holes were later found in the top wing near the petrol tank. Unable to catch the Zeppelin, Galpin continued the search and saw another airship at 10.00, 10 miles away, flying at 8,000ft. It was *L.44*. When they were within 3 miles, Galpin saw the Zeppelin drop ballast, put her nose up and climb to 15,000ft. He correctly concluded that it had been warned of their presence by *L.46*. The H.12 returned to Yarmouth, with just enough petrol to make it.

Kapitänleutnant Hollander reported on the action. He said he had first seen the plane from about 2 miles away. He had dropped most of his ballast but the airship was slow to climb and the plane got to within about 1,000 metres of *L.46*. He steered east to try to draw the enemy towards the German seaplane station at Borkum Island, and fired at it with two machine guns. The action lasted about twenty-three minutes before the seaplane broke off. Hollander said he sent out radio messages because of the danger to other airships. At about 11.00, two squadrons of German seaplane fighters and one squadron of land-based fighters took off, but H.12 No. 8666 was well away.

The 'Large America' flying boat played a major role in the defeat of the Zeppelin, but it had one weakness: with an endurance of just six hours, it was restricted to operations in the narrow part of the North Sea between East Anglia and the coast of Holland.

At the end of 1916, the Royal Navy began to experiment with lighters, special craft designed to extend the range of H.12 'Large America' flying boats. Lighters were unpowered boats strong enough to be towed behind destroyers at a speed of 20-25 knots. The final design was a steel boat about 56ft long, with a beam of 16ft and a height above the water of about 7ft. The lighters were fitted with flooding tanks, so the stern of the boat could be submerged and a flying boat winched onto it. Compressed air would then fill the tank, so the lighter would return to its normal position to be towed at speed. It could then be towed across the North Sea, conserving its fuel, to conduct missions against German targets off the Friesian Coast. When the lighter and flying boat got to their operational position, the loading procedure would be reversed and the H.12 refloated to take off. By November 1918, the Navy had thirty-one of these lighters. They were first used in anti-Zeppelin operations on 19 March 1918, when flying boats were taken into the German Bight. By 18 May, there had been four operations.

21 August 1917

'Q' type Navy Zeppelin *L.23*: By the late summer, the Germans were understandably cautious using Zeppelins off the Dutch coast. They didn't expect the same level of opposition further north, which meant they could use older 'Q' type Zeppelins for scouting missions. Oberleutnant zur See Bernhard Dinter took over *L.23* on 14 June, having previously been second officer to Kapitänleutnant Waldemar Kolle on Schutte-Lanze and Zeppelin airships. He was only 28; it may be that the Airship Service had to use inexperienced commanders as the death rate climbed. On the morning of 21 August, Dinter, with Leutnant zur See Otto Hamann as second officer, set out on a routine patrol from Tondern in *L.23*. His task was to look for enemy ships off the coast of Denmark. At about 04.30, he sighted HMS *Yarmouth*, a light cruiser, on what seemed to be a minesweeping operation, following the warship at what he believed to be a safe distance. He did not know he was flying into a trap, as HMS *Yarmouth* was a primitive aircraft carrier, with a 20ft-long wooden platform on its front gun turret. On it ready to take off was Sub Lieutenant Bernard Arthur Smart, RNAS, in a Sopwith Pup fighter aeroplane. He was probably feeling apprehensive, not because of the Zeppelin, but because he had never taken off from the platform before – not even on a training flight. At about 05.30, *Yarmouth* was given the order 'Fly your aeroplane', and with the cruiser steaming at full speed into the wind, Smart gave the engine of the Pup full throttle and was released, reached flying speed before the end of the platform and took off. He climbed to 7,000ft, with the Zeppelin about 15 miles away. He must have been sighted as he neared the Zeppelin, as *L.23* sent a radio signal – 'Am being attacked by enemy forces' – then silence. Smart flew above *L.23* and fired two burst from his machine gun at the stern. He reported that flames shot out of the airship's hull and it rapidly became a roaring furnace. *L.23* hit the sea and burnt out off the coast of Lodbjerg, Denmark; all eighteen crew men were killed. Smart quickly sighted his fleet, landed in the sea near HMS *Prince* just fifty-nine minutes after taking off from *Yarmouth*. The boat that rescued him was also able to retrieve the engine and machine gun from the Pup.

The Germans sent out a sea plane to search. It saw a large patch of oil and petrol, with a few wooden fragments, probably from a propeller, floating in the sea. It was all there was left of Zeppelin *L.23*. Smart was awarded a DSO for his courageous mission, and would get another ten months later for his part in destroying several more Zeppelins.

21/22 August 1917

Eight airships set out to bomb central England. The raid was a failure, with only little damage caused. The British records for the raid are poor. The cause of this is probably the overall military situation. Normally, soldiers awaiting deployment to France performed observation duty, but by mid-1917, due to the Battle of Passchendaele, there were far fewer men available. Many of the observation duties were passed to special constables, but there were fewer of them, and they often lacked the necessary skills. As the Zeppelins now operated over England at up to 20,000 feet, spotting was also much more difficult.

'R' type Navy Zeppelin *L.35*: Kapitänleutnant Herbert Ehrlich, operating from Ahlhorn, had to turn back when he was near Scarborough because it was getting light, and returned early to base.

'R' type Navy Zeppelin *L.41*: Hauptmann Kuno Manger left Ahlhorn and crossed the coast at midnight, intending to attack Hull. He got near the city but was turned back by anti-aircraft fire. He bombed Paull, Hedon, Preston and Thorngumbald. A number of buildings were damaged in Hedon and one man injured. According to Joseph Morris, author of *German Air Raids on Britain 1914-1918*, the bombs were dropped promiscuously and damaged two chapels, one Primitive Methodist and one Roman Catholic. A number of British aircraft followed *L.41* out to sea, but as Manger was flying at about 20,000ft they could not get near enough to attack. A 'Large America' flying boat was sent to intercept *L.41* as it neared Ahlhorn, but was unable to find it.

'S' type Navy Zeppelin *L.42*: Kapitänleutnant Martin Dietrich, flying from Nordholz, had engine problems and could not attack Hull, so attacked ships off Spurn Point.

'T' type Zeppelin *L.44*: The engine issue seemed to have been solved, though considerable problems with altitude sickness remained when Kapitänleutnant Franz Stabbert set out from Nordholz in *L.44*. It seems he bombed near Lincoln, but there were no casualties and little damage was done.

'R' type Navy Zeppelin *L.45*: Kapitänleutnant Waldemar Kolle, flying from Tondern, attacked warships off the Yorkshire coast near Withernsea.

'T' type Navy Zeppelin *L.46*: Kapitänleutnant Heinrich Hollander flew from Ahlhorn. The only surviving reports indicate that he saw the lights of a big city which he thought was Sheffield, but could not get there because of headwinds so dropped his bombs on Louth in Lincolnshire. The British have no record of any bombs in the area at that time.

'R' type Navy Zeppelin *L.47*: Kapitänleutnant Michael von Freudenreich, embarking from Ahlhorn, claimed to have bombed Grimsby. However, the British have no records of any such attack.

'U' type Navy Zeppelin *L.51*: Kapitänleutnant Walter Dose, flying from Nordholz, reported he had compass problems and returned to base early.

5 September 1917

The British launched an attack using a new strategy, combining the Curtiss H.12 with the Airco D.H.4 in an attempt to intercept Zeppelins at high altitude over the German Bight. The D.H.4 was probably the best anti-Zeppelin aircraft of the war. One shot down *L.70*, the last Zeppelin to raid England in August 1918. The early model had a RAF 3A 17-litre 'V' 12 cylinder 250hp engine. It had a top speed of about 120mph and could operate at 20,000ft. The tactic was that the H.12 and D.H 4 operated in pairs, the H.12 navigating and communicating with the shore while the D.H.4 attacked the Zeppelin.

'T' type Navy Zeppelin *L.44*: Kapitänleutnant Franz Stabbert flew from Ahlhorn.

'T' type Navy Zeppelin *L.46*: Kapitänleutnant Heinrich Hollander flew from Ahlhorn.

For this attack, the H.12 was once again No. 8666: the pilots were Flight Lieutenant Robert Leckie and Squadron Commander Nicholls, with two petty officers as wireless operator and mechanic. The D.H.4 was flown by Flight Lieutenant Gilligan and Observer Lieutenant Trewin. At about 13.00, they saw two Zeppelins, *L.44* and *L.46*, about 30 miles from Terschelling. The D.H.4 fired at *L.44*, but had engine trouble so could not get high enough to endanger the Zeppelin. The D.H.4 had been hit in the radiator, probably by shrapnel fired from a German warship, and the engine eventually seized. Gilligan landed in the sea, with the H.12 landing to pick them up. However, there was a problem. With six men aboard, the flying-boat could not take off in the rough sea and had to taxi back. During the evening, the petrol ran out with the six men in the middle of the North Sea. The H.12 then drifted, and the men were not rescued until 8 September, obviously by then in a very poor physical state.

24 September 1917

Two Zeppelins bombed batteries in strategic positions at Sworbe and Zerel on Oesel Island (now Saaremaa in Estonia) during Operation Albion.

'R' type Navy Zeppelin *LZ.113*: This was commanded by Kapitänleutnant Walter Zaeschmar.

'R' type Navy Zeppelin *LZ.120*: Kapitänleutnant Johann von Lossnitzer was in command of this airship.

Both these Zeppelins were transferred to Navy command in June 1917. This mission was the start of Operation Albion, the invasion by German troops of Russian islands in the Baltic. The main problem for the airships during the operation was the supply of hydrogen gas to top-up after missions. There were three bases, at Seddin, Seerappen and Wainoden. The Seddin base was built at Stolp in East Prussia (Slupsk, Poland) near the city of Danzig (Gdansk, Poland). This base had gas production facilities, but they were reduced because of an explosion in June, and there were small gas production plants at Seeruppen (Lyubilno, Russia) or Wainoden (Vainode, Latvia). The nearest fully operational gas plant was at Stettin in East Prussia (Szczecin, Poland) or the North Sea bases, and hydrogen cylinders had to be transported hundreds of miles by rail up the Baltic coast. Some preliminary bombing had taken place in early September when railway junctions were raided at Walk (Valga, Estonia) and Wolmar (Valmiera, Estonia) east of the Gulf of Riga.

24/25 September 1917

This attack on England again showed the weakness of the height climbers. The sky was cloudy, and this, combined with the altitude of the Zeppelins, made navigation difficult and accurate bombing almost impossible. Three people were injured and damage was caused to the value of £2,210. The height also made ground observations difficult, and it is one of the most poorly recorded raids of the war.

'R' type Navy Zeppelin *L.35*: Kapitänleutnant Herbert Ehrlich, operating out of Ahlhorn, was seen crossing the English coast at 00.05, and flew westward. At 02.30 he was near Barnsley, but saw lights in the direction of Rotherham. Ehrlich bombed the Parkgate Steel Works and Silverwood Colliery north of Rotherham. The lights that attracted Ehrlich were put out before he reached his target, and although some damage was done – largely broken glass - there were no casualties. Twenty-five bombs fell in a line between Thurnscoe and Ryecroft.

'R' type Navy Zeppelin *L.41*: Hauptmann Kuno Manger, flying from Ahlhorn, crossed the Yorkshire coast at Hornsea at 01.27 and made for Hull. He flew across the city from north-west to east, at about 16,000ft, dropping sixteen bombs at around 02.40. Three women were injured, but little damage was caused. Manger dropped four more bombs on Marfleet, which landed in a field. He was then caught in a searchlight and fired on by anti-aircraft guns at Paull, before dropping four more bombs at Preston. He was sighted in the Paull searchlight by Lieutenant W.W. Cook in a B.E.2e. Cook had previously tried to target Zeppelin *L.55*, but could not reach its height. He had the same problem with *L.41*. He was over Beverley at 14,500ft, but the Zeppelin was at 16,000ft and he could not reach it. He lost sight of the Zeppelin when the searchlight was switched off.

'S' type Navy Zeppelin *L.42*: Kapitänleutnant Martin Dietrich, from Nordholz, had engine trouble and turned back before reaching the coast. He reported dropping his bombs on shipping in the Humber. It may be that *L.42* was the third Zeppelin attacked by Lieutenant William Cook that night. After losing *L.41*, he saw another Zeppelin and followed it out to sea for 60 miles. Cook reported he got to within 800 yards of the Zeppelin and fired four magazines from his Lewis gun at it, without effect. On his return to base, Dietrich found two bullet holes in his gas cells; he said he had seen aeroplanes below the ship, but didn't say he was attacked.

'T' type Navy Zeppelin *L.44*: Kapitänleutnant Franz Stabbert operated out of Ahlhorn. A GHQ report suggested this may have been the Zeppelin spotted in Suffolk near Elsmwell at 03.20 by an aeroplane from No. 75 Squadron, and lost near Bungay at 03.35. It was difficult to make more accurate observations because of the cloud.

'T' type Navy Zeppelin *L.46*: Kapitänleutnant Heinrich Hollander, operating out of Ahlhorn, had the dubious honour of having Peter Strasser as his passenger. *L.46* crossed the coast near Grimsby and dropped most of its bombs near Cuxwold in Lincolnshire. It seems Hollander saw the lights of a RFC airfield. The bombs landed in an open field without causing any damage. With his bombs gone, Hollander made for the coast and was seen crossing near Spurn Head at 03.00.

'R' type Navy Zeppelin *L.47*: Kapitänleutnant Michael von Freudenreich flew from Ahlhorn. There are no more details of his participation in the raid.

'R' type Navy Zeppelin *L.50*: Kapitänleutnant Roderich Schwonder operated from Ahlhorn. Again, there are no further details.

'U' type Navy Zeppelin *L.51*: Kapitänleutnant Walter Dose flew from Nordholz and returned early.

'U' type Navy Zeppelin *L.52*: Oberleutnant zur See Kurt Friemel operated out of Nordholz and also returned early.

'V' type Navy Zeppelin *L.53*: Kapitänleutnant Eduard Prolss, flying out of Nordholz, had Sheffield as his target but was held back by strong headwinds. He dropped his bombs in the Boston area of Lincolnshire without causing any damage.

'V' type Navy Zeppelin *L.55*: Kapitänleutnant Hans Kurt Flemming flew out of Nordholz and crossed the Yorkshire coast at Bridlington at 00.15, flying towards Scarborough and Whitby. It appears Flemming knew roughly where he was because he then attempted to bomb the works at Skinningrove, a previous target for Zeppelin attacks. He dropped six bombs which landed 4 miles south of the works without causing any damage. *L.55* was then caught in the Skinningrove searchlight and fired on by anti-aircraft guns, but was able to escape the searchlight beam and made for the coast. It was followed by a B.E.2e aeroplane flown by Lieutenant William Cook of the RFC. In his first attack of the night, he was unable to reach *L.55* at 16,000ft, and the Zeppelin escaped. It seems that Flemming dropped the rest of his bombs in the sea near Staithes.

The most remarkable thing about the raid was the heroism of Lieutenant William Wallace Cook. He was a New Zealander of 76 Squadron RFC, based at Helperby in Yorkshire. He took off in his B.E.2e at about 01.00, with a patrol line between Helperby and Shipton. He saw a Zeppelin caught in searchlights neat Middlesbrough at about 16,000ft. He chased the Zeppelin but was unable to get above 10,000ft. Cook lost the airship when the searchlight went off. It seems this Zeppelin was *L.55*. A 60mph wind was blowing him out to sea, so it took him some fifty minutes to get back to his patrol line, by this time flying at about 14,500ft. He then saw another Zeppelin caught in a searchlight over Hull. This must have been *L.41*, and he turned towards Hull, losing the Zeppelin when the searchlight was turned off. He carried on with his patrol and saw yet another Zeppelin in the light before dawn. This must have been Dietrich in *L.42*. Cook got within 800 yards of the airship and chased him 60 miles out to sea, firing four magazines of ammunition.

He was unable to match Dietrich's height and had to turn back because he was low on fuel. After flying for about five hours, he got back over the coast near Flamborough Head, and landed in a field 400 yards from the shore. He was awarded the Military Cross for his mission, for what was described as an 'intelligent and determined sortie which only failed because of bad luck'.

H.A. Jones, in *The War in the Air*, records Cook was ill-rewarded for his attempts to attack the airships, due to the fact the B.E.2e was outclassed in speed and ceiling by the latest type Zeppelins.

1 October 1917

These Zeppelins again attacked targets in the Baltic in preparation for Operation Albion. They took off from Seerappen and Wainoden to bomb to the east of the Riga Basin, hitting the small ports of Salismunde (now Salacgriva in Latvia) and Sophienruhe. The towns were poorly defended, and Kapitänleutnant Gartner reported he attacked in *L.37* from only 4,100ft.

'R' type Navy Zeppelin *L.30*: Oberleutnant zur See Heinz Bodecker commanded the airship for this raid.

'R' type Navy Zeppelin *L.37*: This Zeppelin was commanded by Kapitänleutnant Gartner.

'R' type Navy Zeppelin *LZ.120*: Kapitänleutnant Johann von Lossnitzer took charge of the airship for this raid.

8 October 1917

'W' type Navy Zeppelin *L.57*: The Naval Airship Service planned a mission to send ammunition and medical supplies to the army of General Paul von Lettow Vorbeck in East Africa. *L.57* and *L.59* were lengthened for this mission. On a test flight at Juterbog, Kapitänleutnant Ludwig Bockholt's *L.57* crashed into the doors of its shed and burst into flames. The Zeppelin was completely destroyed, but the crew were uninjured.

11 October 1917

During Operation Albion, 23,000 German troops embarked on nineteen transport ships at Libau and sailed for Tagga Bay on Oesel Island (Saaremaa).

They landed on 12 October, by 17 October all of Oesel had been captured, and on 19 October Dago Island (Hiiumaa, Estonia) was taken. The Zeppelins escorted the fleet, and provided aerial reconnaissance.

'R' type Navy Zeppelin *L.30*: Oberleutnant zur See Heinz Bodecker took off from Seerappen and flew north-east to watch over the Riga Basin.

'R' type Navy Zeppelin *LZ.113*: Kapitänleutnant Walter Zaeschmar flew north to the mouth of the Finnish Gulf and bombed the Sworbe (Sorve, Estonia) batteries on the way home.

'F' type Navy Shutte-Lanz *SL.20*: Kapitänleutnant Guido Wolff took off from Seddin to accompany the fleet.

15 October 1917

Of the four Zeppelins left in the East - *L.30*, *L.37*, *LZ.113* and *LZ.120* – three set out to bomb Pernau (Pernu, Estonia) in the Gulf of Riga, the last operational Russian naval base in the gulf. All claimed to have bombed the centre of the town, despite anti-aircraft fire.

16 October 1917

Operation Albion was a complete success, and with Russia out of the war the Baltic Airship Command was disbanded. By November 1917, most of the airships were taken out of service. Zeppelins *L.37* and *LZ.113* were deflated and hung up in sheds at Seddin. *L.30* and *LZ.120* were deflated and hung up at Seerappen. Schutte-Lanz *SL.8* was scrapped, and only *SL.20* was deemed good enough for service over the North Sea, going to Ahlhorn, only to be destroyed a few weeks later in a hangar fire.

'R' type Navy Zeppelin *L.37*: Kapitänleutnant Gartner took off from Seerappen to bomb Pernau, returning to base with serious damage to the port midships engine gondola due to a fire on the flight.

'F' type Navy Shutte-Lanz *SL.20*: Kapitänleutnant Guido Wolff took off from Seddin to bomb Pernau, but did not reach the target due to engine trouble. He returned to Seddin after a flight of thirty-one hours.

Chapter Twelve

The Silent Raid: 19/20 October 1917

Politics in the German High Command were the real motive behind the last major Zeppelin raid of the war on 19/20 October 1917. The Army had given up using airships for reconnaissance or bombing, And was using twin-engine Gotha bombers, or four-engine 'Giant' bombers, for the bombing of London. General Ludendorff considered the use of aluminium and other strategic materials in Zeppelins a waste of resources. Not surprisingly, Vizeadmiral Reinhard Scheer, Commander of the High Seas Fleet, and the Navy High Command fundamentally disagreed with this. They needed Zeppelins for purely naval purposes, reconnaissance and mine clearance, and also saw strategic bombing by Zeppelins as important for the war effort. While there was ample evidence that the bombing of London was more effectively carried out by aeroplanes, Gothas operating from near the Belgian coast did not have the range to bomb the industrial Midlands or North. The debate raged over much of 1917, going as far as the Kaiser for resolution. He largely decided in favour of the Army. Zeppelin production was to be cut from two per month to one every two months. This was barely above the attrition rate to replace airship losses. There were also to be strict limits on the number of Zeppelins the Navy operated, and they were to concentrate on reconnaissance. Bombing was seen as a luxury, no longer affordable. Scheer and the Leader of Airships, Fregattenkapitan Peter Strasser, agreed on the need for spectacular mass raids by 'height climbers' as a game-changer to push the argument their way. Plans were made for thirteen Zeppelins to raid the English Midlands in the autumn on a day when weather conditions were favourable.

The raid on 19 October was the last major Zeppelin effort of the war, with eleven Zeppelins setting out to bomb Middle England. Their principal targets were to be Sheffield, Manchester and Liverpool. The raid became known as the 'silent raid' because the airships flew above 16,000ft; due to the wind direction they were not heard from the ground, and the anti-aircraft guns around London did not fire as they failed to see the Zeppelins above the cloud base. Although the raid caused a lot of damage – 250 bombs were dropped, causing £54,346 worth of damage, with thirty-six people killed and fifty-five injured – it was a disaster for the Naval Airship Service. The weather forecast before the raid had been inaccurate, and the Zeppelins were caught in a gale on the way home, which led to the loss of five ships.

The decision to take off was made at short notice on the morning of 19 October. Peter Strasser phoned the thirteen commanders from his head-quarters at Ahlhorn, ordering them to be ready to take off before noon. It is significant that two Zeppelins – *L.42* (Kapitänleutnant Martin Dietrich) and *L.51* (Kapitänleutnant Walter Dose) – were unable to take off because high winds prevented them being taken out of their sheds at Nordholz.

We have reasonably good records of the action of each Zeppelin, with German combat records used by Douglas Robinson and British intelligence reports analyzed by H.A. Jones. Jones wrote: 'As they moved westward the movements of six of them were fairly closely followed by the Admiralty and a warning issued at 4.00pm (16.00) from Whitehall that indications pointed to an airship raid in the Midlands and North.' There are, however, gaps in the records, and they are not as good as the detailed routes we have for raids earlier in the war. There are a number of reasons for this. The most import-ant is the weather: the raid took place on a cloudy night and the Zeppelin commanders were mostly lost. They were aware that the British Admiralty was monitoring their radio signals, and were much more aware of the need to maintain radio discipline. They still made calls asking for their positions, as radio bearings were for much of the raid their only means of navigation, and these were faithfully recorded by the British. In many ways, these sig-nals are the best sources of information we have. There were fewer records made by observers on the ground, as they often couldn't hear let alone see a Zeppelin 20,000ft above them. Obviously, the locations where bombs fell were recorded. Using all these factors, we can trace the route of each Zeppelin, although we have to accept there are gaps in the record. What follows are details of the movement of each Zeppelin.

'R' Type Navy Zeppelin *L.41*: Hauptman Kuno Manger was an expe-rienced commander, with ten raids on England to his credit. He took off from Ahlhorn at about 11.30 in Zeppelin *L.41*, with Manchester as his tar-get. Just after take-off, he reported the weather was flat calm as he flew over the Friesian island of Norderney at 9,000ft. Later in the afternoon, he had to change course several times to go around thunderstorms. He crossed the Yorkshire coast near Spurn Head at 18.45. In his combat report, Manger said he had targeted Manchester, bombing a brightly lit big new factory and an iron foundry with blast furnaces. The British had good records of his progress which show he was nowhere near Manchester. They believe he dropped three bombs at Scampton, Lincolnshire, near the aerodrome of 33 Squadron RFC; aircraft were awaiting orders to take off at 19.40 when the bombs landed. No one had heard the Zeppelin and it was long gone before they were able to take off. He was then observed circling near Derby at 21.40, was west of Birmingham at 22 50 and seems to have dropped most of his bombs in the West Midlands area between Netherton, near Dudley, and Barnt Green, near Birmingham. Local records seem to confirm this, and match what Manger said he saw. He dropped sixteen bombs on the Grazebrook foundry and blast furnace at Netherton, damaging some railway wagons near Hall Lane Farm. There is a story that the farmer there found some bombs on his land the next day, and rather than call the police hired three men to take them to Dudley police station on a horse and cart. *L.41* then flew a few miles south-east and dropped more bombs on the Hayward Forge at Halesowen, described locally as lit up like a Christmas free. A bomb fell on Mucklow Hill but did not explode and a large HE bomb hit Halesowen Golf course at Leasowes. Nearby Quinton School recorded many of its pupils truanted to look at the crater. It seems *L.41* then turned and flew over the Austin Motor Works at Longbridge in Birmingham. Manger dropped five bombs; three failed to explode, one man was injured and some buildings damaged, to a cost of about £500.

A correspondent for the *Dudley Herald* newspaper gave a very full description of the damage, and though because of censorship he could not identify where the bombs fell, he had obviously personally seen the damage and interviewed eyewitnesses. The *Herald* was published on a Saturday, and as the raid occurred late on Friday, details were not published until 27 October. It reported that an eyewitness said:

> The hostile aircraft passed over here about 22.55 on Friday night. The first notice was the noise of the engines, and it was first thought it was an aeroplane, as the noise it made did not seem sufficiently loud for a Zeppelin. No notice of air-raid action had been received. Three bombs were dropped in quick succession, followed by bumps and flashes. [The witness is hearing the different sounds of high explosive and igniting incendiary bombs.] Half a minute elapsed before two more fell. Even then not many thought it was a hostile aircraft, many persons being under the impression that anti-aircraft guns were firing blanks. The Zeppelin must have been travelling at a great height and very fast for it was not audible for more than three minutes.

After further interviews and research, the reporter wrote:

> The attack on several towns was made by the enemy aircraft at
> 10.50pm, but so sudden and swift was the visit that thousands of
> residents lay in their beds undisturbed and did not know an air-
> raid had been made on the districts until the following morning.
> It is marvellous that though 15 to 20 bombs, both high explosive
> and incendiary were dropped that the only causalities consisted of
> the death of a cow and the destruction of a number of pigeons ...
> People were generally unprepared for the attack, no official warn-
> ings having been given in any of the districts. It was remarkable no
> casualties were recorded considering all the works in the districts
> were in full swing ... The first bomb which appeared to be a high
> explosive one fell in a field close to a colliery.

It was here the cow and pigeons were killed. It seems likely the bomb was a
300kg one, as the reporter recorded that windows were broken to a radius
of half a mile. The Zeppelin then dropped a number of incendiary bombs,
which fell in open fields and did no damage. Another 300kg HE bomb seems
to have been dropped about three-quarters of a mile from the first, in a field,
again without causing much damage, though 'the explosion made a large
hole in the ground about 12 feet deep and slight damage was occasioned to
a property some 200 to 300 yards away ... pieces of this bomb were picked
up several hundred yards away'. A night-watchman working in the area was
blown over by the blast, fortunately without injury, and his hut destroyed.

The *Dudley Herald* reporter also puts the story of bombs being carried
to Dudley police station into context, and makes it less exciting (and stupid)
than the tale of a horse and cart, full of unexploded bombs, clip-clopping
over the cobbles of Dudley, on a Saturday morning, to the police station:
'Two other incendiary bombs were dropped both of which fell in a field,
burying themselves in the ground. These were later dug out and conveyed to
the police station. Another fell to the rear of a house, destroying the building
and killing a set of valuable pigeons.'

Another eyewitness said: 'As the bombs descended a great light illuminated the sky, and the stench from the fallen incendiary bombs was that of
burning tar.' This seems to be the only record we have that Manger used a
parachute flare in the raid to try to illuminate his target, whilst the smell of
the incendiary bomb was precisely that of burning tar: they were made from
a tube of thermite wrapped in tar-covered rope.

As the paper was published a week after the raid, it was also able to record some of the press and public reactions. There was considerable anger at the failure of the warning system:

> Having regard to the elaborate precautions taken to ensure the safety of workshops and factories in one of the localities visited by the Zeppelins on Friday night it is surprising that on this occasion the first intimation of danger was provided by the actual dropping of bombs ... the public and the workers whose lives were gravely endangered are undoubtedly indignant over the failure to give proper warning.

We don't know for sure why warnings were not given; there is nothing in the official records. It seems probable that the Zeppelin was simply not seen or heard by ground observers who were usually soldiers or special constables. It seems to have been unobserved after it left the Derby area, and crossed the Black Country by accident. Manger undoubtedly saw the various lights and furnaces, and bombed them. Because of the gale-force winds, *L.41* was travelling too fast for the bomb aimer to take aim, and luckily the bombs mainly fell on farm land just on the western edge of the Black Country. Such is the luck of war: if *L.41* had been a mile or so further east, the bombs would have been in the middle of streets of workers' housing, with doubtless dozens of casualties.

His bombs gone, Manger set course for home. Affected by gale-force winds, he was unable to fly north-east to cross the North Sea, his normal route home, so went south-east down the Thames Estuary and over part of Kent, leaving England north of Dover and crossing the French coast at Gravelines, near Dunkirk. He flew south-west across northern France, and was seen above the British sector of the Western Front at La Bassee at 04.50. Fearing an air attack in daylight, Manger requested an aeroplane to escort him and one was dispatched to take him beyond Brussels. *L.41* eventually returned to Ahlhorn at 15.08, almost out of fuel after twenty-six hours and thirty-nine minutes in the air, sustaining some damage in a heavy landing. The British GHQ, with their usual objectivity, so different from the press, wrote in a secret document after the raid: 'Manger handled his ship well in the circumstances. He bombed from about 16,500 feet.'

'T' type Navy Zeppelin *L.44*: Kapitänleutnant Franz Stabbert had an interesting career, having been interned in Norway after crash-landing

Zeppelin L.20 near Stavanger. After seven months in captivity, he escaped and returned to Germany. Stabbert was soon returned to active service. He was assigned to the latest Zeppelin, the 'height climber' *L.44*, in April 1917. He had raided England three times in *L.44* but none of the raids were successful, there being problems due to lack of experience in operating the new high altitude Zeppelins. The crew suffered severely from altitude sickness and had engine problems due to the evaporation of radiator water at high altitude. Though the raids were a failure – there were no casualties and little damage was done – they did at least demonstrate some of the problems that needed to be solved in operating the 'height climbers'. By October 1917, the engine issue seems to have been solved, though considerable problems with altitude sickness remained.

On 19 October, Stabbert left his base at Ahlhorn near Bremen at about 12.00. His target was London, but Stabbert quickly got into trouble as the weather changed to a north-easterly gale. It is unclear exactly what happened after that as all his logs were lost. It seems *L.44* crossed the coast east of the Wash at 19.45, being observed near Peterborough at 20.30, and dropped a number of bombs near Bedford at 21.00. Two men were injured by them between Elston and Kempston. The airship was then pushed south-east by the wind and flew down the south-east coast, being spotted at Herne Bay at 21.40, where Stabbert dropped several bombs. After this he was seen at 21.52 between Dover and the North Foreland, by which time it seems he had major engine trouble and was drifting, with Stabbert only having partial control of his craft. From Dover, he crossed the Channel and spent much of the night over northern France. It also seems likely that his position was known by French radio intercepts – the French had a number of radio monitoring stations – and *L.44* exchanged messages with *L.49* and *L.50*, as well as asking for fixes of its position. When he reached the Western Front in daylight, at about 06.40, crossing French lines at St Clement near Luneville in Lorraine, the French defences were fully aware a Zeppelin was in the area. He was fired on by French 75mm anti-aircraft artillery from the 63rd Colonial Artillery Regiment. The first salvo missed, and Stabbert increased height to 5,800 metres, according to French observers. *L.44* was hit by an incendiary shell in the second salvo and immediately burst into flames, the airship coming down near the town of Chevenannes. All eighteen crew members were killed. The bodies of most were badly burned, but five were found some distance from the wreck, which indicates they jumped to escape the flames. The French published photographs of the bodies of the crew, some still recognizable, including Oberleutnant zur See Armin Rothe,

the Executive Officer. Most of the crew are buried at the Military Cemetery at Gerbeviller, France.

'R' type Navy Zeppelin *L.45*: Before he took off from Tondern, Kapitänleutnant Waldemar Kolle – a fairly inexperienced commander, making only his third raid on England – was telephoned by Peter Strasser from his headquarters in Ahlhorn. Strasser told him: 'The weather conditions are good, Kolle, go right into the interior.' Though the weather advice was completely wrong, and led to the loss of *L.45*, Kolle did go to the interior of England, and that night he and his crew were to kill thirty-six people, the only Zeppelin commander on the raid to inflict fatal casualties.

L.45 left Tondern at 12.20 in good weather, its intended target being Sheffield. By 16.20, Kolle was aware of gale-force winds at his operating height of 20,000ft. Because of heavy cloud cover, he was unable to calculate his position, but pressed on into the interior, realizing the wind was pushing him to the south. The British observed *L.45* crossing the Yorkshire coast at Withernsea at 20.20. It was next seen near Leicester at 21.50, and an F.E.2b attempted to intercept it, but could not reach its altitude. At about 22.30, Kolle saw a number of lights which he believed to be Oxford: they were in fact Northampton. British reports indicate twenty-two bombs were dropped on the town, with three women being killed in Parkwood Road: Eliza Gammons, aged 52, the wife of a railway bricklayer, and her twin daughters Lily and Gladys Gammons, aged 13. There were a number of press reports about their deaths, which unusually were caused by an incendiary bomb. The report said that eight bombs were dropped on the small town, two HE and six incendiary. One incendiary bomb went through the roof of a workman's cottage and entered the room where Mrs Gammons and her two daughters slept. The flaming missile burned the mother to a cinder and seriously burned the children. They and other members of the family were able to escape from the upstairs windows by jumping into blankets held by neighbours. Sadly, Lily and Gladys died later in hospital from their burns. They are buried in Dallington Cemetery, Northampton, with their mother.

After this, Kolle and his crew, still lost, flew south, attempting to reach the coast. At about 23.30, the second officer, Oberleutnant zur See Karl Schuz, saw a large concentration of dim lights and realized *L.45* was over London. The Zeppelin was travelling too fast for accurate bombing, going south-east across the city. Schuz dropped a number of HE bombs on Hendon, damaging the Graham White Aviation factory and a number of houses. A minute later, he dropped more bombs on Cricklewood railway station. This left *L.45* with three 300kg bombs. Schuz dropped the first near Piccadilly Circus, seriously damaging the Swan and Edgar Department Store on the junction with Regent Street, killing seven people - three were off-duty soldiers - and injuring twenty more, including two soldiers, a sailor and a police constable. The bomb made a crater 100ft wide and 5ft deep. One of the victims was so mutilated that only her jewellery identified her as a woman. Kolle then took *L.45* over the Thames. His next 300kg bomb hit Camberwell, destroying three houses, a doctor's surgery and a fish and chip shop at 101 and 103 Albany Road at the junction with Calmington Road, killing twelve people. We know the names of six of the Camberwell victims: Edwin T. Balls (3); Raymond N. Balls (5); Alice Glass (21); Emily Glass (8); Emma Glass (53); and Stephen Glass (20).

The last 300kg bomb hit 13-17 Glenview Road in Hither Green, killing fourteen people. Their names are recorded on a memorial in Lewisham Cemetery: Francis Sarah Grant (32); Edith L. Jenner (8); Annie Kingston (18) and her following six siblings; Bridget Mary Kingston (16); Mary Elizabeth Kingston (11); Kathleen Violet Kingston (10); Richard Kingston (8); Thomas John Kingston (6); Edith Elizabeth Kingston (3); Elsie Margery Milgate (13); Leonard Alfred Milgate (8); Edith Mabel Milgate (18); Samuell Lilly Milgate (53), who was the father of the three children above and died later in hospital;. Edith Mabel Milgate (18) and William James Turner (13), nephew of the Kingstons, who was visiting them at the time of raid.

With all his bombs gone, Kolle lost height to 16,000ft to escape the gale-force winds. At about midnight, over Chatham, a B.E.2e night fighter from North Weald, flown by Second Lieutenant Thomas Pritchard of 39 Squadron RFC, gave chase. Kolle climbed to 20,000ft and lost the fighter. Pritchard, a South African, was awarded the MC for his action that night. He died in December that year following a flying accident.

Back at altitude, *L.45* was pushed further south. The crew suffered from altitude sickness and were unable to carry out their normal duties. Lack of routine maintenance led to engine failure, and a fuel leak was not noticed. During the night, *L.45* flew across France, passing near Amiens, Compiegne and Auxerre. By dawn they were over Lyons and were fired on by anti-aircraft guns, but were too high to be troubled. In daylight, a third engine failed and Kolle lost height and became aware of his position. He realized he was too far south to reach Germany, but attempted to get to neutral Switzerland. However, *L.45* was running short of fuel, and at 10.00 Kolle crash-landed in the shallow River Bueche near Sisteron, in Alpes-De-Haute-Provence in southern France. Kolle managed to destroy the Zeppelin with a flare pistol, but the crew of seventeen were captured. They spent the rest of the war in PoW camps, but all survived. They were interrogated by Royal Marine interrogator Major Bernard Trench, who used his standard pattern of combining menace about a possible trial for murder, a boastful demonstration of his almost encyclopaedic knowledge of the Zeppelin Service and his intelligence network. Kolle said he acted as an officer should and said little; however, he was a man with an extremely good memory. As soon as he could, he wrote down everything Major Trench had told him and arranged for a prisoner in the camp being repatriated to smuggle it out in the heel of his shoe. It got to Peter Strasser in April 1918, and it is said five men were shot as a result of the Germans discovering how much Trench knew, three in Tondern and two in Nordholz.

It is ironic that Kolle was lost for most of the raid. London was not an intended target, and was found completely by accident. *L.45* killed a total of thirty-six people, with three in Northampton and the remainder in London. He holds the dubious honour of killing more people than any other Zeppelin commander in a single raid. It would be little comfort to the victims to know the Zeppelin was completely lost when the bombs were dropped. He survived the war and put his memory to good use when he wrote a number of magazine articles about his service as a Zeppelin commander.

'T' type Navy Zeppelin *L.46*: Kapitänleutnant Heinrich Hollander was an experienced commander when he took off from Ahlhorn at 12.20 with Oberleutnant zur See Richard Frey as his second officer. His target was the English Midlands, and he intended to cross the coast at the Humber. Like other ships that night, *L.46* was forced southward by gale-force winds and could make little forward progress. But Hollander seems to have had better navigation skills than most of the other commanders, and was more aware of his position by dead reckoning. He decided he had no chance of reaching far into the interior, so attempted to bomb Norwich. In his combat report, he claimed to have bombed the city from 19,400ft at 22.30. His bombs actually landed harmlessly outside Happisburgh on the Norfolk coast. He left the English coast behind at about 23.00 and decided to return to base across neutral Holland because of the wind. He crossed the Scheldt Estuary in darkness and was not seen by Dutch defences. He crossed into Germany over the Ruhr, where he was fired on by German anti-aircraft guns. He reached Ahlhorn at about 09.00, but spent about three hours circling because of fog. He landed safely at about 12.00, after twenty-three hours and thirty-seven minutes in the air.

On 21 April 1918, there was a serious fire at Ahlhorn which destroyed four airship hangars and five airships - *L.46*, *L.47*, *L.51*, *L.58* and *SL.20*. Ten sailors and four civilian workers were killed, and thirty men seriously injured. Hollander broke his leg during the incident and spent months in hospital, and he never commanded a Zeppelin again but did survive the war.

'R' type Navy Zeppelin *L.47*: Kapitänleutnant Michael Freudenreich was an experienced commander, the veteran of six previous raids on Britain. He took off from Ahlhorn at 12.15 with a crew of nineteen. His second officer was Oberleutnant zur See Horstmann. In his combat report, he said he crossed the Yorkshire coast at Scarborough at 20.30, later seeing the lights of a city which he thought was Leeds from 14,800ft. He knew he was being blown southwards by the strong winds, and reported bombing a city which he thought was Nottingham at 22.00 He released 1,000kg of bombs, but was travelling too fast in the strong winds to drop his one remaining 300kg bomb and three 100kg bombs. He reported dropping these on a blast furnace near Ipswich at 23.40 just before he crossed the coast. The British were able to track his fight accurately and reveal that Freudenreich was in fact further south than he thought. He crossed the coast at Sutton on Sea in Lincolnshire, north of the Wash. The bombs he thought he dropped on Nottingham fell harmlessly in fields in Rutland, while the Ipswich bombs fell west of the city in fields, both causing no damage. Radio bearings picked up by the British located *L.47* near Ostend before midnight. The airship returned home over neutral Holland at low altitude, was fired on by Dutch soldiers and moved out to sea. It then travelled home along the Friesian coast and arrived at Ahlhorn at 12.40, almost out of fuel, after twenty-four hours and twenty-five minutes in the air.

'U' type Navy Zeppelin *L.49*: Kapitänleutnant Hans Karl Gayer was an inexperienced commander who had only taken part in one previous raid over England. He took off from Wittmund, near Wilhelmshaven, at13.54, with Oberleutnant zur See Delin as second officer. Like many of the commanders on the raid, he was hopelessly lost. He claimed to have crossed the coast at Scarborough and bombed anti-aircraft batteries, airfields and a railway. British ground observations tell a markedly different story. They say he crossed the coast near Holkham in Norfolk and then flew over Norwich. He dropped forty-two bombs as he flew over, most of which landed west of the city, killing some cattle and damaging farm buildings but causing no human casualties. We can speculate whether his report that he bombed military targets was in fact a fabrication, as he was captured and interrogated by the formidable Major Trench. It may be he actually realized he had bombed Norwich, but had been told bombing cities was forbidden under the Geneva Convention and was threatened with trial for murder, a tactic used to encourage co-operation by Trench.

Gayer was pushed south by the gale and crossed the coast near Folkestone at about 23.00. It appears he then planned to return home over Holland, but was pushed by the winds over the Pas de Calais. He gained altitude and saw *L.44* ahead of him, which he followed for most of the night. It was probably the case that the airships could see each other at a considerable distance above a carpet of cloud. It apparently seemed to him that Franz Stabbert, the experienced commander of *L.44*, knew the best route back. The fact that Stabbert had wrecked his Zeppelin at Stavanger in Norway after bombing Dundee in similar gale conditions probably wasn't considered. We know that the French Intelligence Service was monitoring the radio transmissions to and from the Zeppelins, similar to the Admiralty in London. There are documents that suggest they jammed signals or even sent false radio bearings to the Zeppelins. The main radio transmitter was at the Eiffel Tower radio station. There is no doubt that the route of each airship across France was followed through the night. They did not send out night fighters, but at dawn several squadrons were waiting, knowing where the Zeppelins were.

At dawn, Gayer was still following Stabbert in *L.44*, along with Schwonder in *L.50*. From later interrogation of the crew, it seems the commanders had been communicating during the night and all believed they were over Holland. Gayer saw a burst of flak around L.44 and then it bursting into flames. Still believing Stabbert had been hit by Dutch anti-aircraft fire, it seems Gayer panicked. He certainly did the worst thing possible in the circumstances: he turned west and descended, flying not into Belgium as he thought, but further into France, away from German-occupied territory. Flying at 6,500ft, he was spotted by five Nieuport fighters from Escadrille 152, a squadron called the 'crocodiles' because of the insignia painted on the aeroplanes' fuselage. The fighters attacked. Luckily for Gayer, they carried only solid and tracer ammunition; it seems the French observed the Hague Convention and did not use incendiary bullets in day fighters. The fighters punctured but did not set alight the gas cells of the Zeppelin. Unable to climb to avoid the fighters, Gayer decided to land, putting *L.49* down in a wood near Bourbonne-les-Bains. The ship was only slightly damaged. The ignition mechanism designed to set alight a ship to avoid capture failed, and Gayer's Very pistol misfired, allowing the French to capture a complete 'height climber'. Gayer and his crew were captured, and the Zeppelin was examined in great detail over the next few months by the Allies. It is said that the first American rigid airship, the *Shenandoah*, was largely based on information from *L.49*. Gayer spent the rest of the war in a French PoW camp; he and his crew were interrogated by the redoubtable Major Trench, and undoubtedly much useful information was gained.

'R' type Navy Zeppelin *L.50*: Kapitänleutnant Roderich Schwonder was another inexperienced commander; he had only been involved in one previous raid on England. He took off from Ahlhorn at 13.27, with Oberleutnant zur See Westphal as second officer. He was completely lost in the gales and cloudy conditions. In his interrogation after the flight, he claimed to have bombed Grimsby and Hull. In fact, the British had a reasonable record of his actual position. He crossed the coast at Clay next the Sea in Norfolk at 20.45, and left north of Harwich at 21.50. There was no record of his bombs landing, so it is likely they were dropped in the sea. Pushed south-east by the gale, Schwonder saw Zeppelin *L.44* at some time during the night, and along with Zeppelin *L.49* followed it. Just after dawn, he saw *L.44* shot down near St Clement, and along with *L.49* attempted to fly away from the guns. In his report, he said he thought he was over Holland and was being fired on by Dutch guns, so he turned south into what he thought was German-occupied Belgium. This was the worst thing he could do, as he went further into French territory, flying south-west away from the German side of the Western Front. Totally lost, he descended to try to find a landmark to locate his position. He found a railway, but from the shape of the carriages recognized they weren't German. A building with the sign 'Cafe du Centre' confirmed his suspicion. As he circled, he passed over Bourbonne-les-Bains and saw the undamaged *L.49* on the ground, and also spotted French fighters chasing him. Realising he could not escape in daylight, he decided to crash the airship to prevent its use by the enemy. *L.50* hit the ground near Dammartin-sur-Meuse, about 10 miles from the *L.49*. The front gondola was torn off in the impact, and sixteen crew members – including Schwonder – escaped and were captured, but four others remained in the hull of the ship. It is possible they had been injured in the impact. The hull, now much lighter with the loss of the front gondola, rose in the air and floated southward. It reached an altitude of 23,000ft and could not be reached by French fighters who pursued it to Frejus on the Mediterranean coast at 18.30. The hull was followed by seaplanes until darkness, but it and the four crew members were never seen again. The crew who survived spent the war in a French PoW camp.

'U' type Navy Zeppelin *L.52*: Despite his lower rank, Oberleutnant zur See Kurt Friemel was probably the best if not the most experienced commander on the raid. He had been the second officer on Heinrich Mathy's *L.13* and was involved in ten raids on England. He gained his own command and avoided the fate of Mathy and the crew of *L.31* on 1 October 1916. With a crew of nineteen and Leutnant zur See Fritsche as second officer, *L.52* took off from Wittmund at 13.35. Friemel crossed the Lincolnshire coast near Theddlethorpe at 19.30, his target being Sheffield. He was spotted near Northampton at 20.50, and it seems he then decided to head for London. He is recorded as dropping thirteen bombs near Hertford and thirteen more on Waltham Marches, which injured a man and damaged some houses. He was seen and chased by a B.E.2c fighter, but it could not climb to engage him. *L.52* was reported as crossing the French coast near Etaples and then the British trenches on the Western Front at St Die. Engine problems and the exhaustion of his crew due to altitude sickness meant he was unable to return to base at Wittmund, but crash-landed at Ahlhorn at 15.40, after over twenty-six hours in the air.

'V' type Navy Zeppelin *L.53*: Kapitänleutnant Eduard Prolss, an experienced officer, had taken over command of *L.53* in August 1917. We know little about the route taken by Prolss, as he did not submit a track chart in his combat report; he was probably more honest than most of his comrades in admitting he had little idea where he went during the raid. He said he could not give a precise route because of cloud and strong winds. He took off from Nordholz at 12.15, with Oberleutnant zur See Karl von Proek as his second officer. Prolss believed he crossed the Lincolnshire coast at 19.00, just north of the Wash, was near Cambridge at 20.30, and at 21.30 reached a big city which he believed to be Birmingham. He dropped 2,000kg of bombs, and then flew over another city at 21.30, which had extremely strong anti-aircraft fire and twenty-five to thirty searchlights. He dropped his remaining 1,000kg of bombs and crossed the coast, he thought, near Dover, setting course for Ostend. Because of heavy cloud, he had little idea of his position until the next morning, when he came under anti-aircraft fire which convinced him he was over the Western Front. He continued east, and at 09.10 requested a radio bearing which showed he was near Celle in Germany. He was able to reach Nordholz at lower altitude from there, and landed safely at 15. 45.

The British had rather better records of the route of *L.53* over England than did Prolss, though there are gaps. They observed the Zeppelin crossing the coast at Blakeney, Norfolk, at 18.40. He then flew south to Bedford, where he bombed an engineering works and a military school, which were showing lights. At 21.30, he dropped ten bombs, including a 300kg HE, near Leighton Buzzard, although no significant damage was done. *L.53* flew east of London and reached the coast near Dover at 23.30. It can be said in favour of the navigational skills of Prolss, that he was more accurate than most of his comrades, and at least was honest enough to admit he was lost much of the time. He took part in a number of raids on England after the 'silent raid', but is best known for the unenviable record of being the last Zeppelin commander to die in action when he was shot down in *L.53* by a British Sopwith Camel, operating from an aircraft-carrying towed lighter near the German coast on 11 August 1918.

'U' type Navy Zeppelin *L.54*: Kapitänleutnant Horst von Buttlar-Brandfells, the most experienced airship commander, with twelve raids over Britain to his credit, was assigned to the 'height climber' Zeppelin *L.54* on 16 September 1917. As always, his watch officer was Oberleutnant zur See Hans Schiller. Buttlar took off from Tondern at 12.50; it was his first raid in *L.54*. His provisional targets were Sheffield or Manchester. He reported after the raid that because of the strength of the wind, he had abandoned attacking Sheffield or Manchester but had instead dropped his bombs on Derby and Nottingham from 21,000ft. The British report is very different: *L.54* was observed crossing the Norfolk coast near Happisburgh at 20.55, turned south towards Harwich, and dropped its bombs between Ipswich and Colchester, causing no damage, before going out to sea near Clacton.

Buttlar remains an enigma among Zeppelin commanders. He was not popular in the Zeppelin Service, as it was felt his aristocratic background gave him privileges and allowed him to advance his career, whilst his combat reports either exaggerated his achievements or were outright lies. The British Admiralty intelligence services were scornful of him, describing him as timid and notorious for his pusillanimous conduct. At the time of the 'silent raid', he was by far the most experienced Zeppelin commander and a veteran of bombing missions over England. He was the only commander on the raid with the confidence and experience to recognize the need to alter his altitude to cope with the changing weather conditions. It also seems to be the case that he did this knowing it was against Strasser's explicit orders. He wrote in his report that he bombed Nottingham and Derby from 21,300ft;

whilst he could have genuinely been mistaken about his location, he must have known his altitude. If he had been at 21,300ft, he would have been in the teeth of the gale and blown across France like most of the other ships. We can say he was ultra cautious and timid, or that he displayed initiative and commonsense in flying a course that enabled him to return to base across the North Sea, the shortest and safest route.

Buttlar's decision to fly at a moderate altitude almost caused disaster for him. He was seen and pursued by a B.E.2c flown by Flight Lieutenant Clarence Nunn from Burgh Castle RNAS airfield. Nunn spotted *L.54* about 10 miles north of Great Yarmouth. In his report, Nunn said he was at 8,800ft and the Zeppelin at 5,000ft, but because of engine trouble he was unable to catch it.

L.54 returned to Tonder at about 08.45. Buttlar yet again got back in one piece, having spent twenty hours and fifty minutes in the air, much less than any other returning commander. Caution paid off, and certainly helped in the award of the *Pour le Mérite* (Blue Max), Germany's highest military honour. Buttlar may not have been the bravest or best Zeppelin commander, but he was a shrewd political operator.

'V' type Navy Zeppelin *L.55*: Kapitänleutnant Kurt Flemming took off from Ahlhorn at 12.36. His second officer was Oberleutnant zur See Kohlhauer. Flemming reported after the raid that he was hampered by heavy cloud and gale-force winds, despite which he claimed to have crossed the Yorkshire coast south of Flamborough Head at 20.30. He said he went on to bomb Mappleton and Hull at 21.25 with 2,000kg of bombs, and then, pushed south by the wind, bombed Birmingham with the remaining 1,000kg.

The British intelligence report differed greatly from this, though it was lacking in detail. *L.55* was observed over the Lincolnshire coast at 19.30. It dropped six bombs at Holme, south of Peterborough, and then flew south, possibly following the route of the Great North Railway line. Flemming dropped seventeen bombs between Hitchin and Hatfield, injuring one man and causing some property damage. Still moving fast because of the gale, the Zeppelin crossed the coast near Hastings.

We have more details about the rest of Flemming's flight using information gathered after he landed in Germany. After he crossed the English coast, he was totally lost, and believing he was over enemy territory flew at high altitude. At about 02.00, he lost the three engines. This was bad, but even worse was the loss of the forward engine, which powered the radio. He still had a small battery-powered emergency radio, but it did not have the power to reach German bases so he was unable to request a radio bearing.

He ordered his crew to tear up all the attack orders and attack maps. At about 03.00, he was fired on by anti-aircraft guns, but was too high for them to reach him. Though he did not know it, he was crossing the Western Front between St Quentin and Reims. He then experienced more engine trouble and was largely drifting. At dawn he saw two aircraft thousands of feet below him, so he flew even higher, reaching 24,000ft. For some reason he then believed he was over Maastricht in Holland; he thought flying east he would soon be over Germany near Aachen. He then used the emergency radio to ask for orders and was told to return to Ahlhorn, but was not given a bearing of his true location, which was near Darmstadt, about 125 mile south-east of where he thought he was. Knowing he was over Germany, Flemming descended through the clouds and found himself over a heavily forested area. He flew around looking for landmarks and found a railway station, the platform sign saying 'Immelborn'. Using a railway guide a crew member had fortuitously carried on the raid, they found that they were in Thuringia, in central Germany, about 200 miles from their base. By this time they were low on fuel, so circled to find a place to land. At 17.15, they crash-landed in a forest clearing at Tiefenort in Thuringia. *L.52* was severely damaged; the damage and remote location meant the airship could not be recovered, so it was scrapped, bringing the total loss in the raid to five Zeppelins. It seems Flemming was not blamed for the debacle, being assigned to a new ship, the *L.60*, in April 1918. This was destroyed in its shed at Tondern by British fighters operating from an aircraft carrier on 19 July. Flemming survived the war and later worked for the Zeppelin Company. He was to die in a Zeppelin in the *Hindenburg* disaster at Lakehurst, New Jersey, USA, on 6 May 1937.

An analysis of the 'silent raid' has to judge it as a major disaster for the German Navy. Even so, it was a close run thing. The major cause of the failure was the very inaccurate weather forecast. With the exception of Buttlar, none of the Zeppelin commanders had any real idea of their positions. Operating at 20,000ft over thick cloud made accurate bombing impossible. The need to return to base over Holland or France because of the gale was the reason for most of the losses. Altitude sickness made routine in-flight maintenance of the airships, in particular the engines, impossible, which was the prime cause of the losses. But the British were lucky: there were a number of attempts by fighters to intercept the Zeppelins, all of which failed, as no fighter could get near a 'height climber' at 20,000ft. Paradoxically, the commander who was most in peril was the ultra cautious Buttlar in *L.54*, who was experienced enough to avoid the gale by flying at a much lower altitude, and was chased by a fighter. While French fighters were involved in the capture of a number of airships, this was in daylight, and was mainly caused by crews crippled by altitude sickness. In any arms race, the most that can be expected is a window of opportunity before enemy technology catches up. The Germans had this during much of 1917. By mid-1918, the Allies had fighters that could operate at 20,000ft.

In more favourable weather conditions, the raid could have been the most costly of the war. Kuno Manger in *L.41* bombed steel works and blast furnaces, surrounded by working-class housing, in the area between Dudley and Birmingham. The cost was only one man injured and £500 of damage. Hans Karl Gayer in *L.49* flew over Norwich but his bombs hit the outskirts of the city, killing only cattle and damaging farm buildings. Franz Stabbert in *L.44* almost bombed Bedford; as did Eduard Prolss in *L.53*. All these commanders were completely lost. Luck was on the side of the British, and the bombs did little damage. That luck ran out when Waldemar Kolle in *L.45* dropped his bombs; he was completely lost when his twenty-two bombs hit Northampton. Eliza Gammons certainly ran out of luck when an incendiary bomb came through the roof into her bedroom and burned her to a cinder, while her twin daughters died shortly afterwards in hospital from their burns. Kolle found himself over London by chance. Three 300kg bombs killed thirty-three people. Every victim in the 'silent raid' was killed by Kolle and *L.45*. He killed thirty-six people on 19 October 1917, more than any other Zeppelin commander in a single day.

In many ways the person responsible for the failure of the raid was Peter Strasser. It seems he decided at short notice to take advantage of favourable weather conditions, without considering indications they would severely worsen. We have to note that there were thunderstorms on the Friesian coast, and that two Zeppelins – *L. 42* and *L.51* – were unable to take part in the raid because high winds prevented them being taken out of their sheds at Nordholz. Though weather forecasting was far less advanced in 1917, and weather at high altitude little understood, the British certainly believed there were reasons for caution. H.A. Jones wrote in *The War in the Air*:

> Great Britain lay in an area of high pressure over the Bay of Biscay … there were two low pressure areas over Iceland and Southern Scandinavia … the Icelandic depression was deep and was rapidly approaching our north-western shores. There was superficial calm over England and the North Sea, and up to 10,000 feet the winds were calm, no more than 20 mph. But above that the strength of the wind doubled, above 20,000 feet a gale was raging.

We don't know exactly when the observations were made, but they were certainly accurate.

Even more telling is Strasser's lack of understanding of the affects of altitude sickness. Not only had he read numerous reports about the inability of his crews to operate at high altitude, but he had experienced it himself on earlier raids. Perhaps he thought courage and determination could overcome anything: it couldn't. Zeppelin crew were human, like anyone else, and subject to the same laws of physiology. He literally threw caution to the winds, and it cost him five Zeppelins and four crews. Though there would be a few more raids on England, this the last major attack of the war.

Chapter Thirteen

The end game: November 1917 and 1918

With Russia out of the war and America sending an increasing number of troops, Germany had to go on the offensive to try to get a favourable compromise peace. Germany's allies were growing weaker, and needed more and more German support. It was known that a number were seeking a separate compromise peace.

The German campaign of unrestricted submarine warfare was still dangerous, but the convoy system ensured enough essential supplies got through. The British blockade was very effective; the civilian population of Germany was now hungry. The actions of British naval aeroplanes near the German coast made minesweeping operations by Zeppelins difficult, as airships had to operate at high altitudes. There were few Zeppelin raids on England, and these were largely ineffective because airships could only operate at great height because of intelligent observation and tracking systems, and British aeroplanes now able to operate at 15,000–20,000ft. The Gotha and 'Giant' bombers were the cause of most of the bombing casualties in Britain, although only airships could bomb the industrial Midlands and North.

The French were unable to mount any offensives following the mutiny, and Prime Minister Lloyd George had refused British commander-in-chief Haig any reinforcements to be slaughtered in pointless attacks. Germany's Ludendorff offensive of April–July 1918 came as a surprise to the Allies and was initially successful. It has been described as a 'brilliant tactical success and a strategic failure'. By July, the offensive had halted after several significant attacks. The Germans had lost 500,000 casualties, the Allies somewhat more, but the German Army was exhausted. Allied troops were able to advance through the Hindenburg Line and the war of movement started, finally ending the trench stalemate. The Germans were desperate for peace, hoping the 'fourteen points' of President Wilson would save them. By November, Austria, Bulgaria and Turkey were beaten, Ludendorff was sacked, the Kaiser forced to abdicate and the Germans asked for an armistice.

21/25 November 1917

'W' type Navy Zeppelin *L.59*: Kapitänleutnant Ludwig Bockholt took part in one of the best-known operations of the war, a flight from Jamboli (now Yambol) in Bulgaria to East Africa to supply the troops of General Von Lettow-Vorbeck. Bockholt's *L.59* had been lengthened to 743ft to give it a gas capacity of 2,365,000ft^3 of hydrogen, enabling it to carry 11 tons of ammunition and 3 tons of medical supplies from Bulgaria to German East Africa. It was to be a one-way mission of 3,600 miles, with the Zeppelin crew remaining with Lettow-Vorbeck until the military situation allowed them to return to Germany. The Kaiser naively thought that if Germany was able to hold on to one of its colonies, it would help in any future peace conference. Bockholt left Jamboli at 08.30 on 21 November. He flew down the coast of Turkey and crossed the coast of Africa about a day later, then crossing the Libyan Desert. The operation was a failure, as Lettow-Vorbeck's troops were being overrun by the British, and *L.59* was recalled. Bockholt had reached Sudan, about 125 miles west of Khartoum, when he got the recall order, at about 02.30 on 23 November. It took another day to reach the coast of Africa. In all, *L.59* made a ninety-five-hour flight from Jamboli to Sudan and back, covering 4,200 miles. With the Africa mission cancelled, it was decided that *L.59* would remain at Jamboli and operate in the Mediterranean. No more one-way missions were planned.

5 January 1918
The Ahlhorn disaster

The cold grey days of January prevented any Zeppelin operations, and crews were doing routine maintenance work. A fire started in Shed II at the Ahlhorn base, in the early evening. Within seconds, the shed was alight and two explosions occurred, which led to a fire in Shed I. The second pair of sheds a half mile from the first pair, Shed III and Shed IV, also caught fire. Five airships were completely destroyed:

'F' type Navy Schutte-Lanz *SL.20*: Kapitänleutnant Guido Wolf.

'T' type Navy Zeppelin *L.46*: Kapitänleutnant Heinrich Hollander.

'R' type Navy Zeppelin *L.47*: Kapitänleutnant Michael von Freudenreich.

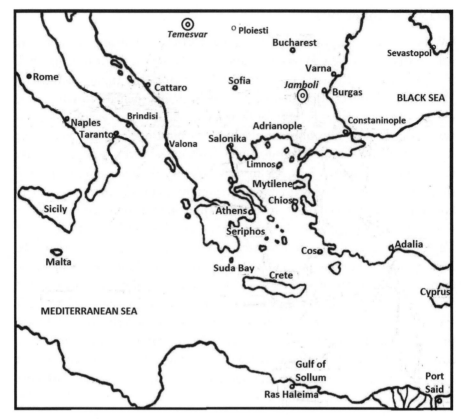

Map 9: Operations over the Mediterranean

There were two main Zeppelin bases: Temesvar, in Hungary (Timisora, Romania) and Jamboli, Bulgaria (now Yambol).

31 January 1916, 17 March 1916 and 5 May 1916. *LZ.85* bombed Salonika from Temesvar on the last raid. It was shot down and the crew captured.

27 July 1916, *SL.X* (10) from Jamboli exploded in the air near Sevastopol.

27 September 1916 *LZ.81* shot down over Bucharest, crash landed.

March 1917 *LZ.97* from Temevar bombed Valona, Brindisi and Imbros. *LZ.101* from Jamboli bombed Lesbos, Lemnos and Imbros.

21/25 November 1917 *L.59* from Jamboli return flight to Africa.

10/11 March 1918 *L.59* from Jamboli bombed Naples.

17/22 March 1918 *L.59* from Jamboli set out to attack Port Said in Eqypt and Suda Bay in Crete.

18 April 1918 *L.59* from Jamboli set out to bomb the British Fleet at Malta. Exploded in the air near Brindisi.

'U' type Navy Zeppelin *L.51*: Kapitänleutnant Walter Dose.
'V' type Navy Zeppelin *L.58*: Korvettenkapitan Arnold Schutze.

A committee of inquiry was held after the fire, but was unable to reach any conclusion about its cause. Sabotage remained a potential cause in the minds of many of the old Zeppelin crews interviewed by Douglas Robinson. While it is possible the first fire could have been started deliberately, the way the fire spread was a surprise to everyone. In many ways this was the end of the Airship Service as an effective force. Ten members of the division were killed, along with four civilian workmen, thirty men were seriously injured and 104 slightly injured. Kapitänleutnant Heinrich Hollander of *L.46* was one of the injured with a broken leg. It probably saved his life; he never flew a mission again.

10/11 March 1918

'W' type Navy Zeppelin *L.59*: It is less well known that Kapitänleutnant Ludwig Bockholt's Africa airship bombed Naples from Jamboli on 10 March 1918. *L.59* took off at 06.30, flying across the Adriatic from Scutari (now Shkoder in Albania) to Manfredonia in Italy, and then across Italy to Naples. There are several reports of the raid. It appears the city was not blacked out, and *L.59* hit the naval port and city gas works, as well as a steel mill at Bagnoli. Bockholt reported he dropped 6,400kg of bombs from 12,000ft. Fourteen people were killed and forty injured, mainly in the city centre. Bockholt returned to Jamboli the next day at 19.42, after more than thirty-seven hours in the air.

12/13 March 1918

In this raid, five Zeppelins set out to bomb the Midlands and North of England. They began in clear weather, but there was solid cloud cover over England. One man was killed during the bombing, and damage done to the tune of £3,474. Two crewmen in Zeppelin *L.53* died in an unusual accident.

'V' type Navy Zeppelin *L.53*: Kapitänleutnant Eduard Prolss flew from Norholz. According to the British report, he reached the Yorkshire coast at 22.00 but did not cross and returned home. Prolss reported he attacked Hull with 3,000lb of bombs, which must have fallen in the sea. It seems likely Prolss made an honest mistake in his report, as flying at 20,000ft accurate bombing was becoming more and more difficult.

Prolss had problems on landing at Nordholz. He signalled the mechanics in the engine gondolas, with the electric telegraph, to slow or stop the engines, but the engine in the rear continued at full speed and Prolss had to climb steeply to avoid hitting the shed. The propeller in the rear gondola hit the ground and broke, and the engines stopped. *L.53* was then able to land, and the rear gondola was investigated. Four mechanics were unconscious. An exhaust pipe had split and the mechanics were poisoned by carbon monoxide. Two men were revived in the fresh air, but the other two died.

'V' type Navy Zeppelin *L.54*: Kapitänleutnant Horst von Buttlar raided England for the last time on 12 March. Flying from Tondern, he claimed to have bombed Grimsby and said he had come under heavy anti-aircraft fire. One of the gas cells of *L.54* was damaged and empty, and whilst it is possible that this was caused by anti-aircraft fire, it could also have been due to ice particles thrown by the propellers. The British believed Buttlar dropped the bomb load out at sea; some bombs were reported as having fallen near a group of British armed trawlers which fired at *L.54*. They didn't hit the airship, which returned safely to Tondern.

Buttlar gives a detailed description of this raid in his autobiography. He says after bombing, his ship was hit by several clouds of shrapnel and two of the middle gas cells were completely empty. Not only did *L.54* lose lift, but the empty cells put a strain on the hull, which eventually cracked. At the time he said he did not take kindly to Hans von Schiller, his watch officer, asking him if the ship broke in half would he prefer to take command of the bow or the stern. They managed to keep the ship in the air using the anchor line to hold the sections together. They kept the ship in the air by dumping all the spare parts and eventually got back to Tondern.

A few weeks later, he got a telegram from the Kaiser awarding him the *Pour le Mérite*. After a night celebrating with his crew, he went to his ship in the morning and found on the front of the control car a larger-than-life Blue Max, painted by a master hand. It didn't last long: *L.54* was destroyed when British Sopwith Camels bombed its shed three months later.

'V' type Navy Zeppelin *L.61*: In December 1917, Kapitänleutnant Herbert Ehrlich was assigned to another Zeppelin, *L.61*. a much more advanced high altitude machine. This was its first raid, flying from Wittmundhaven. The North of England was again the target, but because visibility was poor – there was solid cloud below the Zeppelins flying at 16,000–18,000ft – accuracy was poor. Zeppelin commanders claimed to have bombed Leeds, Bradford and Grimsby, but British records show these cities were untouched. The raid was largely ineffective, only one man being killed and £3,474 worth of damage done. Ehrlich reported he attacked a heavily fortified place on the Humber, but the British have no record of his bombs. It is probably fair to Ehrlich to say he genuinely believed he had attacked a city – the fact he didn't try to name it makes it more believable – but he was bombing through cloud and had no real idea where his bombs landed.

'V' type Navy Zeppelin *L.62*: Hauptmann Kuno Manger, operating from Nordholz, thought he had bombed Leeds and Bradford; in fact he dropped twenty-seven bombs about 6 miles north of Howden. They damaged a pub and some housing.

'V' type Navy Zeppelin *L.63*: Kapitänleutnant Michael von Freudenreich, flying from Nordholz, crossed the Yorkshire coast at Hornsea and it seems followed the railway line to Hull. He dropped six bombs on Hull, hitting houses and allotments in Southcoates Avenue, Southcoates Lane and Whitworth Street. Other buildings damaged were Paragon Station, the Naval Hospital and Holy Trinity Church. Six more bombs were dropped at Sutton and Swine, killing a cow, and he also damaged gardens in Cottingham and left a huge crater in Warne. One person died of shock.

13/14 March 1918

A further attempt was made to raid the North of England two days later. Three airships set out, but Peter Strasser recalled the Zeppelins because of a change in the weather. However, Martin Dietrich disregarded the order and bombed Hartlepool.

'S' type Navy Zeppelin *L.42*: Kapitänleutnant Martin Dietrich flew from Nordholz. Several hours into the flight, Strasser received a report of a change in the weather, revealing that the Zeppelins were flying into a strong northerly wind, so he ordered them to turn back. *L.52* and *L.56* did so, but it seems Dietrich disobeyed the order, claiming poor radio reception. He crossed the English coast near Hartlepool at 21.15, found the town well lit – for once it was a clear night – and dropped his twenty-one bombs on the West Hartlepool Docks from 18,000ft. Eight people were killed and thirty-nine injured, with considerable damage to shops and houses. A report made in Hartlepool at the time said that the Zeppelin crossed the coast heading north at about 21 30. It was at a high altitude and not visible from the ground. It seemed to have cut its engines when over the town and 'glided in'. Bombs landed on Middleton Beach and Old Town. Sheds on the NER railway were damaged, and damage was also caused in Exchange Street, Burkbeck Street, Temperance Street, Frederick Street and Whitby Street.

As Dietrich crossed the coast returning to base, he was followed by an F.E.2d pusher biplane, piloted by Second Lieutenant C. Morris, with observer Second Lieutenant R.D. Linford. They chased *L.42* out to sea, following it at 17,300ft but well below the height of the Zeppelin.

The weather report was accurate and Dietrich was held up by a strong headwind all the way home, getting back to Nordholz at 09.25. He was called to see Strasser that evening, expecting at least strong words. Strasser initially seemed quiet and angry, but then smiled and said: 'I name you Count of Hartlepool' because of his successful mission. Strasser recorded the raid as 'additional to a scouting mission'.

'U' type Navy Zeppelin *L.52*: Oberleutnant zur See Kurt Friemel, operating from Wittmundhaven, returned early from the raid after receiving the recall order from Strasser.

'V' type Navy Zeppelin *L.56*: Hauptmann August Stelling, flying from Wittmundhaven, also returned early as ordered.

20/22 March 1918

'W' type Navy Zeppelin *L.59*: Kapitänleutnant Ludwig Bockholt set out from Jamboli at 03.53 to bomb the British base at Port Said in Egypt, but had to turn back about 3 miles from the target: he had arrived at the heavily defended target much later than planned, because of a headwind, and dawn was breaking. Later in the flight, Bockholt went to Suda Bay in Crete to attack the British naval base, but could not release his bombs because of cloud cover. He landed back at Jamboli at 07.16 on 22 March after over fifty-one hours in the air.

12/13 April 1918

In this raid, five Zeppelins attacked the English Midlands and North. Once again the high-flying Zeppelins were hampered by cloud cover. Seven people were killed and twenty injured, with damage caused to the value of £11,673.

It can probably be regarded as the last successful Zeppelin operation; those killed were the last to die as a result of Zeppelin bombing.

'V' type Navy Zeppelin *L.60*: Kapitänleutnant Hans Kurt Flemming left Tondern at 13.02 and crossed the Yorkshire coast near Spurn Head. According to British reports, *L.60* was only over land for about an hour. Flemming claimed he had bombed Leeds, but the GHQ report show thirty-four bombs landed at East Halton and Thornton Saxby in Lincolnshire without causing any damage. (Presumably GHQ is mistaken with Thornton Saxby (which does not exist), and actually meant Thornton Curtis.) *L.60* returned to Tondern at 09.00 the next day.

'V' type Navy Zeppelin *L.61*: This was Kapitänleutnant Herbert Ehrlich's last raid. *L.61* left its base at Wittmundhaven at about 14.07, crossing the English coast at about 20.45 at Withernsea in Yorkshire. Ehrlich's target was Sheffield; he recorded in his combat log that he was over Sheffield at an altitude of 18,400 feet at 22.07, dropping all his bombs between 22.17 and 22.35. He was in fact over Widnes and then Wigan. He dropped two bombs at Bold, near Widnes, on the road between Warrington and Prescott, one of the bombs damaging the milestone there. The stone was moved after the war to Victoria Park in Widnes, and today has a plaque describing events. *L.61* then flew north to Wigan: the British reported that the blast furnaces of the Wigan Coal and Iron Company were in operation. Eight HE bombs fell on the suburb of Lace, injuring a man and causing some damage. Ehrlich dropped fifteen HE bombs on Wigan, killing seven people and injuring twelve. The last four 300kg bombs fell in open fields near Aspull, damaging cottages and injuring four people. In the whole raid, seven people were killed, twenty injured and £11,673 worth of damage done, most of it by *L.61*. With his bombs gone, Ehrlich climbed to 22,000ft. His log shows he crossed the coast near Spurn Point at 00.30, but British observers noted he passed over the coast later than that, near Hull.

It demonstrates the strength of British air defences that Ehrlich's problems were not over when he was back over the North Sea. An F.2a twin engined flying boat had left Great Yarmouth at 03.30 to find a Zeppelin sighted some 60 miles from there. The flying boat crew and that of *L.61* saw each other at about 04.45, but luckily for Ehrlich it was still dark enough for him to get away. *L.61* landed back at Wittmundhaven at about 11.00.

The Wigan casualties, the last people to die in England as a result of Zeppelin attacks, on 12 April 1918, were: Margaret Ashurst (33) of 156 Platt Lane, Wigan; Mary Cumberbirch (24), who died in hospital; Walter Harris (31), of 181 Whelley, Wigan; Alfred Harris (4 months) of 181 Whelley, Wigan; Samuel Tomlinson (49) of 25 Harper Street, Wigan; Jane Tomlinson (56) of 25 Harper Street, Wigan; and Jane Winters (29) of Union Workhouse, Wigan.

'V' type Navy Zeppelin *L.62*: Hauptmann Kuno Manger made the last raid on the English West Midlands. He was assigned to a new Zeppelin, *L.62*, on 29 January 1918. He left Nordholz at about 12.57; his intended target was the industrial Midlands. At 22.05, he bombed a lit night flying field; he thought was near Lincoln, but in fact it was at Tydd St Mary, about 40 miles south-east of Lincoln. Manger then claimed to have bombed Nottingham, but no traces of his bombs were found by the British. He claimed to have gone on to bomb Birmingham with the rest of his 300kg (660lb) bombs, but it seems he was flying further south than he calculated. He said he saw the damage done by the 300kg bombs as black craters on the lit-up streets. We now know where the bombs actually fell: it seems he dropped two 300kg bombs, close together, one south of Coventry on the Baginton sewerage works, near the present day Coventry Airport. The next bomb fell on Whitney Common, killing two cows and making a crater 25ft wide and 8ft deep. In a recent newspaper report, a man who lived in the area in the 1930s said the 'Zeppelin crater' was widely known and used by boys on their bikes, like a modern BMX track.

Manger continued west, dropping his last two bombs on the Birmingham area. The first landed on the Manor Farm in Shirley, and the second the Robin Hood Golf Course in Solihull. A lot of windows were broken in the Hall Green area, but there was no other damage. H.A. Jones remarks in *War in the Air* how lucky it was that more damage wasn't done. If Manger had been 2 or 3 miles further north, he would have bombed the centre of Coventry and Birmingham, undoubtedly causing considerable casualties.

Manger was under attack from anti-aircraft fire and fighters during the attack. He was fired at by guns in Coventry and Birmingham. According to official reports, he was attacked by Lieutenant Cecil Henry Noble-Campbell, from B Flight 38th Squadron RAF, who took off from Buckminster, near Melton Mowbray, in an F.E.2b. Noble-Campbell was a New Zealander who had previously served as a sergeant with the Wellington Mounted Rifles in the Gallipoli campaign.

Another pilot, Lieutenant William Alfred Brown, took off in an F.E.2b from Stamford to intercept the raiders. He reported seeing *L.62* but could not catch it. Nobel-Campbell reported that he had been patrolling at 16,000ft when he attacked the airship, unfortunately entering the history books as the only pilot to have been shot down by a Zeppelin. He said he chased *L.62* for about a half hour, failing to hit it. He was fired at by the crew in the gondolas, suffering a head wound, and his fighter's propeller was broken. He made a forced landing at Radford near Coventry. Brown also landed there, the pilots only then discovering they had been chasing the same Zeppelin. There is some mystery about the circumstances of the injury to Nobel-Campbell, as Manger did not mention a fighter attack in his combat report. The F.E.2b was an old design with a performance only slightly better than the B.E.2c; it had a top speed of about 80mph and a ceiling of around 16,000ft. It is unlikely that Manger was as low as this when under anti-aircraft fire, as his log shows he reached 21,650ft during the flight. It is therefore difficult to understand how the F.E.2b and the Zeppelin got close enough to exchange fire. It has been suggested that Nobel-Campbell and Brown were attempting to reach the Zeppelin and shooting at it: in the dark, did Brown shoot Nobel-Campbell, luckily only wounding him? We will never know for sure. Manger's problems were not over, however. As he went home, *L.62* came under anti-aircraft fire near Norwich. He was hit and a gas cell damaged, lost a lot of height but returned safely to Nordholtz at 11.30.

'V' type Navy Zeppelin *L.63*: Kapitänleutnant Michael von Freudenreich left Nordholz at 13.19. Freudenreich thought he was bombing Grimsby, but British records show he approached Lincoln from the south-east and was fired on by the anti-aircraft gun at Brauncewell. Freudenreich dropped a number of heavy bombs but they fell in a field east of Metheringham. *L.63* then flew southward, dropping six more bombs on Fleet and Little Sutton, causing little damage. The airship went back out to sea over the Wash, returning to Nordholz at 10.10.

'V' type Navy Zeppelin *L.64*: Korvettenkapitan Arnold Schutze had Peter Strasser on board; they took off from Nordholz at 13.00. British records show they approached Lincoln but did not attack the city, presumably because of the good blackout. There were lights showing at Skellingthorpe and Doddlington, which received fourteen bombs, damaging an engine shed and railway track in Skellingthorpe but only breaking windows in Doddlington. *L.64* returned to Nordholz after more than twenty-six hours in the air at 15.23.

18 April 1918

'W' type Navy Zeppelin *L.59*: *L.59*'s last flight was a bombing raid on the British fleet in Malta. Kapitänleutnant Ludwig Bockholt, with Leutnant zur See Heinrich Maas as second officer, left Jamboli in the early morning to cross the Balkans and the Adriatic, on course for Malta. When it reached the Strait of Otranto, near Brindisi, *L.59* flew over a German U-boat at about 700ft. The submarine commander reported that at 21.30 lights were noticed in the air: probably shrapnel bursts. He saw the Zeppelin explode in a huge flame, which lit the horizon as light as day for a short time and then fall into the water. It seems likely that *L.59* was shot down by Italian anti-aircraft fire, though no one claimed to have shot her down. When a search was made by German naval vessels near Durazzo a droppable petrol tank was found floating in an oil slick, along with some pieces of wood. All the crew of twenty-two were missing, presumed killed.

10 May 1918

'V' type Navy Zeppelin *L.56*: Kapitänleutnant Walter Zaeschmar was operating out of Wittmundhaven.

'V' type Navy Zeppelin *L.62*: Hauptmann Kuno Manger was operating out of Nordholz.

Mystery surrounds the final flight of Zeppelin *L.62*. It took off from Nordholtz on a scouting flight on the morning of 10 May. The airship was seen by a German ship about 10 miles north-west of Helgoland, flying low. It was observed flying into a large cloud, and seconds later there was a loud explosion. *L.62* had broken into two pieces and fell into the sea a blazing wreck. Five bodies were recovered but the entire crew were killed. It has never been established what happened, although Peter Strasser thought the cause of the explosion was lightning in the cloud. The rumour among Zeppelin crew veterans interviewed by author Douglas Robinson, many years after the event, was that it was sabotage.

For many years it was thought by British historians that *L.62* had been shot down by a flying boat flown by Captain T.C. Pattison and Captain A.H. Munday, with an NCO wireless operator and engineer on board. At about noon, the Admiralty picked up wireless signals from a Zeppelin off Helgoland. The flying boat left Killingholme in Lincolnshire to intercept. And at about 15.30, near Borkum Lighthouse, they saw a Zeppelin at about 8,000ft, a mile away. They climbed to attack and opened fire. They saw the port midship engine slow down and the Zeppelin drop bombs and ballast, but lost sight of it and thought they had destroyed it. When GHQ received information about the destruction of *L.62*, they believed Pattison and his crew had shot it down. This is the version that appears in the official history by H.A. Jones.

However, Douglas Robinson, using German archival material and interviews with surviving Zeppelin crews in the 1960s, has a different explanation. Kapitänleutnant Walter Zaeschmar had taken off from Wittmundhaven in Zeppelin *L.56*, and at 15.50 had seen a flying boat about 7 miles away. He dropped ballast and climbed to 21,700ft, with the flying boat climbing in pursuit and reaching about 16,400ft. Zaeschmar did not see the flying boat firing, as it was between him and the sun. After about an hour, the flying boat turned away. Because of the shortage of ballast, Zaeschmar returned to base at 21.15. Because of the times recorded, it seems certain that *L.62* was not shot down by the flying boat: *L.62* was destroyed in the morning, and the encounter between the flying boat and *L.56* was in the afternoon. It seems there was no doubt that Pattison fired at the Zeppelin, but because they were almost 4,000ft apart no damage was done to *L.56*.

19 July 1918

In probably the most effective British attack from the sea, Navy Zeppelins *L.54* and *L.60* were bombed and destroyed in the airship sheds at Tondern by Sopwith Camels.

Two flights of Sopwith Camels took off from HMS *Furious*, with the aim of destroying the Zeppelins in their sheds. The pilots were (first flight) Captain W.D. Jackson, Captain W.F. Dickson and Lieutenant N.E. Williams, and (second flight) Captain B.A. Smart, Captain T.K. Thyne, Lieutenant S. Dawson and Lieutenant W.A. (Toby) Yeulett. From 1 April 1918, they were all in the RAF, as the RFC and RNAS had been combined to form the Royal Air Force. For some time, however the officers kept their old rank titles. The pilots had spent some time training for the mission at Turnhouse airfield (now Edinburgh Airport), bombing markings on the grass supposedly the size of the airship sheds at Tondern.

HMS *Furious*, a cruiser converted into an aircraft carrier, left Rosyth in Scotland on 17 July with the 1st Light Cruiser Squadron and accompanying destroyers. It carried the seven Sopwith Camel fighters, each with two 50lb bombs. The force reached the area of the Lyngvig lightship off the Danish coast early on 18 July, but the operation had to be postponed for twenty-four hours because of thunderstorms. The first flight then took off at 03.20 and flew the 80 miles to Tondern in about an hour. Captain Thyne did not take part as he had to return to the fleet because of engine trouble. In his report, Captain Jackson said the three aeroplanes in the first flight arrived at 04.35 and observed two very large sheds. They attacked from about 70ft, opening fire and bombing the largest shed, which burst into flames. The resulting fire rose at least 1,000ft and the entire shed was destroyed. There was some limited opposition, which increased as the Germans got over their surprise. The second flight, which arrived at about 04.45, was met by more organized fire, and it seems one Sopwith was hit, losing a wheel, but all flew away.

There is an interesting report by Horst von Buttlar in his book. He was living off the base with his wife, about a half mile from the airfield, when he was woken by the whirring of a propeller. He went to the window of his flat and saw a British aeroplane fly over and bomb the airfield. The shed in which his Zeppelin was kept was on fire, the flames burning 'in a terrible straight column'. A second aeroplane flew over, followed by a third. The sailors from the base were firing with rifles at the planes; they were too low for the anti-aircraft guns to fire at them. The English pilots could be seen quite plainly, waving in a most friendly way at the Germans. One of the planes seemed to be in trouble, losing a wheel and hitting a high tension cable, but managed to fly away. Writing some years after the events, Buttlar said he admired the brave British airmen, who during the attack had refused to fire their machine guns at his men, just waving at them, concentrating on their targets.

Putting together all the information we have, we now know that several bombs hit the largest double 'Toska' shed, destroying Zeppelins L.54 and L.60 inside. More limited damage was done to the smaller 'Tobias' shed, destroying the captive balloon and some of the gas equipment. One Zeppelin crewman was seriously injured and several air and ground crewmen slightly injured. Only two of the Sopwith Camels got back to the fleet, and they both ditched in the sea. HMS Furious was able to launch aircraft efficiently, but the technology to safely land aircraft onboard still needed to be perfected.

Captain Dickson was picked up by HMS Violent at 05.45, and was awarded the DSO for his part in the raid. Captain Bernard Smart got back to the fleet at 06.30, earning a bar to the DSO he received ten months before for shooting down Zeppelin L.23. Captain Jackson, Lieutenant Williams and Lieutenant Dawson all landed near Esbjerg in Denmark and were interned; Jackson was later to escape. Lieutenant Toby Yeulett was not seen alive again. It seems likely his aircraft was damaged by the gunfire when he lost a wheel or when he hit the electricity cable. His body was washed up on the Danish coast on 24 July, and he is buried in Haurvig churchyard in Denmark.

The raid had destroyed two Zeppelins, and probably more importantly it led to the end of Tondern as an active station as it was seen as vulnerable to attack. Defences were increased at Nordholz, and only Ahlhorn – far from the sea – was regarded as safe.

2 August 1918

'V' type Navy Zeppelin *L.53*: Kapitänleutnant Eduard Prolss was flying out of Nordholz.

'V' type Navy Zeppelin *L.64*: Korvettenkapitan Arnold Schutze was operating out of Ahlhorn.

This was the last encounter between flying boats and Zeppelins. *L.53* and *L.64* were on a scouting mission about 42 miles north-west of Terschelling. Schutze saw a 'large American' type flying boat and five large bi-planes about 6,500ft under the Zeppelin. They were climbing towards him. When they were about 4,000ft below him they started firing, Schutze dropped all his bombs on them in a vain attempt to hit them, and dropped ballast and climbed to 19,000ft. The British aeroplanes broke off the attack and flew south at about 08.20.

5/6 August 1918

On the last Bank Holiday Monday of the war, this was the final act in the Zeppelin campaign against England. Peter Strasser never gave up the belief that precision night bombing would win the war. The *L.40* class of Zeppelins, the 'height climbers' able to operate at 20,000ft, had limited success, but even if the crews were able to cope with the lack of oxygen and intense cold at that height, a basic problem remained: if you couldn't navigate and bomb accurately from 9,000ft, you certainly couldn't from 20,000ft. By 1918, fighter aircraft could out-climb the Zeppelin. It is fitting that Strasser accompanied the last bombing raid of the war in his latest, most developed Zeppelin, *L.70*. It was shot down by a D.H.4 two-seater, an aeroplane that outperformed the Zeppelin in every way.

The weather conditions did not help the Zeppelins, a fairly strong westerly wind slowing them down. There was heavy cloud cover at low altitudes, whilst above the clouds at 20,000ft there was very good visibility. Five Zeppelins took off in the early afternoon. It seems that finally German radio discipline was effective, as they were not picked up by wireless. They were first reported at about 21.10, well before sunset, by the Leman Trail Lightship 30 miles south-east of Happisburgh, Norfolk.

The British air defence system worked perfectly, the airships being tracked as they approached the Norfolk coast as dusk fell. Thirteen aircraft took off from Great Yarmouth Air Station. Ten flew inland to wait for any Zeppelins that crossed the coast, whilst three flew out to sea to intercept. They saw three Zeppelins at about 17,000ft.

We have very full reports from the RAF pilots in the action and the combat reports of the surviving Zeppelin commanders, which give a clear account of events that night.

'V' type Navy Zeppelin *L.53*: Kapitänleutnant Eduard Prolss left Nordholz at 12.55. He crossed the North Sea in a group of three airships with *L. 65* and *L.70*. He had intended to bomb Nottingham or Sheffield, but at 22.10 he saw a Zeppelin falling in flames, and decided, taking into account the brightness of the evening, to give up on any attempt to go far inland. Using radio bearings, he calculated he was over Boston in Lincolnshire, which was completely covered by clouds when he dropped his bombs. The British calculated he was about 65 miles east of Cromer in Norfolk and all the bombs fell in the sea. Prolss got back to Nordholz at 04.50. He would live to fight another day, but not for long.

'V' type Navy Zeppelin *L.56*: Kapitänleutnant Walter Zaeschmar left Wittmundhaven at 14.10 and crossed the North Sea with *L.63* some 30 miles south of the main group of three. At 21.45, he reported seeing the lights of Yarmouth ahead of him, and *L.53*, *L.65* and *L.70* a long distance away but easily visible against the evening sky. At 22.15, he saw an airship in that group burn and fall through the clouds to the ground, where it continued to burn for some time. He continued the raid and saw lights through a hole in the clouds, which he took to be Norwich; he dropped all his bombs from 20,400ft. British records show his navigation was more accurate than other commanders, as his bombs fell into the sea off the coast, but not far from Norwich. *L.56* returned to Wittmundhaven at 05.15.

'V' type Navy Zeppelin *L.63*: Kapitänleutnant Michael von Freudenreich took off from Ahlhorn at 12.47 and flew across the North Sea with *L.56*. He had little idea of his position. Like the other commanders, he was using the new Telefunken radio location system, which used a radio signal from the shore stations. While it was safer than the old system where the Zeppelin transmitted the signal, it was no more accurate, actually probably less so. Freudenreich was unable to check his position at 21.45 as his stopwatch had failed, and had to wait for the next signal at 22.15. He got a bearing, but it was very inaccurate. At more or less the same time, he witnessed the end of *L.70*. He said he saw a Zeppelin about 5 miles away; it caught fire with a large flame, stood up vertically and fell. Because it was not fully dark, he was not sure of the cause, but expected it was an aeroplane. He turned north and climbed to 20,700ft. He thought he was on the north side of the Humber, and was fired on by a gun battery. He dropped all his bombs on the guns, and turned for home. The British have no record these bombs. He returned to Ahlhorn at 04.05.

'V' type Navy Zeppelin *L.65*: Kapitänleutnant Walter Dose left Nordholz at 13.35, crossing the North Sea with *L.53* and *L.70*. He had some problems with his airship, which would only reach 17,700ft on the crossing, despite dropping some bombs and most of his ballast. He was only about 2 miles from *L.70* when he saw it burn. He saw a small light which immediately spread and the whole ship was in flames, breaking into pieces before it entered the clouds. Immediately after this an aeroplane attacked *L.65*. Dose turned north to try to escape, and then believed he was fired on by a ground battery; he dropped all his bombs in reply and to gain altitude. Dose was being attacked by Egbert Cadbury and Robert Leckie in their D.H.4, who turned towards *L.65* after shooting down *L.70*. They reported that while firing at *L.65* they saw a fire in the gondola of the airship. It seems that this was a mechanic in the port midships engine gondola who lifted a blackout curtain while the gondola light was on. We know that during the attack Cadbury's engine stopped and Leckie's gun jammed. Dose had a very lucky escape, as when he got to Nordholz there were said to be 340 bullet holes in his gas cells. He landed safely at 05.55. Dose was to survive the War.

'X' type Navy Zeppelin *L.70*: Kapitänleutnant Johann von Lossnitzer was a fairly inexperienced Zeppelin commander. He had spent some time in the Baltic as commander of *LZ.120*. He was Peter Strasser's Adjutant and his particular favourite, sharing his enthusiasm for the development of the Zeppelin as a weapon of war. It is often said one of the many mistakes Strasser made that night was giving command to a man as inexperienced as Lossnitzer. However, in reality it seems that while the formal commander was Johann von Lossnitzer, with Leutnant zur See Kurt Kruger as his executive officer, in practice the ship was commanded by Peter Strasser.

L.70 was the latest ship in the airship force, a huge machine, 693ft long and 78ft in diameter. With seven engines, it could operate at 23,000ft and reach almost 80mph. Lossnitzer and Strasser took off from Nordholz at 13.13. Flying at the head of a 'V' formation with *L.65* and *L.53*, Strasser sent his final radio message to his commanders at 21.00. At about 22.10, the aircraft attacked. It seems that *L.70* was attacked almost simultaneously by two aircraft. The man credited with the kill was Major Egbert Cadbury, with Captain Robert Leckie as his observer. Cadbury, of the Birmingham chocolate family, had participated in the destruction of *L.21* almost two years before. Leckie had been part of the crew of a Curtis flying boat that shot down Zeppelin *L.22* the year before. They were flying a D.H.4 two-seat light bomber armed with a forward-firing synchronized Vickers gun and a Lewis gun in the rear cockpit. It was powered by a 375hp 20-litre V.12 Rolls-Royce Eagle engine. It was the best anti-Zeppelin aeroplane, capable of about 125 mph and a ceiling of 22,000ft. They took off from Yarmouth at 21.05. Cadbury said he saw three Zeppelins about 40 miles away in a 'V' formation immediately on leaving Yarmouth. By 22.20, he had climbed to 16,400ft and attacked the first Zeppelin from the front, flying slightly to port and below it. Leckie said he fired a magazine of Pomeroy explosive ammunition from his Lewis gun at the rear of its hull; he aimed at the bow and concentrated his fire on a spot about three-quarters of the way aft. A fire started quickly, which spread along the length of the Zeppelin. It fell as a blazing mass, hitting the sea north of Wells-next-the-Sea, off the Norfolk coast. The crew of twenty-two were all killed.

Lieutenant R.E. Keys, with Air Mechanic A.T. Harman as his observer/gunner, had also taken off from Yarmouth, at 20.55, also in a D.H.4. Keys saw the Zeppelin and attacked at 17,000ft from about 75-100 yards with his front (Vickers) gun. This jammed, so he turned so Harman could fire his Lewis gun. Harman fired about seventy rounds of armour piercing and tracer and the airship burst into flames from the stern before falling into the sea. GHQ accepted that both aeroplanes had attacked, but the victory was given to Cadbury and Leckie, who were both awarded the DFC.

After this, both Cadbury and Keys attacked *L.65*. Cadbury's engine cut, which prevented him raising the nose to fire his Vickers gun because the aircraft would have stalled; when the engine restarted, he flew 500ft below the Zeppelin so Leckie could fire upwards. After a few rounds, the Lewis gun jammed. Cadbury saw a brief burst of light from the Zeppelin; it was a mechanic in the port midships engine gondola raising a blackout curtain. Unable to use his guns, Cadbury turned for home. Because of the heavy cloud cover, he got lost on the way back and landed at Sedgeford near King's Lynn at 23.05. Keys also attacked, Harman firing one complete drum and about a quarter of another, which he reported hit the Zeppelin. Then his engine lost power, some of the cylinders cut completely and he broke off the attack. He too got lost in the clouds, so descended and flew west until he saw a flare path. He landed at Kelstern, Lincolnshire, some 100 miles from Yarmouth.

The other airplane from Yarmouth that flew out to sea to intercept the Zeppelins was a D.H.9, a machine with a much poorer performance than the D.H.4. It is possible that this aeroplane, piloted by Captain B.G. Jardine with Lieutenant E.R. Munday as observer/gunner, did reach and fire at Zeppelin *L.65*. We shall never know, as they failed to return, presumably drowned in the North Sea. The heavy cloud cover was difficult for the RAF as well as the Zeppelins, four airmen being killed. As well as Jardine and Munday, Lieutenant F.A. Benitzin in a Bristol Fighter was killed in a crash-landing at Atwick, his observer being badly injured. Lieutenant G.F. Hodson in a Sopwith Camel was also missing, presumed killed.

Parts of the Zeppelin were recovered and examined by the British, as were the bodies of a number of crew members. However, following protests from local people, they were not buried in the locality but were given military funerals at sea.

Egbert Cadbury (1893-1967) became an Air Commodore. When he left the RAF, he became managing director of the Cadbury Company and was knighted. Robert Leckie (1890-1975) became an Air Marshal and Chief of Staff of the Royal Canadian Air Force during the Second World War.

With the death of Peter Strasser, the position of Leader of Airships was given to Korvettenkapitan Paul Werther. He had previously been commander of ground troops and the airship schools. He made proposals for new larger Zeppelins able to operate at 26,000ft. It is interesting whether these machines could have been built, given the technology of the time. It would not have been difficult to build an airship capable of reaching the height: a longer hull with more gas bags and a weight reduction would enable it to reach the altitude. Today, weather balloons can reach 100,000ft. The problem would be keeping the crew alive. At that height, not only would oxygen masks have been necessary but some form of pressure suits for the crew.

Without Strasser, the proposals were given short shrift. Strasser's supporter on the Naval Staff, Admiral Reinhard Scheer, had been made Chief of the Naval Staff, with his role as Commander in Chief of the High Seas Fleet taken by Admiral Franz Hipper. Hipper made an obvious but telling point that clouds often prevented effective scouting from 20,000ft; the problem could only get worse at 26,000ft. He was firmly of the view that aeroplanes were developed enough for reconnaissance missions in the

German Bight; some Zeppelins would be kept for long-distance scouting missions, but they would have a minor role with the High Seas Fleet, although attacks on England were useful in that they helped the Army by tying down great amounts of defensive equipment and manpower.

11 August 1918

'V' type Navy Zeppelin *L.53*: This was the last Zeppelin to be shot down in the war. Kapitänleutnant Eduard Prolss took off from Nordholz to scout the area between Terschelling and the Dogger Bank South Lightship. At about 07.00, he saw a force of British ships. When they spotted him, they made smokescreens and went out across the North Sea, Prolss following at high altitude. He was flying into an ambush.

At the end of 1916, the Royal Navy began to experiment with lighters, special craft designed to extend the range of H.12 large 'America' flying boats. Lighters were unpowered boats strong enough to be towed behind destroyers at a speed of 20-25 knots. The final design was a steel boat about 56ft long, with a beam of 16ft and a height above the water of about 7ft. The lighters were fitted with flooding tanks, so the stern of the boat could be submerged and a flying boat winched onto it. Compressed air would then fill the tank, so the lighter would return to its normal position to be towed at speed. It could then be towed across the North Sea, conserving its fuel, to conduct missions against German targets off the Friesian Coast. When the lighter and flying boat got to its operational position, the loading procedure was reversed and the H.12 refloated to take off. By November 1918, the Navy had thirty-one of these lighters.

Once the design of the flying boat lighter had been perfected, another use was proposed: the 'flying off platform'. This was simply a flat wooden deck on the lighter so that fighter planes, in practice Sopwith Camels, could take off from the deck. The destroyer steaming at full speed into the wind would enable a Camel to take off from the 56ft platform. A number of successful trial flights were made, many by Lieutenant Stuart Culley. He had a Camel N6812 modified for anti-Zeppelin operation. Flotation bags were fitted into the fuselage so the aeroplane would float after landing in the water, and the synchronized Vickers machine guns were removed and replaced by upward-firing Lewis guns.

Zeppelin *L.53* was shadowing ships from the Harwich force on 11 August. Four destroyers were towing lighters. Three had H.12 flying boats, and one, HMS *Redoubt*, a lighter with a flying off platform. Stuart Culley sat on it in his Sopwith Camel, the fighter held on the deck of the lighter with a quick-release strap. The destroyer steamed into the wind at full speed, the combination of the speed of the destroyer and the wind speed allowing the fighter to accelerate at full throttle to take-off speed.

Cully took off at about 09.00. The Zeppelin was at about 19,000ft, and it took the Sopwith Camel about an hour to climb to 18,000ft and get near *L.53*. The last 1,000ft were difficult, with the Camel close to stalling. Culley then attacked *L.53* head-on, from below. It was here that the modifications made to the Camel paid off: the weapons system was similar to that on the B.E.2c two years before. This time Culley had two upward-firing Lewis guns fitted to the top of the wing on Foster mounts. When he fired, the port gun jammed almost immediately, but he used a complete ninety-seven-round drum of explosive and incendiary ammunition. The Sopwith then lost height in a stall, and Culley looked back at the Zeppelin. He saw flames along its side, and a moment later there was an explosion and he watched the blazing Zeppelin fall 3 miles into the sea, with two or three men jumping from the blazing hull. By the time *L.53* hit the sea, the wreck had burned itself out, leaving only a cloud of smoke. All nineteen crewmen were killed.

Culley used the smokescreen to locate and return to the fleet. He landed in the sea close to HMS *Redoubt*. After he was rescued, the Sopwith Camel N6812 was winched aboard, little damaged from its adventure. It can still be seen today, hanging from the ceiling of the Imperial War Museum in London, its twin Lewis guns pointing upwards to the roof, a fitting tribute to the defeat of the Zeppelin.

13 October 1918

'V' Type Navy Zeppelin *L. 63*: Kapitänleutnant Gerhold Ratz was operating out of Ahlhorn.

'V' Type Navy Zeppelin *L.65*: Oberleutnant zur See Werner Vermehren was flying out of Nordholz.

This mission was routine: its only claim to fame is that it was the last combat mission flown by the Naval Airship Service. The airships were ordered to take off at about 10.00 to provide reconnaissance for a minesweeping operation north of the Dogger Bank. Four battleships from the High Seas Fleet were to provide protection for the minesweepers. The mission was a failure, as cloud prevented any useful observations and both Zeppelins returned before dark, *L.63* to Ahlhorn and *L.65* to Nordholz.

Chapter Fourteen

The Scuttling

On 29 October 1918, a revolution broke out in Germany. It started in the High Seas Fleet. To understand this, we need to briefly look at the political situation at the time. By October 1918, Germany was falling apart under Allied military pressure. All its allies were seeking separate armistice arrangements. The de facto political leaders, Hindenburg and Ludendorff, were desperately seeking to end the war. The leaders of the Navy then behaved with extraordinary stupidity, making plans for a last-ditch attack on the British Navy, a mission they claimed would improve armistice conditions. Everyone knew it had no chance of success, and it was essentially a suicide mission to save the honour of the German Navy. The rank and file sailors were having none of it. Mutiny broke out, first at Kiel, then spreading to all the ports, reaching Cuxhaven within days. By 9 November, most ships were flying the red flag and were controlled by workers' and sailors' councils. Sailors began hunting down their officers, stripping them of rank insignia and decorations.

The uprising soon spread all over the country, in particular Berlin. Soldiers refused to fire at sailors and workers who entered their barracks to raise the red flag over them. They were joined by soldiers and more workers, and within days there was a real threat of revolution, the Army High Command realizing that massive political changes were necessary to preserve their power. The Kaiser was forced to abdicate, and the leader of the Social Democrat Party (SPD), Friedrich Ebert, became Chancellor. For his own reasons, Ebert was as keen to prevent revolution as the generals were. The SPD had split over the issue of war credits, and its left wing, the Independent Social Democrats (USPD), who had opposed the war, were moving to support the revolution. In the wings waited the group Ebert feared the most, the *Spartakusbund* (Spartacus League), who supported a Bolshevik-type revolution.

When he was installed in office, Ebert was telephoned by the First Quartermaster of the Army, General Wilhelm Groener. He said the Kaiser had gone into exile in Holland and Field Marshal Hindenburg intended to march the Army back to Germany. He indicated that the Social Democratic Government would be accepted as legitimate, and that the soldiers' councils would be 'dealt with in a family spirit'. Ebert asked what the Army wanted. He was told it wanted total support in maintaining discipline and order in the Army, and food supplies and rail transport for the Army. Most importantly, the Army expected the Government to fight against Bolshevism, and would place itself at the disposal of the Government for such a purpose.

The Armistice was signed in the early morning of 11 November, and came into effect at 11.00 that day. The terms drawn up by the Allied military were designed to ensure that Germany would be unable to resume the war. Germany was to withdraw from all occupied territories in the West and Alsace Lorraine. The Allies would occupy the west bank of the Rhine and 50 miles east from several bridgeheads over the Rhine. Germany was to surrender most of its aircraft, artillery and machine guns. Most of the fleet was to be interned in Allied ports. The Treaty of Brest-Litovsk and Bucharest would be void, though the territories would not be returned to the Bolshevik Russians but would become independent; decisions that are still a cause of conflict 100 years later.

Airships were covered by a clause that said: 'All Naval aircraft are to be concentrated and immobilized in German bases to be specified by the Allies and United States of America.' This meant that all the surviving airships were to be taken to their sheds and deflated. An Allied commission was to inspect all bases to ensure they had been disarmed according to the Armistice conditions. The airship delegation was led by the British airship pioneer, RAF Brigadier E.A.D. Masterton. Accompanied by Kapitänleutnant Von Buttlar, they inspected all the North Sea bases and other officers examined Friedrichshafen. At the Zeppelin works, according to Ernst Lehmann in his 1927 book *The Zeppelins*, construction of Zeppelin *L.72* continued as the airship had not been handed over to the Navy. However, the Armistice delegation soon ensured it was put into storage.

Nordholz was governed by the Cuxhaven Workers' and Sailors' Council. This was a state of affairs not popular with the ex-officers of the Airship Service. In his autobiography, Von Buttlar describes in some detail his role in the scuttling of the Zeppelins. He describes the revolution at Cuxhaven with contempt: 'When I think of the way our people allowed themselves to be deluded in those days, I can only hold my head in horror.' He said his combat crews remained loyal to the Kaiser and previous regime, though some of the fitters and cleaners were insubordinate, but they were kept in order by loyalists who beat up any agitators. 'The crews who had come in touch with the enemy held aloof from the whole of this disgraceful foolery.' While this may be true, we have to remember that Buttlar wrote this in 1931, before the Nazi takeover but when Germany was increasingly governed by parties of the extreme right.

During the late 1918 and early 1919, Germany was in a state of civil war. In January 1919, the first ever democratic election was held in Germany and the SPD won a majority, though most of the large cities were still controlled by the Workers' and Soldiers' Councils. All the North Sea ports, including Cuxhaven, were under the control of revolutionary sailors. The Social Democratic Government used the right-wing Freikorps to put down the revolution. They feared Bolshevism: fourteen years later they got Hitler.

It was in this situation that the Treaty of Versailles was imposed on Germany. One of the terms of the Armistice was that the High Seas Fleet be disarmed and sent to the British base of Scapa Flow in the Orkney Islands. It remained there, the ships with a skeleton crew, from December 1918 to June 1919. One of the decisions of the final peace treaty at Versailles was that most of the High Seas Fleet was to be handed to the various Allies. Discussions took place among officers, led by Admiral von Reuter, and a decision was taken to scuttle the surrendered High Seas Fleet. On 21 June 1919, the sea cocks were opened on the ships in Scapa Flow and fifty-two warships, including fourteen battleships, were sunk.

The same was to happen to the Airship fleet. Buttler wrote that a 'little council of war' was held the day before the scuttling of the High Seas Fleet and it was agreed the 'enemy shall not have any Zeppelins either'. On 23 June 1919, a group of conspirators entered the Zeppelin sheds at Nordholz and Wittmundhaven, unchallenged by guards from the Sailors' Soviet. They slackened off the suspension tackles and let the deflated airships crash to the floor. The weight of the fragile duralumin structures did the rest, crushing the framework and damaging the ships beyond repair.

All the Nordholz ships – *L.14*, *L.41*, *L.42*, *L.63* and *L.65* – were destroyed, and at Wittmunhaven *L.52* and *L.56* were destroyed. The plot was discovered in other bases and some Zeppelins were handed over to the Allies. Douglas Robinson interviewed a member of a Zeppelin flight crew almost forty years later, who told him: 'We weren't thinking about the Allies getting the ships, we didn't want them falling into the hands of those dammed Communists in Berlin.' Such a comment probably sums up much of the tragedy of German history in the twentieth century.

The Allied Control Commission ensured the other Zeppelins were surrendered. France had *L.72*, *LZ.113* and a commercial airship, the *Nordstern*; Britain the *L.71* and *L.64*; Italy the *L.61*, *LZ.120* and a commercial airship, the *Bodensee*; Belgium the *L.30*; and Japan the *L.37*. After getting as much technical information as they could, most of the Allied nations scrapped the surrendered Zeppelins over the next few years.

Only the French put one into service, *L.72* being renamed *Dixmunde* and making a number of flights, including one of 118 hours over the Sahara Desert. It was commanded by a French Navy airship man, Lieutenant Jean du Plessis de Grenedan. On 21 December 1923, on a long-distance flight over Algeria and Tunisia, it exploded in a thunderstorm over the Mediterranean. Fifty people were killed, ending the French airship programme.

In the months after the Armistice, the Zeppelin Company produced two commercial airships at Friedrichshafen: *LZ.120* (*Bodensee*) and *LZ.121* (*Nordstern*). They were much smaller than the war airships, about 400ft long with a diameter of 61ft, with three engines. The *Bodensee* was completed in August 1919 and made 103 flights, many with paying passengers; its captain was Hans Kurt Flemming, a veteran of many bombing raids. A few of its flights were between Berlin and Stockholm. It was handed over to Italy as part of the post-war reparations in December 1919. The *Nordstern* was not completed; it was seized by the Allied Control Commission in December 1919 and handed to France.

The Zeppelin Company did well from the reparations programme. It kept its designers and workers employed, though *LZ.126* – a Zeppelin 'built in Germany by German workers and engineers, paid for with German money, but which belongs to America', as an editorial in the *Berlin Morning Post* put it – became the USS *Los Angeles*, built for the US Navy. It was flown over the Atlantic by Hugo Eckener and Ernst Lehmann on 12/15 October 1924, covering over 5,000 miles and spending about eighty-one hours in the air. Before it went into service in America, its hydrogen was replaced with helium, which is probably the main reason it lasted until 1939.

The Zeppelin Company went into partnership with Goodyear of Akron, Ohio, to produce airships in the USA. They produced two – the *Akron* and *Macon* – both of which crashed in bad weather. Most of the crew of *Macon* survived, but those of *Akron* died when it crashed into the sea. This ended the American airship programme. Goodyear developed the much smaller non-rigid Blimp, which was probably the most successful military airship.

The Zeppelin Company produced a number of very large passenger airships during the Nazi era: the *LZ.126* (*Los Angeles*, which served in the US Navy), *LZ.127* (*Graf Zeppelin 1*), *LZ.129* (*Hindenburg*) and *LZ.130* (*Graf Zeppelin 2*). It also made, in partnership with the Goodyear Company in the USA, *ZRS.4* (*Akron*) and *ZRS.5* (*Macon*). They continued to use hydrogen as a lifting gas, which led to the best-known airship disaster of them all. On 6 May 1937, the *Hindenburg* was nearing the ground at Lakehurst, New Jersey, when people saw a small glow in the tail, and within seconds the whole of the back of the Zeppelin was on fire. The disaster was captured in a newsreel film and the commentary by Herb Morrison is probably remembered by anyone who has heard it. In tears, he shouted: 'This is one of the worst catastrophes in the world .... Oh, the humanity and all the passengers!' There were ninety-seven people on board, of whom thirty-six died. Many escaped because the Zeppelin was near the ground when the fire started, and as the hydrogen burned away the airship hit the ground and they were able to scramble out. Among the dead were Ernst Lehmann and Hans Kurt Flemming, both of whom had survived the war as Zeppelin commanders, worked for the Zeppelin Company and died as many of their comrades did twenty years before in a burning airship.

The Zeppelin Company produced one more airship, the *LZ.130 Graf Zeppelin II*, in 1938. This was taken over by the Luftwaffe and carried out the last military missions of any Zeppelin. The passenger area was fitted with electronic surveillance equipment, and the airship flew along the borders of Poland, Czechoslovakia, the Netherlands and Britain to spy on electronic and radar defences. *LZ.130* made two missions in international waters off the coast of Britain. The first was in May 1939, a two-day mission along the East Coast, and in early August 1939 another two-day mission to Scotland. It is not clear whether the Germans gained useful electronic intelligence. However, at the start of the Battle of Britain the Luftwaffe concentrated on attacking RAF radar sites, but as far as we know never successfully jammed them.

The most successful airship operations in the Second World War are little-known and involve the humble Goodyear Blimp. The US Navy had 150 of these in fifteen squadrons. The 'K' type was 250ft long, with a diameter of 57ft, and was used for convoy protection and anti-submarine patrols. It was the proud boast of the 'Blimp' service that no ship in a convoy protected by a Blimp was ever sunk by a U-boat. They were only ever used where there was no danger of aeroplane attack, like the East or West Coast of the USA, or the Mediterranean late in the war. Filled with helium, they could fly low and slow over a convoy, missions often lasting over twenty-four hours. The only US Navy Blimp lost in action shows what they couldn't do. The captains were ordered to stay out of range of enemy ships and report their position to destroyers or aeroplanes. On 18 June 1943, *K.74* was off the Florida coast when it picked up a U-boat on radar. As the submarine was approaching a tanker and a freighter, the captain decided to attack. The lookout on *U.134* saw the Blimp and fired at it with a 20mm cannon; the crew of *K.74* fired back with a machine gun and attempted to drop depth charges. The cannon fire punctured the envelope of the Blimp, which landed in the sea. After eight hours, nine of the crew of ten were rescued. One man, Machinist's Mate Isadore Stessel, was attacked by a shark and drowned just before rescue - the only Blimp crewman killed by enemy action.

The defeat of the Zeppelins is a story of courage and horror. Most of all it is about an arms race which the Allies won, mainly due to British organization and technology. The Zeppelins were very effective terror bombers in 1915 and 1916, but they didn't really stand a chance. They could only survive by operating at higher and higher altitudes, and the higher they went, the less effective they were.

The most significant factor in the defeat of the Zeppelins was that the British and French had developed an effective system of tracking them, generally using radio location signals sent by the Zeppelin commanders themselves. Commanders remained too reliant on bearings sent from their HQ. Up to 1918, because the Zeppelins transmitted a signal which was triangulated on-shore and a bearing sent back in code to the Zeppelin, the British were able to use the same system of triangulation to locate the position of the airship. They did not have to wait and decode the bearing signal. They had the position before the Zeppelin commander did. In any system of triangulation, accuracy improves the larger the angle measured, so the British measurements got more accurate as the airships neared the coast, and the German locations less accurate.

It is ironic that the last warlike mission carried out by a Zeppelin was in 1939. The *Graf Zeppelin*, in the guise of showing the flag, flew along the South Coast of Britain, spying on radar installations to map their locations and frequencies. During the Battle of Britain, the Luftwaffe first targeted radar sites as they realized that the British air defence system could only work with accurate information about the range, height and direction of attacking aircraft. The British didn't need radar in 1916 and 1917: the Zeppelins provided radio location signals for them.

The British air defence system was the real long-term gain of the Zeppelin and Gotha attacks. The combination of radio/radar location and ground observations, reporting to regional centres and thence to central control, beat the Germans in 1918 and 1940. The scene of information being constantly updated and displayed on a large map table, with counters moved around by WAAFs with croupiers' rakes, while commanders watched and issued orders to operational commanders from a balcony above, evolved directly from 1918 to 1940. Obviously there were massive updates, as very few fighters had radio in 1917, but the system of patrol lines and telephone control to aerodromes defeated the Zeppelins. The updated system would likewise defeat the Luftwaffe.

The second most important factor in the Zeppelins' defeat is simple; they could not navigate in the dark. All airship commanders were excellent navigators. The naval commanders performed very well in co-operation with surface warships in daylight reconnaissance and minesweeping operations, but at night even the best navigators like Mathy were lost most of the time. This made them all over-reliant on wireless bearings, and we have already seen how dangerous this was, but it also made them largely ineffective. There are very few occasions when airships hit targets of military importance. The Telefunken radio location system introduced in 1918, where signals were transmitted from ground stations and bearings measured on special stop watches, didn't make the situation better, and was probably less accurate than the shore-based system. It also seems to be the case that Zeppelin commanders never really understood just how dangerous radio signals were. Radio discipline improved over England, but they still chattered away (in Morse of course) near their home bases; hence the success of naval aeroplanes.

The cities most targeted were those easiest to find. London had obvious strategic value but was also easy to find from East Anglia or the Channel, mainly because of the River Thames and Blackwater River. London was also well lit, even with the blackout; once they found it, Zeppelins could usually find their way around because of the Thames. The defences of London were a mixed blessing; searchlights, anti-aircraft guns and aeroplanes made it a dangerous place, but also provided a beacon for others. The other city most often bombed was Hull, largely because it was easy to find on the Humber.

Zeppelins were virtually defenceless against aeroplanes. Airships' machine guns were generally useless; occasionally aeroplanes had bullet holes on landing, but there is no evidence that they deterred attacks. There is only one dubious recorded example of a Zeppelin shooting down an attacking aeroplane, which was when Zeppelin *L.62* was attacked by Lieutenant Nobel-Campbell near Coventry. Though the FE.2b of Nobel-Campbell was shot down, all the evidence points to a friendly fire incident. The Zeppelin commander does not mention a fighter attack in his report.

It took the Royal Flying Corps an inordinate length of time to recognize that the Lewis gun with incendiary ammunition was the way to shoot down Zeppelins, but once they did, in the autumn of 1916, they were very successful. The only defence the airships had was height, and for several months the 'height climbers' were able to operate above the ceiling of the fighters. However, this led to a real decline in the usefulness of the airships. They had difficulty in navigation at 9,000ft; at 20,000ft they were lost most of the time.

Flying boats had some success in shooting down Zeppelins, in daylight, near their home bases; the 'height climber's were able to avoid them by operating at altitude, though this created more problems than it solved. It made effective naval reconnaissance and minesweeping impossible.

Zeppelins were very conspicuous and vulnerable on the ground. At the beginning of the war, British air raids on airship sheds were a real problem for the Germans. It was only the advance of the German Army to the west that restricted this. By 1917, Britain had primitive aircraft carriers, and fighter aeroplanes launched from them were able to bomb the North Seas bases, as well as attack Zeppelins in the air. The Tondern attack was particularly successful, and would undoubtedly have been repeated on the other North Sea bases had the war gone on. During the war, four airships were destroyed by bombing raids on their sheds.

Zeppelins needed a ground crew of several hundred men, not to service them but to get them in and out of their sheds, to take off and land. There were a number of accidents when airships suffered major damage after being caught by the wind when taken out of their sheds. The revolving shed at Nordholz, which could be rotated so the doors faced the wind, was a partial solution but too expensive for general use. About twenty airships were destroyed because of the weather, usually high winds, although snow and ice also caused crashes. It is difficult to be precise about airships destroyed by the weather, as other factors such as engine failure or pilot error were usually involved.

Zeppelins had to be landed at or very near a base with hangar facilities. There are many examples of airships, usually with punctured gas cells, landing in friendly territory but too far from a base to be quickly returned. Almost always, one or two nights in the open, tethered to trees or buildings, buffeted by the wind, would damage them beyond repair. They were so fragile they could not rest on the ground uninflated; they would collapse under their own weight. Rigid airship sheds were literally 'hangers', the Zeppelin was suspended from the roof and all maintenance work done in the shed.

The most commented-on Achilles' heel was the use of hydrogen as a lifting gas. The Germans were aware of just how inflammable it was, but they were fighting a war, which is a dangerous business. All aeroplanes were inflammable; Zeppelins were full of petrol, oil and bombs, and were covered with linen tightened with cellulose dope. All were very inflammable, and hydrogen was just another risk to be taken. In no way can this justify the use of hydrogen in post-war civilian airships; it was far too risky, and led to many needless deaths. The incendiary bullet was the death knell of the Zeppelin as a bomber. It was not only effective, but had a tremendous morale effect.

An airship on fire could be seen by other Zeppelins crews from up to 100 miles away; talk in the mess about 'whether to jump or burn' was a powerful symptom of real fear. In all, eleven airships were shot down in flames by aeroplanes using incendiary bullets. Three were shot down by anti-aircraft fire and one brought down by a bomb dropped from an aeroplane.

More airships were destroyed by hydrogen fire in other ways than by being shot at. Six exploded in the air, probably as a result of being struck by lightning. Nine airships caught fire on the ground, usually as a result of landing accidents, though in some cases like the Ahlhorn disaster the cause was unknown; the danger of hydrogen was that if one airship caught fire, it was likely others nearby would also burn.

The most common reason for the destruction of an airship was anti-aircraft fire. It was the main cause of the destruction of twenty-two, mainly early in the war. Only three Zeppelins were shot down in flames by anti-aircraft fire, all near the Western Front by French guns. It is quite surprising how many airships were hit and came down without catching fire. The most common sequence of events was that the airship was hit by shrapnel or rifle fire, which punctured the gas cells, though quite often a shell would go right through the airship without exploding. The airship, leaking gas, would lose height, and if they were lucky they would reach a base and crash-land without major damage. If they didn't reach a base, they were usually in trouble, as without a ground crew to handle it a Zeppelin, even if landed safely, would usually break up if left on the ground. The crew were usually uninjured, and if they got to German-held territory would fight another day. It they didn't, they would end up in PoW camps. Though Zeppelin crews were often threatened during interrogation with being put on trial for murder, this never happened, and they were usually well treated as PoWs in Britain or France. On a number of occasions, Zeppelins lost so much gas they had to crash-land at some speed. The commander would try to land in a lake or a forest to lessen the impact; occasionally some of the crew would get out and others couldn't. There are a number of cases of airships hitting the ground, losing a gondola and most of the crew escaping, leaving a few crew members in a much lighter, uncontrollable airship floating away in the wind, most never to be seen again.

A number of airships landed in the sea; whilst they were likely to be uninjured, this was a much more risky business for the crews, as though a Zeppelin would float for some time, it would eventually sink. The lucky ones were picked up by German ships, others by Allied ships and captured. Some, like the wretched crew of *L.19*, drowned in the cold North Sea.

I covered many of the museums and memorials in some detail in my last book, *Zeppelins Over the Midlands*. The museums at the former Zeppelin bases of Nordholz and Tondern are both excellent. At Nordholz, a few miles from Cuxhaven, is Aeronauticum, the *Deutsches Luftschiff und Marineflieger museum*. It probably has the best collection of Navy Zeppelin artefacts in the world. The museum carefully relates the history of German naval aviation, covering everything from the Zeppelin raids, through the Cuxhaven Soviet to the air-sea operations in the Nazi era. There are a number of exhibits from *L.19*, including most of the letters in bottles from crew members. The exhibits are obviously labelled in German, though some have an English translation. Aeronauticum has a large collection of modern naval aircraft, ranging from a Fairey Gannet to a MIG 21. In summer, the museum is open most days, though visitors should note that in winter the museum is closed on Mondays. It is always worth noting that museums in Germany and indeed much of Europe are usually open on Sundays but close on Mondays, so check before making a special journey. The museum's address is:

Aeronauticum
Peter Strasser Platz
D 27639 Wurster Nordseekuste
Germany
(www.aeronauticum.de)

The Zeppelin and Garrison Museum Tonder is smaller, on what was until recently a Danish Army base. The museum is maintained by volunteers and has limited opening hours, generally just summer weekends. Details are on the really good website. The address is:

The Zeppelin and Garrison Museum
Gasvaerkvej
DK 6270 Tonder
Denmark
(www.zeppelin-museum.dk)

The Zeppelin Museum at Friedrichshafen covers the history and technology of Zeppelins in a lot of detail. There is much more on the civilian role and modern developments than in other museums. It is also possible to have a flight in a Zeppelin from Friedrichshafen. Over 100 years ago, well-heeled customers could fly low and slow around Lake Constance, in perfect safety, according to the DELAG publicity. As the modern airships are filled with helium, it is now safe. The airships still fly low and slow, and readers can check the excellent website to decide if they are well-heeled enough. The hangar is at Bodensee Airport, Friedrichshafen (www.zeppelinflug.de)

The Brussels Army Museum has a number of parts from *L.30*, including an engine gondola. The Zeppelin was taken to Belgium as war reparations in 1919.

France took over *LZ.113* in 1920, and its rear engine gondola can be seen at the Musee de L'air, Le Bourget, near Paris.

In Britain, the Imperial War Museum has an interesting and well-presented collection of Zeppelin artefacts. Most are at the Lambeth Road London site, as is the Sopwith Camel No 6812 in which Lieutenant Stuart Culley shot down Zeppelin *L.53* on 11 August 1918. Other interesting exhibits at Lambeth include the sub-cloud car from *LZ.90*, jettisoned near Manningtree in Essex, and a charred map and badly damaged binoculars from the wreckage of *L.31*. The B.E.2c, which for decades hung from the roof, has been moved to IWM Duxford.

The RAF Museum has a number of interesting items and good First World War material at Hendon and Cosford. As is the case with the IWM, most Zeppelin raid artefacts seem to be at the London site at Hendon. There are various parts from shot-down Zeppelins and *SL.11*. The Hendon museum has a B.E.2, an early B.E.2b rather than the model generally used as a night-fighter, the B.E.2c.

The best museum to appreciate the anti-Zeppelin war is the Stow Maries Great War Aerodrome. This, like Nordholz and Tondern, was an active aerodrome from 1916 to 1918. Construction started in 1915 on one of the aerodromes that formed the defensive circle around London. In September 1916 it housed 37 (Home Defence) Squadron RFC. Though most of the operations of 37 Squadron were against Gotha and other aeroplane attacks, aircraft took off to intercept Zeppelins on a few occasions, in particular during the 'Silent Raid'. Lieutenant Louden Pierce Watkins, the man who shot down *L.48*, was a member of 37 Squadron, though not based at Stow Maries at the time.

Since 2010, the aerodrome has been the subject of a conservation programme to preserve historic buildings and restore it to its original 1917 appearance. Though it will take several years to restore all the buildings, it has the feel of a place where history was made. There are several flying displays, many with original or replica First World War aeroplanes, during the summer. The airfield is generally open from Friday to Sunday, though it has different summer and winter hours: it is always better to check on the excellent website.

The address is:

Stow Maries Great War Aerodrome
Hickmans Lane,
Purleigh, near Maldon
Essex. CM3 6RN
(www.stowmaries.org)

The final major museum to mention is the Shuttleworth Collection, near Biggleswade, which has probably the best collection of flying First World War aircraft in the world. There are many flying days in the summer. The museum is open every day; but opening times vary seasonally. The address is:

The Shuttleworth Collection
Old Warden Aerodrome
Near Biggleswade
Bedfordshire SG18 9EP
(www.shuttleworth.org)

One of the best things about the centenary of the Great War has been the massive increase in research and interest in the period. The Zeppelin raids have been of particular interest to local historians, And there have been a lot of very interesting regional BBC programmes. Several local museums have incendiary bombs on display. Incendiary bombs were rarely completely destroyed. The ones that worked left just a few bits of rusty metal, but the ones that didn't are more interesting, often having the coating of tar-covered rope almost intact.

The commemoration of victims is variable and seems to be based on the interest historians had in recording the names 100 years ago. More and more of the names of the victims are becoming known, but it is a slow process. The military aspects of the raids were well covered in the 1920s and 1930s, the work of Henry Albert Jones being particularly useful. Added to this, we have the various books and articles written by Zeppelin commanders and crewmen. While these show that what people remember in times of stress does not always match the facts seen in the cold light of day, the Zeppelin attacks are among the best-recorded operations of the war. Research by Douglas Robinson in the 1960s, and more recently Ian Castle and Ray Rimmel, have added to our knowledge of Zeppelin and anti-Zeppelin operations. What happened on the ground and the identification of victims is the area where more research is needed. While GHQ, police and fire brigade reports tell us where the bombs fell, they rarely name the casualties. Normally, newspapers would have done this, but because of the iron hand of DORA (the 1914 Defence of the Realm Act) they could not be named. Even when they had family and friends to remember them, after 100 years memories fade and victims are forgotten.

When I started researching the events around my grandmother's moments of terror in Wednesbury, I was initially surprised to find out how much was available about Max Dietrich and Zeppelin *L.21*. The problems started when I tried to find out about the other victims. In Wednesbury, events on the ground were recorded by a historian in 1920. In other towns there were newspaper reports but no names. I had to rely on cemetery records or the 1911 Census to get death certificates for many of them. The situation is well illustrated by the victims of the 'Silent Raid'. Kapitänleutnant Kolle in *L.45* dropped most of his bombs on Northampton and the northern suburbs of London. Three people were killed in Northampton, and their names are known. He had only three large 300kg bombs left when he reached central London. The first landed near Piccadilly Circus, near the Swan and Edgar Department Store. It killed seven people, including three off-duty soldiers. We do not know any of their names. The next bomb exploded in Camberwell, killing twelve people in Albany Road. After the war, a memorial was erected nearby, but over time, as the area was redeveloped, the memorial was lost and with it the names of some of the victims. The last bomb fell at Glenview Road in Hither Green. After the war, a memorial was erected in Lewisham Cemetery and as a result we know the names of the fourteen victims. A similar situation exists in many towns and cities all over the UK.

While the crews of airships shot down over England are quite properly remembered in a memorial garden at Cannock Chase German War Cemetery, the names of probably half of the 557 airship victims are now unrecorded. It is more galling to realize that the Government actually has the information, but so far has refused to make it available in a usable form. Every death caused by enemy action had to have a coroner's inquest, which issued a death certificate; most of the coroner's inquest records are missing, but all the death certificates still exist. A copy is held centrally in the General Register Office and another locally in Register Offices. Birth, marriage and death records are public documents, which means that anyone can buy one. However, Register Offices are not allowed to disclose information on a certificate; they can only supply a certificate. This leads to a Catch 22 situation where a death certificate can only be obtained on a named person, but we don't know the names of many of the victims. There are General Record Office indexes which give the name, age, registration area and quarter of the year a person died (or was born or got married). It would be relatively easy for this information to be made available.

Genealogy is one of the most popular pastimes in much of Europe and America. The provision of online information is a multi-million pound or dollar industry. The best known company is probably Ancestry, but there are many. British birth, marriage and death information could be put online at no cost to the Government. There have been petitions to Parliament to do this, but the only response has been bureaucracy at its best: 'Current legislation does not permit the register entries to be available online and information can only be provided in the form of a certificate.'

Visiting many of the bombed cities demonstrated what I found in my research in the Midlands for my last book, that much of the Midlands and North of England have been damaged by de-industrialization. Quite a few of the streets bombed between 1915 and 1918 survive. The late Victorian terraced house is the great survivor of both world wars, and is little changed in over 100 years. They were built to house workers for industry. The industry has gone, but the houses remain. Most towns had war memorials erected at the end of the war. Whether Zeppelin victims were included seems to have been a random decision made at the time. If they were, the names of the victims are remembered and have found their way into books and websites. If not, they are unremembered; they deserve better.

There are dozens of memorials to Zeppelin victims throughout the UK. The centenary has led to old ones being refurbished or found and re-erected, and new ones erected. I will just mention my favourite, which happens to commemorate the last raid of the war. On 12 April 1918, Kapitänleutnant Herbert Ehrlich in Zeppelin *L.61* dropped two 300kg bombs at Bold near Widnes. One landed on the Prescot to Warrington Road (now the A 57), severely damaging the milestone at Bold, which had to be replaced. An unknown official, obviously a person with a sense of history, had the milestone erected at Victoria Park in Widnes. For many years it remained there, hardly remembered. In 1978, a local historian, who had seen the Zeppelin as a young child, began a campaign to have it re-erected on a display plinth with plaques describing the events of that night. It is a fine memorial, not only to civic pride in Widnes but to the seven people *L.61* went on to kill a few minutes later in Wigan. In this case, as we know their names, we can remember them.

Airships destroyed in the Great War

Zeppelin works No	Army Service No	Navy Service No	Date of Demise	Cause of destruction
LZ.20	Z.V		16 Aug 1914	Shot down by AA fire. Crew captured. Russia
LZ.22	Z.VII		16 Aug 1914	Shot down by AA fire. Crew captured. France
LZ.23	Z.VIII		23 Aug 1914	Shot down by AA fire in France. Crew escaped
LZ.24		L.3	4 Mar 1915	Caught in storm. Crashed. Crew interned. Denmark
LZ.25	Z.IX		8 Oct 1914	Bombed in shed by British aeroplane. Dusseldorf
LZ.27		L.4	4 Mar 1915	Caught in storm. Some of crew killed. Others interned. Denmark.
LZ.28		L.5	6 Aug 1915	Hit by AA fire, crash landed behind German lines. Crew uninjured
LZ.29	Z.X		21 Mar 1915	Shot down by AA fire. France.
LZ.30	LZ.XI		20 May 1915	Caught fire in shed accident. Russia
LZ.31		L.6	16 Sept 1916	Burnt out in shed while being filled with hydrogen. Fuhlsbuettel
LZ.32		L.7	4 May 1916	Shot down by AA fire of British warship. Most of crew killed
LZ.33		L.8	4 Mar 1915	Shot down by AA. Crew survived. Belgium

Appendix One (*Continued*)

Appendix One (*Continued*)

Zeppelin works No	Army Service No	Navy Service No	Date of Demise	Cause of destruction
LZ.34	*LZ.34*		21 Mar 1915	Shot down by AA. Crash landed. Russia
LZ.35	*LZ.35*		13 Apr 1915	Shot down by AA fire. Belgium
LZ.36		*L.9*	16 Sept 1916	Shed fire along with *L.6*. Fuhlsbuettel. No crew injuries
LZ.37	*LZ.37*		6/7 Jun 1915	Bombed in air by British aeroplane. Most of crew killed. Belgium
LZ.38	*LZ.38*		7 Jun 1915	Bombed in shed by British aeroplanes. Belgium
LZ.39	*LZ.39*		18 Dec 1915	Hit by AA fire. Crash landed. Some of crew killed. Russia
LZ.40		*L.10*	3 Sept 1915	Struck by lightning. All crew killed. Germany
		L.12	9/10 Aug 1915	Hit by AA fire over England Landed in sea. Crew rescued. Belgium
LZ.44	*LZ.74*		8 Oct 1915	Crash landed in Eifel mountains, Germany. Crew survived
LZ.47	*LZ.77*		21 Feb 1916	Shot down in flames by AA fire. All crew killed. France
LZ.48		*L.15*	31 Mar/1 April 1916	Hit by AA fire over England. Crashed in sea. Crew captured
LZ.49	*LZ.79*		29 Jan 1916	Hit by AA fire, Paris. Crash landed. Belgium
LZ.50		*L.16*	19 Oct 1917	Crash landed in River Elbe from Nordholz. Some crew injured

Appendix One (*Continued*)

Appendix One (*Continued*)

Zeppelin works No	Army Service No	Navy Service No	Date of Demise	Cause of destruction
LZ. 51	*LZ.81*		27 Sept 1916	Hit by AA fire, Bucharest. Crash landed. Crew survived.
LZ.52		*L.18*	17 Nov 1915	Hydrogen fire in shed. Some of ground crew killed. Tondern
LZ.53		*L.15*	28 Dec 1916	Burned in shed following landing accident by *L.24*. Tondern
LZ.54		*L.19*	About 2 Feb 1916	After raid on England, hit by AA fire over Holland. Crew all drowned in North Sea
LZ.55	*LZ.85*		5 May 1916	Shot down by AA fire, Salonika. Crew captured
LZ.56	*LZ.86*		4 Sept 1916	Crash landed at Temesvar, Hungary. Most of crew killed
LZ.59		*L.20*	2/3 May 1916	Caught in gale over Scotland. Crash landed in Norway. Most of crew interned
LZ.60	*LZ. 90*		7 Nov 1916	Wrecked in violent gale at Wittmundhaven. No injuries
LZ.61		*L.21*	27/28 Nov 1916	Shot down in flames by British aeroplane near Lowestoft. Crew all killed
LZ. 64		*L.22*	14 May 1917	Shot down by British flying boat off Texel Island. Crew all killed
LZ.65	*LZ.95*		21 Feb 1916	Hit by AA fire. Crash landed. Crew uninjured. Belgium

Appendix One (*Continued*)

Zeppelin works No	Army Service No	Navy Service No	Date of Demise	Cause of destruction
LZ.66		*L.23*	21 Aug 1917	Shot down in flames by British fighter launched from warship off coast of Denmark. Crew all killed
LZ.69		*L.24*	28 Dec 1916	Destroyed in shed. Landing accident when frame damaged due to cross winds. *L.17* destroyed in same fire. No injuries
LZ. 72		*L.31*	1 Oct 1916	Shot down in flames by British aeroplane, Potters Bar. Crew all killed.
LZ.74		*L.32*	22/23 Sept 1916	Shot down in flames by British aeroplane, Billericay. Crew all killed
LZ.76		*L.33*	23/24 Sept 1916	Shot down by AA fire. Crew captured. England
LZ.78		*L.34*	27/28 Nov 1916	Shot down in flames by British aeroplane near Hartlepool. Crew all killed
LZ.82		*L.36*	2 Feb 1917	Crash landing on Weser Estuary, Germany. No injuries
LZ.84		*L.38*	28/29 Dec 1916	Crash landing due to bad weather. Crew uninjured. Russia
LZ.85		*L.45*	19/20 Oct 1917	After raid on England, caught in gale. Crash landed in France. Crew captured
LZ.86		*L.39*	16/17 Mar 1917	Shot down in flames by AA fire, France, after raid on England. Crew all killed

Appendix One (*Continued*)

Appendix One (*Continued*)

Zeppelin works No	Army Service No	Navy Service No	Date of Demise	Cause of destruction
LZ.87		*L.47*	5 Jan 1918	Burnt in shed, Ahlhorn Germany
LZ.88		*L.40*	17 June 1917	Crash landed near field at Nordholz. Airship completely wrecked. No injuries
LZ.89		*L.50*	19/20 Oct 1917	Raid on England, caught in gale over France. Crash landed. Most of crew captured, some killed when wreckage floated away from crash over sea
LZ.92		*L.43*	14 Jun 1917	Shot down in flames by British flying boat off Vlieland. Crew all killed
LZ.93		*L.44*	19/20 Oct 1917	After raid on England, shot down in flames by AA fire over France. Crew all killed
LZ.94		*L.46*	5 Jan 1918	Burned in shed, Ahlhorn, Germany
LZ.95		*L.48*	16/17 Jun 1917	Shot down in flames by British aeroplane near Harwich. Most of crew killed
LZ.96		*L.49*	19/20 Oct 1917	After raid on England, caught in gale, crash landed in France. Crew captured
LZ.97		*L.51*	5 Jan 1918	Burned in shed, Ahlhorn, Germany
LZ.99		*L.54*	19 Jun 1918	Destroyed in shed by British fighters launched from aircraft carrier. Tondern
LZ.100		*L.53*	11 Aug 1918	Shot down in flames by British fighter launched off lighter. Crew all killed

Appendix One (*Continued*)

Appendix One (*Continued*)

Zeppelin works No	Army Service No	Navy Service No	Date of Demise	Cause of destruction
LZ.102		*L.57*	8 Oct 1917	Crash landed in gale force winds, caught fire. Ship destroyed. Preparing for mission to Africa at Juterbog
LZ.104		*L.59*	18 Apr 1918	Exploded in air, near Brindisi, Italy. Crew all killed
LZ.105		*L.58*	5 Jan 1918	Burnt in shed. Ahlhorn
LZ.106		*L.61*	10 May 1918	Blew up in air, near Cuxhaven. Probably struck by lightning. Crew all killed
LZ. 108		*L.60*	19 Jun 1918	Destroyed in shed by British fighter launched off aircraft carrier. Tondern
LZ.112		*L.70*	5/6 Aug 1918	Shot down in flames by British fighter off Lowestoft. Crew all killed

Schutte-Lanz works No	Army service No	Navy service No	Date of demise	Cause
SL.2	*SL.II*		10 Jan 1916	Ran out of fuel, Luckenwalde, Germany. Damaged in crash landing. Decommissioned as beyond repair
SL.3		*SL.3*	1 May 1916	Crashed in the Baltic. Crew rescued
SL.4		*SL.4*	11 Dec 1915	Caught by wind when shed doors opened in a gale. Wrecked on field.

Appendix One (*Continued*)

Appendix One (*Continued*)

Schutte-Lanz works No	Army service No	Navy service No	Date of demise	Cause
SL.5	*SL.V*		5 July1915	Crashed due to bad weather. Giessen, Germany
SL.6		*SL.6*	18 Nov 1915	Exploded in air, north of Seddin, Germany. Crew all killed
SL.9		*SL.9*	30 Mar 1917	Struck by lightning in Baltic. Crew all killed
SL.10	*SL.X*		27 Jul 1916	Exploded in air over the Black Sea. Cause not known. Crew all killed
SL.11	*SL.XI (SL.11)*		2 Sept 1916	Shot down in flames by British aeroplane near Cuffley. Crew all killed
SL.12		*SL.12*	28 Dec 1916	Crash landed at Ahlhorn. Airship destroyed
SL. 13	*SL.X111*		8 Feb 1917	Wrecked by shed collapse. Leipzig
SL.14		*SL.14*	9 May 1917	Badly damaged on field at Wainoden. Dismantled as beyond repair
SL.20		*SL.20*	5 Jan 1918	Destroyed in shed at Ahlhorn

Parseval Works No	Army Service No	Navy Service No	Date of demise	Cause
PL.19		*PL.19*	25 Jan 1915	Crashed in Baltic due to ice damage. Crew captured. Russia

Appendix Two

Name changes of towns and cities

Anyone who tries to follow the airships on a modern map of the Eastern Front will be disappointed, as virtually all the towns with German names now have different names. During the Great War, an independent Poland didn't exist. There were three parts to what is now Poland, in Germany, Russia and Austro-Hungary. The names changed in 1918. The borders of Poland again changed in 1945, when much of East Prussia was incorporated into Poland or Russia. With the break-up of the Soviet Union, the process continued, names changing with the political situation.

In the West, the situation is less complex. The most obvious example is the airship base at Tondern. Germany annexed the Danish area of Sonderjylland in 1864, and it became part of Schleswig Holstein. It was returned to Denmark in 1920, and Tondern became Tonder. It still has a very good museum telling the story of the Zeppelin base. In Belgium, almost everywhere has two names: French and Flemish. I try to use the common modern English spelling: Ypres rather than Ieper.

Allenstein	Olsztyn, Poland
Arensburg	Kuessaare, Estonia
Batum	now in Georgia
Bialystok	now in Poland
Dago Island	Hiiumaa, Estonia
Danzig, East Prussia.	Gdansk, Poland
Dunamunde	Daugavgriva, Latvia
Dunnaburg (the castle: Dvinsk is the town) Dunamunde	Daugavpils, Latvia
Dvinsk	Daugavpils, Latvia
Grodno	Hrodna, Belarus
Insterburg	Cherngakovsk, Russia

Appendix Two (*Continued*)

Appendix Two (*Continued*)

Jamboli	Yambol, Bulgaria
Konigsberg Kovno	Kaliningrad, Russia
Kovno Jamboli	Kaunas, Lithuania Yambol, Bulgaria
Lemburg	Lviv, Ukraine
Libau	Liepaja, Latvia
Loetzen	Lotzen
Lomza	now in Poland
Lyck (Luck)	Elk, Poland
Luninietz	now Luninets, Belarus
Malkin	Malkina Gorna, Poland
Mlawa, Russia	now Mlawa, Poland
Mudros	Moudros, Greece
Mytilene	Lesbos, Greece
Novogeorgievsk	now in Ukraine
Oesel Island	Saaremaa, Estonia
Ossovets	Osowiec
Parnau	Parnu, Estonia
Pillau	Baltiysk, Russia
Posen	Poznan, Poland
Pultusk	now in Poland
Rovno	Rivne, Ukraine
Salismunde	Salacgriva, Latvia
Salonika	Thessaloniki, Greece
Schniedemuhl	Pila, Poland
Scutari	Shkodra, Albania
Seemuppen	Ziemupe, Latvia
Seerappen Seemuppen	Lyubilno, Russia Ziemupe, Latvia
Siedlze Seerappen	Siedlce, Poland
Stettin	Szczecin, Poland
Stolpce	Stowbtsy, Belarus
Seddin, airship base at Stopl	now Slupsk, Poland

Appendix One (*Continued*)

Appendix Two (*Continued*)

Sworbe Stettin	Sorve, Estonia Szczecin, Poland
Temesvar, Hungary	Timisoara, Romania
Tirnova, Bulgaria	now Tirnova, Moldova
Tluscz	Tloszcz, Poland
Tondern	Tonder, Denmark
Valona	Vlore, Albania
Vilna	Vilnius, Lithuania
Wainoden	Vainode, Latvia
Walk	Vakga, Estonia
Windau	Ventspils, Latvia
Wolmar	Valmiera, Estonia

Bibliography

Documents and Articles

Intelligence Section, GHQ Home Forces. Secret document. Probably written by Lieutenant Colonel H.G. de Watterville. Air raids 31 January – 1 February 1916, 2–3 September 1916, 23 September - 2 October 1916. HBM Government. GHQ. HF (1) November and December 1916.

David Mechan, 'The Silent Raid, The Untold Story', *Cross and Cockade International*, Vol 45/4(2014).

The Rev W.L.T. Merson, 'Zeppelin Raid on Walsall', *Borough of Walsall Programme of the Peace Celebrations* (1919).

Chris Percy and Noel Ryan, *Lincolnshire Aviation in World War 1* (Airfield Research Group, 2012).

Mick Powis, 'Zeppelins over the Black Country', *Blackcountryman*, Nos 3 & 4, Vol. 29 (1996).

Mick Powis, 'The Last Zeppelin Raid on the Black Country' Blackcountryman, No. 3, Vol. 49 (2016).

E.W. Sockett, article in *Fortress*, No. 13 (May 1992).

Walsall Local History Centre, *Walsall Chronicle No. 8: Walsall at War*, Walsall Library and Museum Service.

'The War Budget. A photographic Record of the Great War', The *Daily Chronicle*, various editions (1914-1918).

'Wolverhampton and the Great War', Wolverhampton Archives and Local Studies (2014).

Newspapers

Black Country Bugle, August, September, October 1983; July, November 1994.

Daily Sketch, February 1916.

Derby Telegraph, 1916 and article 2014.

Dudley Herald, 1916.

Express and Star, February and March 1916, and articles by Mick Powis 25 January 1996 and 6 January 2000.

The Guardian, 4 April 2001.
Hartlepool History Now and Then, 2016.
Ilkeston Advertiser, 1916.
Ilkeston Pioneer, 1916.
The Lincolnshire Star, 1916.
Loughborough Echo, 1916.
Stoke on Trent Sentinel, 2014.
Tipton Herald, 1916.
Walsall Herald, 1916.
Walsall Pioneer, 1916.
Wednesbury Herald, 1916.

Books

Ian M. Bott, *The Midlands Zeppelin Outrage* (Black Country Society Publications, 2016).
Douglas Botting, *The Giant Airships* (Time-Life Books, 1981).
Alec Brew, *The History of Black Country Aviation* (Alan Sutton, 1993).
Horst Treusch von Buttlar-Brandenfels, *Zeppelins over England* (George G. Harrap, 1931).
Ian Castle, *London 1914–17: The Zeppelin Menace* (Osprey, 2008).
Christopher Cole and F.G. Cheeseman, *The Air Defence of Great Britain 1914–1918* (Putnam, 1984).
Gwynne Dyer, *War* (The Bodley Head, 1986).
Stephen Flinders and Danny Corns, *Stanton. Gone but not Forgotten* (Ilkeston and District History Society, 2013).
Bill Gunston, *Night Fighters: A development and combat history* (Patrick Stephens, 1976)
Henry Albert Jones, *The War in the Air* (Clarendon Press, 1931).
Alan Judd, *The Quest for C. Mansfield Cumming and the Founding of the Secret Service* (Harper Collins, 1999).
Peter Kirk, Peter Felix and Gunter Bartnik, *The Bombing of Rolls-Royce at Derby in two World Wars - with diversions* (Rolls-Royce Heritage Trust, 2002).
Ernest A. Lehmann and Howard Mingos, *The Zeppelins. The Development of the Airship, with the Story of the Zeppelin Raids in The World War* (J.H. Sears, 1927, reprint P.S. Chapman, 2014).
Cecil Lewis, *Sagittarius Rising* (Penguin, 1983).
Ian Mackersey, *No Empty Chairs* (Pheonix, 2012).
Joseph Morris, *German Air Raids on Britain 1914–1918* (Naval and Military Press, 1993; first published by Sampson Low, Marston, 1925).
Derek Nicholls, Chris Smith, *The Great Tipton Zeppelin Raid* (Tipton Civil Society, 2016).

Raymond Rimell, *The Airship VC* (Aston Publications, 1989).
Raymond Rimell, *The Last Flight of the L.48* (Windsock, 2006).
Raymond Rimell, *The Last Flight of the L.31* (Windsock data file special, 2016).
Raymond Rimell, *The Last Flight of the L.32* (Windsock data file special, 2016).
Raymond Rimell, *Zeppelin* Vol. 1 (Albatros Publications, 2006).
Raymond Rimell, *Zeppelin* Vol. 2 (Albatros Publications, 2008).
Raymond Rimell, *Zeppelins at War! 1914–1915* (Albatross Publications, 2014).
Douglas H. Robinson, *The Zeppelin in Combat* (Schiffer Publishing, 1994).
Richard M. Watt, *The Kings Depart. The German Revolution and the Treaty of Versailles 1918-19* (Pelican, 1973).
Jerry White, *Zeppelin Nights: London in the First World War* (Vintage Books, 2015).
James Wyllie and Michael McKinley, *The Code Breakers: The Secret Intelligence Unit that Changed the Course of the First World War* (Ebury Press, 2015).

Maps

Henry Albert Jones has a fairly detailed GHQ map of the route of each Zeppelin over a 10 miles to the inch Ordnance Survey Map of the time. While this appears to be very detailed, putting the routes of all the Zeppelins on one page makes it look rather like spaghetti. I am not sure how accurate it is. Certainly Jones has been able to plot the position of each Zeppelin recorded by ground observers; however, the nicely curved paths shown for each Zeppelin probably owe a lot to artistic licence. Though the Zeppelins certainly circled looking for targets, any attempt to portray this on a small-scale map is questionable.

I have found two types of map particularly useful. The first is the modern edition of the humble *A to Z* or *Philips Street Atlas* of the bombed areas. Drawn to a scale of about 4in to the mile, they are very useful in plotting the course of the Zeppelins and locating where the bombs landed. The second are the Godfrey Edition *Old Ordnance Survey Maps* reproduced at a scale of about 15in to the mile. Most date from between 1900 and 1910; they not only show the changes in the name of roads over 100 years, but often allow houses to be identified.

Websites

There are numerous websites on the First World War and Zeppelins. I have found those below particularly useful. With the centenary of the outbreak of the war in 2014, many local newspapers and local history societies produced articles on different aspects of the conflict, with quite a few on the

Zeppelin raids. There are too many to separately quote here, but it is well worth using Google to look at a location and Zeppelin; as the 100th anniversary of the Armistice draws near, many more will doubtless appear.

www.aeronauticum.de

Website of the Aeronauticum Museum at Nordholz, with some sections in English.

www.crossandcockade.com

Website of the British magazine about all things concerning First World War aviation.

www.zeppelin-museum.dk

Website of the Zeppelin and Garrison Museum Tonder, on the site of the old Tondern airship base, now part of Denmark. A very good website, with many pictures of the base, ships and crews. Almost everything in English.

www.frontflieger.de

Website commemorating German airmen who died in the First World War, with good section on Zeppelin men. Some sections in English.

www.loughborough-rollofhonour.com

Certainly the best British website on the Zeppelin raids from a local point of view. Has a list of all the Loughborough victims and many of the damaged buildings in the town.

www.pugetairship.org

American website of the Puget Sound Airship Society. Good pictures and post-war material.

http://denkmalprojekt.org

German war memorial website. Includes some Zeppelin men, mainly officers.

www.iancastlezeppelin.co.uk

Very good website which intends to give details of all air raids on the UK from 1914-1918. Incomplete at the time of writing, as there is a lot of material.

www.ww1hull.org.uk

Kingston upon Hull War Memorial 1914-1918. Good website with names of Zeppelin victims and the people of Hull in the Great War.

https://livesofthefirstworldwar.org/community/2933

Imperial War Museum website with a list of the soldiers from the Manchester Regiment killed in Cleethorpes.

www.pixnet.co.uk/oldham-hrg/world-war1

Oldham Historical Society has more on the soldiers killed at Cleethorpes; most were from the Oldham area.

www.scotlandswar.ed.ac.uk

Good details of bombing in Edinburgh, but no names of victim. Contains Police and Fire Brigade reports.

www.chrishobbs.com/sheffieldfirstairraid1916

Details of Sheffield victims and locations.

www.stedmundsburychronical.com

Good website with plenty of bomb damage pictures, mainly from post-cards. Covers much of East Anglia: Great Yarmouth, Lowestoft, Sudbury, Woodbridge, Ipswich and Bury St Edmunds.

http://hhtandn.org

Hartlepool history then and now. Good details of the air raids, but sadly victims are not identified.

www.bridgetonowhere.friendsofburgesspark.org.uk

Good details of *L.45* attack on Camberwell.

http://lewishamwarmemorials.wikidot.com

Lewisham War Memorials, with details of *L.45* victims in Lewisham.

Index